NORMAN BEL GEDDES DESIGNS AMERICA

HARRY RANSOM CENTER,
The University of Texas at Austin, and the
MUSEUM OF THE CITY OF NEW YORK

DONALD ALBRECHT, Editor

ABRAMS, *New York*

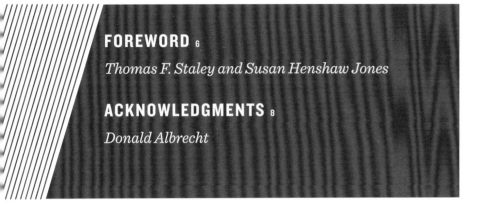

FOREWORD

Thomas F. Staley
and Susan Henshaw Jones

orman Bel Geddes (1893–1958) was an innovative American stage designer, director, producer, architect, industrial designer, futurist, and urban planner. Most active from the 1920s through the early 1950s, Geddes was an iconoclast who questioned the status quo while working within it, a paradoxical figure made up of equal parts visionary and pragmatist, a serious inventor and inveterate promoter, a naturalist and industrialist, a democrat and egoist. Geddes pursued his work with missionary zeal, and his streamlined cars and airplanes, theatrical spectacles, and sky-high revolving restaurants were conceived not only to thrill the general public but also to foster emotional and psychological change. Ultimately, he sought nothing less than the transformation of modern American society through design.

Geddes created and promoted a dynamic vision of the future and communicated his vision through immersive theater productions, visual spectacles, and books such as *Horizons* and *Magic Motorways*. His best-known project, the Futurama exhibit in the General Motors "Highways and Horizons" pavilion at the 1939–40 New York World's Fair, was seen by some 27,500 daily visitors who exited with a pin proclaiming "I Have Seen the Future."

Norman Bel Geddes Designs America is the first book to focus on and fully explore every aspect of the life and career of this complex and influential man. We are pleased that the Harry Ransom Center and the Museum of the City of New York have joined forces to develop this project, showcasing the extraordinary collection of Geddes's work at the Ransom Center, which came to the University of Texas in 1958, and highlighting the efforts of one of New York's leading cultural figures. The book and the accompanying exhibition, titled *I Have Seen the Future: Norman Bel Geddes Designs America* and presented at both of these institutions, reach the public through the efforts of numerous individuals. From start to finish, the project was expertly directed by Cathy Henderson, associate director for exhibitions at the Ransom Center. The exhibition was organized by Donald Albrecht, curator of architecture and design at the Museum of the City of New York, who also edited this volume. We wish to thank all of the scholars who contributed to planning the project, many of whom wrote essays for the book. We gratefully acknowledge the efforts of Abrams, the book's publisher.

The programs of the Ransom Center and the Museum of the City of New York depend on the generosity of its friends and supporters. This book was made possible through the cooperation of the Edith Lutyens and Norman Bel Geddes Foundation, Inc., and through the generous support of the Graham Foundation for Advanced Studies in the Fine Arts; Furthermore: a program of the J. M. Kaplan Fund; and Janet and Jack Roberts. Planning support for the exhibition was provided in part by a grant from the National Endowment for the Humanities. Additional support for the exhibition was provided by the Marlene Nathan Meyerson Family Foundation and an FAIC/Tru Vue Optium® Conservation Grant. We are grateful to IBM for in-kind support.

THOMAS F. STALEY
Director, Harry Ransom Center
University of Texas at Austin

SUSAN HENSHAW JONES
Ronay Menschel Director,
Museum of the City of New York

ACKNOWLEDGMENTS

Donald Albrecht

I n the fall of 2008, Cathy Henderson, associate director for exhibitions and Fleur Cowles executive curator at the Harry Ransom Center, University of Texas at Austin, contacted me about working with the Ransom Center on this book and the exhibition it accompanies. The intervening years have brought me in touch with a remarkably intelligent and dedicated group of people without whom this project would not have happened. After the center received a planning grant from the National Endowment for the Humanities in 2009, the project took flight through a pair of meetings in Austin that gathered leading scholars. Those scholars helped shape the project's content, and many eventually contributed essays to this book. I want to acknowledge the members of that committee: Tom Borders, Andrea Gustavson, Linda Dalrymple Henderson, Christopher Innes, Katherine Feo Kelly, Christopher Long, Nicolas Maffei, Jeffrey Meikle, Danielle Sigler, and Larry Speck. It was especially rewarding to work not only with these scholars but also with graduate students at the University of Texas and alumni as well as outside scholars, who conducted original research in the center's Norman Bel Geddes archive and contributed essays. I also want to thank the following individuals at the Ransom Center: Helen Baer, associate curator of performing arts; Megan Barnard, assistant director for acquisitions and administration; Bridget Gayle, academic affair coordinator; Christine Lee, director of marketing; interns Allison Devereux, Susannah Jacob, and Rachel Platis; Lisa Pulsifer, associate curator for education and public engagement; Margie Rine, associate director for development; research associate Rick Watson; and photographer Pete Smith.

Without the extraordinary support of James Male, Justine Tenney, and Norman Posner, trustees of the Edith Lutyens and Norman Bel Geddes Foundation, Inc., neither the book nor the exhibition would have been possible.

Natalie Shivers provided expert editorial advice on all the essays, and I'm especially grateful for her work on my own introduction. I thank Thomas Reynolds for his copyediting advice. At Abrams, my gratitude goes to Eric Himmel, Andrea Danese, Sarah Gifford, Kat Kopit, and Jen Graham. Finally, I want to thank Cathy Henderson for asking me to work on this great project and for making the process fun and stimulating all along the way.

DONALD ALBRECHT
Guest Curator and Editor

INTRODUCTION

Donald Albrecht

hen you drive on an interstate highway, attend a multimedia Broadway show, dine in a sky-high revolving restaurant, or watch a football game in an all-weather stadium, you owe a debt of gratitude to Norman Bel Geddes.[1] A Promethean figure who was equally comfortable in the realms of fact and fantasy, Geddes was both a visionary and a pragmatist who had a significant role in shaping not only modern America, but also the nation's image of itself as leading the way into the future. He was a polymath who had no schooling or professional training in the activities he mastered, which included designing stage sets, costumes, and lighting; creating theater buildings, offices, nightclubs, and houses, as well as their furnishings, from vacuum cleaners to cocktail sets; and authoring oracular books and articles that landed him and his prophesies on the front page of newspapers across the country. To Americans between the world wars, he was nothing less than the "grand master of modernism," the impresario who gave visual form to Aldous Huxley's prophetic 1932 novel *Brave New World*.[2]

Geddes's imagination seemed sui generis. "In the process of evoking the natural beauty of industrial objects," *Fortune* magazine said of Geddes's approach, "he begins with a question: What is a bed?"[3] Geddes's explorations ranged across media and spanned vast differences in scale, from the conception of an individual product—a counter scale, for example—to the design of the factory where it would be manufactured, to the city where the factory would be located, to the world of the future where that city might one day exist. The same was true of his theater designs—he designed the buildings as well as the imaginary worlds within them. Even cars he saw as part of a larger Geddes-designed ecosystem of massive highways and newly planned cities.

Geddes's expansive portfolio also included the design of Hollywood movie sets, the development of new forms of media such as model photography, and the reconception of the graphic design of newspapers and magazines. As Americans became wealthier after World War II and sought sunny climates and the excitement of exotic vacation locales, Geddes created glass-walled ranch houses in Boca Raton, Florida, and chic and colorful resorts in Mexico and the Bahamas.

Even his hobbies, according to one press account, showed "breath-taking originality and capacity for detail that forever astounds [*sic*] one."[4] For his own amusement, he made a film of insects mating and another in which, reportedly, ants reenacted the saga of Helen of Troy. He built a miniature golf course in his apartment before the sport became a national craze. He created war games that were played by as many as twenty-eight people over a vast model, and an electronic horse race game that attracted Manhattan's elite to his apartment, where he kept a veritable zoo of pet monkeys. Underlying Geddes's amazing array of efforts were themes that can be traced throughout his career: his commitment to the power of unfettered imagination and the primacy of the individual, his fascination with nature as a model for imitation, and his belief in the possibility of a utopian future. And Geddes's showmanship became his trademark.

From his childhood on, Geddes was also a strong believer in the spiritual value of art and the idea that art as well as architecture and design could make people's lives psychologically and emotionally richer. As an adult he adopted a practical vision for business, influencing the behavior of American consumers and helping to make the industrial and theater design professions into modern businesses. Believing that communication was a key factor in shaping the modern world, Geddes popularized not only his many realized projects, but also his visionary prognostications about futurist cities, streamlined ocean liners, and flying cars through drawings, models, and photographs. These were exhibited in museums and published in promotional brochures and books with aspirational titles such as *Horizons* (1932) and *Magic Motorways* (1940).

As one of the twentieth century's leading futurists, Geddes believed that a brighter tomorrow awaited Americans, and that it was just around the corner. He saw great differences between the quick tempo of the United States and the slower pace of Europe. In Europe, "dreams take centuries," Geddes recounted in his autobiography, *Miracle in the Evening* (1960), where he describes the experience of seeing the French medieval monastery Mont-Saint-Michel.[5] Not so in America: "It happens that the United States has seized upon more of the fruits of industrialism than any other nation," he wrote in *Horizons*. "We have gone further and more swiftly than any other. To what end?"[6] While Geddes answered the question of what the future would bring in many forms—his visionary articles boasted titles like "Dreamlining Tomorrow" and "Ten Years from Now"—his most notable effort was his Futurama display for the General Motors "Highways and Horizons" exhibition at the 1939–40 New York World's Fair, which adopted the motto "I Have Seen the Future." Futurama's giant model of America in 1960, complete with glass-clad skyscrapers and multilevel superhighways, gave Depression-era Americans genuine hope for a better future within their lifetimes. It was Geddes, more than any designer of his era, who created and promoted a dynamic vision of the future with an image

 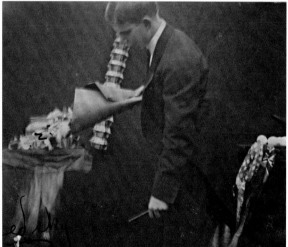

FIGURE 1 (LEFT)
Norman M. Geddes in his "Indian dress," c. 1900. Photograph by unidentified photographer, 3 x 5 in., 7.6 x 12.7 cm

FIGURE 2 (RIGHT)
Norman M. Geddes as Zetskey, Boy Magician, c. 1909. Photograph by unidentified photographer, 4 x 3¼ in., 10.1 x 8.3 cm

that was streamlined, technocratic, and optimistic. Today, as seen in the "retro-futurist" looks of theme parks, animated television programs, and popular novels, Geddes's vision of the future continues to shape and inspire the twenty-first-century American imagination.

MIND OVER MATTER: 1893–1916

As recounted by Geddes with characteristic melodrama in his autobiography, his youth was part Horatio Alger, part Houdini, a perfect first act for a successful entrepreneur-in-training. Norman Melancton Geddes was born in Adrian, Michigan, in 1893. As his father was in and out of various jobs and had died by the time Geddes was fifteen, he and his

strong-willed mother struggled financially. Starting at an early age, Geddes was inspired by his mother's faith in Christian Science, a religion and philosophy that espouses the power of the mind over the physical world. A range of influences proved formative to Geddes's poetic and emotional expression of the power of the spirit to create art—these included Christian Science, as well as the works of the esoteric philosopher P. D. Ouspensky and Claude Bragdon, an architect and writer, who saw natural forms as the only suitable inspiration for the buildings of a truly democratic America. As a child, Geddes took to playacting, sporting Native American dress at a time when movies and tourism were dramatizing the American West and its people. Performing as Zetskey, Boy Magician, Geddes also fostered his interest in mind-over-matter persuasion, a skill he would use later to convince clients to buy his ideas.

Geddes showed an early aptitude for drawing, attending classes at the Art Institute of Chicago and the Cleveland Institute of Art, and working as an illustrator for advertising companies in Chicago and Detroit. From 1915 to 1916, Geddes and his first wife, Belle Sneider, published a magazine called *Inwhich*—"in which" Geddes told his readership what he thought on numerous topics of interest to him. (At that time, Geddes joined his and Belle's first names to become Norman-Bel Geddes, a moniker he kept, without the hyphen, after their separation in the mid-1920s.[7]) Geddes's fusion of the practical (advertising) and the visionary (his spiritually based magazine) reflected larger American interests of the time as manifested in the formation of the nation's consumer culture. This combination also characterized American merchants, starting in the late nineteenth century, when department store owners like John Wanamaker used such devices as theatrical displays of clothing, sometimes bathed in colored lights; scenographic store windows; and even an organ to create dramatic, at times quasi-religious, auras around their products that transfixed customers and induced them to give up their Calvinist proscriptions against the material world and buy.[8] From early on in his life, Geddes was steeped in this consumer culture, as some of the books in his library attest. Reflecting his interest in the role of psychology in advertising and consumer behavior, Geddes's library included *Wild and Tame Advertising, or, How to Become a Director of Publicity in One Lesson* (1914) and *Instincts in Industry: A Study of Working-Class Psychology* (1918). Even as Geddes abandoned the lofty, spiritual language of Christian Science in favor of a pragmatic industrial design practice in the late 1920s, he retained a near-religious belief in art's ability to transform people's lives—and to sell products and ideas.

like Geddes aimed to free the theater from the strictures of bourgeois realism and to create settings for a new generation of playwrights, such as Eugene O'Neill, who were exploring deeper psychological and emotional depth in their work. New Stagecraft designers like Adolphe Appia and Edward Gordon Craig in Europe and Robert Edmond Jones, Lee Simonson, and Geddes in America used broad strokes of color, dramatic lighting, simplified detail, and exaggerated and abstracted settings and costumes. In his work for the theater, Geddes wasn't content to serve as designer, and he sometimes took on the roles of director and producer so he could have complete control over a production.

Geddes's first theatrical work was done under the patronage of oil heiress and arts pa-

SETTING THE STAGE: 1916–1927

In the initial phase of Geddes's professional career, from 1916 to 1927, he focused on theater design and theater spaces, beginning in Los Angeles and continuing in New York. At the time, Geddes adapted for the American stage the principles of the so-called New Stagecraft movement in Europe. Americans

tron Aline Barnsdall in Los Angeles. His concept of "unity of effect," in which sets, costumes, and lighting were conceived holistically, is evident in his construction of a miniature stage model for his production of *Thunderbird* (1914–17) and other plays such as *Nju* of 1916, which featured a highly abstract and minimalist set of only six screens. His work for Barnsdall established a lifelong habit of making models to aid clients in visualizing his ideas. For Barnsdall, Geddes also proposed a children's theater, an early example of his intent to design both the contents and the container. Through Barnsdall Geddes met Frank Lloyd Wright, who helped to inspire his lifelong fascination with architecture.

Soon realizing that only New York, with its prestige, vast audiences, and well-oiled publicity apparatus, could fulfill his ambitions to become a theatrical impresario on the order of P. T. Barnum or Florenz Ziegfeld, Geddes left Los Angeles for New York in 1917. While the move ultimately caused a rift with Barnsdall, Geddes achieved rapid success. Through the patronage of New York investment banker Otto Kahn, Geddes worked for the Metropolitan Opera as well as the Chicago Opera Company, for whom he designed the sets, costumes, and lighting of *Boudour Ballet* (1919–20). While its design showed the exotic influences of Ballets Russes master Léon Bakst, it was also modern in its use of plastics, rather than traditional materials such as wood and cloth for scenery. Geddes's adoption of plastic was an early intimation of his and other American designers' fascination with new, industrial materials in the 1930s.

Broadway, though, was the natural habitat for the ambitious Geddes during the 1920s, a decade characterized by innovative productions and artists. In their musicals, composers such as Irving Berlin and George Gershwin were creating a new, jazz-inflected popular music idiom, while writers Eugene O'Neill, Oscar Hammerstein II, and Mae West tackled taboo subjects such as race, psychology, and sex. Geddes's advanced ideas on stage design meshed well with these other cutting-edge developments. After designing a revival of *Erminie* in 1920, Geddes worked on Restoration comedies (*The Rivals* in 1922 and *The School for Scandal* in 1923), Ziegfeld's Follies in 1925, and Cole Porter's *Fifty Million Frenchmen* in 1929. Later acclaimed as the "Leonardo of our Theater" by critic and historian Kenneth Macgowan, Geddes would ultimately design nearly one hundred Broadway plays and operas, many of which adopted the expressive stylization of the New Stagecraft.[9] "Pure realism is heavy, flat. It has no elasticity," one critic noted of the outworn mode that he felt Geddes was revolutionizing. "The impressionistic, toward which our better stage designers are now leaning, has no limitations in the richness of beauty and meaning that it can portray."[10] At the same time, not all of Geddes's experimentation was aesthetic—he also proposed technical innovations that transformed theater production. His sets for the 1928 play

figures such as the German impresario Max Reinhardt, with whom Geddes worked in New York.

Far more successful and important than *The Divine Comedy* for his future work was Geddes's 1924 New York production of *The Miracle*, a staged version of a medieval legend about a nun, which was directed by Reinhardt. As the designer of the show's scenery, costumes, and lighting, Geddes pulled off an artistic and technical tour de force. He remade the interior of the Century Theatre into a Gothic

The Patriot, for example, featured an elaborate set of quick-changing mobile architectural elements, a technology he would later apply to postwar housing.

While these productions provided Geddes with considerable fame, it was his never-realized staging of Dante's *The Divine Comedy* (1920–24) that was most significant as an early example of his career-long attempt to create emotionally rich experiences. Eschewing realism and adopting abstraction, the play grounded his work within the theories and practices of Expressionism, distorting reality so that the outside objective world would be "filtered through the internal subjective world of the artist's emotions in an attempt to express an inner reality—the psychological reality behind appearances."[11] In the 1910s and 1920s Expressionism influenced the visual arts, architecture, music, and the theater, where it was primarily associated with German productions by

cathedral, complete with dramatic lighting filtered through stained glass windows, pews instead of theater seats for the audience, and incense wafting through the air. Geddes's technical innovations for the production included mechanization of movable scenery; devices for quick costume changes; and the creation of a single switchboard, manned by one electrician, who controlled the direction, color, and focus of the play's lighting. In New York *The Miracle* played for twenty months, subsequently traveling to eleven cities for a three-year tour.

The Miracle solidified Geddes's reputation as a multitalented theatrical genius. Its success attracted the attention of Hollywood film producer Jesse Lasky and, in turn, commissions for production design work from directors Cecil B. DeMille (*Feet of Clay*, 1924) and D. W. Griffith (*Sorrows of Satan*, 1925). Geddes's film work was characterized by its

FIGURE 9 (LEFT)
Geddes costume design (male slave dancer) for Boudour Ballet, *1919–20. Watercolor on paper, 10 x 15 in., 25.4 x 38.1 cm*

FIGURE 10 (MIDDLE)
Geddes costume design (yellow dancer) for Boudour Ballet, *1919–20. Watercolor on paper, 10 x 15 in., 25.4 x 38.1 cm*

FIGURE 11 (RIGHT)
Geddes ensemble scene for Boudour Ballet, *1919–20. Watercolor on paper, 19 x 11 in., 48.2 x 28 cm*

CALAMITY IN HOLLYWOOD - ONE OF CECIL B. DEMILLE'S YES-MEN SAYS "NO!"

visual spectacle and dramatic lighting. In *Sorrows of Satan*, he depicted a climactic battle between good and evil with high-contrast lighting—Satan rendered in dark shadows—and a swirling mass of angels and demons traversing a grand stairway.

More important for Geddes's future career, *The Miracle* fused theater and architecture, creating an immersive environment that transformed passive audience members into active participants in the drama that surrounded them. As such, this new concept of the theater could realize the transformative effects Geddes sought in all his art. To the architect and writer Claude Bragdon, an early influence on Geddes, his fusion of color, light, and movement would release in theatergoers "those great primal orgiastic tides of thought and feeling." Bragdon went on to compare this theater to a new kind of church, where the lighting technician is "like the organist in the choir-loft . . . master [of] an art which may usher the human spirit into realms at which music itself now beats in vain."[12]

INDUSTRIAL DESIGN AND ARCHITECTURE: 1927–1937

Eager to move beyond the theater and broaden his influence over American society, Geddes branched out in two directions around 1927, adapting his flair for theater to architecture and interior design and pioneering the new field of industrial design. As early as 1922, Geddes had designed New York's Palais Royal Cabaret Theatre—one of his first architectural settings. It featured walls decorated with life-size dancing figures imitating the chic patrons who visited the club, thereby merging architecture and theater. While working on set designs for DeMille in the mid-1920s, Geddes also designed a real structure for him, the Island Dance Restaurant, which suffused diners in theatrical-style lighting; in 1929, Geddes revived this unbuilt commission as one of his many proposals for the Chicago Century of Progress International Exposition. Around 1927, Geddes fused these architecture-as-theater projects with his burgeoning interest in industrial design by creating shop window displays and mannequins (among his first object designs) for the Franklin Simon stores in New York. "The window is the stage," Geddes noted, "and the merchandise the players."[13] So startling was

the effect that the windows were reported to have stopped Manhattan traffic, garnering yet more press for Geddes. "Shoppers besieged the window," *The American* magazine declared. "The crowds swelled to such proportions that police reserves needed to be called out to clear the way!"[14]

The Franklin Simon windows launched Geddes full-throttle into industrial design, and over the next ten years he produced dozens of designs for home appliances such as stoves and vacuum cleaners, bedroom furniture, and decorative objects, from soda siphons to cocktail sets. In designing these products Geddes sought to update every aspect of the home, achieving ever-greater ease and cleanliness. While his furniture designs often lacked pizzazz, perhaps because the medium was too traditional for an avid futurist like Geddes, new technologies, for example radios, were more interesting to him as a medium for a new streamlined aesthetic. Working for various companies such as Majestic and Philco, Geddes helped domesticate the look of radio receivers by transforming them from intimidating assemblages of electronic components into displays of sophistication and prosperity. In all of this work, Geddes showed a far greater interest in an object's external form than its internal workings, often sheathing those workings in smooth, streamlined curves.

Launching his industrial design career in the late 1920s, Geddes was a founding member of the field. The first generation of designers, including Raymond Loewy, Henry Dreyfuss, and Russel Wright, established this new profession without the benefit of formal education. Propelling their efforts was a trend among American businesses and manufacturers to increase sales by means of style and design. This trend was succinctly expressed in advertising executive Earnest Elmo Calkins's essay "Beauty the New Business Tool," published in the August 1927 issue of the *Atlantic Monthly* magazine. "The appeal of efficiency alone is nearly ended," Calkins wrote. "Beauty is the natural and logical next step."[15] The early industrial designers created many of the products that still define contemporary American life today, from telephones to transportation vehicles and elegant yet casual dinnerware.

It was through these products that Geddes and his generation defined the concept of streamlining. For them, the principles of streamlining shaped both the forms of their vision for America and the process by which that future would be achieved. Everything from household items to buildings should be designed in curving, unornamented shapes, while products would move from design studio to consumer homes on well-coordinated and frictionless paths. Largely through Geddes's popularizing efforts—one magazine singled him out as "the man who streamlined the world"[16]—this concept became ubiquitous during the economic downturn of the Great Depression, when hard times spurred com-

FIGURE 14

Geddes designs of dancing couples for the Palais Royal Cabaret Theatre, c. 1922. Watercolor, 19¾ x 28½ in., 50.1 x 72.3 cm (left); 20 x 28½ in., 50.8 x 72.3 cm (middle); 19¾ x 28¾ in., 50.1 x 73 cm (right)

FIGURE 15 (OVERLEAF)

The Geddes-designed interior of the Palais Royal Cabaret Theatre, c. 1922. Photograph by unidentified photographer, 14 x 11 in., 35.6 x 27.9 cm

FIGURE 16 (TOP LEFT)
View of the Barberry Room ("Elbow Room") street facade, c. 1938. Geddes designed this private dinner club, an addition to the Berkshire Hotel on East Fifty-second Street, for New York City's literati in 1937. Alexander Woolcott originally named it the Elbow Room. Photograph by Richard Garrison, 7½ x 9¼ in., 19 x 23 cm

FIGURE 17 (TOP RIGHT)
View of the Barberry Room ("Elbow Room") main dining room, "showing the air of spaciousness provided by the parallel mirror walls," c. 1938. Photograph by Richard Garrison, 9½ x 7¼ in., 24.1 x 18.4 cm

FIGURE 18 (BOTTOM)
Geddes-designed dinner plate with Barberry Room monogram, c. 1938. Lamberton/Scammell china, 10½ in., 26.7 cm diameter

panies to use striking design as a means to increase consumer sales.

Among his peers, however, Geddes stood out as a designer of real products who also took his imagination into truly visionary realms. His vast transportation networks, for example, comprised floating airports, flying cars, airplanes large enough to function as aerial hotels, and ocean liners that housed two thousand people. To announce the historic significance of these and other visionary projects, Geddes opened *Horizons* with the simple declaration: "We enter a new era." He then followed this assertion with highly detailed and persuasive models and drawings to illustrate the virtually invisible line that the practical visionary Geddes drew between them and reality. So strange were these visionary schemes that one magazine, describing Geddes as a designer who "sees a big future for daring ideas," felt compelled to ask its reluctant readership in the article's headline: "Are YOU Afraid of the Unexpected?"[17]

During this period Geddes also designed more functional yet theatrical factories, offices, and nightclubs. Among the most notable was the Toledo Scale Company's factory. The Ohio-based company commissioned two of Geddes's most famous, never-realized designs: his reimagining of their signature product—a counter scale—and his redesign of the firm's entire factory complex. Here, Geddes took his idea of the transformative theater and applied it to the factory, where he imagined work to be an uplifting enterprise. Similarly, Geddes designed the offices of the J. Walter Thompson advertising agency in Manhattan, where sleek walls hid all of the messy accoutrements of business to create a stage set of streamlined corporate efficiency. (In 1933 Geddes married Frances Resor Waite, niece of the president of the J. Walter Thompson agency, further strengthening his relationship with the company.) Another significant commission was Manhattan's Barberry Room nightclub of 1938, where Geddes installed mirrors on facing walls to reflect the images of patrons amid the club's spectacle.

In the 1930s, Geddes also participated in some of the era's great American world's fairs. Such expositions, located in cities from San Francisco to Chicago to New York, provided Depression-weary Americans with glimpses of a brighter future in the form of spectacular modernist pavilions filled with the latest technologies, products, and media. While Geddes's General Motors Futurama made him a star of the 1939–40 New York World's Fair, he also provided numerous projects that fused theater and architecture for Chicago's 1933–34 Century of Progress International Exposition. His most spectacular proposals included a twenty-five-story tower comprising a slender core surmounted by a cantilevered, three-tier revolving restaurant, anticipating Seattle's Space Needle of 1962, and a group of domed theater buildings, one of which Geddes hoped would house his *Divine Comedy* spectacle.

Although none of Geddes's designs for the Chicago fair were realized, the 1930s proved to be the decade of his greatest acclaim. Geddes, architect Hugh Ferriss, critic Lewis Mumford, and designer Paul Frankl presented their ideas for the future in the *Annual of American Design* in 1931, while Geddes also figured in Sheldon and Martha Cheney's important book *Art and the Machine* (1936). Geddes's fame also earned him a place in the *New Yorker* magazine as the subject of a cartoon, which made fun of his ubiquity in the offices of corporate America and his desire to redesign the entire world, down to the level of biscuits. Enhancing his reputation as an impractical visionary, *Fortune* magazine described the extravagant Geddes as "a bomb thrower" whose ideas "cost American businessmen billions of dollars."[18]

A BIGGER WORLD: 1937–1945

Not willing to constrain his efforts to theater sets, automobiles, and nightclubs, in the late 1930s Geddes also sought to reshape the entire American landscape. In 1937, when Geddes was asked by the J. Walter Thompson agency to create an ad campaign for a new form of gasoline, he envisioned a Shell Oil City of Tomorrow. With this project, pitchman Geddes became urban visionary, focusing on decentralization as key to the improved city. Represented by a massive model and dramatically photographed for magazine publication, Shell's City of Tomorrow featured overpasses with ramps that permitted drivers to change direction without crossing traffic, the segregation of residential from business and industrial areas by green space, and the routing of through-traffic around the city center. Geddes forecast what we now recognize as global positioning systems with "automatic in-car traffic control," directed in part by television feeds of local traffic conditions.

Although Shell's City of Tomorrow was born as an advertising campaign, it addressed serious issues of contemporary urbanism. Similarly, after a hiatus of about eight years from the theater, in the

seek ways to remedy the problems of urban youth. Demonstrating his wide range of aesthetic expression, Geddes followed the gritty, hyperrealistic *Dead End* with grandiose abstract sets for *The Eternal Road* (1937), a musical drama directed by Max Reinhardt with music by Kurt Weill, who had recently emigrated from Hitler's Germany. Depicting anti-Semitic events in medieval times, the play sought to engender sympathy for the plight of the Jews in Nazi Germany.

FIGURE 19 (LEFT)
Catalog cover for the International Theatre Exhibition at Amsterdam, January–February, 1922. Geddes's designs for The Divine Comedy *and* King Lear *were featured.*

FIGURE 20 (RIGHT)
Arthur Strawn, "Grand Master of Modernism" article, New York Herald Tribune, *March 1, 1931.*

mid-1930s Geddes returned to Broadway for two productions, *Dead End* and *The Eternal Road*, which addressed significant social and cultural topics with his characteristic design flair. While Geddes laid the foundation for his concepts of an immersive and transformative theater design by the late 1920s, those concepts were enhanced in Sidney Kingsley's play *Dead End* (1935), which Geddes produced and in which he employed set, sound, and lighting designs to contrast the plight of poor urban adolescents against an adjacent affluent neighborhood. The play proved so effective in conveying its social message that it spurred First Lady Eleanor Roosevelt to

In their visual drama and engagement with contemporary social issues, Shell's City of Tomorrow, *Dead End*, and *The Eternal Road* proved to be valuable dress rehearsals for Geddes's final project of the 1930s: Futurama, the General Motors pavilion at the 1939–40 New York World's Fair, dedicated to "building the world of tomorrow." One of the most popular attractions at the fair, Futurama proved to be the pinnacle of Geddes's career. This feat of imagination and its impact on the national consciousness highlights Geddes's talents as a modeler, futurist, and urban planner. Geddes's design of the Futurama exhibition was the culmination of his holistic approach: The audience experience was choreographed from entrance to exit as people traveled over a huge model of 1960 America, complete with highways that bisected cities and wove through mountains and valleys, bringing people breathtakingly close to nature. The model's national roadways anticipated the 1950s interstate highway system. Although some argue that the audience experience was akin to moving consumers like products along an assembly line, there is no question that Futurama represented a vision of an egalitarian America (automobility for all!) that was shaped to the last detail by a godlike Norman Bel Geddes.[19] As visitors left the exhibition, they were given buttons stating "I Have Seen the Future"—visible proof of their trip into the future.

Courtesy Kemp Starrett from the "New Yorker"
"Gentlemen—I Am Convinced That Our Next New Biscuit Must Be Styled by Norman Bel Geddes"

How original was Geddes's vision of an auto-centric America in 1960? Such ideas were already prevalent at the time. "Outside the fairgrounds," Owen D. Gutfreund has noted, New York's master builder, Robert Moses, was at work, "remaking the metropolitan area along these auto-centric lines, and the public seemed to embrace each new project as a step into the future." Still, enormously popular exhibitions such as Futurama "created even more converts" to an America dependent on the car.[20]

While the exhibition inside the Futurama pavilion was the focus of the public's attention, its sculptural, curvilinear exterior was equally im-

pressive. Here, Geddes, who was never a licensed architect, showed his interest in the work of such German modernists as Erich Mendelsohn, whom Geddes met in 1924. Mendelsohn's work represented a more dynamic form of modernism than the more puritanical International Style. With Geddes's Futurama pavilion, he cast a shadow on other architects, including Eero Saarinen, who worked on the Futurama pavilion in Geddes's office in 1938 and whose TWA Terminal at New York's Kennedy Airport shows its influence. The modernist lineage

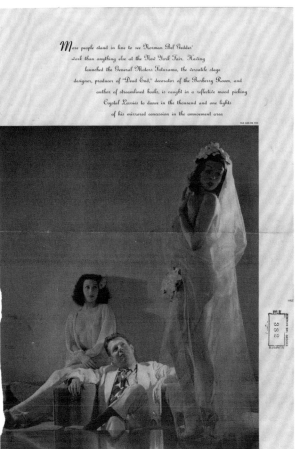

established by Mendelsohn, Geddes, and Saarinen continues today in the work of such architects as Santiago Calatrava.

Following the success of Futurama, Geddes sought ways to influence American car culture and its imprint on the nation's landscape. Less than three months after Futurama opened, Geddes wrote to President Roosevelt with material outlining Futurama's "enormous popularity . . . as indicated by the nation-wide press use of the subject

FIGURE 21 (LEFT)
Kemp Starrett Geddes-themed cartoon in The New Yorker, *December 10, 1932.*

FIGURE 22 (RIGHT)
Feature on Geddes's Crystal Lassies novelty for the 1939–40 New York World's Fair in Town & Country, *August 1939. Geddes's burlesque show of mirrored reflections of very scantily clad women was one of many offered in the Amusement Area of the World's Fair, sharing space with Salvador Dalí's "Dream of Venus" and the Cavalcade of Centaurs as well as the more family-friendly Aquacade choreographed by Billy Rose.*

matter, and the consequent editorial comment."[21] Roosevelt responded by appointing Geddes to work on preliminary planning for the National Motorway Planning Authority, which influenced the interstate highway system. Geddes further disseminated his ideas with the book *Magic Motorways*, announcing that "there are too many cars" and proposing a more tempered approach to their accommodation, including still-valid ideas such as minicars for city driving, suburban subway systems, and "park and ride" areas for commuters living outside the city's core.[22]

By the second year of the New York World's Fair, war was declared in Europe, and the United States entered the conflict in 1941. This prompted Geddes to convert his interest in war—he had invented a popular war game in the mid-1910s and owned an extensive library on the subject—into serious wartime activities. He applied the model-making skills he had developed for Futurama to the fabrication of elaborate miniatures of land and sea conflicts that would give Americans front-row seats on the battlefront. Like his models of *The Divine Comedy* in the 1920s or those of Shell's City of Tomorrow in the 1930s, these miniatures were convincingly photographed (with clouds and smoke made of cotton) as part of the grandiosely titled and extravagantly marketed Norman Bel Geddes Process. Proclaimed by New York's Museum of Modern Art as "a new form of picture journalism" that educated the public about the war, these images were featured in *Life* magazine, while the models themselves were displayed at the museum in 1944.[23] By the end of the war, Geddes was using this process to realistically depict the building of the Egyptian pyramids and the Panama Canal for the *Encyclopaedia Britannica*. With the Bel Geddes Process, Geddes not only exponentially expanded his arsenal of visualization tools, but also pointed American design in a new, largely unexplored direction beyond the creation of discrete objects toward the creation of information systems. This field would be advanced in the late 1950s by designers such as Charles and Ray Eames and George Nelson in their exhibitions and books for IBM and the United States government.

TOTAL LIVING: 1945–1958

At the end of World War II, in 1945, the United States emerged as a rich and powerful nation, a seemingly ideal environment for Geddes to realize his most visionary dreams. Yet, sadly, circumstances conspired against him. In failing health—Geddes had a heart attack in 1944 and afterward suffered increasingly from high blood pressure—he was further depressed by the death of his wife, Frances Resor Waite, in 1943.[24] Around the same time, his business partners left the office for a competitor; Geddes wanted to focus less on consumer research and engineering and more on design, while they did not. Although the years between 1944 and 1947 were successful ones—including designs of a new Coca-Cola vending machine, as well as window displays, radios, luggage, and boats—Geddes's financial situation soon turned sour. A few years after the war, business had fallen off by fifty percent, and Geddes closed his large office in 1946.[25]

No longer at the epicenter of American industrial design after World War II, Geddes nonetheless remained a prescient visionary who, though often not successful in realizing his vision, was involved in virtually every field that defined Cold War America, from television to suburbia to urban renewal. Between 1944 and 1947, for example, Geddes's office worked for postwar powerhouse IBM on the design of business machines and workstations. (Eliot Noyes, one of Geddes's employees at the time, went on to design the famous Selectric typewriter for IBM after leaving Geddes's office.) Urban planning continued to preoccupy Geddes. Although attempts to send Futurama's vast model around the world as a kind of mobile cultural ambassador of the American way of life didn't materialize, Geddes's interest in the American city advanced in 1945 when he was invited to come up with a comprehensive plan for redeveloping Toledo, Ohio. The core problems to be solved in the "Toledo Tomorrow" project included transportation and traffic flow, and Geddes reiterated many of the concepts developed for Shell Oil and Futurama. His plans for an associated air terminal were evidence of his strikingly prescient understanding that mass air transit would become commonplace at a time when such services had just been introduced in

MAGIC MOTORWAYS

NORMAN BEL GEDDES

America. Sadly, this project, like so many of Geddes's postwar efforts, was not realized.

After the war, Geddes returned to the performing arts and creating innovative spaces for them—his first love and the field of his earliest successes. (When Geddes turned his attention to his autobiography shortly before his death in 1958, he chose to focus it exclusively on his early career in the theater.) He worked until 1949 for Ringling Bros. and Barnum & Bailey Circus. In addition to creating dynamic posters, Geddes designed modular cages and wagons with improved fittings that facilitated easy transfer from rail to ground transport. He also discarded the traditional peaked circus tent in favor of a domed construction which allowed a huge, completely unobstructed space

accommodating as many as two thousand people and a five-ring circus—a revolutionary rethinking of a traditional structure. Reconceiving a historic form of entertainment, Geddes also worked for the newest entertainment media, and in the 1950s, collaborated with television pioneer Frank Stanton on a series of unbuilt studio facilities in Manhattan that sought to mechanize television production in the same way Geddes had mechanized theater sets in the 1920s. Television viewers were also considered in Geddes's never-built design for an open-air sports stadium with a retractable roof for the Brooklyn Dodgers, while moviegoers were the audience for an unrealized film version of *The Miracle* in Cinerama.

A theatricalized form of architecture—in which the movement of masses of people added drama and where people could see and be seen—also characterized Geddes's postwar work. His Copa City in Miami of 1948, a nightclub-cum-theater, department store, and radio or television studio, was a veritable fun house of transparent and reflective surfaces that outshone the Barberry Room of the 1930s. The next year Geddes proposed a General Motors "consumers' building," which was, in effect, a vertical version of Futurama—a multistory structure in which people moved via swooping ramps,

FIGURE 24 (RIGHT)
Rendering of consumers' building cutaway to show ramp system and auditorium, c. 1949. Charcoal and gouache on paper, 17¾ x 22 in., 45 x 55.9 cm

FIGURE 25 (BOTTOM RIGHT)
Rendering of a generic (ABCD) consumers' building, originally pitched to General Motors, 1949. Charcoal and gouache on paper, 20⅞ x 21½ in., 53 x 54.6 cm

FIGURE 26 (BOTTOM LEFT)
Rendering of consumers' building interior with imagined exposition, c. 1949. Charcoal and gouache on paper, 23⅝ x 9⅝ in., 60 x 24.4 cm

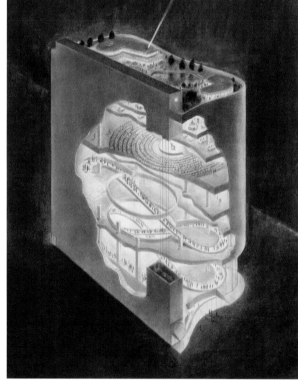

and large windows on the street turned their movement into urban theater. Geddes also applied his innovative ideas for mobile sets—most famously used for the 1928 Broadway production of *The Patriot*—to architecture, best seen in the moving components of his Expand-A-House, as well as his climatically efficient Walless House, with its garage-door-like walls that pivoted up to open and close the residence depending on the weather.

While these projects are fascinating, they are little known. Most people's awareness of Geddes's work—if they know it at all—dates to the 1930s. Why this blind spot in our understanding of his full achievement? There are several reasons for Geddes's obscurity. Unlike other founding members of the industrial design profession, he closed his office before he died, leaving no successor firm. Also, he died before publishing an autobiography that presented his design, as well as his theatrical, legacy.

Other industrial designers memorialized their work in hagiographic volumes: One of Geddes's protégés, Henry Dreyfuss, cemented his reputation as a serious thinker and designer in his books *Designing for People* (1955) and *The Measure of Man* (1960); Raymond Loewy, as shameless a self-promoter as Geddes, staked out an exalted role for himself in his 1979 book *Industrial Design*. And, unlike Dreyfuss's telephone or Russel Wright's dinnerware, which are still in circulation, Geddes's most iconic project, Futurama, exists only in images—even his best-known work was ephemeral.

This publication and the exhibition it accompanies seek to address this gap in Geddes scholarship. To tell a comprehensive story, the resulting book has been organized into two parts: The first features six thematic essays that interpret Geddes's work in the context of broader themes that were central to his achievements—spirituality, business

FIGURE 27

Norman Bel Geddes & Co. design for a Ringling Bros. and Barnum & Bailey Circus poster, c. 1942. Watercolor and tempera on board, 28½ x 19¼ in., 72.4 x 48.9 cm

FIGURE 28 (TOP)
Rendering of the exterior of Geddes's redesign of a circus tent for Ringling Bros. and Barnum & Bailey Circus, c. 1940. Pencil on paper, 23¼ x 16½ in., 59 x 41.9 cm

FIGURE 29 (BOTTOM)
T. Kautzky rendering of Geddes-designed interior of a circus tent for Ringling Bros. and Barnum & Bailey Circus, c. 1940. Tempera and conté on paper, 22¾ x 17 in., 60.3 x 43.1 cm

practice, architecture, consumer culture, nature and transportation systems, and futurism. The second part of the book contains eleven project essays, each of which explores an aspect of his work, from his designs for plays and theaters to his furniture and domestic appliances, graphic designs, and models. The book and exhibition are the first to focus on Geddes since the 1970s and by far the largest in scope. They also serve as showcases for the extraordinary Geddes archive at the Harry Ransom Humanities Research Center at The University of Texas at Austin.

Coincidentally, the publication of this book comes one year after the U.S. Postal Service issued a block of stamps devoted to American industrial designers: Geddes (represented by his stylish 1940 Patriot radio) and his protégés make up a third of the dozen designers featured in the series—an indication of his significance and long-lasting influence. Beyond the design of products and the imagining of fantastic schemes, Geddes played a seminal role in shaping the expectations and behavior of American consumers and helping to transform both the industrial and theater design professions into modern businesses. A paradoxical figure made up of equal parts visionary and pragmatist, serious inventor and inveterate promoter, naturalist and industrialist, democrat and egoist, Norman Bel Geddes sought nothing less than the transformation of modern American society through design.

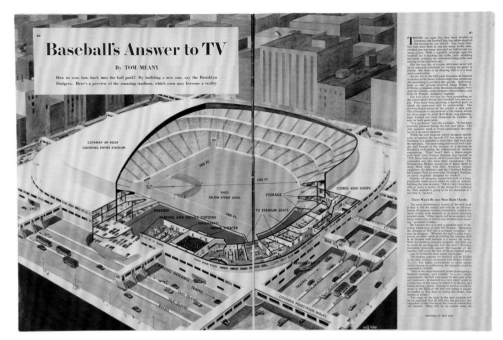

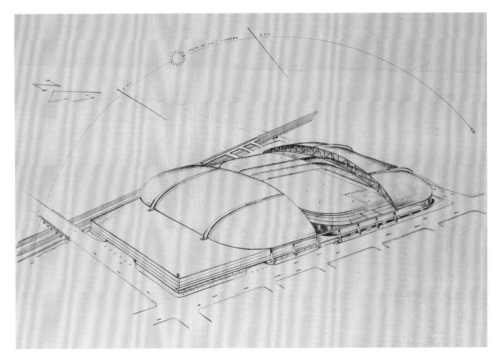

FIGURE 30 (TOP)
Tom Meany article "Baseball's Answer to TV" in Collier's, *September 27, 1952.*

FIGURE 31 (BOTTOM)
John A. Dilliard perspective drawing of Geddes's design for an all-weather, all-purpose stadium, never built, for the Brooklyn Dodgers, 1949. Pen and ink, 25 x 22 in., 63.5 x 55.9 cm

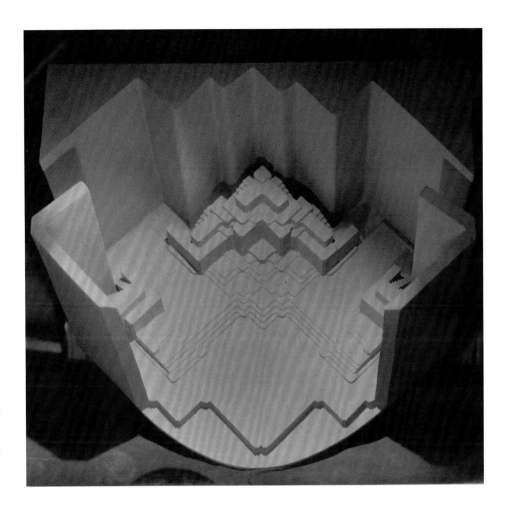

FIGURE 32 (OPPOSITE TOP)
*Robert Edmond Jones
set for an unidentified play from Geddes's
research files, not dated.
Photograph by unidentified photographer,
12 x 6½ in., 30.5 x 16.5 cm*

FIGURE 33 (OPPOSITE BOTTOM)
*Geddes set design drawing
("Archangel Michael
sweeping his sword
beneath Satan's feet") for
the film* Sorrows of Satan,
*1924. Charcoal on board,
28 x 21 in., 71.1 x 53.3 cm*

FIGURE 34 (TOP)
Geddes model set for
Jeanne d'Arc, *c. 1925.
Photograph by Francis
Bruguière, 11¼ x 9 in.,
29.6 x 22.9 cm*

FIGURE 35 (BOTTOM)
*Production still for the
film* Sorrows of Satan,
*1925. Photograph by
unidentified photographer,
10 x 8½ in., 25.4 x 21.6 cm*

COLOR SCHEME

MAJOR DOMO : GROUND HAT · UMBRELLA
BLACK WITH VERMILION STRIPES · SPOTS
GOLD · VEIL DUST · SHOES VERMILION ·
RUFF EDGED WITH GOLD ·

LATE CLOWN : GROUND HAT WHITE WITH
ULTRAMARINE · STRIPES SPOTS EMERALD ·
RUFFS WHITE · SHOES EMERALD ·

CART 1510 : CART ORANGE · FLOWERS WHITE ·

DONKEY 1511 : HARNESS ORANGE · RUFF
WHITE ·

CLOWN BAND MASTER · DRIVER · MUSICIANS :
GROUND WHITE · POMPONS RUFFS BLACK ·

CLOWN BARKER : BLACK AND WHITE ·

DONKEY 1601 : BODY POWDERED WHITE ·

FLOAT 1600 : GROUND WHITE PATTERN
LETTERING · FOOTLIGHT CERULEAN BACK
DROP EMERALD · PUNCH VERMILION JUDY YELLOW ·

HOOP CLOWN : GROUND WHITE · STRIPES
VIOLET · RUFF WHITE EDGED WITH VIOLET ·
SHOES VIOLET ·

UMBRELLA CLOWN : GROUND HAT WHITE ·
STRIPES YELLOW · RUFF WHITE EDGED IN
YELLOW · SHOES YELLOW ·
UMBRELLA : GROUND WITH · STRIPES YELLOW ·

MIDGET CLOWN : COAT BLACK · SPOTS
VERMILION · COLLAR WHITE · TROUSERS
EMERALD AND WHITE STRIPES · STOCKING
BLACK AND VERMILION CHECKS · WIG VER-
MILION · HAT BLACK ·

RUNABOUT CLOWN : LOWER AND UPPER
GROUND EMERALD · CENTER GROUND
BLACK · STRIPES COLLAR AND CUFFS
WHITE · SHOES POMPONS VERMILION ·

BALLOON CLOWN : GROUND WHITE · STRIPES
SHIRT CERULEAN · WIG ORANGE ·

FLOAT 1800 : AIRPLANE YELLOW AND
WHITE · STAYS STRIPED · DERRICK AND
TRUCK VERMILION · WHEELS BLACK ·
FLOWERS YELLOW ·

AERO CLOWNS 1806 1807 : STARCHED
SHIRT WHITE HAT TIE BLACK STOCKING
GREEN SPOTS SHOES YELLOW · BRACES
CERULEAN · TROUSERS ROSE · DRAWERS
ORANGE ·

AERO CLOWN 1808 : WAIST BLACK ·
RUFFLES ROSE · WIG EMERALD ·

AERO CLOWN 1809 : LOWER AND UPPER
GROUND ROSE · CENTER GROUND WHITE ·
STRIPES CUFFS COLLAR EMERALD ·
SHOES POMPONS CERULEAN ·

AERO MECHANICS : GROUND CERULEAN
PATTERN HAT WHITE · SHOES AND
FEATHERS EMERALD ·

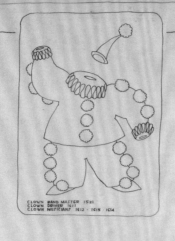

CLOWN BAND MASTER 1521
CLOWN DRIVER 1511
CLOWN MUSICIANS 1612 · 1613 · 1614

CLOWN BARKERS
1615 · 1616

BALLOON CLOWN
1704

MAJOR DOMO
1501

DONKEY 1511

BAND LEADER
1521

CLOWN CART 1510

DONKEY 1601

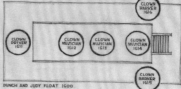

CLOWN
BARKER
1616

CLOWN
DRIVER
1611

CLOWN
MUSICIAN
1612

CLOWN
MUSICIAN
1613

CLOWN
MUSICIAN
1614

CLOWN
BARKER
1615

PUNCH AND JUDY FLOAT 1600

HOOP
CLOWN
1701

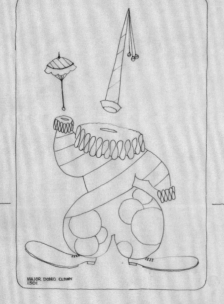

MAJOR DOMO CLOWN
1501

CURB LINE

HOOP CLOWN 1701 ·
UMBRELLA CLOWN 1703

1 CLOWN MAJOR DOMO

1 CLOWN BAND MASTER

PUNCH & JUDY

1 DRIVER · 3 PUPPETS · 3 CLOWN MUSICIANS · 2 CLOWN BARKERS

1 HOOP CLOWN · 1 M

PUNCH AND JUDY FLOAT 1600

DRAWING 6

UNITS 1500 · 1600 · 1700 · 1800 · 1900
SCALE OF ½ INCH EQUALS 1 FOOT

CHRIST

FIGURE 38

Geddes drawing of Punch and Judy, clowns, and airplane floats for a Macy's Christmas parade, October 12, 1926. Pencil, ink, gouache, and watercolor on paper, 91½ x 41 in., 232.4 x 104.1 cm

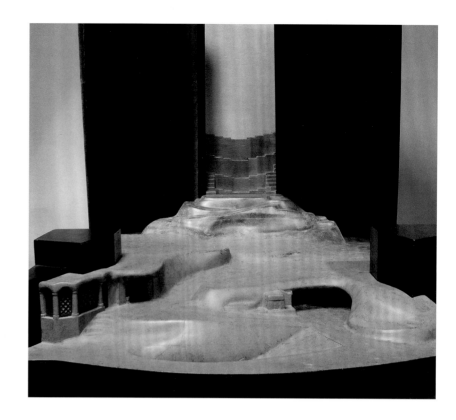

FIGURE 39 (TOP)
Geddes model of the stage set for The Eternal Road, *c. 1937. Extensive restoration was done on the model in the 1960s. The model originally seems to have had a light-colored cyclorama, probably in gray. Wood and plastic, 51 x 49 x 39 in., 129.5 x 124.5 x 99.1 cm*

FIGURE 40 (BOTTOM RIGHT)
Bel Geddes (pointing up) during construction of The Eternal Road *set, c. 1937. Kurt Weill is standing second from left. Photograph by Metropolitan Photoservice, 8 x 10 in., 20.3 x 25.4 cm*

FIGURE 41 (BOTTOM LEFT)
Stage set for The Eternal Road *under construction, c. 1937. Photograph by Edward Gruber, 8 x 10 in., 20.3 x 25.4 cm*

FIGURE 42 (OPPOSITE)
Joseph Macauley as Angel of Death in The Eternal Road, *c. 1937. Photograph by Edward Steichen, used with permission of the estate of Edward Steichen, 10 x 8 in., 20.3 x 35.4 cm*

ENDNOTES

1 Some project descriptions in this essay are drawn from texts written by Cathy Henderson and others in the preparation of planning and implementation grants to the National Endowment for the Humanities.

2 "Grand Master of Modernism" was an article published in the *New York Herald Tribune* (March 1931), while the article "A Designer's 'Brave New World'" was published in the *New York Times Book Review* (18 December 1932).

3 "Norman Bel Geddes," *Fortune*, vol. 11 (July 1930): 51–57.

4 Chesla C. Sherlock, "The Man Who Streamlined the World," *Opportunity* magazine, vol. 30 (April 1938): 12, 28, 41.

5 Norman Bel Geddes, *Miracle in the Evening: An Autobiography*, edited by William Kelley (Garden City, NY: Doubleday & Company, 1960), 278.

6 Norman Bel Geddes, *Horizons* (Boston: Little, Brown, 1932), 4.

7 Belle and Norman had two daughters, Joan and Barbara. Barbara Bel Geddes had a successful acting career in theater, film, and television.

8 For information on consumer culture and department stores I am indebted to William Leach, *Land of Desire: Merchants, Power, and the Rise of a New American Culture* (New York: Pantheon Books, 1993).

9 Kenneth Macgowan, "Leonardo of Our Theater," *Theater Arts Monthly* 45 (January 1961): 63–65.

10 F. V. Frazer, "The New Magic of the Stage," *Broadhurst Theater: The New York Stage Magazine* (no date): 10, 34.

11 For a full discussion of Geddes and Expressionism, see Nicolas Paolo Maffei, "Designing the Image of the Practical Visionary: Norman Bel Geddes, 1893–1958," a thesis submitted in partial fulfillment of the requirements of the Royal College of Art for the degree of Doctor of Philosophy, February 2000.

12 Claude Bragdon, "A New Kind of Theatre by Norman Bel Geddes," *Architectural Record* 57 (March 1922): 170–182.

13 "Norman Bel Geddes," *Fortune* (July 1930): 51.

14 M. K. Wisehart, "Are YOU Afraid of the Unexpected?" *The American* magazine (July 1931): 71–73, 85.

15 Earnest Elmo Calkins, "Beauty the New Business Tool," *Atlantic Monthly* (August 1927): 144–156.

16 Sherlock, 12.

17 Wisehart, 71.

18 George Nelson, "Both Fish and Fowl," *Fortune*, vol. 15 (February 1934): 43–44, 88.

19 Maffei in his dissertation credits the connection between Futurama's ride and an assembly line to a 1992 article by Roland Marchand as well as to a critic of Geddes's time. See page 249.

20 Owen D. Gutfreund, "Rebuilding New York in the Auto Age: Robert Moses and His Highways" in Hilary Ballon and Kenneth T. Jackson, eds., *Robert Moses and the Modern City: The Transformation of New York* (New York and London: W.W. Norton and Company, 2007), 89–90.

21 The fair officially opened on 30 April 1939. The letter is dated July 21 of that year.

22 Norman Bel Geddes, *Magic Motorways* (New York: Random House, 1940), 11.

23 The quote appears in a booklet published by the museum in conjunction with the exhibition "Norman Bel Geddes War Maneuver Models Created for *Life* Magazine," which was presented at the museum from 26 January to 5 March 1944.

24 Geddes married two more times, first to Anne Howe Hilliard and then to Edith Lutyens.

25 Maffei, "Designing the Image of the Practical Visionary," 269–70. In his thesis, Maffei further explains that Geddes subsequently opened "a smaller office with a staff of twelve devoted to 'design' rather than 'administration' as Geddes put it"; letter from Geddes to Mr. and Mrs. Windsor Lewis (Barbara Bel Geddes), 7 August 1952, family correspondence, File 960, Geddes Papers.

FIGURE 43 (TOP)
Rendering, signed only "Lutz," of Colonial Hotel Nassau, aerial view, 1954–56. Gouache on board, 29 x 18 in., 73.7 x 45.7 cm

FIGURE 44 (BOTTOM LEFT)
Rendering, signed only "Lutz," of Colonial Hotel Nassau patio, 1954–56. Gouache on board, 11 x 15 in., 27.9 x 38.1 cm

FIGURE 45 (BOTTOM RIGHT)
Rendering, signed only "Lutz," of Colonial Hotel Nassau front elevation, 1954–56. Gouache on board, 11 x 15 in., 27.9 x 38.1 cm

NORMAN BEL GEDDES AND A SPIRITUAL PHILOSOPHY OF ART AND INSPIRATION

Danielle Brune Sigler

ith *Horizons* and Futurama, Norman Bel Geddes ensured his place in the pantheon of visionary designers. While he planned the future, he also became known for his salesmanship and very earthly pursuit of commercial and financial success. Yet, in the 1910s and '20s, in the earliest phases of his career, Geddes espoused a lofty, spiritually based philosophy of art and inspiration—one with roots in his mother's belief in Christian Science and Theosophy, a religious tradition popular among his fellow artists. The 1932 publication of *Horizons*, his major treatise on the importance of good industrial design, marked a decided shift in Geddes's focus. While insisting that the designer could and should be an artist, Geddes no longer emphasized the importance of the spiritual qualities of art—focusing instead on the emotional and functional appeal of an object and the careful, studied problem-solving approach of the designer.

Norman Melancton Geddes's religious upbringing began with the rigid Methodist faith of his mother's parents in Newcomerstown, Ohio (FIG. 1). As a boy, Geddes chafed at required attendance at church services and Sunday school and the strict religious conservatism of his grandfather, whom he later labeled a "spiritual bully." As an adult, Geddes vividly recalled episodes that exposed the hypocrisy and narrow-mindedness of the faith of his mother's family.[1] This Methodism dominated Geddes's childhood until he, his brother, and his mother, Lulu Yingling Geddes, moved to Ann Arbor, Michigan, to run a boarding house near the University of Michigan.[2] Geddes's younger brother, Dudley, whose left leg was one inch shorter than his right leg, began to experience physical and emotional difficulties because of the discrepancy. Lulu Geddes availed herself of the medical resources of the university and a friend on the faculty of the medical school, but when traditional medicine did not offer Dudley a cure, she turned to Christian Science, a faith still in its infancy.

Christian Science had been growing in popularity since its founder, Mary Baker Eddy, published *Science and Health* in 1875. Eddy taught that humans could work toward the perfection of Jesus and break free from their perceived limitations through reading and study. For Eddy, the seen world and apparent

obstacles could be overcome through a belief in the divine. Freeing oneself from disease and disability was just one portion of this teaching, but one with a significant appeal to the mother of an ailing son. Geddes recalled that his mother began reading Mary Baker Eddy's writings and going to Christian Science church services and testimonial meetings. After a few months, his mother "began taking Dudley into her bedroom for an hour or more, reading and discussing thoughts she had located in the Bible and their interpretation of Mrs. Eddy[']s *Science and Health* book."[3] After almost a year of this study, Geddes reported that Dudley had begun to walk more easily and that "within twenty months after Mother began talking and praying with Dudley, his short leg had lengthened to within one sixteenth of an inch of the other one."[4] The healing was so striking that it impressed not only the family, but also the professor of medicine whom Lulu Geddes had consulted. He appended his name to one of the many testimonies she submitted to Christian Science publications. In this testimony, Lulu Geddes also noted that, in addition to helping Dudley's leg, Christian Science had provided her with relief from mental and physical ailments.

Though Geddes would later explain that "neither [Dudley] nor I ever embraced Christian Science,"[5] he did devote attention to Christian Science during his years in Detroit, where he had moved in 1913 and commenced work as a commercial illustrator. His income soon permitted him to rent a small house and to bring his mother and Dudley to live in the city. Among the books in his Detroit library was his own copy of *Science and Health*, a Christmas gift from his mother. Geddes's study of *Science and Health* encouraged his mother to such a degree that four months later, on the eve of his twenty-first birthday in 1914, she wrote him a letter praising his new spiritual birth.[6] The underlining, brackets, and annotations in Geddes's *Science and Health* support his mother's appraisal of his investment in the study of Christian Science and reveal his specific interest in the role of the spiritual in Christian Science. His engagement with the religion was not limited to reading and study; Geddes also sought assistance from Christian Science practitioners for psychological

and physical problems while in Detroit. Evidence of the influence of Christian Science theology appears in Geddes's earliest public writing and, perhaps even more important, Christian Science provided Geddes with an entrée into a broader, mystical world.

As it did for Geddes's sometime collaborator, choreographer Ruth St. Denis, Christian Science proved a point of departure for expansion into other religious traditions that were gaining in popularity in the era.[7] Theosophy, one of these emerging religions, acknowledged the existence of, and offered the possibility of communion with, something beyond the seen world. Theosophists sought "the aggregate of the knowledge and wisdom that underlie the Universe"[8] and, while there was an official organization, the Theosophical Society, to foster this effort, countless Americans like Geddes pursued the wisdom of the universe without a formal connection to the Society.

Theosophy and related strains of esoteric religion offered Geddes a more fluid approach to the spirit than that provided by Christian Science *and* they united his interest in the spiritual with his passion for art and creation. Art, for many mystics and Theosophists of Geddes's era, retained a unique status. The Russian philosopher and mystic P. D. Ouspensky asserted that "Art is a powerful instrument of knowledge of the nuomenal world: mysterious depths, each one more amazing than the last, open to the vision of man when he holds in his hands this magical key."[9] Given the value placed on art and its status within these belief systems, it is little wonder that they were part and parcel of the creative world in which Geddes moved early in his career. His friends and collaborators, including St. Denis, her partner Ted Shawn, and architect Claude Bragdon, embraced various forms of these mystical faiths and integrated them into their work. Their correspondence and writings are filled with the language of the spiritual. Bragdon saw his own colleagues as likely "spiritual brothers" to Geddes.[10] And, as Geddes prepared to embark on a major project, his close friend Jacob Weintz wrote to him, "May God weld your possibilities into an idealistic reality and give you the power to project" and signed off "Inshallah!"[11]

In June 1915, Geddes began sharing his thoughts through the "idealistic reality" of *Inwhich,*

a magazine "in which I say just what I think." The breadth, tone, and even the design of the magazine owed much to Roycroft founder Elbert Hubbard's little magazine, *The Philistine* (**FIG. 2, 3**).[12] Hubbard's magazine, written entirely by Hubbard, proved to be an apt model for Geddes, whose own aspirations saw their incarnation in the scope and personality-centered nature of Hubbard's Roycroft empire. Writing to Weintz a few months into the magazine's run, Geddes commented on what he viewed as the unique feature of *Inwhich*: "It is the only personal book published. That is it is the only book where one person rules—bodily puts his own personality. There was a book—The Philistine as published by Elbert Hubbard at East Aurora—but Elbert is dead and so is the Philistine. . . . Do not for the world compare Inwhich with the Philistine. It is different in every way—except that it is a personal book and is similar in size."[13] Geddes's protest notwithstanding, readers were quick to make the connection between *Inwhich* and *The Philistine*, given that the first issue of *Inwhich* appeared just one month after Elbert Hubbard perished aboard the *Lusitania*. One reader wrote, "You were quick to grasp the opportunity when Fra Elbertus disappeared," and another, "By the shadow of Davy Jones, has the sea given up its dead or is it only a reincarnation of the spirit of our lamented Elbert that has given us In Which?"[14] Thus, a twenty-two-year-old Geddes had positioned himself as philosopher and espouser of general wisdom (**FIG. 4**).

Hubbard and *The Philistine* provided Geddes with an instructive model, both for his magazine and his larger career aspirations.[15] Geddes adopted Hubbard's authorial voice and followed Hubbard's lead in expounding on any and every subject that attracted his attention. Over the sixteen-issue run of *Inwhich*, subjects included billboards, World War I preparedness, profiles of people he admired, and of course, the theater. Unlike Hubbard, Geddes also incorporated a fair amount of spiritual and religiously themed content, including poems about Jesus and God, a short story told from the perspective of a man crucified with Jesus, and poetry by and a profile of an invented mystic by the name of Maq Yohaan. The spiritual emphasis appealed to others, including

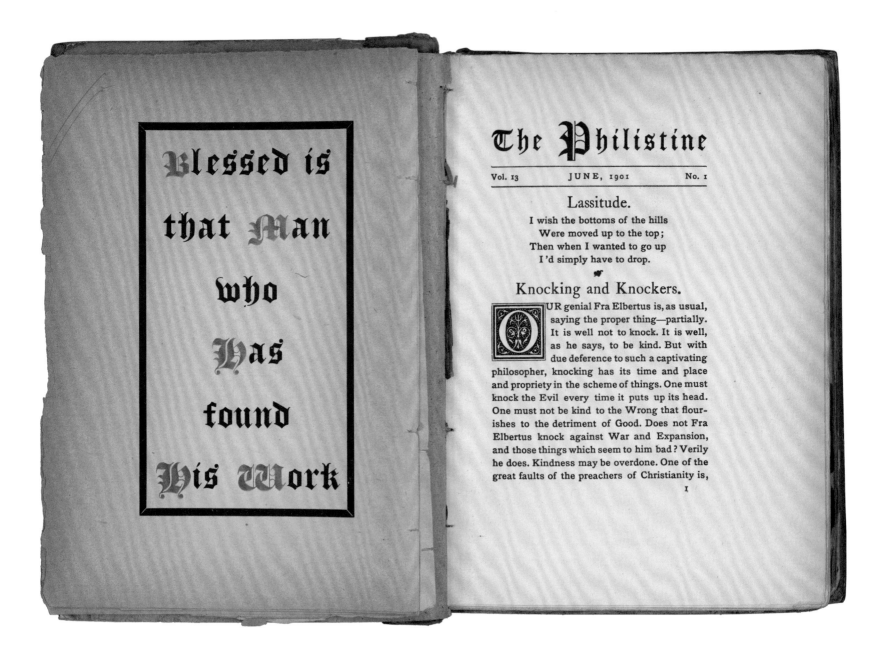

FIGURE 2

Interior pages of Elbert Hubbard's magazine, The Philistine, *June 1901.*

the advertising manager of the Society of Modern Art, who called *Inwhich* "that ray of sunshine which seems to radiate the great eternal,"[16] and the Occult Book Concern (New York), which deemed *Inwhich* an appropriate venue for advertising.

The spiritual also permeated Geddes's discussions of art, a topic at the heart of a magazine dedicated "to all who are striving to bring about the Reign of Life in Art." He began the inaugural issue, "Art and life! Improve one and you better the other . . ." and clearly believed that art had the potential to profoundly affect the world. In the second issue of *Inwhich*, Geddes explained the true appeal of art: "When we look at a beautiful object," he argued, "we are not admiring a work of art but the spirit of art, spiritually created beauty calling out spiritual recognition."[17] This spiritual component of art was fundamental to Geddes's conception. For Geddes, art was not "substance, but a spiritual

accomplishment,"[18] created by communing with the divine. In the essay "Genius-Talent-Cleverness," Geddes explained that genius was "the power God gives man at a specific moment to carry out His ideas." [19] From Geddes's perspective, any individual had the option to experience genius; he or she just needed to develop his or her innate divine nature.[20] Isolation was essential to this process, and Geddes turned to a centuries-old quote from Sir Thomas Browne to express his thoughts on the subject: "Be able to be alone. Lose not the advantage of solitude, and the society of thyself; nor be only content but delight to be alone and single with Omnipresency."[21] Geddes believed that isolation and struggle set the stage for a connection with the divine, and he would soon find it to be true in his own life.

Although Geddes abandoned *Inwhich* shortly after his August 1916 move to Los Angeles, the intellectual currents running through the magazine

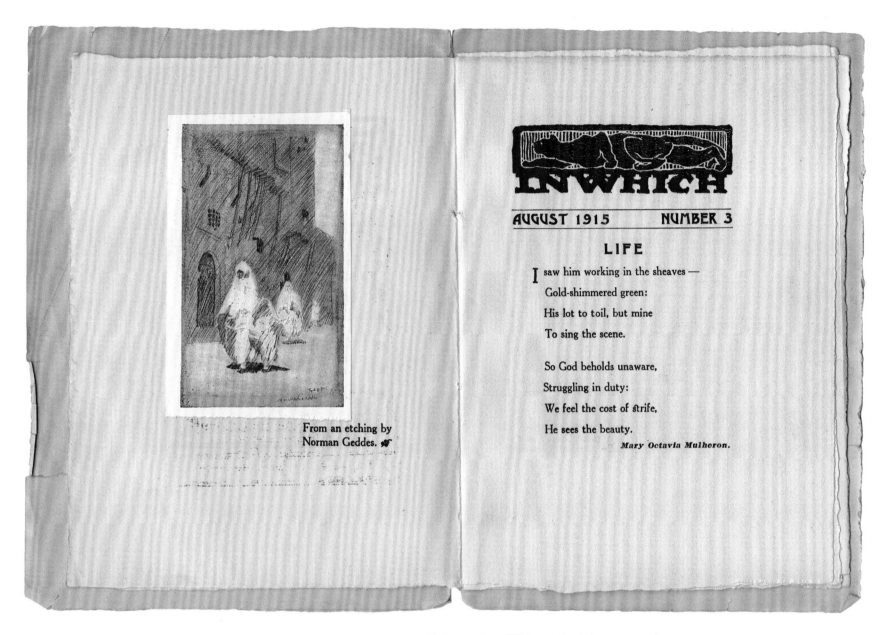

From an etching by
Norman Geddes.

INWHICH

AUGUST 1915   NUMBER 3

LIFE

I saw him working in the sheaves —
Gold-shimmered green:
His lot to toil, but mine
To sing the scene.

So God beholds unaware,
Struggling in duty:
We feel the cost of strife,
He sees the beauty.

Mary Octavia Mulheron.

remained vital to his life and work. Even after Geddes moved to New York and met with one of his first great successes—designing the set for a revival of the musical *Erminie*—the quest for spiritual inspiration was not far behind. Geddes spent most of 1921, "one of the most depressing"[22] years of his life, waiting for a new project to come his way or for inspiration to strike. When inspiration finally did strike, it came to him in a quiet moment of isolation and anxiety and involved an apparently metaphysical phenomenon. The resulting effort was ultimately published in 1924 as *A Project for the Theatrical Presentation of The Divine Comedy of Dante Alighieri.*

In the preface of the book, Geddes carefully detailed his moment of inspiration: As he battled distraction, he had eliminated items from his work-space until he faced a bare wall. Staring at the wall, Geddes began to notice "a palpitation as of [*sic*] some

sort of life was there."[23] He realized that no one else would be able to see it, that it was in his imagination, yet "the wall pulsated just as surely as my own body did. . . . The spot would glow as a coal that is breathed upon."[24] The palpitation's rhythm and appearance varied night to night until finally:

I was being drawn toward that burning hole in the wall, all the time, turning round and round, like a corkscrew. My body grew hotter and hotter. I rose to my feet, to throw the illusion off, and reeled dizzily into the next room and across it into a bookcase. I grabbed a book without reading the title. . . . It was the first volume of Norton's translation of Dante's Divine Comedy."[25]

This set Geddes on a path to create a "dramatic visualization" of *The Divine Comedy*. Beyond the initial inspiration to grab the volume of Dante, his

FIGURE 3
Interior pages of Geddes's little magazine, Inwhich, *August 1915.*

interaction with the palpitating wall became fundamental to his design, "the form that I could not forget was the never ceasing movement round and round" (FIG. 5).[26]

And yet Geddes set forth this account of a rather mystical-sounding inspiration without the explicit use of the language of religion or spirituality that he used in *Inwhich*. His motivation for this is unclear, but it may have been an effort to be taken seriously by those who did *not* subscribe to the role of the spiritual/metaphysical in art. Those who saw a link between art and the divine would likely have read into the description the language that Geddes left out. When Geddes turned his attention to teaching a new generation of theater professionals, his notes left no question that he continued to believe

that the spiritual played a fundamental role in the creation of art.

In late fall of 1921, Geddes began offering a theater design course. He required prospective students to apply, limited the class size, and presented twenty lessons, once a week for four hours.[27] He advertised the class as a "practical course in the visual elements of dramatic production," and yet his course lecture notes are filled with language and theories that would strike some as anything but practical. The twenty design lessons varied from year to year and with the level of the class, but Geddes consistently included broad discussions of art and inspiration. "Art," Geddes wrote in his lecture notes, "transports us from the common human plane to one of aesthetic exaltation. . . . Great art is

FIGURE 4

A young Geddes with Helen Belle (Bel) Sneider, c. 1915. Photograph by unidentified photographer, 5 x 3¼ in., 12.7 x 8.3 cm

eternal and universal in its appeal."[28] Geddes persisted in his belief that truly great art was marked by a spiritual quality that was inherent in an artistic creation and that spoke directly to the spirit of the viewer. This was not evidence of "technical dexterity but a spirit radiating from the work which moves us emotionally thru the aesthetic sense."[29] In this capacity, art was wholly unique: "Art is a quality which exists in certain works of man, and it exists nowhere else for the reason that it is not physical but a psychic force . . . "[30]

As he had in the pages of *Inwhich*, Geddes continued to envision the role of the artist as a "person who is capable of creating a state of mind within himself that makes him a medium or aesthetic phenomenon."[31] Thus, true art could not be produced through training in technique or emulation of others, but had to be born of a real, spiritual connection. Geddes explained that to prepare for this "connecting link," one must "clear your mind as a battleship clears deck for action."[32] Or, in more mystical terms, the artist must work toward "the spiritual state of mind under which condition the work will be done."[33] Doing so would permit the artist to achieve genius, which Geddes now described not in the language of Christian monotheism but in the language of Theosophy:

Man: merely interpreter of ideas on earthly plane.
Genius: a reflection of eternity in works of art.
A genius is connecting link between his fellow-men
here, and eternity there.[34]

FIGURE 5

Geddes scene rendering ("Circles of agonizing souls and immense wavering shadows in a glare of crimson") for The Divine Comedy, *c. 1921. Geddes derived the circular features evident in this preliminary sketch for* The Divine Comedy *project from an inspirational vision. Sanguine on paper, 11½ x 9¼ in., 29.2 x 23.5 cm*

A PRIMER OF HIGHER SPACE (THE FOURTH DIMENSION)

by

Claude Bragdon

1913 : THE : MANAS : PRESS
ROCHESTER : NEW : YORK

The language used here reveals the extent to which Geddes had embraced the Theosophical notion of the multiplane universe. The artist was no longer connecting with a male, monotheistic God, but reaching out to "eternity" and seeking "a higher plane of creative expression" in the theater.[35]

Geddes's design lectures also reveal his interest in one of the prominent features of esoteric religion of the early twentieth century—the possibility of the fourth dimension. The concept of the fourth dimension had evolved apart from Theosophy proper, though some Theosophists saw it as a useful concept that could be adapted to their own purposes.[36] It had roots in the development of non-Euclidean geometry and speculation that there existed, beyond conventional human perception, another spatial dimension.[37] By the late nineteenth and early twentieth centuries this theory had captured the attention of a wide range of thinkers in the United States: Artists, scientists, and mystics alike saw promise in the concept of the fourth dimension. Geddes most likely encountered the idea through Claude Bragdon, whose work was vital to its popularization in the United States.[38] Though not all formulations of the fourth dimension included a spiritual component, Bragdon's and Geddes's did.

In his own copy of Bragdon's 1913 *A Primer of Higher Space (The Fourth Dimension)* (FIG. 6), Geddes underlined "The light of things known serves but to reveal a greater abysm of mystery beyond the threshold of consciousness." Geddes, too, believed that there was a great deal beyond common human perception. For Geddes, like Ouspensky before him, art provided a special and unique avenue for accessing higher planes of knowledge. Art exemplified the "undefinable" quality shared by the fourth dimension.[39] In his notes for his design course Geddes wrote, "God and Art happen to be in the fourth dimensional class and we three dimensional people do not fully comprehend them."[40] For Geddes, though, the true artist (along with mathematicians and philosophers) had the potential to perceive and appreciate reality beyond three dimensions—making the abysm of mystery increasingly accessible.

Thus Geddes's *practical* theater design course argued for the spiritual as an essential quality of great art, encouraged young theater designers to commune with it as a first step in their work, and proposed the possibilities of fourth dimensional thinking. He recommended Ouspensky's *Tertium Organum* and Bragdon's *Beautiful Necessity* alongside Charles E. Pellew's *Dyes and Dyeing* and Talbot Hughes's *Dress Design*. And yet few of his students would have been surprised by this particular bent of his teaching. Not only was he in keeping with popular trends among creative artists of the period,[41] but Geddes also had come to be known specifically for the mystical qualities of his plays. One of his earliest critics had remarked favorably on Geddes's desire to create a unique "spiritual atmosphere" for each of his plays and his success in bringing "the abstract, the hidden, illusive and vital force" to the surface of his productions.[42] Bragdon himself saw Geddes's proposed Theater Number 6 building as a potential venue for "dramatic representations" that could range through many countries, styles, and periods, "even through the Fourth Dimension and the Eternal Now."[43] And, after 1924, Geddes's reputation as a man with a "mystical" genius was cemented by his association with the highly successful production of Max Reinhardt's *The Miracle* and the publication of *A Project for the Theatrical Presentation of The Divine Comedy of Dante Alighieri*.[44] Public perceptions of Geddes began to change, however, as he moved into the field of industrial design—heralded by his 1932 book *Horizons* (FIG. 7).

There are threads of Geddes's earlier work in *Horizons*. He relied on the same confident authorial voice he had borrowed from Hubbard, sought to share his designs with the world as he had done with *The Divine Comedy*, and attempted to alter the assumptions and expectations of a new generation as he had done in his theater design courses. Geddes still acknowledged a spiritual component to human life, but it was no longer central to his thinking about the creation and understanding of art.[45] Art, however, remained vital to Geddes's enterprise. Indeed, art was to be the inspiration for the new era he envisioned.[46]

In *Horizons*, Geddes argued that art was moving in a new direction that was less a matter of "frames, pedestals, museums, books and concert halls" and "more to do with people and their life."[47]

Art was coming to the people in the form of everyday objects and buildings. It would no longer be remote— nor would artists. Geddes paid particular attention to his justification of the commercial designer as an artist—a matter of decided importance to a man who had always perceived himself as an artist.[48] Geddes, however, sought to dispel misguided notions of artists as "intriguing and mysterious" people who "live[d] on" inspiration.[49] This shift represented an important break for a man whose *Divine Comedy* project provided a compelling description of inspiration and who taught his own students about the importance of finding inspiration by connecting with "eternity." There was apparently no room for this model of inspiration in his new field. Design, as Geddes defined it, was "the opposite of accidental."[50] It was "deliberate thinking, planning to a purpose."[51] If Geddes still envisioned a role for spiritual inspiration in this thinking and planning, he did not share it in *Horizons*. Instead, he argued, originality and inspiration "must take root from the conditions and functions of the problem involved."[52]

As Geddes discussed the qualities of these resulting well-designed objects, he noted "the governing factor as to what is pleasing to the eye is the *idea*, which is of an emotional nature—an emotion of pleasure, satisfaction, excitement, exhilaration, stimulation."[53] He attributed the "stirring beauty of airplanes" not to a spiritual quality connecting with the viewer, but the fact that the design of a plane "was in keeping with the purpose it serves."[54] Time after time in *Horizons*, Geddes emphasized that what people responded to in art or in a well-designed object was an emotional quality. A powerful spiritual connection was no longer the standard by which Geddes measured great art.

Norman Bel Geddes, the "mystical genius" of the theater, had repositioned himself as a visionary industrial designer and, in doing so, had abandoned the language and teachings of esoteric religion that marked his earliest work. In a world where Geddes could confidently assert that "art will be achieved by the machine—inspirationally and technically,"[55] there seemed little role for the spiritual. *Horizons*, however, did not represent a complete break with his previous philosophy. Even as he moved away from

the fundamental role of the eternal in art and inspiration, Geddes retained his faith in art itself and its ability to improve the world. He was as optimistic as ever and envisioned a new era dawning in which "a refrigerator may be beautiful, that a factory need not be an eyesore, and that a school classroom, in its own way, may be as beautiful as a church."[56]

FIGURE 7
Horizons (1932) marked Geddes's shift away from an emphasis on the spiritual qualities of art.

I did not believe in God as defined by mother or grandmother. I did believe that the earth and what was on it was a speck in a universe and that there were powers in this universe way beyond the imagination of man[,] that these were evident in faint flashes from the unknown of what our ignorance terms mysticism.

Norman Bel Geddes in a draft of his autobiography[57]

★ ★ ★ ★ ★ ★ ★ ★

HORIZONS

A GLIMPSE
into the
NOT FAR-DISTANT FUTURE,
a future that will see many if not all of our present
notions of form cast into the discard—when, through
the influence of new design, most of the features of our
everyday life will take on new aspects for the greater
economy, efficiency, comfort and happiness of our lives.

NORMAN BEL GEDDES

ENDNOTES

1 Geddes's autobiography reveals the extent of his disdain for organized religion. Geddes originally did not include churches in his most defining project, Futurama, but added them after the public expressed concern. Warren Susman notes the omission of churches in his *Culture as History* (New York: Pantheon Books, 1984) as does David Gerlernter in *1939: The Lost World of the Fair* (New York: Free Press, 1995).

2 Norman's father was absent during significant portions of his childhood. His mother and his mother's family fill most of his recollections in his autobiography. Norman received word while living in Ann Arbor that his father had died.

3 Draft of autobiography, Box 52-A, Folder 653.17, Geddes Papers.

4 Ibid.

5 Norman Bel Geddes, *Miracle in the Evening* (New York: Doubleday & Company, 1960), 29. Geddes offered a longer explanation of their disinterest in Christian Science in an earlier draft of the book. Geddes's autobiography appeared posthumously and was edited by William Kelley. In the early drafts, Geddes either left the manuscript untitled or used the title "I Designed My Life."

6 Letter from Lulu Yingling Geddes to Norman Geddes, April 1914, Box 96, Folder 960.5, Geddes Papers. This letter appears in *Miracle* and earlier autobiography drafts, but Geddes or an editor altered obvious Christian Science references, including the capitalization of "truth" and "principle." Geddes (or an editor) also added punctuation for clarity. *Miracle*, 133.

7 According to Susan Tenneriello, like Geddes, Ruth St. Denis's "theological orientation was founded in . . . Christian Science" but later expanded to include Theosophy. In "The Divine Spaces of Metaphysical Spectacle," *Performance Research* 13, no. 3, 124–38. Quotation from p. 126. In a diary entry, Belle Sneider noted that she had met St. Denis and her husband, Ted Shawn, with Norman while they were still living in Detroit. Jeffrey Meikle argued that Christian Science "contributed" to Geddes's later beliefs about artistic creation. "Norman Bel Geddes: A Portrait," *Rassegna* 60 (1994): 6.

8 H. P. Blavatsky, *The Key to Theosophy* (London: The Theosophical Publishing Company, Limited, 1889), 56.

9 P. D. Ouspensky, *Tertium Organum* (Rochester, NY: Manas Press, 1920), 236.

10 Letter from Claude Bragdon to Geddes, 29 April 1921, Box 95, Folder 957.49, Geddes Papers.

11 Letter from Jacob Weintz to Geddes, 15 May 1915, Theater Box 176, Folder J-2, Geddes Papers.

12 Geddes's awareness of and interest in Hubbard was significant. Among the books in Geddes's library is a bound edition of volume 13 of *The Philistine* from 1901. *Inwhich* more closely resembles the design of *The Philistine* in this volume than the design of the magazine in 1915 when Geddes began printing *Inwhich*. Geddes also owned two copies of Hubbard's best-known work, *A Message to Garcia* (1899), and later recommended it to his design course students. Before their marriage, Norman and Belle Sneider met at East Aurora and dined at Roycroft. In a letter to Norman, Belle referred to Elbert and Alice Hubbard's relationship and the integration of their work as a model for Norman and Belle's relationship. Norman also listed Miriam Hubbard, Elbert and Alice's daughter, on a list of *Inwhich* subscribers he sent to Brentano's bookstore.

13 Letter from Geddes to Jacob Weintz, 29 September 1915, Theater Box 176, Folder J-2, Geddes Papers. In his letter to Weintz, Geddes mistyped "different" as "differebnt" and "similar" as "similara." Geddes did include work by other writers, including Max Eastman and Helen Belle Sneider (both before and after they were married). He altered the magazine's slogan from "In which I say just what I think" to read "In which we say just what we think" a few months after his marriage to Belle and their mutual adoption of Norman-Bel Geddes as a signature for their work.

14 Letter from reader to Geddes, 3 August 1915, and letter from Sallie Kennedy to Geddes, 19 June 1915, Theater Box 175, Folder J-3, Geddes Papers.

15 Geddes was accurate in claiming a significant distance from Hubbard's Arts and Crafts movement–inspired philosophical outlook. Elbert Hubbard does, however, provide historians with a compelling new perspective through which to understand Geddes's career and the apparent inconsistencies between his philosophical ideals and his desire to be commercially successful.

16 Letter from H. D. Abbott to Norman Geddes, 23 December 1915, Theater Box 176, Folder J-3, Geddes Papers.

17 Norman Geddes, "Art?" *Inwhich*, no. 2 (July 1915): n.p.

18 Ibid.

19 Norman Geddes, "Genius-Talent-Cleverness," *Inwhich*, no. 10 (March 1916): n.p. In this essay, Geddes retained a fairly traditional Christian perspective of the divine as male and singular.

20 Ibid.

21 Norman Geddes, "Simplicity," *Inwhich*, no. 2 (August 1915): n.p.

22 *Miracle in the Evening*, 247.

23 Norman-Bel Geddes, *A Project for a Theatrical Presentation of The Divine Comedy of Dante Alighieri* (New York: Theatre Arts, Inc., 1924), 8.

24 Ibid.

25 Ibid., 8–9. In an earlier draft, Geddes had added the line "I wasn't dreaming, I was wide awake" immediately following "hotter."

26 Ibid., 13.

27 Geddes would continue teaching permutations of this course intermittently throughout his career.

28 Design course lecture notes, Theater Box 153, Folder Y-7, Geddes Papers.

29 Design course lecture notes, c. 1922, Theater Box 153, Folder Y-1, Geddes Papers.

30 Ibid.

31 Design course lecture notes, Theater Box 153, Folder Y-10, Geddes Papers. In his notes, Geddes misspells "phenomenon" "phenomenom."

32 Design course lecture notes, Theater Box 153, Folder Y-2, Geddes Papers. This language mimics Geddes's description of his inspiration in *A Project for a Theatrical Presentation of The Divine Comedy* that he and the wall were "clearing for action."

33 Design course lecture notes, Theater Box 153, Folder Y-10, Geddes Papers.

34 Design course lecture notes, Theater Box 153, Folder Y-2, Geddes Papers.

35 Design course lecture notes, c. 1922, Theater Box 153, Folder Y-1, Geddes Papers. Theosophists believed that the universe comprised seven planes. The earthly was the most basic and accessible to the common person.

36 Linda Dalrymple Henderson, *The Fourth Dimension and Non-Euclidean Geometry in Modern Art* (Princeton: Princeton University Press, 1983), 45.

37 Henderson, chapter 1.

38 For more on Bragdon's importance to popularization and development of conceptions of the

fourth dimension, see Henderson, 186–201. Henderson notes Geddes's friendship with Bragdon and the incorporation of the fourth dimension into Geddes's course lecture notes. See Henderson, 234–35.

39 Design course lecture notes, Theater Box 149, Folder J-3, Geddes Papers.

40 Ibid.

41 Some advocates of the New Stagecraft, including Kenneth Macgowan, also saw a role for the spiritual. In Macgowan's *The Theatre of Tomorrow* (1921), he focused on capturing spiritual qualities onstage and did not devote the time to its role in inspiration that Geddes did. Geddes provided images for and directed his students to *The Theatre of Tomorrow*. Macgowan referred to Geddes as a "young and brilliant designer" in the book.

42 Bruce Bliven, "Norman Bel-Geddes: His Art and Ideas," *Theatre Arts Magazine* 3, no. 3 (July 1919): 181.

43 Claude Bragdon, "Towards a New Theatre," *Architectural Record* 52, no. 3 (September 1922): 171–82. Quotation on 180.

44 R. Dana Skinner, in "The Play," *Commonweal* 4, no. 12 (28 July 1926): 308, observed, "It is typical of the mystical quality of his genius that his greatest complete achievement to date was the cathedral setting for *The Miracle*, and that his greatest project now well toward realization is the dramatic presentation in majestic form

of Dante's *The Divine Comedy*." For Geddes, any production could have a spiritual quality. Thus the fact that *The Miracle* and *The Divine Comedy* were religious in nature was not fundamental to his artistic program. However, the specifically religious content of both of these projects likely encouraged others to view Geddes as a man with particular, spiritually oriented gifts.

45 He explained that sunshine and light are "both physical and spiritual assets" (138) and that Americans do not give enough attention to living spiritually, favoring the material instead (158). In the concluding chapter, he wrote, "It is essential that [the artist] should be an explorer and delve into the future, both spiritually and materially" (280) and argued that mastering the machine would "yield not only purely physical but aesthetic and spiritual satisfaction" (293).

46 Ibid., 5.

47 Ibid., 7.

48 This line of thinking is not entirely born of Geddes's career shift. As early as 1915, he argued that artists need not be conventionally defined: "We do not have to paint to be artists; art bows to her farmers and blacksmiths as well as her sculptors and poets." Geddes, "Art?"

49 *Horizons*, 9.

50 Ibid., 17.

51 Ibid.

52 Ibid., 18.

53 Ibid.

54 Ibid., 20.

55 Ibid., 292.

56 Unidentified author, "Geddes and Howe Form Partnership," *New York Times* (29 May 1935): 19.

57 Draft of autobiography, Box 52-A, Folder 653.39, Geddes Papers.

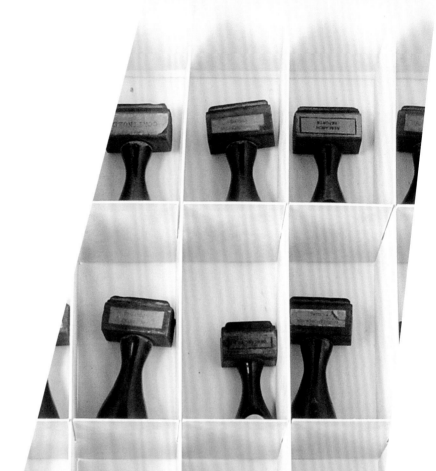

2

PRACTICAL VISION AND THE BUSINESS OF DESIGN: NORMAN BEL GEDDES INCORPORATED

Nicolas Paolo Maffei

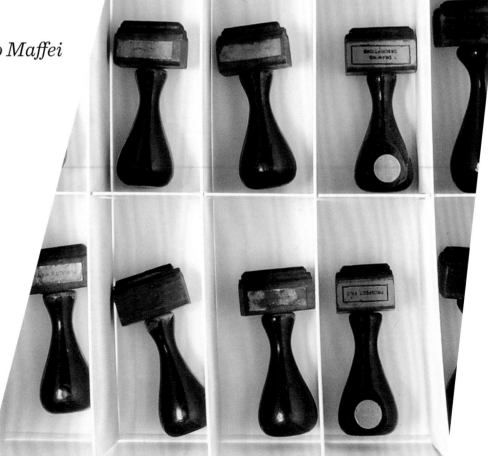

s a founder of the American industrial design profession in the 1920s, Norman Bel Geddes profoundly shaped the field, providing a practical training ground for the next generation while imparting a visionary outlook to both his contemporaries and his successors. Many of America's leading industrial designers apprenticed with Geddes or worked in his office, including Henry Dreyfuss, Russel Wright, and Eliot Noyes. After World War II, leading industrial designers adopted many of Geddes's business strategies and aspects of his visionary social agenda—while rejecting his theatricality and grandiosity.[1] This essay explores the promotion, staffing, and organization of the office, examining it as a machine for gaining clients, producing designs, and keeping the Geddes name in the public mind. This investigation also documents how Geddes created the image of the American industrial designer as a utopian, but practical, visionary.

Geddes's bold creations, unswerving idealism, and inflated ego led many of his contemporaries to alternately brand him a genius and an unrealistic dreamer. Henry Dreyfuss considered Geddes the "only authentic genius this [industrial design] profession has ever produced."[2] But Dreyfuss also came to believe that Geddes's flamboyance cost him many commissions. George Nelson, who would later become an influential postwar designer, agreed and described Geddes as "dynamic" and "volubly articulate," "a born showman, the P. T. Barnum of industrial design," and a "bomb-thrower" who "cost American industry a billion dollars" through retooling and "join[ing] the redesign movement," a reference to Geddes's notion that everything needed to be redesigned.[3] At the height of Geddes's industrial design success in 1941, the *New Yorker* called him an "intense, wild-haired . . . supersalesman [who] moves from one grandiose venture to another, leaving chaos, and usually an awed but somehow satisfied client," noting that his critics considered him "impractical and visionary" compared to his "businesslike" contemporaries.[4]

The image that Geddes cultivated over his lifetime, however, was one of vision and expertise—the industrial designer as organizational mastermind and creative seer who infused mass-produced goods with an aura of glamour and optimism. To sell his services to new clients, Geddes depicted himself as a practical visionary. He fused the rhetoric of the rational engineer with the visionary artist. He did so by mimicking modernist designers like Le Corbusier, borrowing philosophies from technocratic idealists, and engaging in technological forecasting. This approach, developed and articulated in his 1932 monograph, *Horizons*, and publicized in numerous articles in both the popular and trade press, helped shape the image of industrial design in the early 1930s and played an important role in legitimizing the profession during its first decades in the 1930s and 1940s.

In a tribute to the designer, Dreyfuss reiterated Geddes's notion of practical vision, noting the "tremendous influence" the flamboyant designer had exerted over him and "will continue to exert over all designers." In his own career, Dreyfuss drew on such fundamental Geddes principles as creating designs that subordinated the parts to the whole—which Dreyfuss termed "cleanlining"—and adopted a holistic approach to design that encompassed architecture, fine art, and craft. Dreyfuss, who had apprenticed for three years with Geddes, explained that "to be an industrial designer is to breathe an atmosphere that Norman Bel Geddes helped to create." He "was the modern counterpart of the 15th century master craftsman. To back his often grandiose schemes, he turned to today's businessmen just as the master craftsmen turned to the Medici. And like his 15th century predecessor, Norman could turn his talents in any direction." Dreyfuss described Geddes as "both a practical man and a visionary." His ideas "were built, manufactured, staged. And their impact was unforgettable. But equally powerful were the ideas that never left the drawing board, the dreams that remained dreams. . . . [S]omehow they got into the air and were absorbed by hundreds of other designers, who drew inspiration, in some unaccountable way, from a man they may never have known."[5]

While Geddes mentored many of his future industrial design competitors—Henry Dreyfuss and Russel Wright both worked as his theater apprentices—his large and highly systematized office became the training ground for numerous others, including Eliot Noyes and senior members of Harold Van Doren's office.[6] In 1946 Geddes claimed that of

America's "hundred leading designers . . . at least half" had apprenticed in his office. Most likely referring to Dreyfuss and Wright, he added that "two of my six leading competitors are among this group." Probably referring to Harold Van Doren's office and his former partners, including Peter Schladermundt and Roger Nowland, he concluded, in "the office of my leading competitor six of his eight highest paid men are of this category."[7]

Long before he trained his future competitors, Geddes developed his own self-promotional skills in his magazine, *Inwhich*, produced monthly by Geddes and his fiancée Helen Belle Sneider from 1915 to 1916.[8] *Inwhich* joined the hundreds of little magazines, such as the *Little Review* (1914–29) and *The Dial* (1920–29), which published articles on avantgarde art and ideas and proliferated in the United States after 1912.[9] Geddes used his magazine primarily to promote himself as a newly fashioned visionary artist. In it he introduced his recently created name, Norman-Bel Geddes.[10] The magazine was distributed to prominent individuals from the worlds of art and commerce, including the renowned illustrator Edward Penfield; the retailer John Wanamaker; the editor of *The Masses*, Max Eastman; and the wealthy theater dilettante Aline Barnsdall.[11] The range of recipients reflected the extent of Geddes's ambitions and was testimony to his skill for self-promotion.[12] Later in his career Geddes would hone this public relations technique to perfection, strategically publishing his designs and ideas in articles, pamphlets, and books and sending copies to potential clients and supporters.

Geddes believed that the "most unique feature" of *Inwhich* "is that it is personal. Being a book in which I say what I think . . . it is the only book where one person rules—bodily puts his own personality."[13] Geddes's fascination with personality reflects a wider American phenomenon. After the first decade of the century, the notion of the movie star emerged along with the industry of celebrity.[14] The management of persona as a means of shaping public perception would be famously scrutinized in *Public Opinion*, written in 1922 by Walter Lippmann, who wrote of "stage-manage[d]" and "constructed personalities," and "great men . . . known to the public

only through a fictitious personality," resulting in "at least two distinct selves, the public and . . . the private."[15] In a letter to *Inwhich* business manager Jacob Weintz, Geddes described himself as a manufactured celebrity, designed for public consumption. "By personal I mean this. Keeping Norman Geddes, who ever he is, in the book [*Inwhich*] all the time. Make him felt. Keep it published by Norman Geddes instead of published by the Inwhich publishing Co [*sic*] or words to that effect." The inner cover of each copy of *Inwhich* read: "BEING A BOOK INWHICH IS SAID WHAT I THINK. PUBLISHED EVERY MONTH BY NORMAN-BEL GEDDES."[16] Geddes's carefully crafted personality would remain a key tool in promoting and developing his design business.

Another promotional tool exploited by Geddes was his background in stage design. In 1932, nearly five years after America's first major industrial design offices were established, the cultural commentator Gilbert Seldes observed: "Two of the most powerful influences" on the origins of industrial design were "advertising agencies and the makers of scenery for the theatre."[17] Raymond Loewy had worked in fashion illustration, Walter Dorwin Teague had for many years been a successful advertising illustrator, and Dreyfuss and Geddes had maintained significant careers in stage design.[18] While Geddes was quick to proclaim the relevance of his theater experience to his industrial design career, he was less open about his advertising past (**FIG. 1, 2**).[19] He described his transformation from stage design to industrial design as a natural evolution and saw numerous commonalities between the two professions. He believed they both depended on detailed planning and seamless presentation and insisted that each must be "done with an eye to pleasing and intriguing the on-looker. Industry . . . would be stagnant otherwise and certainly could not achieve popular success."[20]

Geddes's shift from stage to industrial design was not surprising; for many years he had seamlessly mixed theatrical and commercial design. While producing the artistic *Inwhich* magazine, he broadcast his services as a designer of personal monograms.[21] As a young advertising artist Geddes had been obsessed with stage design. And throughout his industrial design career he maintained a

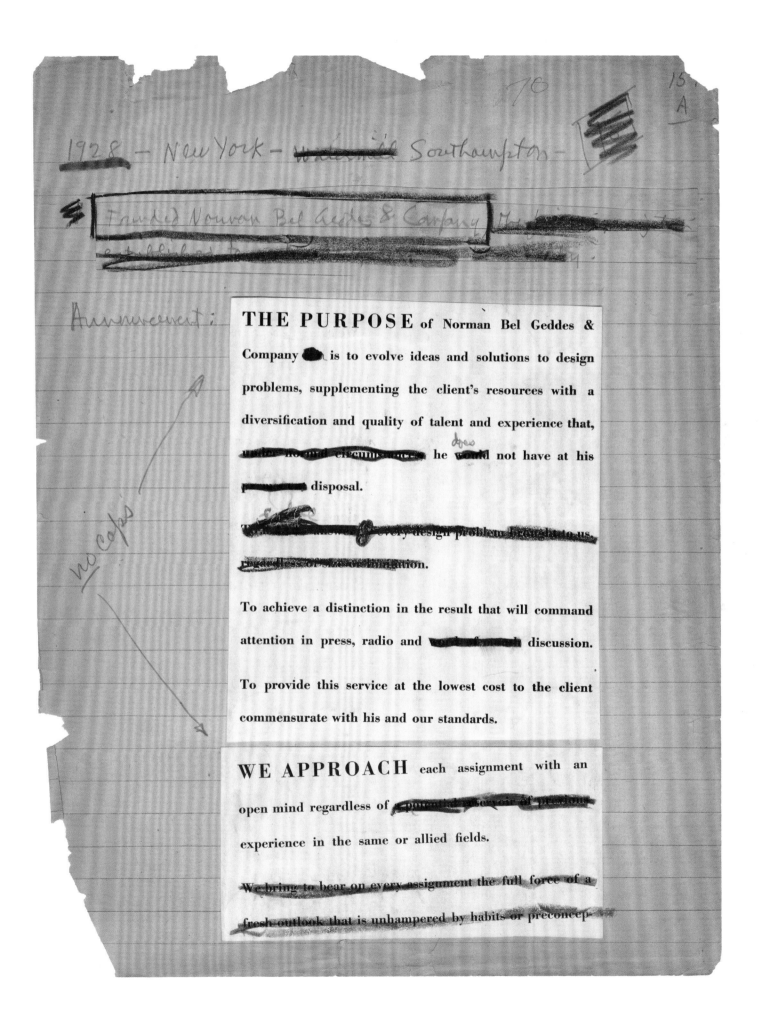

1928 — New York — ~~Watermill~~ Southampton —

~~Founded Norman Bel Geddes & Company~~

Announcement:

no caps

THE PURPOSE of Norman Bel Geddes & Company ~~Inc.~~ is to evolve ideas and solutions to design problems, supplementing the client's resources with a diversification and quality of talent and experience that, ~~under no and circumstances~~ *does* he ~~would~~ not have at his ~~permanent~~ disposal.

~~To ~~~~every design problem brought to us, regardless of our specialization.~~

To achieve a distinction in the result that will command attention in press, radio and ~~other forms of~~ discussion.

To provide this service at the lowest cost to the client commensurate with his and our standards.

WE APPROACH each assignment with an open mind regardless of ~~potential reservoir of previous~~ experience in the same or allied fields.

~~We bring to bear on every assignment the full force of a fresh outlook that is unhampered by habits or preconcep-~~

FIGURE 3

W. K. Kesley article "A Peep into the Future by the Spectacular Norman Bel Geddes, in the Detroit News, *Sunday, January 1, 1933.*

substantial sideline in theater arts. By 1927 he described industrial design as a hybrid profession, balancing the "opposites" of the businessman and the artist. Believing he possessed this "peculiar blending," he viewed his own mental discipline as key in combining "practical" and "aesthetic" thought.[22] Geddes recognized the need for imagination and fantasy in both stage and industrial design, explaining, "Once he [Geddes] dreamed in the make believe world of the theater. Now he dreams in an industrial world of the future."[23] Accordingly, Geddes's promotional language evolved from that of a dreamy artist to a hard-nosed businessman.

Throughout his industrial design career Geddes published various promotional texts, including articles, press releases, and books, to publicize himself as a forward-looking designer of boundless imagination. In the Geddes office it became standard practice to send his prophetic writings to business contacts in order to attract new clients and retain existing ones.[24] More than any of Geddes's promotional texts, *Horizons*, published in 1932, helped to secure his popular image as a technological prophet. Depicting both his unrealized and completed designs, Geddes's visionary book was the earliest monograph by one of America's first generation of industrial designers; monographs on the work of Dreyfuss, Teague, and Loewy appeared years later.[25]

The publication of *Horizons* provided advance publicity for Geddes's designs: his Standard Gas Equipment Co. (SGE) stove, for example, appeared in shops a few months later. Such carefully timed promotion became common practice for the Geddes office and was later described in the office's *Standard Practice* manual. Prior to approaching a client, "an industrial design group is determined," "four or five stories are outlined . . . one [aimed] at a national periodical for popular consumer appeal, another for the leading trade journal written from the view point of the prospective client, another at a literary or highbrow periodical," as well as a "feature newspaper article, a news story, radio and newsreels."[26] These allowed Geddes to speak to a range of audiences, including industrial clients, consumers, and cultural elites, confirming Geddes's desire for continued business and artistic recognition.

As agreed in late 1930, the SGE stove displayed the designer's monogram and the phrase "This product designed by Norman Bel Geddes." The "signed" appliance presented the designer as akin to a named artist and the industrialist as his patron. This image of an enlightened art and design partnership benefited the designer and the manufacturer, and the trend of "signing" mass-produced goods became common practice among industrial designers.[27]

Promoting the Geddes name was essential to the design office. Despite his dependence on a large number of highly trained staff, Geddes underlined the importance of maintaining his name above those of other office members, explaining, "It is necessary and advisable to handle most of our publicity through the channel of Norman Bel Geddes." Geddes believed that "Other partners and associates, on occasion, should be developed, and built up." However, he reminded his staff that "establish[ing] a name requires so many years and such a series of outstanding performances that the bulk of our publicity will be more profitably placed through the Norman Bel Geddes name." Such promotion was "not a job of getting personal publicity for Mr. Geddes," but "only of value when it enhances the status and stature of our business as a whole."[28] Geddes's publicity, whether it was advertising for a stove or a publication on visionary design, continued the personality-driven

in the trade and national press, Geddes was promoted as *the* leader of both aesthetic and scientific streamlining, styling that borrowed from the smooth surfaces of airplane design, on the one hand, and the scientific application of aerodynamic principles, on the other. After 1932, Geddes's futuristic tapered vehicles, first pictured in *Horizons*, were reprinted in newspapers across the country, helping to popularize the style. Such "development work," produced by the Geddes office during "slack time," resulted in the designs of "ovoid ships, cars, and trains, nine-deck airliners, [and] multicellular houses," which, George Nelson noted, "put Norman Bel Geddes in the small

approach first established with *Inwhich*. While this may have led to accusations of egotism, *Industrial Design* magazine defended Geddes's self-centered promotional style: "Geddes was absorbed not in himself, but in any work he was doing at that moment. Yet, he had a tremendous respect for other people's talent and ideas; he only demanded of them the same high standards which he imposed upon himself."[29]

Because of its associations with science and the future, the streamlining phenomenon provided a perfect opportunity to develop the Geddes name and to market his services.[30] The persistent and canny promotion of his aerodynamic visualizations of planes, trains, cars, and boats guaranteed his fame as a visionary designer. During the 1930s and 1940s,

company of Sunday Supplement subjects along with his admirer Stratosphere Piccard, Hugh (City-of-the-Future) Ferriss, and the rocket trip to Mars. These drawings have built the Geddes myth"(FIG. 3).[31]

The influence of the Geddes "myth" would soon be felt in the design studios of America's carmakers. *Horizons* proved an inspiration to many automotive engineers, and Geddes was quickly hired by America's leading manufacturers to aid their publicity and design. In 1933 Chrysler employed Geddes to publicize the Airflow, America's first mass-produced car shaped according to aerodynamic principles.[32] The same year, General Motors hired Geddes to design its twenty-fifth–anniversary commemorative medal (FIG. 4A, 4B). Geddes hoped to secure his reputation

FIGURE 4A, 4B
Geddes promotional images of his General Motors twenty-fifth-anniversary medal, 1933. Photograph, 10 x 8 in., 25.4 x 20.3 cm

STREAMLINING

BY NORMAN BEL GEDDES

Reprinted from the Atlantic Monthly, November, 1934

as a streamlining expert with the publication of his technical article "Streamlining" in the *Atlantic Monthly* in 1934.[33] General Electric's Institute of Aerodynamic Research proclaimed, "Overnight Norman Bel Geddes has become the father of a new type of aero-dynamic engineering."[34] Harold Van Doren acknowledged, "What Geddes did was to dramatize it [streamlining], well before it had really arrived, and so convincingly as to crystallize the scattered forces already tending in that direction."[35]

In their 1936 book, *Art and the Machine,* Sheldon and Martha Cheney viewed streamlining as *the* style of the age and presented Geddes as its trailblazer. Emphasizing his expressive, rather than scientific, use of the style, the Cheneys "credited [Geddes] as having contributed the word 'streamline' to the everyday vocabulary, and with making explicit the streamline as an appearance value, and as a symbol of machine-age style in objects far outside the legitimate field of its scientific application."[36] As a representation of progress and dynamism, they saw even the most ordinary streamlined product as "conspicuous a symbol . . . of the age" as the "symbol of the cross" was to the "medieval mind."[37] Geddes is said to have been "embarrassed" to be called the father of streamlining.[38] However, writing after World War II, he characterized himself "as the father of 'Industrial Design' who put 'streamline' in the dictionary."[39]

Geddes's "Streamlining" article for the *Atlantic Monthly* coincided with his streamlined design work for Chrysler and illustrates the way in which publicity was used as the engine of his design business. "Streamlining" was most likely ghostwritten for Geddes[40] and summarized his thoughts on aerodynamic car design.[41] Detailed and scientific-sounding, the treatise positioned Geddes as a streamlining expert and may have deflected post-*Horizons* criticism of him as an *impractical* visionary. The article provided a brief history of aerodynamic study, from Leonardo da Vinci to the present, and aimed to rectify the lazy use of the term, especially by "advertising copywriters" who have "seized upon it as a handy synonym for the word 'new' . . . using it indiscriminately and often inexactly to describe automobiles and women's dresses, railroad trains and men's shoes."[42] While Geddes was openly critical

of this view of streamlining, as his business grew and sought new clients it increasingly accepted jobs from clients who did not share this perspective.

After its publication, the Geddes office sent copies of "Streamlining" to twelve hundred captains of industry, industrial designers, heads of museums, the industrial press, advertising agencies, and government officials (**FIG. 5**).[43] A letter from Geddes was included and cast the designer as a guardian of scientific streamlining, stating, "Industrial applications [of streamlining] have in some cases been made willy-nilly without apparent basis or benefit." General Motors requested an additional one hundred copies for circulation.[44] The goals of the letter campaign were to gain clients, publicize the office, and inform colleagues of Geddes's preeminence in the field. During this effort Geddes sent staff to prospective clients to discuss the article and offer the services of the office. This follow-up was a common practice at the office and was intended to nurture a strong client base.

Significantly, most respondents complimented Geddes's succinct presentation of aerodynamics and his attempt to guard against its misuse, while a handful congratulated the firm for its canny publicity campaign. The sympathetic reply from Alfred Barr, director of the Museum of Modern Art, was typical of many letters: "It seems to me that streamlining has been an absurdity in much contemporary design." Referring to a Loewy design, Barr noted, "I have even seen a streamline pencil sharpener by one of the highest paid industrial designers." Perhaps revealing his desire to be linked with scientific rather than stylistic streamlining, Geddes underlined Barr's final sentence: "This blind concern with fashion is one of the things which makes it difficult to take the ordinary industrial designers seriously."[45] The architect Ely Jacques Kahn echoed Barr and wrote, "As you so aptly put it, streamlining has, unfortunately, become as much of a fetish as functionalism, and we have streamlined ash cans and breakfast food. Perhaps if we know more of the scientific angle, we may be less inclined to do stupid things with design."[46]

However, another recipient was less concerned with the debates regarding style and science and more intrigued by the effort to erase Geddes's image

FIGURE 6

Geddes and staff with radios, c. 1940s. Photograph by Richard Garrison, 10 x 8 in., 25.4 x 20.3 cm

as the P. T. Barnum of design. "I was impressed by its [the article's] sobriety and believe that for this reason it was an extremely wise step for you to take. I believe that a great many people who read it are going to have a new conception of Norman Bel Geddes & Company. You are of course not blind to the fact that your spectacular history has led people to believe that you are essentially a show man [*sic*]." [47]

This and similar publicity was essential to maintaining the Geddes name and was guided by the office's press relations representative, who, with "many contacts in the newspaper, magazine, book, radio and trade journal field," was "responsible for creating the best possible impression of Norman Bel Geddes and Company . . . through the subtle and expert guidance of public opinion through proper publicity, expertly prepared." [48]

By 1935 opinion polling had become commonplace through George Gallup's American Institute of Public Opinion. [49] And by the early forties the study and practice of shaping public opinion was well established in America, having been famously scrutinized in Walter Lippmann's *Public Opinion*. The Geddes office recognized that a carefully managed public image could determine the response of both prospective clients and consumers. "He [the press relations representative] must also be constantly aware of all our activities that would tend to excite prospective customers and fill them with admiration for our work. . . . [H]e is constantly striving to stimulate new accounts under various disguises. . . ."[50] Such "disguises" might include publicity gained through an article on scientific streamlining or activities seemingly unrelated to industrial design. Articles on Geddes's hobbies and interests found their way into numerous celebrity newspaper columns and were consumed by a public hungry for manufactured personalities and tales of tomorrow. In addition to such publicity, Geddes maintained his office through the sheer strength of his personality. His jovial company as a nightclub companion and regular host of dinner parties helped him to maintain a devoted coterie of businessmen, financial investors, and journalists.[51]

Geddes's public image also relied on the firm's design, planning, and research activities. In *Horizons* Geddes outlined the multiple stages involved in a design job, including extensive research, an activity that he considered essential. At the beginning of the job, all of the relevant staff, including designers, engineers, merchandisers, and researchers, gathered in Geddes's office to discuss the design problem (**FIG. 6**). Design objectives and the means of achieving them, along with a schedule, were agreed on by the group. Geddes considered scheduling of the "utmost importance" and planned jobs six months ahead in general and three months ahead in detail. In 1946 Geddes wrote, "Visualize an office with twenty jobs being worked on at once all having to meet different dates at different period [*sic*] of the work, all interchanging personnel because of specialized abilities, all involving people traveling around the country or on vacation, and allowing for contingencies such as illnesses."[52] Next came a lengthy period of research, which included familiarization with the client's product: its present function; its ultimate function; and its manufacture, sales, and servicing. Geddes's team visited the client's factory in order to match the final design with the available manufacturing technology. Equivalent information was then gathered on the competitors' models, materials, production, merchandising, and servicing. At this point comments from consumers and retailers were solicited—Geddes considered this the most important phase of the design job.[53]

Only following this initial research, "and having established clearly in his own mind and that of

his client what purpose and conditions the product must meet," should the designer apply "himself to the problem of redesign."[54] The job would be organized using a card index system "consisting of several hundred printed forms—covering every phase of every type of work" (**FIG. 7**).[55] Geddes warned that design is more a matter of "*thinking*" than drawing: Only after the "objective" and "facts" were "clearly visualized" may preliminary sketches be completed.[56] Just as he had taught his stage design students in the 1920s to visualize their ideas before drawing them, he recommended that "there is no use putting hand to paper until you can close your eyes and see with *complete* clarity all details of what it is you wish to draw."[57] Following client approval, finished sketches

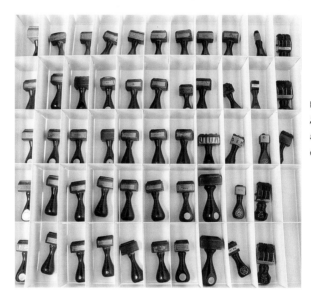

FIGURE 7
Some of the many rubber stamps used in the Geddes office to track projects.

were developed into larger and more detailed working drawings; finally, full-size models were produced.[58] Although Geddes made very few sketches himself, he maintained great control over the design process, insisting, "Every drawing, at every stage of the work, from the preliminary sketches up to the final shop drawings, passes across my desk."[59]

Geddes described how he avoided depending on his client's knowledge, using consumer surveys instead to achieve an independent perspective.[60] Geddes's office highlighted the near-scientific nature of its consumer research: The office "assigned various individuals with proper qualifications to . . . carefully selected parts of the country to make numerous specific inquiries."[61] Among these investigators were

ANNOUNCING OUR
NEW ADDRESS
& TELEPHONE

NORMAN BEL GEDDES & COMPANY

50 ROCKEFELLER PLAZA
PHONE CIRCLE 5-8030
NEW YORK CITY

FIGURE 8A (LEFT)
Cover of Norman Bel Geddes & Company's new address announcement, c. 1939.

FIGURE 8B (RIGHT)
Norman Bel Geddes & Co. staff, c. 1930s. Photograph by Richard Garrison, 10 x 8 in., 25.4 x 20.3 cm

"designers, merchandising specialists, salesmen, [and] engineers: men to get the men's point of view, women to get the reaction of women . . . from the metropolis to the scantily populated rural community."[62] Geddes's "investigators" "mailed in daily" reports which the office "sorted and compiled in statistical form."[63] Appearing in the pages of *Horizons*, such descriptions of highly systematized and rigorous research presented Geddes's design consultancy as essential to any ambitious client. Upon completion of a design project, an official job summary was produced. This was typically used to reflect on the successes and failures of the job, generate publicity, and attract new clients.

As the office grew, design-related research became more entrenched and sophisticated. This was especially apparent in the postwar years. This rigorous approach represented a substantial shift from Geddes's more prosaic consumer and dealer surveys and coincided with a broader national trend in social research.[64] Much of the credit for the transformation in research at the Geddes office belongs to his partner and business manager, Earl Newsom, who had a doctorate in English from Columbia University. Newsom began a career in market research in 1925, working first for *Reader's Digest* and in 1927 for the Oil Heating Institute, where his job was to "help change the public's fears of converting from coal to

oil."[65] Newsom, who joined Geddes's firm in 1933, was interested in mass behavior and the emotional response of "the crowd mind."[66]

The concepts of the "people" and the "Average American" were manufactured in part through the practice of mass polling and opinion surveys, pioneered after 1935 by Gallup's American Institute of Public Opinion.[67] The idea of the "people" became a rhetorical tool for cutting across class, ethnic, and ideological lines to create a sense of national unity and culture.[68] Geddes's office developed and refined its use of consumer surveys from the early thirties. Geddes, however, didn't construct the "people" as a unified and homogenous mass, but rather, with Newsom's help, as a large middle class, which could be divided into a few consumer segments, each of which could be sold a different style at a different price. Such postwar research exemplified the tendency of the Geddes office to offer products targeted at a handful of large consumer segments of average taste and middle incomes.

While in 1934 Geddes employed thirty staff,[69] eight years later seventy-five "experts in . . . color, line, functionalism, merchandising, engineering, and manufacturing" were working in his Rockefeller Center office (**FIG. 8A, 8B**), primarily engaged in "production planning for the post-war period." Geddes explained, "business has never been better in

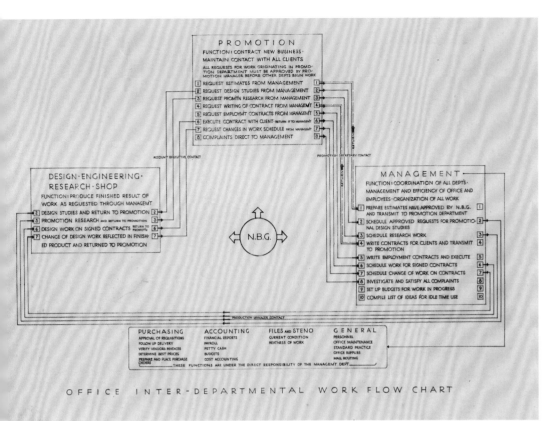

OFFICE INTER-DEPARTMENTAL WORK FLOW CHART

our field."[70] However, he found the firm's intensified design activity and emphasis on consumer research a distraction from his greater interest—unbridled visionary design.[71] The office would soon attempt to rationalize its operations, perhaps in response to Geddes's dissatisfaction with its research focus and increased size.

By the early 1940s the Geddes office had refined its operations, codifying them in its four-volume *Standard Practice* handbook of 1944. The handbook reflected Geddes's mania for order, especially in its emphasis on office efficiency (**FIG. 9, 10**). However, it also announced a new departure for the office—a focus on retaining "a selected number of clients."[72] This goal would be achieved by the coordinated operations of the office's three departments: management, service, and production. The task of client relations was the province of the service department, whose key staff included the service director, who procured design accounts, and the press relations representative, who publicized the work of the Geddes office. The service director ensured that the firm did "everything possible to hold all business and continue all contracts"[73] and oversaw two "salesmen" working in its "No-Sales Department," so named in order to highlight the office's goal of "maintaining a small group of clients," as opposed to growth for growth's sake.[74] Employees were informed that since

the office's inception "we have wasted a large amount of our time in [the] wrong fields of activity" and on "numerous" jobs "that were trivial." The new "policy" was to concentrate on "selected fields of activity and above a minimum price range of $10,000 per contract." Compared to its 1934 fees of $1,000 to $100,000 plus royalties, the office manual presented an image of consistency and moderation.[75] Even as late as 1941, "the bulk" of Geddes's business was made up of "bread-and-butter jobs in the $5,000-fee class."[76] The new policy called for the Geddes office to "stop being a little business . . . and think and perform as a big business. . . . In the past we have solicited nearly 1,000 accounts. In the future we will concentrate on less than 100."[77] The new policy may have pacified clients who feared the exorbitant fees of the Geddes office, which had recently charged General Motors $200,000 for the design of Futurama.[78] In actuality, Geddes's wartime jobs ranged from a one-week assignment for Emerson Radio, which paid $381.66, to a job for International Business Machines (IBM), which began in 1943 and by 1947 was paying $15,000 a month.[79]

The IBM project involved Eliot Noyes, who, after leaving the Museum of Modern Art in 1940 as its first curator of industrial design, worked on a number of Geddes's design jobs from 1945 to 1947, including the redesign of the IBM 562 typewriter, developing it into the influential, ergonomic

FIGURE 9 (LEFT)
NBG Office Inter-Departmental Work Flow Chart, showing Geddes at the nexus of Design, Promotion, and Management. Photostat, 11 x 8½ in., 28 x 21.6 cm

FIGURE 10 (RIGHT)
"Norman Bel Geddes Plans Like a General," in an unidentified newspaper, March 15, 1942.

PERSONAL EFFICIENCY EXPERT

CHARACTER ANALYSIS
FROM HANDWRITING

DeWitt B. Lucas

GRAPHOLOGIST

PROMPT, ACCURATE AND
CONFIDENTIAL SERVICE

664 PUTNAM AVENUE

DETROIT, MICHIGAN

THIS REPORT
WAS PREPARED

SEP 2 9 1924

ALL ANALYSES PERFORMED IN STRICTEST CONFIDENCE

38219

GRAPHOLOGICAL ANALYSIS OF THE HANDWRITING OF:

DICTATED AND
NOT READ FOR
CORRECTIONS

MISS FRANCES R. WAITE.

A Personal Typewritten Analysis

oooooooo

She is very unusually intuitive (even for a woman), this
quality at times overlapping into a pure clairvoyant insight, making her fairly impressionable, and often able to
sense a situation or a condition, or to know the motives
and reliability of others, instinctively. Her will is
more determined and obstinate than firm, strong, or independent, there being the need for more of those inhibitory
qualities which make for firmness and self direction. She
is decidedly original, clever, versatile, and resourceful,
with excellent capacity for invention. She is not averse
to authority and would exercise it at times with a touch
of imperiousness. The type forms of her capital letters
indicate good breeding, cultivation, refinement, artistic
sense, and a love of the beautiful in its various forms of
expression. She seems to show good sense of dramatic values and balance. There is a little more coldness, selfish-
ness, and indifference than is required to provide her with
the proper discretion and self-protection. These qualities

IF THE SERVICE
PLEASE, PLEASE
RECOMMEND IT

A thorough personal
diagnosis, including
a vocational resumé
for five dollars

(OVER)

ALWAYS ENCLOSE A
SELF ADDRESSED AND
STAMPED ENVELOPE

"Executive" model (**FIG. 12**).[80] While continuing his work on the IBM job for Geddes, in 1946 Noyes set up his own architectural and industrial design office with Marcel Breuer in New York.[81]

World War II provided numerous design contracts for the Geddes office, including government war assignments and commercial postwar forecasting. However, it would prove to be an emotional and professional trial for Geddes. In January of 1943, Geddes's wife of ten years, Frances Resor Waite, died (**FIG. 13**).[82] The resulting emotional strain, poor health, and disagreements with his partners, Roger Nowland, Peter Schladermundt, and Katherine B. Gray, profoundly affected his professional life.[83] He became increasingly unhappy with what he considered his partners' emphasis on consumer research at

Street crash, Geddes's futuristic imagery found an eager audience that desired both fantasy and distraction. Maintaining the image of the practical visionary in the increasingly affluent postwar years proved difficult. Such a persona had little relevance and even less resonance. Niels Diffrient, a second-generation industrial designer and partner at Henry Dreyfuss and Associates, explained the change:

. . . judging from what I've seen of Loewy's work, and Geddes's work, and Teague's, I think that they were used to the flourish, and it was drama, it was high drama to them, and they played it like theatre. And they wanted to be stars in their own rights. And when the star era began to wane, I think they all generally lost an interest in it.[89]

FIGURE 11 (OPPOSITE)
DeWitt B. Lucas graphological analysis of the handwriting of Miss Frances R. Waite commissioned by Geddes, c. 1928.

FIGURE 12 (LEFT)
Geddes's own IBM Executive electric typewriter, designed jointly with Eliot Noyes, 1948. Metal and plastic, 20½ x 16½ x 9½ in., 52 x 41.9 x 24.1 cm

FIGURE 13 (RIGHT)
Geddes and Frances Resor Waite, c. 1938. Photograph by Cosmo-Sileo Co., 8 x 10 in., 20.3 x 25.4 cm

the expense of design.[84] Deeply upset with a change in contractual terms that gave new clients ownership of their projects' designs by the firm, Geddes called his partners "rigid" and "unswerving,"[85] telling them, "You people can obviously go ahead and sign it without me."[86] He subsequently broke from his partners,[87] who joined the Harold Van Doren office to become Van Doren, Nowland & Schladermundt in 1944.[88]

The success of Geddes's design office depended on attracting talented staff, organizing a large and complex business, and aggressively promoting the Geddes image. In the years following the 1929 Wall

In the decades after World War II, industrial design emphasized the practical over the visionary, stressing professionalism while discarding the utopian aura that Geddes was so instrumental in forging.[90] However, while the maturing profession turned away from theatricality and grandiosity, it embraced other key strategies developed primarily by Geddes, including consumer and design research, the systematization of the design practice, and the promotion of named (though less flamboyant) designers.

ENDNOTES

1 Dreyfuss and Wright were both stage design apprentices to Geddes in the early 1920s. Eero Saarinen worked for Geddes in 1938 on the hook-shaped facade of the General Motors building at the 1939–40 New York World's Fair. Eliot Noyes worked as a design director for Geddes during the mid-1940s. Russell Flinchum, *Henry Dreyfuss, Industrial Designer: The Man in the Brown Suit* (New York: Rizzoli International Publications, 1997): 26–28; Donald Albrecht, Robert Schonfeld, and Lindsay Stamm Shapiro, *Russel Wright: Creating American Lifestyle* (New York: Harry N. Abrams, 2001), 13; Ursula McHugh, "Gallery 2: Eliot Noyes," *Industrial Design* 7, no. 1 (January 1960): 32–37; Jeffrey L. Meikle, *Design in the USA* (Oxford: Oxford University Press, 2005), 139.

2 Russell Flinchum, *Henry Dreyfuss, Industrial Designer*, 27.

3 George Nelson, "Both Fish and Fowl," *Fortune* 9, no. 2 (February 1934): 90.

4 Geoffrey T. Hellman, "Profiles: Design for a Living—I," *New Yorker* (8 February 1941): 24, 25.

5 G. D. (possibly associate editor Gregory Dunne) with contributions from Gilbert Seldes and Henry Dreyfuss, "Norman Bel Geddes 1893–1958," *Industrial Design* (June 1958): 48–51.

6 Ibid., 51.

7 Geddes to Howard Church, Dean, Art Department, Michigan State College, East Lansing, Michigan, 8 May 1946, Job 972, Syracuse Industrial Design Course; Katherine Gray to Geddes, 2 May 1944, Box 26, Folder 415.1, Geddes Papers.

8 Charlotte Himber, *Famous in Their Twenties* (New York: Association Press), 25–31.

9 Frederick J. Hoffmann, Charles Allen, and Carolyn F. Ulrich, *The Little Magazine: A History and a Bibliography* (Princeton: Princeton University Press, 1947), 2, 4, 5.

10 Geddes to Jake (Jacob Weintz, business manager of *Inwhich*), 29 September 1915, Theater Box 176, Folder J-2, Geddes Papers.

11 *The Masses* was a monthly little magazine of art and socialist politics published between 1911 and 1917. In 1916 Barnsdall gave Geddes an important break in his stage design career when she brought him to Los Angeles to stage productions for her children's theater.

12 Those who received copies included Margeret Whittemore, "Suffrage Leader"; George Stevens, "Director of the Toledo Museum of Art"; Edward Penfield, "Father of Posters"; Oliver Morosco, "Theatrical Producer"; Hiram Kelly Moderwell, "Author—Critic *Boston Transcript*"; Hon. Newton D. Baker, "Mayor of Cleveland"; Maurice Browne, "Manager Little Theatre Chicago"; Winthrop Ames, "Mgr. Little Theatre—NY"; Aline Barnsdall, "Manager—Players Producing Co."; Theater Box 176, Folder J-3, Geddes Papers.

13 Geddes to Weintz, 29 September 1915, Theater Box 176, Folder J-2, Geddes Papers.

14 Warren Susman, *Culture as History: The Transformation of American Society in the Twentieth Century* (New York: Pantheon Books, 1984), 282.

15 Walter Lippmann, *Public Opinion* (New York: Penguin Books, 1946), 4.

16 Geddes to Weintz, 29 September 1915, Theater Box 176, Folder J-2, Geddes Papers.

17 Gilbert Seldes, "Industrial Design," *Saturday Evening Post* (28 May 1932), Flat Box 22, Folder 982.1a, Geddes Papers.

18 Jeffrey L. Meikle, *Twentieth Century Limited: Industrial Design in America, 1925–1939* (Philadelphia: Temple University Press, 1979), 43.

19 Geddes was with the advertising firm of Barnes Crosby Company (c. 1912, Chicago; c. 1914–16, Detroit), the Peninsular Engraving Company (late 1912, Detroit), the commercial art firm Apel-Campbell (c. 1914, Detroit), and the publicity agency Thorson-Seelye (c. 1914–15, Detroit), which he formed with several other young ad men. Dates during this period are approximate as many of Geddes's autobiographical accounts are contradictory. Offprint of "Norman Bel-Geddes," *National Cyclopaedia of American Biography*, Box 112a, Folder 982.3, Norman Bel Geddes, *Miracle in the Evening: An Autobiography*, edited by William Kelley (Garden City, NY: Doubleday & Company, 1960), 126–31.

20 Untitled typed manuscript draft of Geddes's autobiography, n.d., AE-78, ch. 74, Autobiography, Geddes Papers.

21 Untitled article, *Inwhich*, no. 5 (October 1915): n.p.

22 Untitled chapter draft, Theater Box 149, Folder J-3, Geddes Papers.

23 Ibid.

24 Promoting Geddes as a technological prophet became a significant aspect of the office's output and an important source of income and publicity. "19. Books and Articles," 4 September 1945, Job 940, Geddes Papers.

25 Norman Bel Geddes, *Horizons* (Boston: Little, Brown, 1932); Henry Dreyfuss, *Ten Years of Industrial Design: 1929–1939* (New York: 1939), the first of a series of privately published books of his designs; Walter Dorwin Teague, *Design This Day: The Technique of Order in the Machine Age* (New York: Harcourt, Brace, 1940); Raymond Loewy, *Never Leave Well Enough Alone* (New York: Simon and Schuster, 1951). Teague's 1940 book *Design This Day* had the most in common with *Horizons*; it expressed a sympathy with classical Greece, associated technology with progress, and defined design as a civilizing and improving force.

26 "31.6 Press Schedule Planned," *Standard Practice*, "Service Department," Job 940, Geddes Papers.

27 Geddes made a similar arrangement regarding the design of radios for the Philadelphia Storage Battery Company in 1930. See Meikle, *Twentieth Century Limited*, 85, 102; contract between SGE and Geddes, December 1930, Box 13, Folder 267.1, Geddes Papers.

28 "30.8 Press Relations," Box 88, Folder 940.6, Geddes Papers.

29 Dreyfuss et al., "Norman Bel Geddes 1893–1958," 48.

30 Geddes was certainly not the first to apply streamlining to vehicles and other goods. Samuel R. Calthrop patented an "air-resisting train" with tapered front and rear in 1865. By the end of the nineteenth century the teardrop form had been accepted as the ideal air-resistant shape. After 1930 the fad for streamlining took off within car design. In Britain Sir Charles Burney's Streamliner was produced around 1930. In the United States Buckminster Fuller's Dymaxion cars were built after 1933. Donald J. Bush, *The Streamlined Decade* (New York: George Braziller, 1975), 99. In 1930 Geddes did consider his contribution to streamlining significant and recognized that he did not "originate streamlining" but did the "original creative work on them [streamlined designs] and published it in a complete drawings-plans specifications, making it available to any one …" Job 653, Folders AP1–AP12, Geddes Papers.

31 Nelson, "Both Fish and Fowl": 94.

32 James J. Flink, *The Automobile Age* (Cambridge, MA: MIT Press, 1990), 237.

33 Norman Bel Geddes, "Streamlining," *Atlantic Monthly* (November 1934): 553–68.

34 *Horizons: Excerpts from 'Horizons' by Norman Bel Geddes*, Job 237, Geddes Papers.

35 Harold Van Doren, *Industrial Design: A Practical Guide to Product Design and Development*, Second Edi-

tion (New York: McGraw-Hill Book Company, Inc., 1954), 147–48.

36 Sheldon and Martha Cheney, *Art and the Machine* (New York: Whittlesey House, 1936), 64.

37 Ibid., 102.

38 Anthony J. Pulos, "Dynamic Showman: Norman Bel Geddes," *Industrial Design* 17 (July 1970): 60–64. Pulos notes that it was unfortunate that Geddes became associated with stylistic streamlining and that "his designs became paradigms of the mania for speed and the progress it implied that ruled the early thirties."

39 Geddes continued to present himself as a streamlining pioneer even as the popularity of the style decreased. See "Low Cost Houses-Presentation Book," c. 1946–54, p. 51, Oversize Box 9, Folder 460, Geddes Papers.

40 "19. Books and Articles," 4 September 1945, Job 940, Geddes Papers; H. D. Bennett, President, Toledo Scale Company, Toledo, to Geddes, 12 December 1934, Box 175, Folder WA-14b, Geddes Papers. Referring to the "streamlining" article, Bennett wrote, "You will pardon my suspicions of a 'ghost' since I quite distinctly recall your once saying that you never wrote anything, although the 'ghost' has expressed your ideas well."

41 Geddes, "Streamlining," passim.

42 Ibid., 553.

43 Those who received copies included Alfred Barr (Museum of Modern Art, New York), George Howe, Frank Lloyd Wright, Erich Mendelsohn, Richard F. Bach (Metropolitan Museum of Art, New York),

Ernst Wasmuth (publisher of the journal *Wendingen*), Charles Kettering (vice president, General Motors Corporation), Fred Zeder (head engineer, Chrysler Motors Corporation), Henry Ford (Henry Ford Motors), Harvey Firestone (Firestone Tire and Rubber Company), as well as officials at Continental Bakery, Socony-Vacuum Oil Company, and Chase Copper and Brass Company.

44 H. G. Weaver, General Motors Corp., Detroit, to Earl Newsom (Geddes's partner), 14 December 1934, Box 175, Folder WA-14b, replies to "Streamlining," Geddes Papers.

45 The last sentence was underscored in the letter from Alfred Barr to Geddes, 4 December 1934, Box 175, Folder WA-14b, Geddes Papers.

46 Ely Jacques Kahn to Geddes, 28 November 1934, Box 175, Folder WA-14b, Geddes Papers.

47 Fred L. Palmer, Distributors Group, Inc., to Geddes, 30 November 1934, Box 175, Folder WA-14b, replies to "Streamlining," Geddes Papers.

48 "30.8 Press Relations," Box 88, Folder 940.6, Geddes Papers.

49 Susman, *Culture as History*, 158.

50 "30.8 Press Relations," Box 88, Folder 940.6, Geddes Papers.

51 Geoffrey T. Hellman, "Profiles: Design for a Living—III," *New Yorker* (22 February 1941): 27.

52 Geddes to Charman (first name unidentified), 11 March 1946, Job 927, Geddes Papers.

53 Geddes, *Horizons*, 225–27.

54 Ibid., 231.

55 Ibid.

56 Ibid., 232–31.

57 Ibid., 231.

58 Ibid.

59 Ibid., 232.

60 Ibid., 230–31.

61 Ibid., 27.

62 Ibid., 227–28.

63 Ibid., 228.

64 *Recent Social Trends in the United States: A Report of the President's Research Committee on Social Trends*, 1933 (rpt., New York, McGraw-Hill, 1970).

65 "PR counselor Earl Newsom: Management is happier when it's a 'good citizen,'" *Printers' Ink* 14 (February 1958): 70; Job 927, Geddes Papers.

66 Earl Newsom's notion of mass behavior was influenced by Le Bon and Martin. Le Bon viewed the crowd as a single "organism" that was characterized by "barbarian" "spirit" and "unconscious" action. Martin believed the actions of the "crowd mind" to be "unconsciously determined." Gustave Le Bon, *The Crowd: A Study of the Popular Mind*, 1896 (rpt., London: Earnest Benn Limited, 1952), 155–7; Everett Dean Martin, *The Behavior of Crowds: A Psychological Study* (New York: Harper, 1920), 52.

67 Susman, *Culture as History*, 213, 217.

68 During his career, Earl Newsom used information services such as the Elmo Roper opinion surveys and Link Audit, which was started in 1937 and attempted to chart the "climate" of public opinion through interviews. In the 1930s he focused on selling products. In the 1940s he concentrated on fashioning corporate images, identifying and

molding a company's "personality picture." See "PR counselor Earl Newsom: Management is happier when it's a 'good citizen.'" Susman, *Culture as History*, 212.

69 Nelson, 43. Key staff included Worthen Paxton, who was educated in engineering and architecture at Yale and became Geddes's assistant designer around 1934; Roger Nowland, a 1927 graduate of MIT in aeronautical engineering; Peter Schladermundt, another Yale architecture graduate and prior employee of Raymond Hood; and Garth Huxtable, a 1933 graduate in design from the Massachusetts School of Art.

70 Himber, *Famous in Their Twenties*, 26, 38.

71 Letter from Katherine B. Gray of Van Doren, Nowland & Schladermundt to Geddes, 2 May 1944, Box 26, Folder 415.1, Geddes Papers.

72 "30.1 Client Service," Box 88, Folder 940.6, Geddes Papers.

73 Section 30.3, Box 88, Folder 940.6, Geddes Papers.

74 "Standard Practice 31. 31 Prospective Client Service. 31.1 No-Sales Department," Box 88, Folder 940.6, Geddes Papers.

75 Nelson, "Both Fish and Fowl": 43.

76 Hellman, "Profiles: Design for a Living—III": 24.

77 "31.2 Concentration versus Dispersion," Box 88, Folder 940.6, Geddes Papers.

78 Hellman, "Profiles: Design for a Living—III," 29.

79 Emerson Radio, Job 414; International Business Machines, "List of IBM approved assignments 2/3/47," Box 44, Folder 558.1, Geddes Papers.

80 Eliot F. Noyes, *Organic Design in Home Furnishings* (New York: Museum of Modern Art, c. 1941). Kathryn B. Hiesinger and George H. Marcus, *Landmarks of Twentieth-Century Design* (New York: Abbeville Press, 1993), 368. "Employees, Applications and Subcontractors," File 927, Geddes Papers. John Harwood, "The White Room: Eliot Noyes and the Logic of the Information Age Interior," *Grey Room*, no. 12 (Summer 2003, MIT Press): 5–31, 9.

81 Harwood: 10.

82 Unidentified author, "Mrs. Norman Bel Geddes," *New York Star* (21 January 1943): n.p. Chapter 87, Autobiography, Geddes Papers.

83 Ibid.

84 Letter from Katherine B. Gray of Van Doren, Nowland & Schladermundt to Geddes, 2 May 1944, Box 26, Folder 415.1, Geddes Papers.

85 Memo to Mr. Lance and Miss [Katherine B.] Gray from Geddes, 1 December 1943, in reference to the Nash-Kelvinator contract as arranged by Schladermundt, Box 26, Folder 415.1, Geddes Papers.

86 Ibid.

87 Geddes to G. Mason, president, Nash-Kelvinator, 15 March 1944, Box 26, Folder 415.1, Geddes Papers.

88 Letter from Gray to Geddes, 2 May 1944, Box 26, Folder 415.1, Geddes Papers.

89 Quoted in Flinchum, 126 (Niels Diffrient interview with Flinchum, 1 March 1991).

90 Anonymous, "How a Big Design Office Works," *Industrial Design* 2, vol. 2, no. 1 (February 1955): 26–37.

IMAGINING CONSUMERS: NORMAN BEL GEDDES AND AMERICAN CONSUMER CULTURE

Regina Lee Blaszczyk

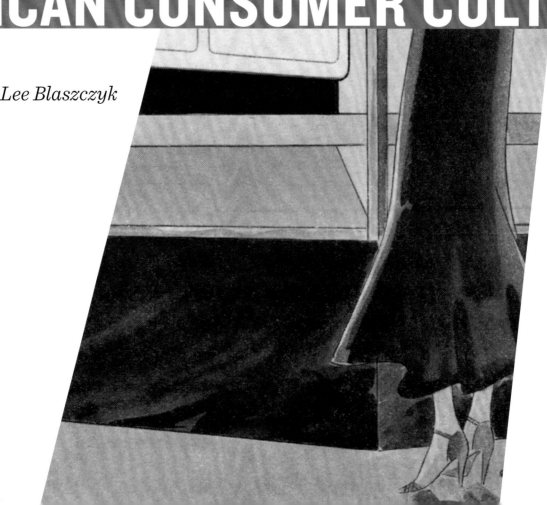

The boom economy of the United States in the 1920s provided Norman Bel Geddes with the chance to move away from his comfort zone of creating theatrical sets and costumes into the uncharted territory of designing for consumer culture. As firms like Nash Motor Car Company and Pan American Airways sought to augment their engineering prowess with design expertise, entrepreneurs with aesthetic skills responded to the opportunity. Geddes, along with Walter Dorwin Teague, Raymond Loewy, and Henry Dreyfuss packaged themselves as consultant industrial designers whose job was to help American businesses create products that would sell.

This essay examines Geddes's career as a consultant designer from the late 1920s through the mid-1950s. It presents case studies that illuminate the designer-client relationship and the consultant's role in consumer culture. A wide selection of businesses—department stores and chain stores, automobile and appliance manufacturers, a transnational airline, costume jewelry factories, and a liquor distributor—allows us to see how Geddes operated over time and in different contexts. While the evidence does not always permit us to see why and how clients hired him, we can explore other important issues. Did Geddes see himself as an aesthetic reformer who sought to improve mass taste, or did he define his role as that of a "fashion intermediary" who interpreted consumer desires? And how did he adapt to the economic and cultural shifts that differentiated the interwar years from the postwar era?[1]

AMERICAN CONSUMER CULTURE

American consumer culture came of age in the early twentieth century. The standard of living in the United States became the envy of economies around the globe. Earlier consumer cultures such as those in Renaissance Florence, Amsterdam in the seventeenth-century Dutch Golden Age, and Victorian London had laid the groundwork, but the United States was the first true mass-consumption society enabled by higher wages, lower prices, geographic mobility, and the permeable boundaries between social classes. For the period of Geddes's industrial design career, from the 1920s through the 1950s, more and more Americans stepped through

the portal of consumer culture and reaped the fruits of abundance.[2]

The American dream was in part defined by consumer culture and access to a middle-class lifestyle. During the Second Industrial Revolution of the late nineteenth and early twentieth centuries, many creature comforts—the single-family home, personal transportation, musical and theatrical entertainments, and fashionable clothing—that had once been available only to the wealthy came within reach of most white-collar and some blue-collar households. With the growing middle-class market, entrepreneurs introduced modern commercial enterprises—the mail-order house, the department store, the mass-circulation magazine—and created occupations—retail buyer, window display artist, advertising account executive, market researcher, industrial designer—to serve consumer culture (FIG. 1).

The 1920s were a critical decade in this evolution. World War I had devastated Europe's industrial economies, but the Western Hemisphere was unscathed. Already a major industrial power, the United States usurped Great Britain's role as the global financial capital. American manufacturers had benefited from the hiatus in transatlantic trade, and when peace returned, many firms channeled their wartime profits into new facilities. Most famously, between 1917 and 1928, the Ford Motor Company built its mammoth River Rouge complex outside Detroit, perfecting the system of interchangeable parts, machine tools, moving assembly lines, low prices, and high wages that forever defined "mass production." General Motors Corporation added flexibility and the concept of the "ladder of consumption" to the system, introducing the annual model change and encouraging Chevrolet owners to aspire to a Cadillac.

By the mid-twenties, America's gigantic mass-production economy faced a new problem. Factories could make large quantities of cars, shoes, and stoves at reasonable prices, but production capacity outstripped demand. Industry had become more efficient, and although the middle class had expanded, many people were still barely getting by. To stimulate consumption, American businesses revamped their efforts in industrial research, advertising,

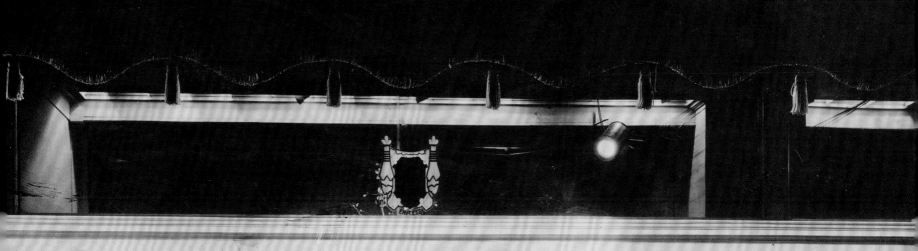

FIGURE I (OPPOSITE)
*Detail of Philadelphia
Gas Works publicity flyer
for* The New Acorn Gas
Range, *c. 1932–33.*

FIGURE 2
*Pre-Geddes Franklin
Simon & Company "Worth
of Paris" window display,
1920s. Geddes sought
to eliminate this type
of clutter with his work*

*for Franklin Simon &
Company between 1927
and 1929. Photograph
by Worsinger Window
Service, 10 x 8 in.,
25.4 x 20.3 cm*

marketing, and product development. Some entrepreneurs saw opportunities from the sidelines. The industrial design career of Norman Bel Geddes was born of this moment.

THE ENSEMBLE IN THE WINDOW

The idea of the consultant designer to industry originated with advertising agencies like J. Walter Thompson in Cincinnati and New York, Campbell-Ewald Company in Detroit, and Calkins and Holden in New York, whose art departments coached clients on the aesthetic aspects of campaigns, logos, brands, and products. Recognizing opportunities, some ad men started their own design consultancies dedicated to market research, style advisement, color counseling, packaging, and product development. Other pathways to this new profession included architecture, interior decoration, and set design for Broadway or Hollywood.

Geddes began his New York consulting business after a youthful dalliance with advertising and a significant career in New York theater. He positioned his office as a mediator between producers and consumers, an aesthetic coach to manufacturers and retailers who wanted to improve their market share. One of his first projects—the window decorations in 1927–29 for Franklin Simon & Company, a Fifth Avenue department store in Manhattan—exposed him to the distinctive challenges of product presentation and corporate branding in the field of fashion merchandising. This account allowed Geddes to test his mettle by combining his theatrical skills with popular ideas about Fordist production economies and French aesthetics. A devotee of the form-follows-function school pioneered by theorists from Horatio Greenough to Le Corbusier, he used this project to evolve the tempered modern style that characterized his designs for consumer culture.

Following the 1925 Paris Exposition, New York's leading department stores began to cast off Victorian clutter for an up-to-date image. Over the previous few decades, these stores had inched away from their origins as dry-goods emporiums, and with the triumph of the "flapper" style after World War I, they became one-stop shopping venues for fashion lovers who appreciated the convenience of ready-to-wear. Before the days of designer fashion à la Ralph Lauren, stores competed on their house brands, filling salesrooms with exclusive merchandise geared to the tastes and buying power of their particular clientele. The merchandise at Franklin Simon & Company, Lord & Taylor, and R. H. Macy & Company was worlds apart. While some stores were part of sourcing groups such as the Associated Merchandising Corporation, there were no national department store chains that stocked the same global brands in all branches. The typical department store was a stand-alone retailer that offered a one-of-a-kind urban shopping experience. In the competition for loyal customers, many department stores borrowed the concept of "the ensemble" from French haute couture and turned it into a mass-merchandising tool. By promoting the vogue for a ready-to-wear outfit with matching accessories, managers hoped to increase sales of their exclusive designs across several departments: dresses, hosiery, millinery, gloves, costume jewelry, and shoes.[3]

The ensemble mode was the rage when Geddes designed the Franklin Simon windows. Department stores advertised new fashions in the daily newspapers, but in the heyday of the walking city, there was no better promotional means than street-level window displays. As the price of plate glass, electric power, and lighting equipment fell in the early twentieth century, sumptuous window displays became a major attraction of every shopping district. After a day's work, consumers put on their good clothes and headed downtown to go "window shopping."

Initially, retailers employed window dressers who had grown up within the trade, but by the twenties they were hiring professionally trained artists as advisers on interior design, architecture, and merchandise. Department stores changed their windows for major holidays such as Easter and Christmas, society events like the debutante ball or the Belmont Stakes, and new fashion arrivals for the spring-summer and fall-winter seasons. In the war of the windows, the merchant with the best displays would often attract the most customers in its price category. To outdo each other, window dressers pulled out all the stops, cluttering the area behind the plate glass with "Grand Rapids antiques, Greenwich

Village screens, anybody's pictures and whatever else appears sufficiently decorative to make people admire the accessories and turn a blind eye to the merchandise."[4]

Saks & Company was no different, its windows stuffed with props that detracted from the luxury merchandise. Trying to break into the world of display window design in 1927, Geddes boldly told Adam Gimbel, a top Saks executive: "Speaking of display windows in general, I do not recall when I have seen any genuine beauty in their composition—in the individual merchandise, yes; but it is the composing of the window, and windows as a whole, that I am concerned with. They are, in nearly all instances, too cold in their attempt to be dignified, too lacking in charm to be persuasive, too 'Show casey' and broken up to have any compelling sales merit, and certainly incapable of kindling that emotional excitement which is the essence of real beauty. Further value— no window in town is sufficiently striking to cause anyone to cross the street to look at it. Novelty is not sufficient, the ideas back of them must be radical— revolutionary."[5]

Although Adam Gimbel shied away from radical change, fellow merchant George D. Simon joined the revolution by inviting Geddes to redo the windows of his family's store. Specializing in imported merchandise, Franklin Simon & Company touted itself as a store of individual shops, presaging the boutique approach that would later make superstars of American designers like Ralph Lauren and Liz Claiborne. Versed in French fashion, George Simon's father, Franklin (the founder and president), and the display staff were receptive to the bright colors, streamlined forms, and holistic approach of modernistic design.[6]

Geddes helped Franklin Simon & Company promote the idea of coordinated fashions and accessories with window displays that embodied the idea of the ensemble. His revolutionary concept was a display system comprised of reusable, standardized, interchangeable parts as a platform for stylish merchandise. In many ways, this display technique of engineering a standardized platform and adding changeable decorative elements paralleled the General Motors approach to flexible mass production. The eye-catching novelty came not from Victorian details, but from the latest visual trickery: dramatic stage lighting, color harmony, and stylized geometric props set against simple, streamlined backdrops. In an interview with *Women's Wear Daily*, Geddes explained: "Unquestionably, there should be some display system, of the utmost flexibility, yet rigid, in imposing on the store's window dresser the necessity of composing his merchandise into patterns endowed with genuine pictorial values. Merchandise and background should always tie up so intimately, so organically, that they become a single artistic entity, as costumes and scenery blend into each other—sometimes—on the stage."[7] In the theater the pared-down European approach to scenography

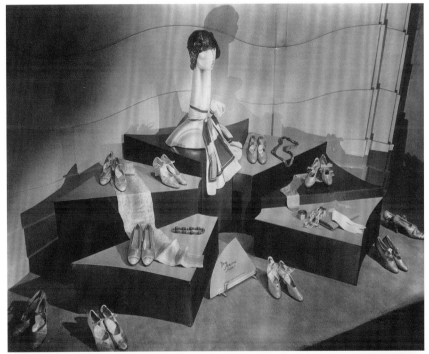

75

called the New Stagecraft (popularized in New York by the Austrian immigrant Joseph Urban) taught Geddes to appreciate simplicity as a tool for keeping the audience's attention on the actors. His windows for Franklin Simon & Company used a similar approach to encourage consumers to stop, look at the merchandise, and "desire it."[8]

COMFORT AND CONVENIENCE IN THE SKIES

Geddes also applied this holistic approach to designs for consumer culture in his cabin interiors for Pan American Airways (FIG. 5). In 1933, commercial air travel was an expensive novelty, but Pan Am founder Juan Trippe saw a bright future for the company in transoceanic flights for business and leisure. Most civilian planes were hollow aluminum shells that delivered the mail, and the few paying customers who braved long flights in makeshift cabins found their trips exhausting. Anxious to develop long-distance tourist travel to Latin America, Pan Am invested in large seaplanes and hired Geddes to outfit these "flying boats," famously known as the Clipper fleet after the swift sailing ships of the old China trade.[9]

The Clipper project presented Geddes with a new set of challenges that forced him out of his theatrical comfort zone. This was the first time that a new fleet of airplanes was outfitted expressly with the consumer in mind. The Clipper interior had to be designed for long flights between Pan Am's home airport in Miami and sightseeing destinations in Latin America. The trip could take five or six days with an overnight stop for refueling and sleeping at a Pan Am hotel every sixteen to eighteen hours. In the air, passengers were free to walk around, but many people were skittish about flying and couldn't relax. The trip needed to be made less stressful for consumers.

As pioneers in corporate branding, Pan Am executives took interior design seriously, realizing that the aircraft itself was part of the total flying experience. The company's purchasing agent, Franklin Gledhill, "was much interested in design" and helped fellow executives understand the importance of homey surroundings for passengers in the air.[10] He told a Geddes representative that "improving accommodations for passengers was the greatest

need in airplane design today."[11] To attract tourists, it was imperative that the Clipper "be the last word in airplane design, inside and out."[12]

Geddes understood the allure of creature comforts, which went hand-in-hand with the need to accommodate the era's gender conventions. In his own flying experience, he had noticed the dearth of female passengers, which he attributed "to the inadequate facilities which are normally provided in air travel." When presented with early cabin sketches, he immediately suggested "separating the toilets for men and women, placing one to the front of the ship and the other to the rear."[13] More women, he argued, could be encouraged to fly by creating an interior that put them at ease. It was one thing to sit next to a strange man on the plane, another to share the toilet with him.

Objections came from the mechanical engineers employed by the airplane builders. Working closely with the Glenn L. Martin Company and the Sikorsky Aviation Corporation, Geddes had to convince these hard-nosed technicians that comfort and convenience were as important as performance. Seeking to privilege their own technical expertise, the engineers didn't always agree that Mrs. Consumer was a priority. Sikorsky was a particularly tough sell, largely because Pan Am hired Geddes after its staff had already drawn up their own specifications for the interior design and ordered the materials. Pan Am then arranged for Geddes to work exclusively with Glenn Martin, but those men could be equally stubborn. When asked to take Geddes's advice on the design, one engineer scoffed, "The present interior is as good as a train coach or a bus, and therefore, should be acceptable for airplane travel."[14]

By 1934, Geddes had succeeded in creating the basic aircraft interior that we know today.[15] The ensemble concept, including color coordination, informed his design. The territory was new and the hurdles numerous. He had to accept the limitations of the Clipper's lozenge-shaped body, compensate for poor ventilation and deafening sound, figure out how to prepare and serve fresh food to the crew and passengers, and design the first ergonomic furniture for long-distance travel. Amenities like carpeting, curtains, fabric walls; a dining area with

tablecloths, silverware, and bone china; separate toilets for women and men; sleeping compartments with bunk beds; a kitchen equipped with an electric stove and refrigerator; and color-coordinated fixtures and fabrics were all part of the new airplane environment (FIG. 6). As with the window displays for Franklin Simon & Company, Geddes's perceptions of consumers' desires and expectations shaped his design choices.

IMAGINING CONSUMERS

How did Geddes know what consumers wanted from department store windows and unfamiliar experiences like air travel? Like other designers, he studied the market using the best available formal and informal methods: door-to-door surveys; interviews with retail buyers, salesmen, and consumers; brainstorming sessions with the client; and statistical analyses of sales trends (FIG. 7). This research was combined with his intuitive understanding of the man on the street, which he had developed over a lifetime of

people watching: studying them in public and private spaces and analyzing their choice of clothes, cars, houses, furnishings, and personal habits.

This practice was typical of how American businesses imagined the consumer during the industrial era. No one used the term "segmented market," but manufacturers, wholesalers, and retailers knew that tastes varied by social origins, location, and income. Factory art directors designed a range of products suited to America's highly differentiated tastes. Mass merchandisers such as Frank W. Woolworth, the dime-store pioneer, developed quantitative methods for analyzing tastes. Managers collected sales data from stores around the country, quantified it to delineate the patterns, and selected the next season's stock based on last season's best-sellers. Even without computers, Woolworth managers knew that merchandise that flew off the shelves in the Italian American neighborhoods of Syracuse might languish among Pennsylvania Dutch farmers in Lancaster.[16] Publishers and advertising agencies added more precision to consumer research. By 1911, the Curtis Publishing Company's commercial research division compiled demographic data on subscribers to the *Saturday Evening Post* and the *Ladies' Home Journal* and shared these reports with corporate advertisers. By the next decade, Madison Avenue advertising agencies like J. Walter Thompson began to study the relationship between ethnicity, social class, and consumer taste, sharing this research with clients in special reports and with potential clients in popular business magazines.

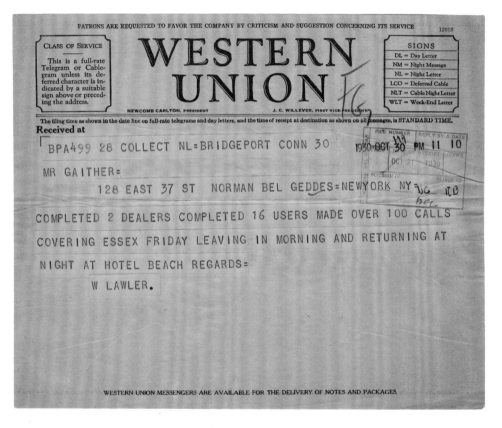

FIGURE 7

Western Union telegram documenting on-the-road research by the Geddes firm for the Standard Gas Equipment Co., 1930.

Factory-employed designers applied these concepts to their work. At General Motors, designers in Harley J. Earl's Art and Colour Section combined an intuitive understanding of consumer taste with hard facts: statistical data on the preferences of GM car owners gathered from franchised dealers. By the late 1920s, they knew which car colors, hood ornaments, and fender shapes were preferred by various income brackets in different sections of the country. At the Homer Laughlin China Company, designer Frederick Hurten Rhead divided the market into segments by income, occupation, ethnicity, gender, and race, ranging from "Mrs. Vassar-Yale" to recent immigrants and "colored" folks. By the late 1920s and early 1930s, at the world's largest automaker and at the world's largest pottery, managers were using design research to introduce the annual model change and the ladder of consumption.[17]

Some of Geddes's clients used similar techniques to update products and reposition brands. Around 1940, the Nash-Kelvinator Corporation of Detroit hired Geddes to work on automobiles and appliances as an aesthetic counterpart to the engineering staff. Aware of Raymond Loewy's recent improvements to GM's Frigidaire line, managers in the Kelvinator appliance division anticipated a general "dolling up" of electric refrigerators and didn't want to be left behind. They wrestled with the matter of class and taste. Market research had revealed that 85 percent of their sales went to households from "the low income brackets" that were upgrading from iceboxes to refrigerators. Kelvinator determined their needs "by getting 300 or 400 women to come in and tell what they like or dislike about their boxes as well as competitive boxes." When the ladies smiled favorably on "simple" rather than "screamish" designs, Kelvinator concluded, "The low income people like good design too."[18] Geddes believed he could improve on this market research technique with the addition of design research.

For Nash cars, Geddes combined insights from a market survey by the American Automobile Association (AAA) and his own consumer-focused design research (**FIG. 8**). His recommendations for postwar cars were based on AAA's analysis of people's impressions about existing models and a control group's reactions to design prototypes. Geddes "approached the problem from a fundamental requirement sense, whereas the general consumer, being non-imaginative and non-creative, is critical in a small sense but does not comprehend the broader possibilities of improvement which are possible."[19] The car buyer lacked the analytical and verbal skills to articulate how a vehicle's comfort, convenience, safety, and utility could be improved and sidestepped the issue by muttering, "I know what I like when I see it." Geddes helped his research subjects visualize possibilities by showing them sketches and models that pointed in new directions.

The Kelvinator project came on the heels of a major standardization effort by the housing industry and the U.S. Department of Commerce to cut construction costs, lower housing prices, and improve the American standard of living. By 1942, most kitchen cabinets and appliances were "interchangeable to conform to any floor plan"—with one exception. "The refrigerator is the only unit out of step with the other equipment, being higher and deeper and not conforming with any basic design scheme."[20] The Kelvinator technical staff advocated designs based on pure utility, but Geddes resisted: "I am not interested in engineers' opinion on styling."[21] In the wider world, professional home economists—a group that identified itself as the voice of the consumer—lobbied for standardized kitchen equipment that could lessen the burden of chores and make housekeeping efficient. Geddes balked at the apparent lack of contact with the living, breathing consumer. "The average housewife does not base her use of her refrigerator on a scientific approach. She stores food according to her particular requirements and in the manner that meets her greatest convenience. It is not sufficient to design a refrigerator on the specifications of the home economics bureaus. The solutions must go further and determine first what the housewife wants and needs herself (since she is unable to visualize the ideal solution for herself), and second, what is required for scientific storage."[22] By contrast, Geddes solicited the consumer's opinion and used it to redesign Kelvinator appliances as stylish components in the kitchen ensemble.

Geddes's consumer-focused approach to innovation had a lasting impact on the American kitchen. From the early 1930s onward, he pushed his appliance manufacturer clients away from cast-iron cabinets that emulated Chippendale parlor furniture toward a streamlined aesthetic. For the Standard Gas Equipment Company in 1932, he introduced a white enameled stove with straight chrome handles, rounded corners, and a legless base. Borrowing mass-production techniques from the auto industry, he invented a modular construction system whereby lightweight enameled panels were clipped onto a steel frame. In terms of housekeeping, the goal was

to eliminate the nooks, crannies, and cabriole legs that accumulated dirt in favor of a clean, practical look that would match any decorating scheme. Again drawing on consumer surveys, he applied this approach to refrigerators that he designed for General Electric (GE), Electrolux, Frigidaire, and Kelvinator from the early 1930s through the early 1940s. The first electric refrigerators, such as the GE Monitor Top introduced in 1927, had unsightly exposed cooling coils on their roofs and small storage compartments. Geddes moved the coils to the back, enlarged

FIGURE 8
Geddes's report for Nash-Kelvinator on car use-body types, 1941–42.

and rearranged the storage space, and using a modular assembly system, created the basic refrigerator design that is still used today.[23]

This consumer-focused approach to product design set Geddes apart from efficiency-minded engineers and home economists and from factory art directors whose style choices were often based on past successes. For Nash cars, his New York staff built life-size mockups of sedans and studied people getting in and out of the vehicle to determine the proper positioning of the seats (FIG. 9).[24] This early form of ergonomic research sought feedback on comfort and convenience from potential users. For Kelvinator appliances, Geddes's office conducted "500 personal interviews with housewives of all income classes in suburban New York and New Jersey." Research subjects were shown design sketches and miniature models of electric refrigerators and were asked to vote on aspects of the interior layout and on the color, shape, and overall appearance (**FIG. 10**).[25] Much like Raymond Loewy, Geddes sought to determine which prototype "makes the greatest concessions, the one most acceptable to the market." His consumer research was applied to product development, with the idea of eventually introducing an "annual design change . . . with the minimum tooling and die changes."[26]

This mode of trying to anticipate consumers' changing expectations was a good fit for the evolving role of the consultant designer as a bridge between the spheres of production and consumption. Very much a man of his times, Geddes navigated around internal corporate roadblocks and gender-based cultural values to develop market research practices that focused on how real consumers reacted to particular products. A memo to Nash-Kelvinator summed it up. Design and development "should be approached from the consumer's point of view only so that the goal set by the specifications is one which

unquestionably will answer any consumer criticism and one which if achieved, makes for real progress, in the design and development of the units."[27]

FLOW-MOTION

In June 1950, Rice-Weiner & Company, a major costume jewelry manufacturer with factories in Providence and a sales office in New York, introduced the Flow-Motion line by Norman Bel Geddes (**FIG. 11**). Jewelry manufacturers, clustered in northeastern states from Massachusetts to New Jersey, competed on price, quality, and style. They employed in-house designers but looked to consultants to give them a creative edge. This latest addition to the Jeray brand produced by Rice-Weiner consisted of ensembles of bracelets, necklaces, earrings, and novelty pins that expressed the idea that form should follow function. The term Flow-Motion referred to the mechanics of the construction and the streamlined look of the neckwear. Each motif in the chain was hung separately so that the necklace could "conform to the shape of a woman's neck as an elastic bathing suit conforms to her body. The result of this flexibility is that any necklace will fit any woman." Jeray president Martin Lasher called it "the first constructivist bit of thinking in jewelry."[28]

Drawing on his experience as a costumer for the stage and screen, Geddes was a keen observer of

FIGURE 9 (LEFT)

Woman stepping out of a Nash car mock-up, c. 1941–42. Photograph by unidentified photographer, 5 x 4 in., 12.7 x 10.2 cm

FIGURE 10 (RIGHT)

Consumer looking at drawing and model of refrigerator, c. 1941–42. Photograph by unidentified photographer, 5 x 4 in., 12.7 x 10.2 cm

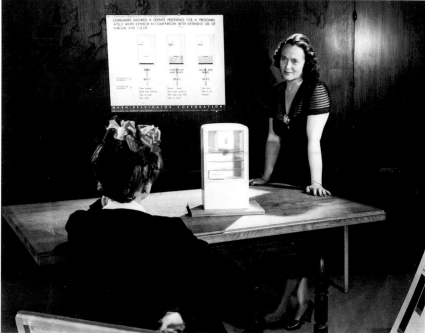

women's dress. Over the years, he grew frustrated with jewelry manufacturers' reliance on traditional motifs, which led to an incongruity between the designs and the natural movement of the body. Geddes defied the decorative conventions of costume jewelry to introduce fluidity and freedom of movement. "Necks and wrists vary enormously in contour. The necklace should lay upon and fit the modulating form of any neckline," he explained. "I have tried to achieve this in my Flow-Motion designs—to complete the artistic composition of the well-dressed women."[29] The wearer of Flow-Motion did not have to check in the mirror to see that her necklace was straight: The design ensured that it moved as she did.

Geddes had experimented with jewelry design in 1940 when he created a line for Trifari, Krussman & Fishel, a well-known Fifth Avenue company that eventually merged with Monet and then Liz Claiborne (**FIG. 12**). During the Great Depression, the proliferation of inexpensive Bakelite plastic novelties whetted consumers' appetites for trinkets in bright colors. By the mid-thirties, the newer acrylic plastics, marketed under the trade names Plexiglas, Crystallite, and Lucite, inspired designers like Gilbert Rohde to play with the concept of clear, colorless, transparent furniture. Geddes's design sketches for Trifari included Cubist earrings inspired by the Bakelite color fad and his now-collectible fish pin with a Lucite belly (**FIG. 13**). As former Trifari executive Irving Wolf recalled, in-house designer Alfred Philippe came up with the idea to introduce a group of "jelly belly" brooches with cabochons fabricated from acrylic bits discarded during the production of military aircraft windshields. Geddes's designs for the fish pin and a swan pin, both patented in 1941, were part of this "Lucite group."[30]

Around 1940, Rice-Weiner had hired the illustrator McClelland Barclay to design a line of jewelry (**FIG. 14**). Since Barclay's death in 1942, the firm had been "seeking another artist or industrial designer with whom to work."[31] In October 1949, the company signed a one-year exclusive contract with Geddes to produce a hundred sketches for bracelets, necklaces, brooches, and earrings.[32] His third wife, Ann Howe Hilliard, was a collaborator, traveling to Providence with him to see the production setup while helping

FIGURE 11 (LEFT)
Geddes Flow-Motion design for the Jeray brand of jewelry, 1950. Copyright © 1950 Rice-Weiner & Company, 8 x 10¼ in., 20.3 x 26 cm

FIGURE 12 (BELOW)
Geddes brooch and earrings design for Trifari, Krussman & Fishel, November 5, 1940. Pencil on paper, 8½ x 11 in., 21.6 x 28 cm

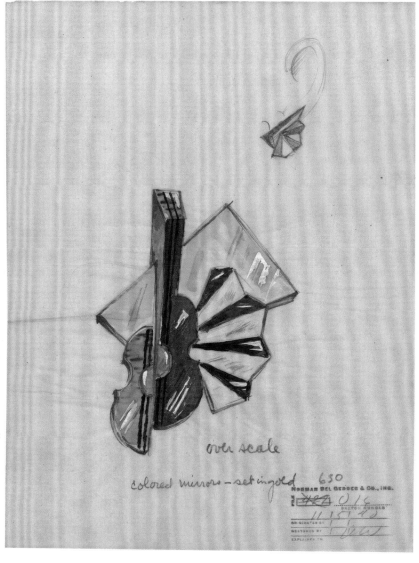

over scale

colored mirrors — set in gold 650

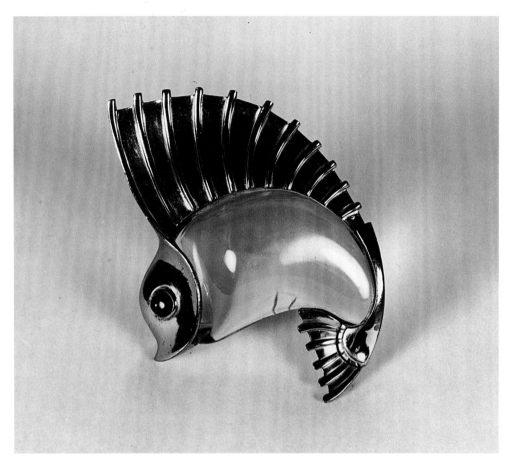

to "turn out distinctive designs appealing both to a prestige and [a] popular market."[33] Ann acted as a consumer surrogate, bringing the woman's viewpoint to the design table.

The letters between Geddes and Rice-Weiner illustrate the challenges of designing fashion accessories for the mass market. To get started, Geddes submitted thirty sketches by his staff, along with thirty-seven drawings by himself and Ann, in a "dozen or more different styles . . . from the conservative to the extreme modern." He thought their sketch for a Venetian Gondola necklace, which consisted of a boat in three to five separate pieces, represented something "entirely new in jewelry." The design suggested a "romantic picture" in a "series of related units" that would "lay more gracefully on the neck than a single piece." "It may seem corny," Geddes wrote, "but I believe that this has great popular possibilities."[34]

The client had a different opinion. "The Gondola series does not particularly impress me," Jeray executive Howard A. Weiner wrote, nor did the sketches of necklaces with jungle tigers, hungry baby birds, or dollar signs (FIG. 15–17). Besides being "conventional and conservative," these ideas could never be stamped out economically on the assembly line. "I had hoped that you would give to jewelry the feeling in the lines and the flow of motion, which you had captured and practically developed in the design field. . . . As a group, these designs do not seem to have the depth, body and rhythm contained, for example, in your 'Futurama,'" referring to the General Motors exhibition at the 1939–40 New York World's Fair. He encouraged Geddes to push the envelope. "I honestly believe that if the harmonies and rhythms of those lines could be introduced to jewelry, it would be a new approach that would demand the highest respect and admiration."[35]

Geddes insisted that his links to the market— his contacts with the press, his understanding of retailing, and Ann's input as Mrs. Consumer—put him in the best position to decide what would sell. Ultimately, the "final decision as to what the public will buy and what they won't buy and which is the highest

FIGURE 15 (TOP)
Unsuccessful Geddes jewelry design (No. 96) for Rice-Weiner, c. 1949. Photostat, 8½ x 11 in., 21.6 x 28 cm

FIGURE 16 (BOTTOM RIGHT)
Unsuccessful Geddes jewelry design (No. 114) for Rice-Weiner, c. 1949. Photostat, 8½ x 11 in., 21.6 x 28 cm

FIGURE 17 (BOTTOM LEFT)
Unsuccessful Geddes jewelry design (No. 100) for Rice-Weiner, c. 1949. Photostat, 8½ x 11 in., 21.6 x 28 cm

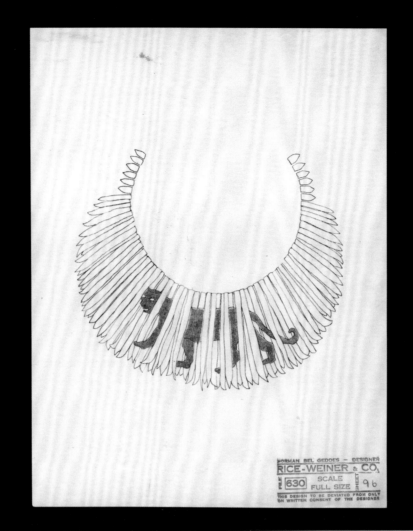

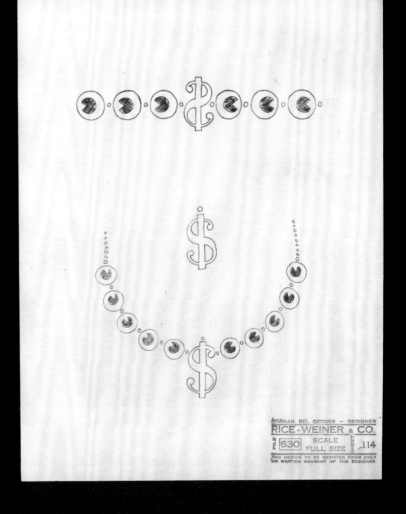

styled item for you to include from the point of prestige" should rest with him. "I know the items which will catch the Publicity Editor's imagination" and would secure the most press coverage in newspapers and fashion magazines.[36] When Rice-Weiner finally agreed to turn his sketches into samples, Geddes insisted on the highest production values. The "better we can make each detail look, without increasing the cost, the more favorable reaction we are going to get from the buyers. And by the 'buyers' I don't mean the public, but the jewelry buyers in the stores. The more quality we give them at the price, the more they are going to be impressed. And this would be especially so in connection with my name."[37]

Both Geddes and his wife pored over the stamped samples from Providence. "If I can study the problems that you had from the manufacturing standpoint, you'll be surprised how much better, and more variety, will get into the future designs. This is more than ever necessary for Mrs. Geddes, who is much less experienced than I with production problems."[38]

"Mrs. Geddes and I like everything"—with some exceptions. Long letters detailed the couple's requests for changes: "I do not like the bracelet at all, it looks like wire junk." Design tweaks were suggested with Mrs. Consumer in mind. "You will note that I have included one new earring unit—a single leaf with a pearl, very tiny, very dainty, very feminine. Mrs. Geddes feels certain that a lot of girls would like it."[39]

Fashion journalists gave high marks to Flow-Motion. *Women's Wear Daily* reported on the press preview at the Hotel Pierre in New York City. "The forms, as one might expect from an industrial and theatrical designer, are not 'strictly modern.' Many have an antique quality . . . yet brought up to date by construction and fit. There's a bit of whimsy in the collection, too, particularly among the socalled [*sic*] gadget pins. Amusing little French poodles, fascinating cat heads with iridescent bead eyes, and devil heads with rolling eyes contribute a conversation quality to the group." The *New York Herald Tribune* commended the up-to-date, moderate styling. "The new Jeray jewelry . . . does not resemble something from Mars, as might be expected from persons

familiar with Mr. Geddes's futuristic thinking." The familiar flora and fauna would put consumers at ease with the designs, but the unique construction made them modern. "Credit for the delicacy and essential femininity of the new designs, Mr. Geddes explained, should go to his wife."[40]

Six months after Flow-Motion's debut, Jeray executive Alex Weiner wrote Geddes with disappointing news. The quick turnover in the fashion trades—the ceaseless quest for novelty—had undermined the whole project. Rice-Weiner did "a very poor job" with Geddes's styles in the fall. The competition copied the designs or swiftly introduced newer creations that caught on. "It seems that after we work six or seven months on getting out a line of samples, the trend changes." After paying Geddes his hefty $5,000 fee, Rice-Weiner was left in the lurch with much of the product unsold. These troubles were exacerbated by a lack of interest in Geddes's designs among department stores, the major customers for prestige costume jewelry. Promoting the Geddes name proved costly and time-consuming, and the jewelry buyers didn't take the bait. Alex Weiner was direct. Since his firm "did not do a good business with these numbers we have to discontinue the use of your name in connection with sales."[41] In jewelry, as in other style industries, success depended not only on artistic creativity but also on the ability to keep up with the incessant demand for novelty.

REVISITING THE RETAIL ENSEMBLE

At the end of his career, Geddes returned to retail display with work for A. S. Beck Shoe Corporation and for Schenley Industries, Inc. These projects reflected his mature vision of the consultant as an intermediary and as a visionary who could anticipate future changes in taste. These projects benefited from his experience with urban retail design but put him face-to-face with the new challenges of suburban stores and with the emerging concept of design as unifying element in corporate branding.

In the late 1940s, most Americans bought their shoes from national chain stores like Sears, Roebuck and Company and J. C. Penney or from regional chains that specialized in men's or women's footwear. The nation's sixth-largest shoe retailer was the

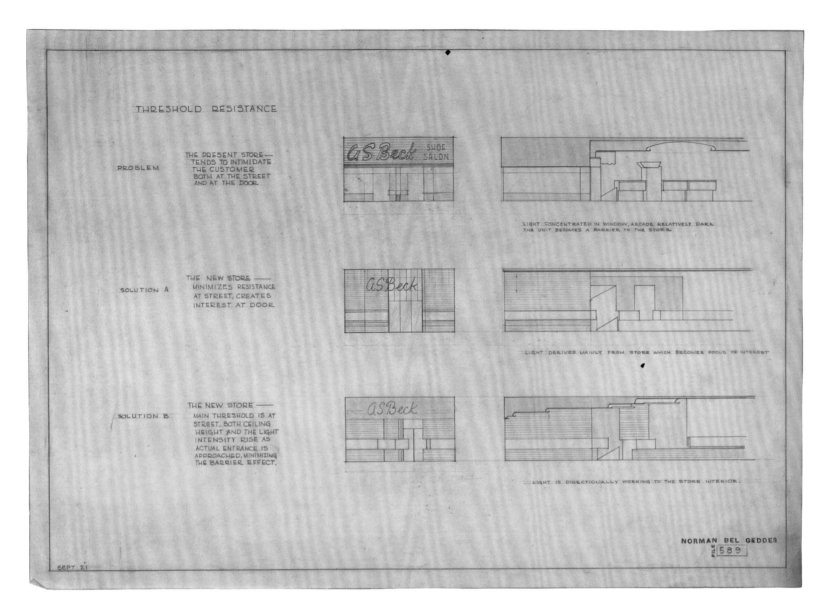

THRESHOLD RESISTANCE

PROBLEM — THE PRESENT STORE— TENDS TO INTIMIDATE THE CUSTOMER BOTH AT THE STREET AND AT THE DOOR.

SOLUTION A — THE NEW STORE— MINIMIZES RESISTANCE AT STREET, CREATES INTEREST AT DOOR.

SOLUTION B — THE NEW STORE— MAIN THRESHOLD IS AT STREET, BOTH CEILING HEIGHT AND THE LIGHT INTENSITY RISE AS ACTUAL ENTRANCE IS APPROACHED, MINIMIZING THE BARRIER EFFECT.

LIGHT CONCENTRATED IN WINDOW, ARCADE RELATIVELY DARK THE UNIT BECOMES A BARRIER TO THE STORE.

LIGHT DERIVES MAINLY FROM STORE WHICH BECOMES FOCUS OF INTEREST

LIGHT IS DIRECTIONALLY WORKING TO THE STORE INTERIOR.

NORMAN BEL GEDDES
589

SEPT 21

A. S. Beck Shoe Corporation, a regional chain with 123 stores, mostly on the East Coast, and $48 million annual sales.[42] As early as 1942, Beck managers realized that their stores needed a face-lift, particularly after Lord & Taylor made footwear-display history on Fifth Avenue in Manhattan, reducing their large windows to "shoe size" by masking the glass to show only the legs and feet of mannequins. Other retailers gradually emulated this model, installing bulkhead windows that elevated merchandise to eye level. Beck wanted to "bring the merchandise up to the customers' eyes"—to "serve the merchandise to him on a platter"—but renovations were put on hold due to the war.[43]

In 1947, Beck executives hired Geddes to modernize their window displays. The chain spent $200,000 annually on window design and construction plus dressers' salaries. The seasonal theme was changed four times per year, but merchandise was changed more frequently, sometimes daily.[44] Beck's

art deco stores had large knee-to-ceiling windows piled high with merchandise and looked woefully outdated (**FIG. 18**). Geddes helped Beck managers see how "the windows might be treated as theatre" with the "full emphasis placed on shoes, background to be secondary."[45] After a trial run, Beck manager Julian E. Hirschfeld reported that he was "thrilled with the result." The "lobbies seem to be filled with people, and the stores say, 'the windows are bringing them in.' . . . It is the first time that I remember ever being able to see the shoes."[46] Geddes secured contracts to rethink the facades, windows, and interiors for Beck's Class A stores in major cities like Atlanta and Chicago. His design suggestions focused on achieving the "maximum standardization and interchangeability" of the components and eye-catching theatrical effects through the judicious manipulation of space, form, light, and color (**FIG. 19**).[47]

Geddes's longstanding interest in retailing led to one of the last commissions of his career, designing display units and stores for Schenley Industries, a large liquor manufacturer-distributor that began as a distillery in Schenley, in western Pennsylvania. Like his work for national oil companies such as Shell and Continental, this project exposed Geddes to a major shift that would transform American consumer culture in the second half of the twentieth century. Most of his pre–World War II commissions had focused on improving human comfort and adding beauty to everyday objects, but Geddes was in part a victim of his own success. By the postwar era, comfort and aesthetics were taken for granted, and consumers increasingly looked elsewhere for novelty. They found it in the low prices, branded disposable merchandise, and drive-to-shopping destinations that became the hallmarks of American consumer culture in the Baby Boomer era.[48]

Schenley—a national company in the big leagues with Seagrams, Hiram Walker, and National Distillers—was grappling with this rising emphasis on convenience and a depressed market for its hard liquor. During the 1940s, founder Lewis Solon Rosenstiel had diversified from his core brand, Three Feathers potato whiskey, into other spirits—beer, rum, wine, vermouth, gin, and cordials—and into penicillin and other antibiotics. Schenley lost market share when consumers turned away from straight whiskies in favor of blends—and tax-free bootlegged booze. By Schenley's estimates in the early fifties, bootleggers made nearly half of the whiskey that Americans drank, leaving legitimate distillers with unsold inventory and declining profits. Diversification had only been partially successful; the firm's beer and wine subsidiaries, including the Blatz Brewing Company, were on shaky ground. By 1951, Schenley's sales had slumped to the lowest levels since the war. Rosenstiel stepped down as president to become chairman and handed the day-to-day operations over to a younger generation of managers.[49]

On behalf of Schenley's new management team, Seymour D. Hesse, the vice president in charge of advertising, hired Geddes as part of its effort to rethink liquor distribution. Before World War II, taverns sold 65 percent of the legal liquor consumed in the United States, but stores now dominated that market. Several factors accounted for this

shift: the seedy reputation of taprooms, spiraling inflation during the Korean War, and the spread of television, backyard entertaining, and stay-at-home culture.[50] Schenley managers thought that cleaner, brighter stores and distinctive merchandising displays might attract customers, build brand loyalty, and increase sales.

Taking cues from the popular Horn & Hardart automat cafeteria, the new team wondered if the self-service idea might work in traditional liquor stores, which catered to men, and in the new suburban supermarkets, which targeted women. Their goal was to create new spaces that showcased the full range of the Schenley brand, providing the consumer with a unique shopping experience that encouraged impulse purchases. Wine was still a novelty in American homes, and Schenley wanted supermarket dispensers that would appeal to the housewife's epicurean interests. Hard liquor was often purchased by businessmen for other businessmen as a goodwill gesture, and Schenley needed "ideas that would add gift interest to our packages." Geddes was asked to create concept designs for self-service liquor stores, supermarket display units, bars and cocktail lounges, and a unique whiskey bottle that would "become [a] trade mark, as 'Pinch Bottle' is to Scotch."[51]

Geddes designed the supermarket dispensers around the automat idea, as shown in his concept drawing for an overhead unit above the checkout counter (FIG. 20). The objective was to stimulate last-minute impulse purchases for the housewife who might like to experiment by cooking with wine or serving it with dinner. The liquor store designs were built around the ensemble concept that had been integral to mass merchandising since the twenties. In an era when liquor clerks still waited on customers, Geddes reconceptualized the store as a stylish warehouse that put goods within reach of the customer. His layouts increased the space dedicated to selling and allowed the store to handle more customers with the same number of employees. His concept drawings included new technologies such as air-conditioning; glass-front, self-service refrigerators; and overhead signs that directed shoppers to the merchandise (FIG. 21). His idea for a curvaceous new Bottle No. 5, the Lady Schenley, was designed to pique the male

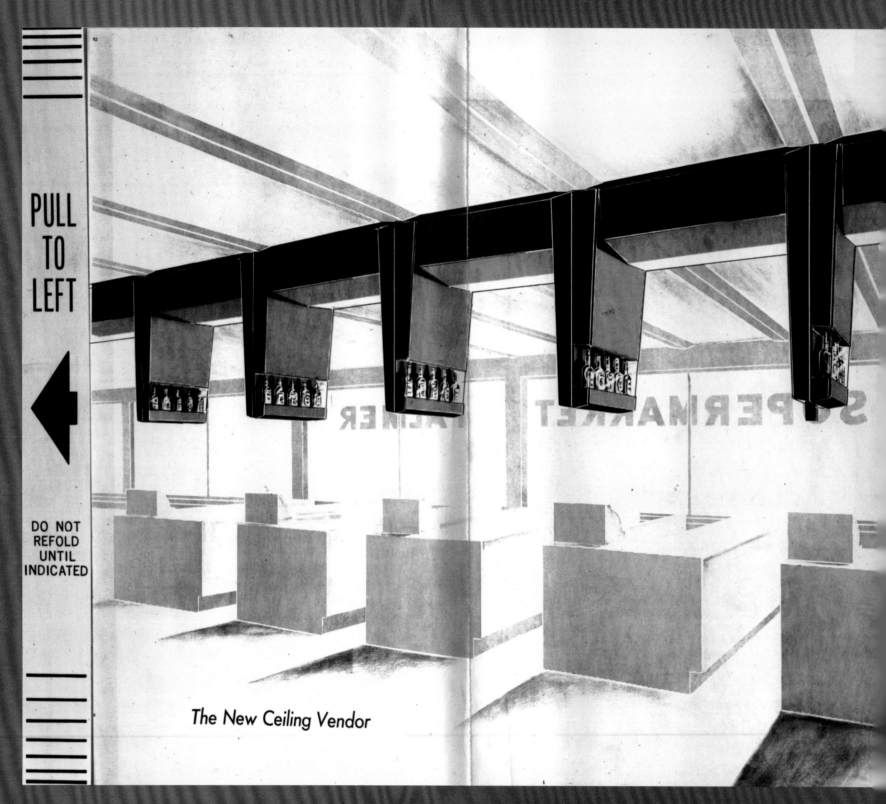

PULL TO LEFT

←

DO NOT
REFOLD
UNTIL
INDICATED

The New Ceiling Vendor

FIGURE 20

Geddes design for an overhead dispenser ("The New Ceiling Vendor") for a supermarket checkout line in his presentation book on "Self-Service Vending Equipment for Supermarkets and New Forms for Whiskey Bottles," c. 1953. Photostat, 17 x 12 in., 43.1 x 30.5 cm

FIGURE 21

Geddes design for a liquor store interior with directional overhead signs, c. 1953. Negative print, 10 x 12 in., 25.4 x 30.5 cm

consumer's interest: "Easy to take hold of—Pleasant to the eye—Curves designed for your hand—Can not slip from your grip—The natural expression of perfect proportion—A firm body—And most of all—good taste" (FIG. 22). Geddes boasted that this program could "do Schenley and the liquor business more good than the Futurama did General Motors and the highway business" for a mere ten percent of the cost![52]

As Schenley managers battled the "moonshine menace," they faced another set of challenges when the U.S. Justice Department launched a series of antitrust investigations against the company, which had grown exponentially through a series of acquisitions and controlled both liquor production and distribution. These headaches were compounded by the blue laws in conservative states. The Oregon Liquor Control Commission, for example, banned the sale of Schenley Reserve—"in its handsome gift box, it's the perfect gift"—because of laws that forbade the marketing of liquor as a present. While Schenley hired Geddes to imagine how liquor could fit into lifestyle marketing, the economic, cultural, and political milieu worked against the realization of that grand plan.[53]

A DESIGNER FOR MODERN CONSUMER CULTURE

The Beck and Schenley projects are a fitting closure to this examination of Geddes and American consumer culture, bringing it full circle to the display concepts for the Franklin Simon department store. Geddes remained committed to the ensemble idea, the consumer viewpoint, and the fusion of standards and style exemplified by design practice at General Motors. During his industrial design career, Geddes served as a bridge between producer and consumer, and in doing so, helped American business appreciate the value of consumer-driven design research and product development.

By the time he worked for Nash-Kelvinator, Geddes had settled into a role as a fashion intermediary, accepting that his job depended on gender-based cultural assumptions. The perception of the primary consumer as a malleable female—"Mr. Geddes said women are more susceptible to new things than men. Thinks they will get a very different reaction

from women than men"—typified the stereotypes of mid-century.[54] Those biases combined with cultural hierarchy to shape his views on social class and mass taste: "Mr. Geddes said that . . . the women's reaction will bear out that it is unusual to get 'class' in a low bracket. It is a difficult problem to lick."[55] Improved Beck window displays tutored the blue-collar shopper on good taste, and the curvaceous Lady Schenley bottle, geared toward men, embodied Geddes's ideas of a malleable female consumer.

To the very end, Geddes was very much a man of the moment, mediating between consumer expectations and client needs. When he died in 1958, the modern world was about to experience a sea change. Competitor Raymond Loewy, another first-generation consultant designer, understood the transition and warned clients to heed the great population shift to the suburbs.[56] Another consultant, Ernest Dichter, a psychologist who advised businesses on consumer motivation, also saw the writing on the wall. Whereas Americans had once treasured their automobiles, Easter outfits, and glistening white appliances, they now identified themselves through intangible status symbols: a college education, a job at a Fortune 500 company, and membership in the right country club.[57] The consumer culture that had made Geddes's career was giving way to a consumer culture that would make him obsolete. His short-lived experience with Schenley Industries was a harbinger of the changing current. Few postwar clients wanted window displays that would attract pedestrians from across the street; they needed backlit Plexiglas signs that would attract drivers speeding by at forty miles per hour.

American consumer society of the 1920s, '30s, and '40s rested on the fundamental premise, inherited from Victorian times, that durable goods were imbued with cultural meaning. The projects discussed in this essay—the retail displays, airplane interiors, kitchen appliances, and costume jewelry—reflected those beliefs. By the 1950s, the treasure-chest era was morphing into an I-want-it-now culture that prized the ephemeral. In the years ahead, a new type of designer—the package designer and the branding expert—would supplant the industrial designer as the great intermediary between the producer and

FIGURE 22
*Rendering of the Lady
Schenley bottle in
Geddes's presentation
book on "Self-Service
Vending Equipment
for Supermarkets and
New Forms for Whiskey
Bottles," c. 1953. Photostat,
10 x 12 in., 25.4 x 30.5 cm*

FIGURE 23

Three manufactured Geddes-designed pins, c. 1950s. Gold-tone, 1½ x 2 in, 3.8 x 5 cm (rooster); 1¼ x 2 in., 3.2 x 5 cm (poodle); 1¾ x 1 in., 4.5 x 2.5 cm (snail)

consumer or between the corporation and its publics. Men like Walter P. Margulies and Walter Landor—whose consulting businesses applied the ensemble concept to corporate identity projects for big businesses like Bank of America, Black and Decker, Chrysler, Citgo, Coca-Cola, Ford, Phillips 66, RCA, and TWA—understood the brand-oriented mentality that came with unbridled prosperity.[58] Geddes had laid the foundation for this transition by making style obsolescence part of the designer's tool kit, but the I-want-it-now attitude would only have befuddled him. History will remember Norman Bel Geddes as the great industrial designer for the modern era. He was indeed a man of his times, dedicated to the streamlined elegance that would be eclipsed by the throwaway consumer culture and the corporate identity projects of the late twentieth century.

ENDNOTES

1   On fashion intermediaries, see Regina Lee Blaszczyk, *Imagining Consumers: Design and Innovation from Wedgwood to Corning* (Baltimore: Johns Hopkins University Press, 2000).

2   Unless otherwise noted, this chapter draws on Regina Lee Blaszczyk, *American Consumer Society, 1865–2005: From Hearth to HDTV* (Wheeling, IL: Harlan Davidson, 2009).

3   On the ensemble, see Regina Lee Blaszczyk, *The Color Revolution* (Cambridge, MA: MIT Press, 2012), ch. 7.

4   "Franklin Simon Displays Treat the Window as a Stage and Merchandise as the Actors," in *Display Methods of Ten Leading New York Stores* (*Women's Wear Daily*, 1928): 13–15 (13, "Grand Rapids"), Box 7, Folder 134.2, Geddes Papers.

5   Geddes to Adam Gimbel, Saks & Company, New York, 18 April 1927, Damaged Box 35, Folder 938.1, Geddes Papers.

6   Christopher Innes, *Designing Modern America: Broadway to Main Street* (New Haven: Yale University Press, 2005), ch. 14; Norman Bel Geddes, *Horizons* (Boston: Little, Brown, 1932), 271; "Franklin Simon Displays," 14.

7   "Franklin Simon Displays," 13 ("utmost flexibility").

8   Ibid., 15 ("desire").

9   Blaszczyk, *The Color Revolution*, ch. 9.

10 Martin Dodge, "Prospect Report: Interior Decoration, Three Trans-Atlantic Air Liners Now Being Built," 5 September 1933 ("much"), Box 15, Folder 291.1, Geddes Papers.

11 Ibid.

12 E. A. Paxton, summary of meeting with Pan American Airways at Norman Bel Geddes offices, New York, 21 November 1933 ("last word"), Box 15, Folder 291.1, Geddes Papers.

13 "Interoffice Conference on Pan American Airways," rough draft of minutes, 26 December 1933 ("inadequate"), Box 15, Folder 291.2, Geddes Papers.

14 "Minutes of Meeting, Trip to Martin Factory," 13 February 1934 ("train coach"), Box 15, Folder 291.3, Geddes Papers.

15 For a retrospective overview of this project, see Pan American Clipper Case History, 15 October 1946, Box 15, Folder 291.1, Geddes Papers.

16 For early market research techniques, see Blaszczyk, *Imagining Consumers,* and Blaszczyk, *American Consumer Society.*

17 On GM, see Blaszczyk, *The Color Revolution*, ch. 10, and Sally H. Clarke, *Trust and Power: Consumers, the Modern Corporation and the Making of the United States Automobile Market* (New York: Cambridge University Press, 2007). On Homer Laughlin, see Blaszczyk, *Imagining Consumers,* ch. 4.

18 "Models of Kelvinator Exhibited," minutes of meeting with Nash-Kelvinator held at office of Norman Bel Geddes & Company, New York, 10 December 1940 (1, "300"; 4, "screamish"; 5, "dolling," "low income"; "simple," "good design"), Box 26, Folder 415.2, Geddes Papers.

19 NBG & Co., typescript on Nash presentation, "Car—Stage 4," 3 March 1943, Box 26, Folder 415.6, Geddes Papers.

20 NBG & Co. to Lawrence Phillips, "Kelvinator Refrig-

erator, Range and Water Heater," 7 January 1942, 1 ("interchangeable"), Box 26, Folder 415.1, Geddes Papers.

21 Geddes, "Nite Letter to Nash, Sunday, March 23, 1941," 24 March 1941, Box 26, Folder 415.2, Geddes Papers.

22 "Ref—Stage 1," three-month progress report on Nash refrigerator research, 29 April 1942, 1–2 (two quotations), Box 26, Folder 415.10, Geddes Papers.

23 Geddes, *Horizons*, ch. 1; Innes, ch. 13.

24 NBG & Co., "Quarterly Report to Nash-Kelvinator Corporation, Passenger Automobile Study—Stage 5," chart 98: Access and Egress 5, Box 26, Folder 415.5, Geddes Papers.

25 NBG & Co., typescript, "Nash-Kelvinator—Stage 3," 22 June 1943, Box 27, Folder 415.10, Geddes Papers.

26 NBG & Co. to Phillips, 6 ("concessions"; "annual").

27 Ibid., 4 ("point of view"); Glenn Porter, *Raymond Loewy: Designs for a Consumer Culture* (Wilmington, DE: Hagley Museum and Library, 2002).

28 "Jeray Jewelry by Bel Geddes Put on Display," *New York Herald Tribune*, 15 June 1950 (offprint); Bud Fox, Bud Fox Enterprises, N.Y., to Geddes, 22 September 1949, both in Box 48, Folder 630.3, Geddes Papers; Francesca Carnevali, "Fashioning Luxury for Factory Girls: American Jewelry, 1860–1914," *Business History Review* 85 (Summer 2011): 295–317.

29 Geddes, *Miracle in the Evening* (Garden City, NY: Doubleday, 1960), 260; Rice-Weiner & Company, press release on Flow-

Motion [1950], Box 48, Folder 630.5, Geddes Papers.

30 Geddes to Trifari, Krussman & Fishel, Inc., N.Y., 21 October 1940, Box 48, Folder 630.1, Geddes Papers: "Irving Wolf and Trifari: A View from the Top," The Trifari Collection: Jewels of the 1940s–1980s, available at http://trifaricollection.com/wolf.html, accessed 27 July 2011, Geddes, Design for a Pin Clip (swan), U.S. Design Patent 129,164, filed 22 July 1941, granted 26 August 1941; Geddes, Design for a Pin Clip (fish), U.S. Design Patent 129,165, filed 22 July 1941, granted 26 August 1941.

31 Bud Fox to Geddes, 15 September 1949; Miss Miele to Geddes, "Semi Precious Costume Jewelry Account," 21 September 1949, both in Box 48, Folder 630.3, Geddes Papers; Rice-Weiner & Company, *Original American Beauty Fashions* (1940), Box 48, Folder 630.4, Geddes Papers.

32 A. H. Geddes, Norman Bel Geddes Corporation, Stamford, Conn., to Rice-Weiner Corporation, N.Y., 18 October 1949, Box 48, Folder 630.3, Geddes Papers.

33 Miss Miele to Geddes, "Rice-Weiner Costume Jewelry," 24 October 1949; Geddes to Howard Weiner, Rice-Weiner & Company, Providence, R.I., 7 November 1949 ("distinctive"), both in Box 48, Folder 630.3, Geddes Papers; "Mrs. Ann Hilliard Wed to Designer," *New York Times* (hereafter cited as *NYT*), 21 December 1944: 19.

34 Geddes to Rice-Weiner & Company, Providence,

22 November 1949, Box 48, Folder 630.3, Geddes Papers.

35 Howard A. Weiner, Rice-Weiner & Company, Providence, to Geddes, 28 November 1949, Box 48, Folder 630.3, Geddes Papers.

36 Geddes to Rice-Weiner & Company, 22 November 1949.

37 Geddes to Messrs. Weiner and Lasher, New York, 28 February 1950, Box 48, Folder 630.3, Geddes Papers.

38 Ibid.

39 Geddes to Rice-Weiner & Company, Providence, 7 March 1950, Box 48, Folder 630.3, Geddes Papers.

40 "'Flow-Motion' Jewelry by Bel Geddes Introduced," *Women's Wear Daily*, 1 June 1950, clipping in Box 48, Folder 630.5, Geddes Papers; "Jeray Jewelry by Bel Geddes Put on Display" ("Mars" and "Mrs. Geddes").

41 Alex Weiner, Providence, to Geddes, 27 December 1950, Box 48, Folder 630.3, Geddes Papers.

42 J. Baum to Geddes, "Volume of Shoe Retailers and Competitors of A. S. Beck," 27 April 1949, Box 45, Folder 573.1; A. S. Beck Shoe Corporation, "Store Locations and New Postal 'Key' Numbers" (1947), Box 45, Folder 573.4, both in Geddes Papers.

43 Julian E. Hirschfeld to B. Daniels, 13 January 1942, Box 45, Folder 573.1, Geddes Papers.

44 Minutes of meetings on A. S. Beck, 5 June 1947; 30 July 1947 ($200,000), Box 45, Folder 573.2, Geddes Papers.

45 Minutes of meeting on A. S. Beck Window Display, 20 June 1947 ("theatre"), Box

45, Folder 573.2, Geddes Papers.

46 Transcription of letter from Julian E. Hirschfeld to Mr. Paxton, 6 August 1947 ("bringing"), Box 45, Folder 573.2, Geddes Papers.

47 Geddes to A. S. Beck, 15 October 1947 ("standardization"); A. H. Geddes to A. S. Beck Shoe Corporation, 17 June 1948, both in Box 45, Folder 573.1, Geddes Papers.

48 Blaszczyk, *American Consumer Society*, Part III.

49 "'Tax-Free' Whisky Seen Cutting Sales," *NYT*, 5 April 1952, 21; John Stuart, "Flood of Whisky Faces Distillers," *NYT*, 7 December 1952, F1; "Schenley Names R. T. Heymsfeld New President," *Wall Street Journal* (hereafter cited as *WSJ*), 16 September 1952: 11; "Liquor Levies," *WSJ*, 1 April 1953, 18; "Liquor: The Schenley Reserves," *Time* (29 September 1952), http://www.time.com/time/magazine/article/0,9171,935789-1,00.html, accessed 20 May 2011.

50 "Stores Now Sell More Liquor than Inns, Group Told," *Washington Post* (hereafter cited as *WP*), 13 November 1951, B10; "Taverns Lose Out in Sale of Liquor," *NYT*, 13 November 1951, 55.

51 S. D. Hesse, Schenley Industries, N.Y., to Geddes, 23 July 1953 ("gift"); "LWK Personal Notes on Conference Between Norman Bel Geddes & Messrs. [Erwin D.] Swann, [vice president, Schenley Distributors] & Hess," 3 April 1954 ("Pinch"), both in Box 57, Folder 680.4, Geddes Papers; "Elected

Vice President of Schenley Industries," *NYT*, 27 August 1954, 24.

52 "For Schenley Industries: A Report by Norman Bel Geddes on Preliminary Studies for Self-Service Vending Equipment and New Forms for Whiskey Bottles," 3 November 1954 ("Lady"), Oversize Box 12, Folder 680.4; "The Store, the Bar, the Lounge," presentation book for Schenley Industries, 13 July 1954, 85 ("Futurama"), Oversize Box 12, Folder 680.5, both in Geddes Papers.

53 Hal Boyle, "Bootleg War Is Considered by Distillers," *WP*, 18 February 1954, 19 ("menace"); "Oregon Bars Schenley Sales, Ads for 10 Days," *WSJ*, 24 November 1953, 2 ("gift").

54 "Models of Kelvinator Exhibited," 2 ("susceptible").

55 Ibid., 4 ("bracket").

56 See records of the Marketing Planning and Research Division, Boxes 138–57, Mss. 62142: Papers of Raymond Loewy, Library of Congress, Washington, D.C.

57 Blaszczyk, *The Color Revolution*, ch. 11.

58 On Margulies, see Tom Pickens, "The Great Corporate Identity Switch," *Passages* 10 (January 1979): 20–23. For Landor, see Acc. 500: Papers of Walter Landor, Archives Center, Smithsonian National Museum of American History, Behring Center, Washington, D.C.

4

ON THE ROAD TO THE FUTURE
Dave Croke

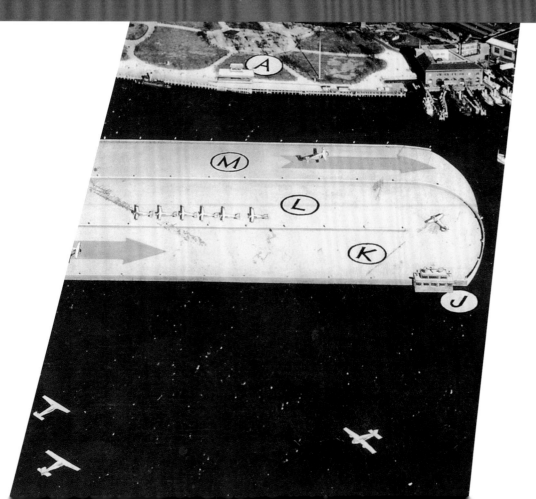

During the 1920s and 1930s, there was enormous popular enthusiasm for transportation technologies and widespread faith in their potential to transform society. Norman Bel Geddes was a major proponent of this belief, with an alluring vision of a seamlessly mechanized future populated by flying cars, yachts, amphibious planes, tanks, and buses. Underlying Geddes's work in this field was his fascination with the concept of the technological sublime—the transcendent, awe-inspiring attributes of structures that, by their magnitude and power, suggest a substitution of artificial design for the natural world.[1] Geddes's designs for mammoth ocean liners and airplanes certainly represented the gigantism of the technological sublime. However, Geddes also felt that autos and more modest industrial objects could fit this concept. His vehicle designs achieved a kind of technological sublimity in their seductively organic forms and their stylization of evolutionary principles, suggesting the substitution of design for nature, not by sheer size, but by nuanced attention to complexity, integration, and fluid motion. Natural evolution and transformation were the essence of Geddes's aesthetic, and, in his transportation designs, he attempted to create a vehicular ecosystem—a totally designed artificial landscape of interconnected vehicles. This essay explores Geddes's transportation designs as a man-made ecosystem and his use of streamlining—a language of smooth, aerodynamic shapes that was rooted in scientific inquiry—in the development of his vehicular designs.

HYBRIDITY AND METAMORPHOSIS: FLYING CARS AND THE WENNER-GREN YACHT

Geddes's affinity for hybrid vehicles was generated by his interest in the theatrics of evolution and transformation. He was one of many midcentury designers who tried to domesticate flight by creating a hybrid vehicle: a personal aircraft that was also an automobile. Indeed, the flying car was perhaps the definitive icon of machine-age futurism. Still a familiar image today, it continues to provoke our nostalgic reflections on yesterday's sanguine vision of technological progress. Modernists like Le Corbusier were deeply enamored of airplanes, which employed cutting-edge industrial materials and rigorous scientific methods

in their engineering. Early commercial designers were also inspired by the technology of flight, borrowing many of their aesthetic cues from the airplane. Indeed, it is impossible to contemplate streamlining without considering the drama of flight and its attendant images. Streamlining depended on aerodynamic principles that originated with the airplane industry. So close was the connection that cynics often denigrated streamlining as nothing more than a slim pretext for superficially aping aeronautic forms in the design of consumer objects.

In Geddes's hands, streamlining embraced an exuberant vision of a fully mechanized landscape and pursued the concept of efficient motion far beyond the narrow issue of air resistance. The airplane, however, as the preeminent technology of the day, remained an important touchstone for his aesthetic. Yet, paradoxically, even as designers looked to the airplane to find the shape of the future, most of them, including Geddes, assumed that the airplane was bound to conform to a familiar pattern of development, following the automobile into the suburban garage. This is precisely where Geddes chose to place his own flying car in a series of meticulously detailed models (**FIG. 1**). As the title of his design manifesto, *Horizons*, suggested, Geddes was preoccupied with the end point of development: the ultimate realization of an innovation's potential to transform society. Thus, if the first flying car was most likely to appear on a military base or, perhaps, in the driveway of an eccentric billionaire, Geddes nonetheless preferred to look to the horizon, imagining the flying car as the next in a series of high-tech consumer products that had already begun to dramatically reshape social reality in the machine age. And while designers like Moulton Taylor and Robert Fulton, who met with limited success in the flying car endeavor, relied on detachable wings, Geddes characteristically attempted a more organic hybrid. His 1945 version employed telescoping wings that retracted into the vehicle's chassis, allowing the driver to take flight whenever it suited him and presenting a visual spectacle far more dramatic than the awkward process of detaching and reattaching wings (**FIG. 2**). Ultimately, this bias toward the sublime and the revolutionary is why none of Geddes's transportation designs was actually produced, but it is also the reason they remain evocative today.

Geddes's interest in achieving vivid exhibitions of transformation and adaptation in his vehicle designs was also represented in the yacht he designed in 1934 for the Swedish industrialist Axel Wenner-Gren. With typical bombast, Geddes claimed that his work would revolutionize the shipbuilding industry. Yet Geddes also admitted that much about his Wenner-Gren design was basically conservative.

streamlined superstructure provided an arresting vision that suggested a significant departure from historical precedent. For Geddes, streamlining was a highly technical pursuit grounded in scientific inquiry, but that did not mean that it yielded forms that were geometric, regular, or constrained. Rather, his streamlined designs were lusciously organic and expressive. By presenting unprecedented design challenges that Geddes met in a characteristically ingenious and theatrical manner, the yacht program

He made no effort to improve existing hull designs, confining his ambition to streamlining the yacht's superstructure in a measure that he tepidly hoped might mitigate the effect of crosswinds. He conceded that any improvement in the ship's overall performance would likely be minimal, since his design would add, by his own estimate, ten tons of weight over traditional arrangements.

The radical nature of his design rested on virtues other than speed, performance, or efficiency. The sculptural quality of Wenner-Gren's

provided an opportunity for Geddes to explore his interest in hybridity—the yacht was both a passenger vehicle and a launching pad for smaller ships—and to propose a definitive representation of his concept of the technological sublime. Indeed, the superstructure of the Wenner-Gren yacht, with its articulated tail section and the sensual orifices of its exhaust stacks, resembled a species of primeval marine life more than any industrial object (**FIG. 3**).

The greatest challenge for Geddes was how to deal with the yacht's lifeboats and launches, which were typically stored on the open top deck of a ship where they could be lowered over the ship's sides with relative ease. Having effectively eliminated the traditional slanted sides of a ship in favor of a fully enclosed, streamlined superstructure, Geddes needed to create a mechanism that could expel lifeboats and launches from the bowels of the yacht. The patented mechanism that he designed for performing this novel contortion became the focal point of his Wenner-Gren design. Several photographs of models undergoing this spectacular transformation were prominently featured in the proposal that Geddes ultimately delivered to Wenner-Gren: In the photos the yacht appears to give birth (**FIG. 4**). It

was not a tinkerer, but he was certainly representative of American traditions of vernacular engineering: a man for whom engineering was not an esoteric specialty but a democratic medium with revolutionary potential. Ultimately, what is most striking about Geddes's work in the transportation field is the fluidity with which he worked across a range of industries, moving with ease from designing cars to designing trains, boats, and airplanes (**FIG. 6–8**). His range of activity was unprecedented in his own time and could not even be contemplated today. In keeping with his populist attitude toward technology, Geddes was both highly confident in his own untutored mechanical acumen and deeply skepti-

FIGURE 3 (LEFT)
Drawing of the Wenner-Gren yacht, c. 1934. Photostat, 15 x 11 in., 38.1 x 28 cm

FIGURE 4 (RIGHT)
Wenner-Gren yacht lifeboat launch mechanism, c. 1934. Digital photograph of model, mixed media, 33 x 12¾ x 8 in., 83.8 x 32.4 x 20.3 cm

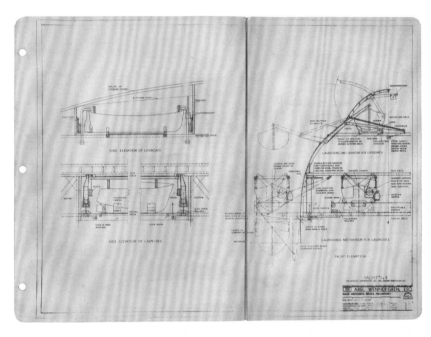

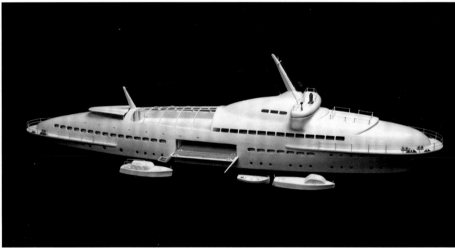

was this spectacle of symbiosis, transformation, and metamorphosis that characterized Geddes's transportation designs (**FIG. 5**).

STREAMLINING: STYLE AND SCIENCE

For Geddes, streamlining was not just a technical design process, but also a fundamentally expressive one. In his sensitivity to the theatrics of industrial design, which included an enthusiasm for ingenious and often unnecessary mechanical solutions and gadgets, Geddes exhibited much of the technological euphoria that had long been characteristic of popular American attitudes toward machines. He

cal of professional engineers with their established hierarchies and traditions.

It is not surprising then that Geddes's relationships with the various engineers with whom he collaborated were rather contentious. His work with the aeronautical engineer Otto Koller devolved into personal acrimony after Koller called Geddes's first proposal for Air Liner Number 4 "an absolute[ly] undesirable design"[2] and then failed to deliver performance specifications for a revised design (**FIG. 8**). During his time at Chrysler, repeated clashes with engineers led to a meeting where Geddes was pointedly reminded that his contract with the

YACHT 1931

THESE photographs, now published for the first time in America, show no dream-ship, but a model of the 231-foot yacht which Norman Bel Geddes has designed for a foreign client who plans a two-year trip around the world. In it the same principles that make the Australian crawl superior to the breast stroke are applied to naval architecture: instead of a hull built to buck the waves and a high superstructure offering great wind-resistance, this craft will have a stainless steel shell shaped to enter and shed green water with a minimum of checking. The shell will be opened or closed (electrically) so that all decks can be used regardless of the weather; and an air-conditioning system with its intake in the foremast will leave the decks clear of ventilators and other obstructions. Motor lifeboats and two launches, stowed within, may be lowered over either side by patent davits also designed by Mr. Geddes' organization. Accommodations are provided for eight passengers, two personal servants, a nurse, a secretary, a crew of thirty, two automobiles. Statistics: beam, 37 feet; draft, 12½ feet; displacement, 1,400 tons; cruising radius, 10,000 miles; power, steam turbine or Diesel; speed, 16 knots; cost (preliminary estimate), $550,000.

DESIGNED BY
NORMAN BEL GEDDES & COMPANY

PHOTOS BY RICHARD GARRISON

FIGURE 5
Unidentified magazine feature about the Geddes-designed Wenner-Gren yacht, 1937.

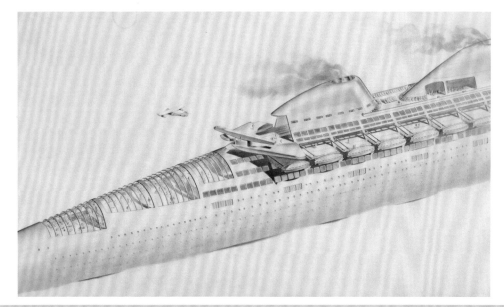

nothing more than a style—a superficial formula that could be applied to virtually any medium. Certainly, Geddes did pursue a number of projects that might be viewed in this light: The tank that he designed for the U.S Army is a conspicuous example. Geddes's tank seems unremarkable, except for its stunning armature, which is streamlined in the deep-sea primeval manner that he favored (FIG. 9, 10). Geddes's claim that the streamlined form would decrease the impact of enemy munitions on the vehicle is, perhaps, plausible. However, it seems a superficial rationalization for his abiding aesthetic preferences when we consider that armor-grade steel could not possibly have been shaped into the graceful curvi-

FIGURE 6 (TOP)
Geddes rendering of his streamlined ocean liner, c. 1932. Pencil on paper, 10¼ x 8 in., 26 x 20.3 cm

FIGURE 7 (BOTTOM)
Streamlined ocean liner model. Norman Bel Geddes, 1932. Wood, paint, 80 x 12 x 16½ in., 203.2 x 30.5 x 41.9 cm.

company specifically precluded his input on engineering matters. Even the marine engineers who agreed to sign off on his Wenner-Gren yacht design remained noticeably aloof in their affirmation. His scheme was deemed acceptable, but they made it clear that he was an interloper whom they viewed warily. Geddes, however, was undeterred by such slights and criticism. He was bolstered by his populist attitude and his adherence to the dogma of streamlining, which provided a golden opportunity for designers to enhance their status through recourse to scientific authority.[3]

However, if streamlining was often a powerful source of coherence and legitimacy for designers, that command remained precarious, for many observers persisted in interpreting streamlining as

linear form that Geddes envisioned. Several other designs, like his bus or his Locomotive Number 1, provided less extreme examples of the same phenomenon, with Geddes producing streamlined shells for what seem like otherwise ordinary designs. As with the Wenner-Gren yacht, Geddes's Locomotive Number 1 took a well-established form and provided a streamlined housing (FIG. 11). In contrast to the ship, however, the shell of Locomotive Number 1 did not transform the conventional architecture beneath it: It remained, simply, a smooth surface over a generic locomotive.

Geddes, however, never adopted a cynical attitude toward streamlining. He always made a conscientious effort to embrace holistic design, attempting, within the limited scope of his engineering capabilities, to introduce innovations that went beyond the artful molding of sheet metal. It is difficult to imagine how a man who came to prominence as a stage designer and had no formal training as an engineer could have been expected to provide a meaningful intervention in the design of modern tanks. Nevertheless, Geddes attempted to rationalize his streamlined design as a functional response to the unique operating conditions that tanks encountered (he even undertook an ergonomic study of the vehicle's interior). And, if his tank design ultimately seemed frivolous and misdirected, nonetheless Geddes's larger vision of a complex vehicular ecosystem did anticipate the design of armaments for World War

II on a more conceptual level, as that conflict relied on a system of highly cooperative machines, many of which were either true hybrids or vehicles that were capable of transformation.

Within that ecosystem, Geddes was particularly interested in the development potential of automobiles. He insisted that the car should not be seen as a mechanical substitute for the horse and was eager to promote and shape its continued development as an independent form. Indeed, much of Geddes's faith in the future, which linked the evolution of technology and society, came from his observation of the spectacular rise of the automobile. Of deep importance to Geddes and his contemporaries, the car

FIGURE 8 (TOP)
Geddes rendering of Air Liner Number 4 (aerial, front view), c. 1929–32. Pencil on paper, 28 x 17½ in., 71.1 x 44.5 cm

FIGURE 9 (BOTTOM LEFT)
Section drawing of Geddes-designed tank for U.S. Army, June 1940. Pencil on paper, 11 x 8½ in., 28 x 21.6 cm

FIGURE 10 (BOTTOM RIGHT)
Side elevation of Geddes-designed tank for U.S. Army, June 1940. Pencil on paper, 11 x 8½ in., 28 x 21.6 cm

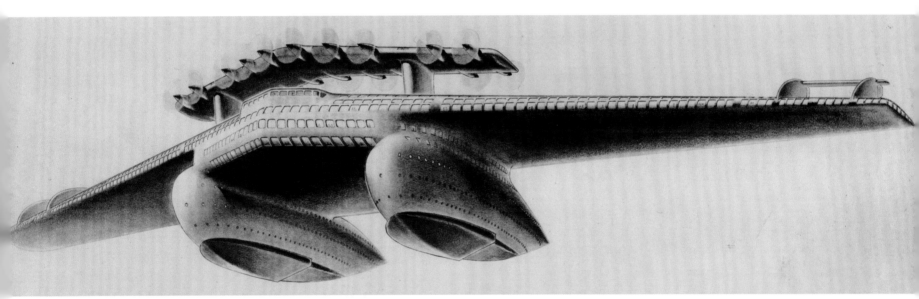

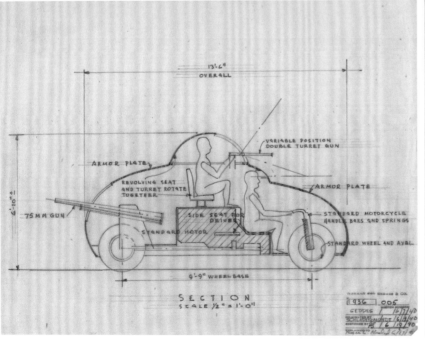

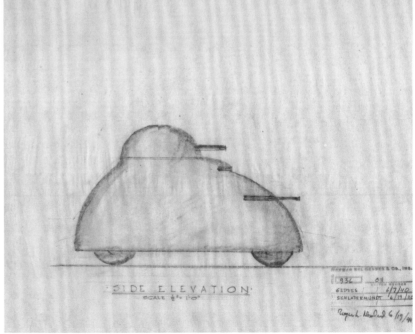

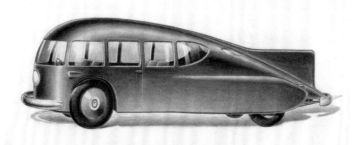

provided a template that designers felt subsequent technologies would follow: innovation followed by rapid technical improvement, widespread dissemination through the consumer market, and propitious social transformation. For Geddes, the auto industry not only presented the opportunity to work on projects that seemed to be of considerable import to society, but it also offered practical inducements. Although Geddes's designs for tanks, airplanes, and ocean liners circulated widely in the press and met with public enthusiasm, they did not generate serious interest from manufacturers.

It was only in the auto industry that Geddes actually came close to seeing one of his vehicle designs mass produced. His first opportunity occurred in 1928 when the Graham-Paige Motor Company asked him to design a series of automobiles. The company wanted him to execute a radical car design that would be suitable for production in five years and then to work backward, gradually introducing the elements of that design, beginning with the 1928 model. Geddes referred to these designs as car numbers 1, 2, 3, 4, and 5, and he placed all of his subsequent automobile designs in numbered sequence, even after he left Graham-Paige. Thus, the streamlined car that he designed five years after Motorcar Number 1 (**FIG. 12**) was called Motorcar Number 8. Of course, Motorcar Number 8 differed relatively little from Motorcar Number 5 because, for Geddes, Number 5 was "the ultimate car"—the perfect form toward which all cars were progressing (**FIG. 13-15**). As Geddes's decision to number his designs sequentially suggests, he viewed all of his car designs as parts of the same ongoing project: the unified, linear progression of automobile development. Although Motorcar Number 9 (**FIG. 17**) had eight unusually small wheels, which were housed in their own mini-teardrop fenders protruding from the vehicle's body, the later model was an unmistakable refinement of Motorcar Number 5—the critical features of the teardrop body, rear engine, and wraparound window were constants. The rear-engine format was especially important to Geddes because it would make the realization of the aerodynamically perfect teardrop form possible. It would also create a superior vantage for the driver by eliminating the visual obstruction of the hood, which must have struck Geddes as a repugnant transfiguration of the horse's ass as viewed from a carriage.

Geddes's work for Graham-Paige became an embittering experience, however, that demonstrated the indeterminate status of streamlining, caught somewhere between style and science, just as Geddes's own identity straddled the roles of artist and engineer. Graham himself did not particularly want to create the "ultimate car" as Geddes conceived of it. Rather, he simply wanted to achieve an evocative style. Graham-Paige was, in fact, an established leader in automotive styling. (The company's 1929 campaign is cited as a conspicuous example of Detroit's growing tendency to depict the automobile as a feminized fashion accessory.)[4] Graham was groping toward a rationalization of the styling process along the lines of Alfred P. Sloan's achievement at General Motors: Create a radical design, slowly introduce its styling features over five years, and repeat the procedure ad infinitum. Geddes exhibited a typically conflicted response to this program of gradually doling out novel design features. As a practical engineer, he recognized Graham-Paige's strategy as necessary to spread out the considerable production costs of introducing a new design. However, as an artist, he decried the vision of an intransigent, parochial public: "There seems to be a kink in the human mind that rejects the absolutely new and bizarre."[5] Ultimately, Graham-Paige decided that even Motorcar Number 1 was too radical. Geddes's designs were shelved, and the company went on to introduce a very modestly streamlined 1932 model that was more similar to the luxurious custom cars of the 1920s than to Geddes's Motorcar Number 1, which had a far more aggressive quality that would have taken streamlining in the direction of muscular bulbousness, as opposed to graceful balance.

The streamlined Graham-Paige Blue-Streak appeared in 1932 at the same time that Geddes's book *Horizons* was published. In it he acknowledged the effects of the stock market crash on the company's decision to cancel his ambitious design. Ultimately, however, he attributed the decision to small minds or "psychological factors in the human make-up that have to do with timidity."[6]

FIGURE 11 (TOP LEFT)
Model of Geddes's Locomotive Number 1, 1931. Photograph by Maurice Goldberg, 10 x 8 in., 25.4 x 20.3 cm

FIGURE 12 (TOP RIGHT)
Clay model of Motorcar Number 1 (convertible) designed by Geddes for Graham-Paige, 1928. Photograph by Maurice Goldberg, 7 1/2 x 9 1/2 in., 19 x 24.1 cm

FIGURE 13 (MIDDLE LEFT)
Geddes sketch of Motorcar Number 8, rear view, 1931, as it appeared in Horizons. *Pencil on paper, 12 x 12 in., 30.5 x 30.5 cm*

FIGURE 14 (MIDDLE CENTER)
Geddes sketch of Motorcar Number 8, side view, c. 1931. Pencil on paper, 17 1/2 x 12 in., 44.5 x 30.5 cm

FIGURE 15 (MIDDLE RIGHT)
Geddes preliminary sketch of Streamlined Automobile "Number 9," c. 1933. Pencil and charcoal on paper, 10 3/4 x 8 3/8 in., 27.3 x 21.3 cm

FIGURE 16 (BOTTOM LEFT)
Geddes model of Motorcar Number 9, without tail fin, c. 1933. Brass and plastic, 18 x 6 x 7 in., 45.7 x 15.2 x 17.8 cm

FIGURE 17 (BOTTOM RIGHT)
Geddes model of Motorcar Number 9, with tail fin, c. 1933. Brass and plastic, 18 x 6 x 7 in., 45.7 x 15.2 x 17.8 cm

Horizons was designed to expand those small minds, and it led directly to Geddes getting a second chance at realizing his dream of mass-producing the ultimate car.

Walter Chrysler was a great admirer of the book, and he seemed to be Geddes's ideal patron. When Chrysler contracted with Geddes in 1933, the company was about to introduce its radical Airflow model, which featured uni-body construction, an independent suspension, and the most aggressively streamlined body yet attempted by the auto industry. Geddes's first task was to do last-minute restyling of the Airflow, but he would also be collaborating on the design of future Chrysler models (**FIG. 18, 19**).

Walter Chrysler's audacious ambitions for the 1936 model year (and beyond) seemed certain to yield the ultimate car. Chrysler wanted to create the new Model T: an inexpensive car that would reverse the auto industry's dependence on styling and re-

Geddes participated, was aimed at improving the appearance of this ungainly feature. The Airflow that was produced sported an art deco grille that spread over much of the hood and had the appearance of a two-dimensional appliqué. Geddes had a hand in the design of this oddly graphic grille treatment. However, all of his models and sketches indicate his search for an alternative solution, attempting to integrate the grille and hood more fully and to eliminate the wide, planar contour of the front end by introducing more of a V-shape, like the inverted prow of a ship (**FIG. 20**).

FIGURE 18 (LEFT)
Airflow brochure for Chrysler Corporation, c. 1933.

FIGURE 19 (RIGHT)
Chrysler Airflow publicity tear sheet, Saturday Evening Post, *December 16, 1933.*

store an ethic of functionalism in Detroit. Geddes, of course, was immediately enthralled by this project, and it occupied most of his attention, even as Chrysler encouraged him to first work on restyling the Airflow (**FIG. 19**). The signature visual feature of the Airflow was an extremely wide hood that arced high over the engine to approximate the streamliner's ideal teardrop shape as nearly as possible in a front-engine car. The last-minute restyling effort, in which

Chrysler had hoped to create a streamlined, rear-engine car with a narrow wheel base that would be significantly cheaper than anything on the road and consistent in its design features over time. Chrysler realized that distribution costs had become the greatest obstacle to introducing a markedly cheaper automobile, and he resolved to reduce the wheel base of his standard model until it could fit perpendicularly into a railroad container, allowing him to ship twice as many cars in the same space. In another example of transformation and symbiosis between vehicles, Geddes worked extensively on this problem, designing a giant hinge that allowed the body of the car to fold in half. Chrysler's ambitious plan to reinstitute functional design in his 1936 models was torpedoed, however, by the poor sales performance of the Airflow. Instead, Chrysler's vision was ultimately realized in the form of the Volkswagen Beetle, which was in its earliest stages of planning in 1936 when Ferdinand Porsche toured Chrysler's facilities. The Volkswagen, with its streamlined body,

ment to progressive design. His version of streamlining was not confined to wrapping products in an aerodynamic package but embraced a larger vision of integration and organicism. So, while Chrysler's engineers scoffed at Geddes's plan to use the tail fin of his ultimate car as the vehicle's gasoline container, noting that storing gasoline above an engine invited catastrophe, they failed to appreciate the importance of this configuration to Geddes. Every previous automobile design featured a gas tank that was perfunctorily bolted to the vehicle's frame, where it remained, essentially, an extraneous thing. Aesthetic

 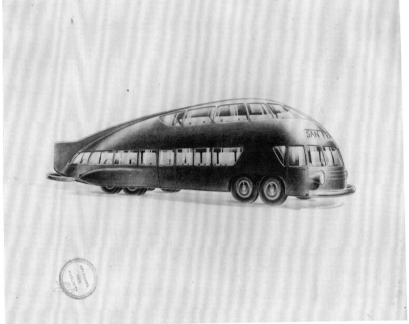

rear engine, light weight, narrow wheel base, minimal styling, immutable design, and rock-bottom price, had all the features that Chrysler envisioned for his 1936 model, and it became the Model T of the globally expanding frontier of the automotive industry during the postwar years.

There was something oddly nostalgic about Chrysler's ambition to create a futuristic streamlined car. Geddes, too, was both committed to progress and interested in resurrecting the original promise of the Model T, which had once seemed the harbinger of a mechanized democratic utopia. Henry Ford, of course, thought that his Model T was the ultimate car. That dream was superseded, but Geddes felt that it could be revived with a radical commit-

streamlining of the type Detroit popularized in the 1930s, which concealed the gas tank under a sensuous sheet metal body, disguised the heterogeneous reality of the mass-produced car without fundamentally altering it. The car remained an assembly of parts: a conglomeration of tanks and wheels and canopies that were gleaned from other sources. In Geddes's scheme, one that integrated the gas tank into the whole of the vehicle in an unprecedented way, the car would have existed independently of these sources and legacies, undertaking its own autonomous evolution. Geddes wanted to offer the spectacle of a machine that mimicked the seamlessly integrated complexity of nature. He wanted to offer a metamorphic version of the technological sublime.

FIGURE 20 (LEFT)
Geddes preliminary sketch of a car for the Chrysler Corporation. Pencil on paper, 11 x 8½ in., 28 x 21.6 cm

FIGURE 21 (RIGHT)
Rendering of Geddes's Motor Coach Number 2, 1932. Photograph by unidentified photographer, 10¼ x 8 in., 26 x 20.3 cm

NATURE: A UNIFIED VISION

Geddes's attempt to create a vehicular ecosystem offered a vision of machines in a network of symbiotic relationships that occupied an autonomous world of man's own devising. He conceived of each project within a larger concept of a totally designed artificial landscape. His 1932 design for a streamlined bus (**FIG. 21**), for instance, was part of an organic unity of transportation systems that included cloverleaf superhighways carrying cars and buses that led to train stations housing streamlined locomotives. On closer analysis it becomes apparent that Geddes had a deeply paradoxical but characteristically modern relationship with nature: The natural world and its organizing principles and forms were a fundamental source of inspiration for his work, but nature itself was something to be surpassed and discarded, and it was ruthlessly excluded from his final vision.

Significantly, all of Geddes's vehicle designs specified air-conditioning as a feature and demanded complete, hermetic enclosures. Because air-conditioning has become so standard, it is easy to overlook the importance of its ubiquitous appearance in Geddes's work, dismissing his persistent emphasis on this feature as mere common sense and not an important element of his exuberant futurism. But air-conditioning was very much a central element of Geddes's audacious vision, and he insisted on it when many of his contemporaries felt that common sense dictated otherwise. For instance, Theodore Ferris, a marine engineer who reviewed Geddes's plans for the Wenner-Gren yacht, generally applauded the design, but added: "There will be quite an element of the old fashioned order who will want to hang on to the tradition of open decks and superstructure and be content with putting up with spray slop, seas coming aboard, and lack of weather protection of this nature."[7] Ferris, whom we must suspect included himself in this "element of the old fashioned order," pointed out that many people found aesthetic attributes in their confrontations with nature and didn't regard convenience as the supreme attribute that a vehicle might offer. What he failed to recognize, of course, was that Geddes's design was not about mere convenience. Geddes himself had an alternative aesthetic vision to offer. The

FIGURE 22
Geddes model for a rotary airport, 1930. Photograph by unidentified photographer, 10 x 8 in., 25.4 x 20.3 cm

FIGURE 23 (ABOVE)
*Color rendering of
Air Liner Number 4
taking off from water,
c. 1929–32 (see also
page 101). Pencil, pastel,
and conté on paper,
12 x 10 in., 30.5 x 25.4 cm*

FIGURE 24 (OPPOSITE)
*Photograph of a model
helicopter and helipad,
c. 1945. Photograph by
Norman Bel Geddes & Co.,
4 x 5 in., 10.2 x 12.7 cm*

FIGURE 25
Geddes gas station design for Socony, c. 1934. Photograph by Richard Garrison, 10 x 8 in., 25.4 x 20.3 cm

trade-off that he presented was not between venerable maritime traditions like spray slop and the dubious convenience of spray-free decks. He wasn't pursuing marginal gains in efficiency or convenience, but rather something sublime.

Geddes's vehicles all presented a reification of the modernist vision: a perspective that prized control and detached observation.[8] In addition to air-conditioning, all of Geddes's designs offered expansive curvilinear windows to allow "perfect unobstructed vision."[9] In certain instances, such as his streamlined bus, these extended windows were nearly the only feature that distinguished Geddes's design from the prevailing standard. Even Air Liner Number 4, a wildly improbable flying cruise ship with a 528-foot wingspan that would have carried 606 passengers and a seven-piece band, staked much of its appeal on providing passengers with a range of observation positions (FIG. 23). As always, Geddes removed the traveler from the landscape in order to offer the landscape as a spectacle for the traveler's consumption. By emphasizing windows and vistas, his designs played with a common trope of the era's advertising, which often depicted powerful men serenely staring out of skyscraper windows as an image of status.[10] Geddes, too, promised the power and prestige inherent in unobstructed vision.

Indeed, all of Geddes's designs straddled a fine line between utopian prophecy and aggressive publicity. This tension is apparent in the volatile relationship between Geddes and the aeronautical engineer Otto Koller. Koller had previously deemed Geddes's Airplane Number 1 "absolute[ly] undesirable," but Geddes returned to Koller in 1931 and asked him to provide performance specifications for his new design, Airplane Number 4. Geddes was eager to include Airplane Number 4 in his upcoming publication, *Horizons,* and when Koller repeatedly failed to deliver the relevant specifications, an exasperated Geddes asked the engineer's subordinates whether Koller understood the value of publicity. Geddes understood publicity intuitively. He recognized that performance specifications were largely irrelevant to the fantastic visions that populated *Horizons,* and he was furious he might fail to meet his publication deadline over something so minor.

Nonetheless, Geddes was unwilling to drop Koller and completely forgo the authority of quantitative data because he genuinely considered himself an engineer, a scientist, and the preeminent spokesman for a future that was imminent. Geddes walked this fine line throughout his career, delicately negotiating between realistic possibilities for the near future and outlandish fantasies. *Horizons* was intended to support these efforts, shifting some of his fantastic designs into the category of the likely near future.

Geddes's affinity for publicity was widely known. The Geddes company's file on Air Liner Number 4, for instance, contains a 1934 newspaper article that provides a helpful perspective here. It begins with an ironic recounting of a local horse breeder's assertion that, for many purposes, horses remain an economical alternative to the automobile and proceeds to a keen skewering of Geddes. Having dismissed the notion that traditional horses might provide valuable service in the modern age, the anonymous author sarcastically ponders the possibilities of an improved horse: "Depend on it, in one shape or another the horse will emerge perfected for everyday use. You will see sketches of the article by Norman Bel Geddes, just to show that there is a near possibility, not just an enthusiast's dream.... It may be equipped with free wheeling, almost certainly with knee action, and, let us hope, with plumbing."[11] In his caricature of Geddes, the author identifies the critical themes of Geddes's work on transportation technologies: his preoccupation with supplanting nature with ingenious machines and his designs' tenuous balance between visionary futurism and crass marketing. However, the writer's image of a horse with plumbing misses the essence of Geddes's mechanical intervention in the natural world. Geddes was determined to move beyond the age of the horseless carriage, when machines served as isolated substitutes for elements in the natural order. In his world of transcendent artifice, highly adaptive machines would have their own autonomous and self-regulating network of relationships. Geddes did not want to employ technology in order to improve the natural world: He wanted to create an artificial world informed by natural principles.

ENDNOTES

1   David Nye, *The American Technological Sublime* (Cambridge, MA: MIT Press, 1994).

2   Letter from Otto Koller to Norman Bel Geddes, January 1930, Box 17, Folder 328.1, Geddes Papers.

3   David Gartman, *Auto Opium: A Social History of American Automobile Design* (New York: Routledge, 1994).

4   Roland Marchand, *Advertising the American Dream: Making Way for Modernity, 1920–1940* (Berkeley: University of California Press, 1985).

5   Geddes quoted by Munro Innes in an untitled manuscript for an article in *Automobile Topics* (New York: Motor Trades Publishing). Manuscript enclosed with letter from Innes to Geddes, 26 June 1929, Box 9, Folder 161.14, Geddes Papers.

6   Norman Bel Geddes, *Horizons* (Boston: Little Brown, 1932), 55.

7   Letter from Theodore Ferris to Norman Bel Geddes, 22 November 1934, Box 16, Folder 302.1, Geddes Papers.

8   Ardnan Morshed, "The Aesthetics of Ascension in Norman Bel Gedde's Futurama," *Journal of the Society of Architectural Historians* 63, no. 1 (March 2004): 74–99.

9   Norman Bel Geddes & Company caption sheet for publicity image of Motorcar Number 9, Box 17, Folder 329.6, Geddes Papers.

10 Marchand, ch. 8.

11 Unidentified author, "Startling Development," *The Record* (17 July 1934), n.p.

FIGURE 26

Geddes-designed Roadable Airplane, not dated. Pencil, pastel, and conté on paper, 11¼ x 9⅝ in., 28.6 x 24.4 cm

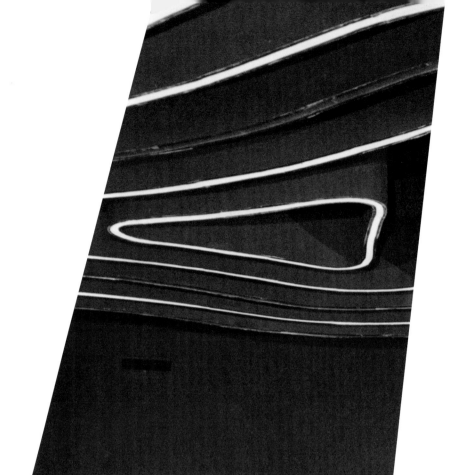

5

"A FEW YEARS AHEAD": DEFINING A MODERNISM WITH POPULAR APPEAL

Jeffrey L. Meikle

orman Bel Geddes was unpredictable, quick to roast subordinates, and quick to forgive. A draftsman recalled Geddes returning to the office after a night on the town, furious that renderings of Futurama and its streamlined building lacked coherence. With a presentation to General Motors only a few hours away, Geddes worked till dawn rescuing the project by giving each drawing a uniform charcoal shading. Always an optimist, he believed "a dream is an idea to be translated into a reality."[1] In a career noteworthy for many unrealized projects, he remained bitter about only one failure, his inability to gain official recognition as an architect. All the same, his career as an architectural designer had considerable influence on commercial modernism during his lifetime and on more avant-garde trends even into the twenty-first century.

Although Geddes was celebrated as a stage designer and an industrial designer, his lack of professional status as an architect rankled. That goal had once seemed within reach. In 1929, serving as consultant to the architectural commission of the Century of Progress International Exposition to be held in Chicago four years later, he won praise for his designs for several theaters and restaurants from Raymond Hood, Paul Philippe Cret, and Harvey Wiley Corbett, prominent architects in the recent skyscraper building boom. None of Geddes's proposals was built, however, owing to their cost as the stock market crashed, the jealousy of Chicago architects, and Geddes's unwillingness to compromise on "my ideal of what it [the exposition] should be."[2]

The fate of Geddes's designs remained uncertain in August 1930 when Ralph Walker, a commission member, invited him to present a "one-man show" at the Architectural League of New York (FIG. 1). By the time the show of models and renderings of Geddes's Chicago proposals opened in November, their viability was all but dead. Even so, a press release quoted praise from commission members. Walker described Geddes's "architectural work" as "highly interesting and unusual," marking "the beginnings of a new architecture." Hood regarded Geddes as "one of the most highly imaginative men now working in the field of architectural design." And Corbett observed that Geddes had made "a real contribution to the progress of architectural thought" by devising "new and delightful forms . . . modern in the best sense of the word."[3] These claims positioned Geddes as potentially the most innovative new figure in American modern architecture. To come into his own, however, he believed he would have to become a licensed architect.

Hoping the show would further his aspirations, the designer instructed that Basil O'Connor, law partner of New York Governor Franklin D. Roosevelt, should be treated well at the opening dinner.[4] The state's educational Board of Regents had already denied a routine application because Geddes possessed neither a high school diploma nor an architectural degree, and he was preparing a petition requesting that the board waive educational requirements as permitted by law. In support, he claimed that many of his stage productions were architectural in scope, that he had designed successful theaters and restaurants, as well as a conference room and auditorium for the J. Walter Thompson advertising agency, and that the nation's "most outstanding contemporary architects" applauded his Chicago designs.[5] Despite O'Connor's lobbying, when Geddes presented himself at the board's Albany office in March 1931, the examiners ignored his portfolio and used "endless technical questions" about plumbing and heating as grounds for denying his request.[6]

Four years later, Geddes again tried to enter the architectural profession by forming a partnership with the architect George Howe (FIG. 2), but they learned almost immediately that it was illegal for a non-architect to be partnered with a licensed architect. After that setback, Geddes briefly referred to himself as an "architecturalist," but he soon abandoned the awkward coinage.[7] Although he continued working on projects encompassing building and construction, he gave up on official recognition and instead relied on architects hired by clients to approve his plans. Even so, Geddes never lost his architectural ambitions. In August 1931, several months after his humiliation in Albany, he signed a contract for a book provisionally titled *My Theories on the Future of Architecture*.[8] When this book, more broadly titled *Horizons*, was published late in 1932, it covered all aspects of his design career, but architecture remained central to his vision of machine-age modernism.

Geddes had become interested in architecture in his late teens when he constructed a model theater to work out the staging of his own plays. By 1914, he was reading about architecture and devising plans for Theater Number 6, a radical structure with an axially oriented stage, later reworked for the Chicago fair. That same year the ambitious twenty-year-old acquired a manual entitled *Principles of Reinforced Concrete Construction*, perhaps to assist in planning the theater's high dome.[9] Within a few years the young stage designer had met Frank Lloyd Wright through wealthy arts patron Aline Barnsdall,

for whom the architect was designing a house and theater in Los Angeles (**FIG. 3**). She asked Geddes to design the stage and its technical equipment. The two men got along well despite the three decades separating them in age. From Wright, Geddes absorbed the idea of architecture's organic essence and the need to work "from the inside out."[10] However, they disagreed when Wright violated his own principles. Rather than allowing Geddes's vision of a stage projecting into the audience to generate exterior form, Wright designed a rectangular theater into which Geddes was expected to insert a traditional proscenium stage. Barnsdall's theater went unbuilt, but the younger man retained Wright's good will and later recalled the "strong sculptural character" of Wright's work as "the most beautiful expression of architectural mass I had ever seen."[11]

Wright's influence on Geddes was mostly inspirational. The latter's work reveals no trace of Wright's Prairie aesthetic, nor of the Mayan idiom of his Los Angeles period. However, Geddes's stage

FIGURE 1 (BELOW)
Architectural League of New York invitation to an exhibition of Geddes-proposed designs for the 1933–34 Century of Progress International Exposition in Chicago, November 18–December 6, 1930. Courtesy of the Architectural League of New York.

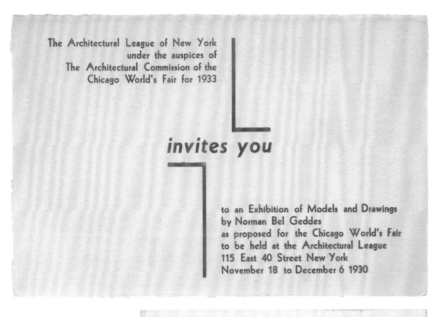

The Architectural League of New York
under the auspices of
The Architectural Commission of the
Chicago World's Fair for 1933

invites you

to an Exhibition of Models and Drawings
by Norman Bel Geddes
as proposed for the Chicago World's Fair
to be held at the Architectural League
115 East 40 Street New York
November 18 to December 6 1930

FIGURE 2 (BOTTOM LEFT)
Flyer announcing the short-lived Geddes/Howe architectural partnership, 1935.

FIGURE 3 (BOTTOM RIGHT)
Aline Barnsdall, her daughter Aline (nicknamed Sugartop), and dogs in front of her Frank Lloyd Wright–designed Hollyhock House, c. 1920s. Photograph by unidentified photographer, 3½ x 5½ in., 8.9 x 14 cm

As another step in his plan, inaugurated eight years ago, of extending his creative activities in design to industry

NORMAN BEL GEDDES

takes pride in announcing the association as active partner with him of the internationally known architect and designer

GEORGE HOWE

who until recently was senior partner in the firm of Howe & Lescaze, Architects, of New York and Philadelphia.

The interdependence of design for industry and commerce and of the architectural and decorative arts is a necessary consequence of our complex business and social structure.

The overlapping of their fields of activity and the common objective and purpose of their work have convinced both Mr. Geddes and Mr. Howe that a coordination of their separate but related activities in a single organization is a logical step.

From a public made conscious of simple eye appeal combined with technical perfection, the demand for original design based on serviceability becomes more and more exacting.

To leaders of industry and to prospective building owners who sense this new and inevitable trend in taste and utility

NORMAN BEL GEDDES GEORGE HOWE & COMPANY INC

is prepared to offer its services for consumer survey, research, design, production, construction and other technical problems from the stage of initial analysis to final solution.

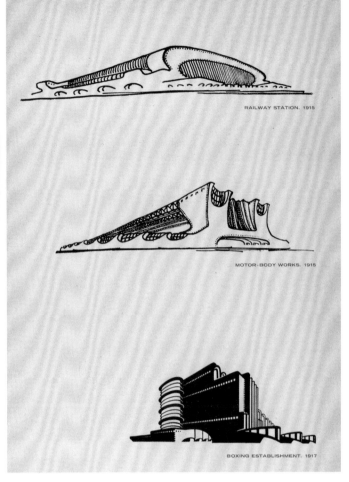

RAILWAY STATION. 1915

MOTOR-BODY WORKS. 1915

BOXING ESTABLISHMENT. 1917

designs assumed architectural heft. For the Chicago Opera in 1919, Geddes launched a ship with forty cast members down a ramp of ball bearings. In 1924 he transformed the interior of New York's Century Theatre into a medieval cathedral for director Max Reinhardt's production of *The Miracle* (**FIG. 4**). Geddes emphasized this project in his licensing petition, but its detailed historicism hardly suggested he was soon to become a machine-age modernist.

His conversion seems to have occurred through a meeting with Erich Mendelsohn, a German Jewish architect who visited the United States in 1924 and introduced Geddes to an expressionist modern style more flamboyant and commercial than the functionalism of the German Bauhaus. Mendelsohn was already well known for dramatic sketches of fantastic buildings with sweeping curvilinear forms and for boldly streamlined department stores, office buildings, and industrial structures. Details of their friendship have not survived, but Mendelsohn was

impressed enough to present Geddes with a sketch of his Einstein Tower at Potsdam, a fantasia of curving ink strokes defining a stubby but powerful eminence lacking right angles, unlike anything else in western architecture (**FIG. 5**).

Especially influential on Geddes was Mendelsohn's book *Structures and Sketches*, which he personally inscribed to Geddes. Several of its visionary studies, in particular a railway station sketched in 1915, prefigured the sculptural streamlining of Geddes's General Motors building of 1939 (**FIG. 6**). Even more striking are three renderings Mendelsohn prepared in 1921 for a competition for a so-called skyscraper for Berlin's Kemperplatz. The drawings reveal a dramatically horizontal structure with three main sections, each asymmetrically set back from the one beneath. Each section comprised three stories—or three bands of glass curving seamlessly round the corners, each band accented by a dark projecting cornice, together creating an impression of a

FIGURE 4 (TOP LEFT)
The set for The Miracle, *Century Theatre, c. 1924–25. Photograph by unidentified photographer, 10 x 8 in., 25.4 x 20.3 cm*

FIGURE 5 (BOTTOM LEFT)
Erich Mendelsohn sketch of the Einstein Tower, originally dated 1919 and presented to Geddes by the architect on November 25, 1924. Ink on paper, approximately 9½ x 11½ in., 24.1 x 29.2 cm

FIGURE 6 (RIGHT)
Erich Mendelsohn's 1915 sketch of a railway station in his book Structures and Sketches.

declare it "so modern . . . it may properly be termed 'modernistic.'"[13]

That last word, suggesting something extreme, serves as a reminder of modern architecture's eclecticism. Even after the postmodern movement of the 1980s revived an awareness of that eclecticism, it remains easy to regard the functionalism celebrated by the Museum of Modern Art (MoMA) as the one true modernism. Geddes's friend Sheldon Cheney offered an expansive account of various modernist currents in *The New World Architecture* (1930), encompassing Claude Bragdon's mystical orientalism, Paul Frankl's skyscraper furniture, Peter Behrens's machine-inflected neoclassicism, and Ludwig Mies van der Rohe's austere minimalism—with space devoted to Geddes's Toledo Scale and Century of Progress proposals. It must have reinforced Geddes's self-image as an architect to read that his theater projects were "the most provocative, prophetic, and intriguing of any of the radical thrusts so far." In his own copy of the book, Geddes marked Cheney's exhortation to go beyond functionalism. Although a designer had to be a rational engineer, "inspiration of an 'artistic' sort" could be turned toward "reinforcement of expressive mass" or "accenting of the revealing line."[14] Two years later, in *Horizons,* Geddes embraced the expressionist credo of Mendelsohn, Cheney, and others when he announced, "Function, once arrived at, is fixed, [but] its expression in form may vary endlessly under individual inflection."[15]

The breadth of Geddes's library suggests he shared Cheney's inclusive view of modern architecture. Not only did he own Werner Gräff's *Innen-räume* (1928), with photographs of austere functionalist interiors, and *Bau und Wohnung* (1927), a catalog of the Weißenhofsiedlung housing exhibition at Stuttgart (a favorite of the purists at MoMA), but also Bruno Taut's expressionist *Modern Architecture* (1929) and Frederick Kiesler's semi-constructivist manifesto, *Contemporary Art Applied to the Store and Its Display* (1929). Birthday gifts from Geddes's young daughters added Le Corbusier's *Towards a New Architecture* (1927) and Frankl's more decorative *New Directions* (1928). By then Geddes's first marriage was failing, and in June 1928 he was at loose ends because his lover Frances Resor Waite,

stack of cooling fins surrounding an unprecedented futuristic machine.[12]

Early in 1929, five years after receiving Mendelsohn's book, Geddes prepared plans for a complex of factory buildings for the Toledo Scale Company, a project also mentioned in his licensing petition. One of the buildings, a three-story laboratory, directly referenced Mendelsohn's Kemperplatz design. Presented at night in a glowing rendering, the laboratory's three horizontal bands of glass, divided by darker overhanging cornices, swept dramatically around a corner (**FIG. 7, 8**). Suggesting a borrowing from the middle section of Mendelsohn's Kemperplatz design, Geddes's rendering also assumed a three-quarter view, emphasizing the building's long side in a manner reminiscent of the German's visionary sketches. Although derivative, the Toledo Scale project, unbuilt owing to the stock market crash, provoked *Industrial Engineering* to

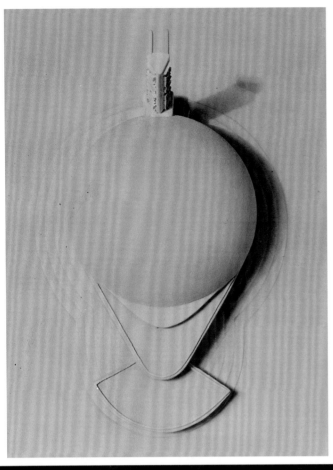

whom he was to marry in 1933, was away in Europe. He implored her to send "any good books or magazines on modern decoration or architecture" she might find.[16] Geddes sought out modernism of all sorts and made it his business to transform it for American consumers. The "modern," he wrote later, "is something that is a few years ahead of popular acceptance."[17]

Geddes's pragmatic definition suggests a rejection of formulas, a refusal to acknowledge elite cultural gatekeepers, and a desire to play to the audience. That was the case with *Horizons,* which critic Douglas Haskell declared lacking in "underlying principles" as its author purveyed "popular mechanics" and "advertising psychology." Even Wright dismissed *Horizons* as a "treatise on popular mechanics" with "little of value to offer either art or industry except as . . . a sort of stage scenery."[18] Actually, *Horizons* did reveal Geddes as a designer whose approach, no matter how popularly slanted, was wholly innovative. From his transportation machines, including motor vehicles, a train, and a

FIGURE 9 (TOP)
Aerial view of the model of Geddes's Theater Number 14. Photograph by Maurice Goldberg, 7½ x 9½ in., 19 x 24.1 cm

FIGURE 10 (BOTTOM)
View of the General Motors Highways and Horizon building that housed Futurama, c. 1939. Photograph by Richard Garrison, 10 x 8 in., 25.4 x 20.3 cm

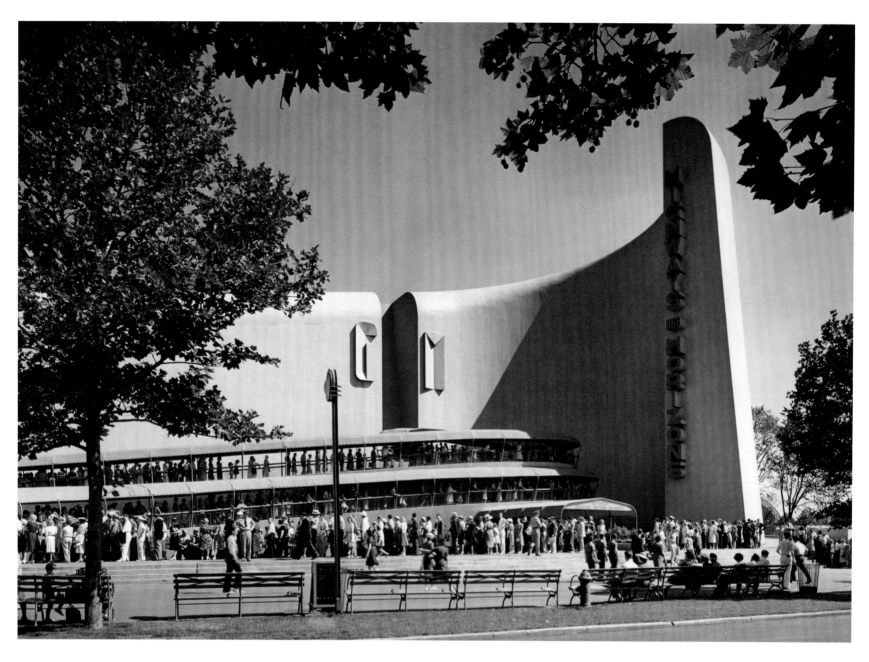

FIGURE II

Vertical concave "hook" enclosing the visitor-packed entry ramps to the General Motors building, c. 1939. Photograph by Richard Garrison, 10 x 8 in., 25.4 x 20.3 cm

huge flying wing intended to transport 600 people, to his architectural designs, Geddes avoided the current vogue for art deco with its angular, mechanistic forms and instead introduced a relatively pure version of streamlining, inspired by aerodynamics and imitated by other designers as it became the major commercial style of the 1930s.

The amazing thing about *Horizons* is the distinctive, personal quality of Geddes's streamlining. His design for a revolving restaurant lacked typical style markers and would have seemed innovative even into the twenty-first century. As for the Toledo Scale factory, though partially indebted to Mendelsohn in style, its streamlining consisted more in its efficient processes—also the case with several airport plans proposed in *Horizons*. The theater buildings, not usually included in discussions of Ged-

des's streamlining, embodied a purity of conception superior to the applied teardrops, rounded corners, and bands of three parallel lines associated with more typical stylistic streamlining of the late 1930s.[19] Photographs of a model of Theater Number 14 revealed a curving marquee typical of new movie theaters (**FIG. 9**). Except for that, nothing about Geddes's design suggested routine styling. Conceived as a theater in the round, it possessed a hemispherical dome whose outer diameter was recessed at the ground level to provide a sheltering overhang. A one-story foyer projected seamlessly from the body of the dome, its two walls meeting in a rounded acute angle. Seen from above, in an "airplane view," the theater evoked the soon-to-be iconic teardrop.[20] All the same, Geddes paid as much attention to the smooth functioning of his theaters as to their smooth forms.

In working to bring about the coalescence of process and style, Geddes was developing his own expressionist variant of modernism. Nowhere was this goal so obviously achieved as in the streamlining of the General Motors building of 1939 (FIG. 10).

Lauded as the triumph of the 1939–40 New York World's Fair, the General Motors building addressed Mendelsohn's dictum that modern architecture required "great masses and bold lines" for "the man in a motor-car, or in an aeroplane."[21] Although viewed mostly by pedestrians, the structure evoked automotive lines. As visitors streamed into the fair's Transportation Zone, they passed beside the General Motors building's long, horizontal northern side, its height slowly rising. Turning a sharp-angled (but rounded) corner to the left, they glimpsed another long horizontal wall, rising still higher, its distant terminus curving out from the building to create a vertically oriented concave screen that visually enclosed two meandering paths, alive with lines of people winding their way upward, then disappearing into a distant slit in the wall (FIG. 11). The building's cool sculptural lines, painted a metallic gray "to simulate Duco finish on automobiles," contrasted with the crowd's nervous energy.[22]

Passing down switchback ramps in an auditorium whose electronic display predicted future automotive congestion on a map of the United States, visitors boarded moving seats for a fifteen-minute ride overlooking dioramas modeling a smooth-flowing cross-country superhighway system and a metropolis of widely spaced skyscrapers, efficient automotive circulation, and elevated pedestrian walkways—all projected for the year 1960. After a

FIGURE 12
General Motors building intersection, showing all four facades, January 31, 1941. Photograph by Richard Garrison, 10 x 8 in., 25.4 x 20.3 cm

close-up view of an urban street intersection bridged four ways for pedestrians, the armchair futurists left their seats, turned a corner, and found themselves outside, standing in a full-size version of that same intersection, gazing up at four variants of modernist building fronts and looking down at streets filled with current General Motors vehicles (**FIG. 12**).

Curvilinear forms, meandering ramps, moving chairs with views of shifting landscapes, and the final shift from model into full-size reality—everything revealed process and form coalescing in a complete embodiment of architectural streamlining. Even Haskell, the critic who panned *Horizons,* became "ecstatic over the strange power of the streamlined complex of General Motors, so like some vast carburetor, sucking in the crowd by fascination into its feeding tubes, carrying them through the prescribed route, and finally whirling them out, at the very center of the display."[23] Geddes was enthusiastic after a visit to the construction site, reporting that the building "looms up and, due to the curved surfaces, it has a sense of power, which is a strange word to use architecturally, that is lacking in all of the cardboard appearing buildings within sight of it."[24] Similar judgments poured from journalists. For anyone remotely interested in architecture and design, Geddes's accomplishment seemed a mature statement of a uniquely American modernism, both flamboyant and functional, foreshadowed in *Horizons* and proclaimed in 1934 by the journal *Architectural Forum* with the statement that if Americans had been "lagging somewhat behind Europe," with streamlining they were finally "developing a national style."[25]

The culmination of streamlining as an American commercial modernism rivaling MoMA's austere functionalism coincided by chance with the culmination of Geddes's prominence as an industrial designer. Both were soon to fade, one a victim of cultural shifts, the other of failing health. World War II brought Geddes military work, but it also took his name out of circulation. However, for a while it seemed he would be able to capitalize on the General Motors building's success. Negotiating a contract to design a Bacardi distillery in Puerto Rico, Geddes was told the client sought a design "more unusual

FIGURE 13 (TOP)
Geddes model of Copa City, Miami, 1948. Mixed media, 27 x 22 x 8 in., 69.6 x 55.9 x 20.3 cm

FIGURE 14 (BOTTOM)
Front facade of Copa City on opening night, 1948. Photograph by Look *magazine, 9¼ x 4 in., 23.5 x 10.2 cm*

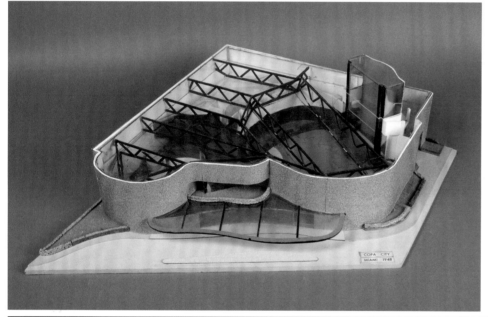

FIGURE 15

Copa City lounge on opening night, 1948. Photograph by Look *magazine, 10 x 8 in., 25.4 x 20.3 cm*

than . . . if done by a regular architect"—something with "a value equal to the imagination put over for the Futurama."[26] Although that deal collapsed, Geddes's renovation of the Ambassador Hotel in Los Angeles for Myer Schine was completed successfully—after the designer told his client that the world's fair had made every hotel in America obsolete by "open[ing] 50 million people's eyes to the possibilities of new ideas."[27] But the remodeled Ambassador was tame compared with another project completed in 1948, one with an obvious debt to the General Motors building. Copa City, a Miami Beach nightclub, marked the fulfillment of the "push button age,"

according to a journalist, while radio newscaster Gabriel Heatter praised it as "the only building of its kind in the whole world," indicating "how the future world will look" (FIG. 13).[28]

Murray Weinger, developer of Copa City, was a risk-taker whose enthusiasm matched Geddes's. After his Copa Cabana nightclub burned in June 1948, he spoke with radio broadcaster Barry Gray from the smoking ruin's entrance. Weinger talked expansively about rebuilding, saying, "Well, my gosh, if I could get a man like Norman Bel Geddes to come down here and do my room, it would be the talk of the country." Geddes, alerted to the broadcast by one of Schine's

FIGURE 16 (LEFT)
Geddes rough interior per-spective drawing of Copa City dining room with revealed trusses, July 25, 1949. Pencil on paper, 21½ x 17 in., 54.6 x 43.1 cm

FIGURE 17 (RIGHT)
Plans of first and second floors of Copa City, Engineering News-Record, *May 12, 1949.*

associates, phoned Weinger immediately and acted like he had personally heard his name invoked on the radio. "Well, let's do it," Geddes suggested. "It won't cost you more than if somebody else did it."[29] In short order they hired a local architect, Norman M. Giller, to prepare working drawings and a contractor willing to "work day and night" with three shifts of workers, a strategy garnering local publicity and bringing Copa City to completion in four months.[30]

Judging from press coverage, Copa City's opening on December 23, 1948, was a major event. Driving along Dade Boulevard, a wide street with a saltwater canal to one side, guests became aware

shops, each enclosed in curving glass walls—two of them placed inside the glass wall to the left and right of the doors, the other shaped like a teardrop, dividing the flow of guests through the two doors and into a foyer (FIG. 14).

From there they passed into a large dining room on the right or a smaller lounge on the left. No right angles marred public areas, and no doors divided these spaces. Even waiters moved through curved one-way baffles connecting kitchen and din-

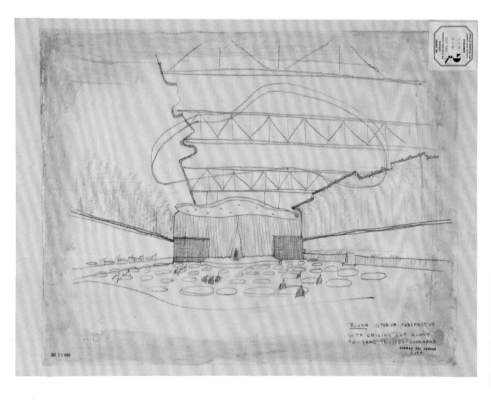

FIGURE 18 (OPPOSITE)
Cover of Copa City *magazine, 1951.*

of the nightclub as a large, apparently windowless structure looming ahead, flowing in a wide-radius curve from a side street. As they pulled closer, however, they caught sight of spotlights on a high horizontal facade, alive with undulating curves, and with a thin, projecting marquee whose free-form shape was cantilevered thirty feet out from the building at its widest point. Guests moved toward either of two wide doors in a long, slightly concave wall of glass that suggested an exclusive new suburban shopping center more than a nightclub. Mannequins in the latest fashions beckoned from three small interior

ing room. Flowing interiors led smoothly through public areas, with partial dividers and shifts in levels defining major spaces. The dining room had a raised stage equipped with rollers so it could be moved forty feet into the room to create an intimate atmosphere. Suspended false ceiling sections with amoeboid outlines relieved the room's general oval shape. On slow nights, an oval interior partition slid down from the main ceiling to decrease the room's size and create the feel of a crowded club. On opening night, however, a capacity crowd of 640 patrons, encompassing "every type of vacationer from jewel

Mizzi Green   Murray   Fields

A New World in Show Business

Kay Thompson   Frankie Laine   Joe

Joe E. Lewis   Healy

Peter Lina Horne and Mary Martin and Lewis

Norman Bel Geddes   Carson Harvey

Copa city

Henny   Frank Sinatra

Jane Froman   Chevalier   Benny

Jimmy Durante Maurice   Milton Berle

miami beach

Frank Sinatra Ritz Brothers   Tony Martin

Sophie Tucker Danny Kaye

Price Georgie Jessel Sam Levenson

Harry Richman Mickey

PRICE TWENTY FIVE CENTS

Billy Vine

adorned society belles to Broadway celebrities and well heeled racketeers," took in a show headlined by comedian Milton Berle (FIG. 15).[31] The smaller lounge, the site of Barry Gray's radio show, had a submerged seating area whose flowing free-form shape was outlined by a low wall and echoed by a shallow dome rising above. This recessed ceiling was dark in color and its outline was repeated by five concentric rings of bright neon. A long bar curved one-third of the way around the room, its seated patrons enjoying a heightened sense of the flowing kinetic energy of shifting spaces and people that marked Copa City throughout.

Although the nightclub attracted huge crowds at first, attendance declined, and creditors forced Weinger to close in April 1949. Seven months later, Copa City changed hands and received a face-lift. A huge neon sign was added, announcing the club, which Geddes had intended to be done by its unique shape alone. Today, sixty years after construction, the building houses an outlet of Public Storage, a nationwide self-storage chain. It has been thoroughly reworked in a twenty-first-century design idiom, but its distinctive footprint gives it away.[32]

Geddes would have approved of this adaptive reuse. In a letter, he discussed a "new principle of construction" for Copa City, opening up "new possibilities for flexibility and economy." The club's roof was supported by interlocking sets of trusses (one set for the dining room, the other for the lounge) resting on hidden piers (FIG. 16, 17). No support piers marred either of the two main rooms, and most of the building's weight was carried through the trusses to exterior walls. Swirling ceilings extended across the entire club, leaving long vistas broken only by changing levels and, in the foyer, by dazzling walls of glass. Wires attached to trusses supported the main ceiling, the suspended false ceilings, and a mezzanine with offices and dressing rooms. Ironically, Geddes's "popular mechanics" approach enabled the destruction of his work at Copa City. As he boasted, the building's "flexibility" allowed a new "room" with "an entirely different shape than the present one" to be "built outside, delivered, and installed as a set of scenery replaces another in a theatre." Beyond that, by providing totally open space, Geddes enabled

the structure's use to be "changed from a cabaret to a loft, garage, theatre, bank or department store."[33] Eight years before Mies van der Rohe completed the universal space of Crown Hall at Illinois Institute of Technology, Geddes was applying functional modernist principles to a structure displaying the aesthetic verve of commercial or expressionist modernism.

Geddes himself associated Copa City with the General Motors building. Shortly before the club's opening, Geddes proclaimed it "the first building done since the World's Fair that seems to have gained from it."[34] If General Motors' Futurama encompassed the world in miniature, then by incorporating shopping into the nightclub experience, Copa City embraced a multifunctional agenda soon to become commonplace in such postwar environments as shopping malls, theme parks, and festival marketplaces. The aesthetic of vast open spaces relieved by sensuous curves, changing levels, shifting materials and colors, and suspended ceilings also paralleled the visual effects of new casinos soon to be built along the Strip in Las Vegas.

Heatter tried to convey these effects in a broadcast the night before Copa City opened. Without "a straight line or a column, or a door," the "freewheeling" interior moved him to exclaim he was "beginning to understand what Professor Einstein meant by time without beginning or ending." Within the Copa, he continued, "nothing begins or ends, anywhere," but instead "curves in a rhythm."[35] The General Motors building had also curved in on itself, leading visitors through a series of spaces filled with dioramas. Visitors to Futurama remained enclosed even after they spilled into the life-size intersection contained entirely within the building. Copa City, despite its sweeping glass entry facade, created enclosed fantasy spaces devoid of any connection to the outside world. In that sense it functioned like the General Motors building, which invited guests to contemplate an imaginary future containing no surprises and therefore conveying a comforting sense of stasis in a perfectly realized artificial environment.

These two idealizations, so similar and yet so different—one based on developing technologies, the other on hedonistic pleasure—both proceeded from Geddes's efforts to create a modern architecture beyond austere functionalism, a modern architecture that would express contemporary life as actually lived and envisioned by ordinary Americans. Some historians have suggested that Geddes's influence, particularly that of Copa City, carried through to the Fontainebleau, the Eden Roc, and other Miami

However, most commercial architects and designers abandoned the rounded, enclosing forms of Geddes's most innovative work and instead employed flaring lines, acute angles, swooping diagonal planes with sharp edges, and a palette of bright colors more jarring and energizing than soothing. To the extent the Googie style was aerodynamic, designers followed the aesthetic of the jet fighter and tail-

Beach hotels designed by architect Morris Lapidus in the 1950s, and more generally to the commercial architecture of the fifties, the coffee shops, restaurants, motels, and shopping centers designed in a style variously referred to as Populuxe or Googie, the latter referring to the name of a popular restaurant in Los Angeles.[36]

finned auto, not the teardrop. While Geddes expected Copa City's undulating facade to serve as its own advertisement, commercial architects in California and Florida relied on huge, idiosyncratic signs as a major part of their architectural statement, a development reaching its apotheosis on the Las Vegas Strip. Rather than turning its back on outside reality,

FIGURE 19

Pann's at night, Los Angeles. Copyright © Jack Laxer.

as Copa City did, Googie architecture engaged with America's automobile culture. Rather than curving round and implicitly completing a protecting circle or sphere, as Geddes's streamlining did, Googie's flaring forms sped ever outward into infinity, paralleling the energy of the open road (FIG. 19).

In 1950 Geddes unsuccessfully proposed that General Motors sponsor a "consumers' building" in Manhattan. Its high, curvilinear, horizontally undulating walls were to enclose a Guggenheim Museum–like spiral ramp down which visitors would walk as they viewed a reinstallation of Futurama. Dramatically open at the entry level like Copa City, the structure would otherwise have been totally enclosed. General Motors probably balked at the project's expense, but it also no longer spoke to the times. Geddes's style, though perfect for the social and cultural needs of the Depression thirties, was not relevant in an era of expansive abundance.

Even so, Geddes's influence on 1950s architecture was considerable, particularly through his association with Eero Saarinen, a young Finnish

American architect who worked as a draftsman for Geddes for several months during the planning of the General Motors building in the spring of 1938. A detailed work estimate prepared for General Motors credited Saarinen with forty-six days on the project, primarily making models, sketches, or final drawings for the exterior of the General Motors building, the exteriors of the four different "buildings" within the life-sized intersection, and the map seen by visitors after entering the building.[37] Three of the four intersection facades were curvilinear: an auditorium building with a dramatic wraparound corner, a department store with deep undulations or corrugations rippling horizontally around the corner, and an apartment building with windows, balconies, and planter boxes running along each story—except where ribbon windows curved around the corner. Only one facade boasted functional modernism's straight lines and glass curtain walls, and that was dedicated to a neon-lit automobile showroom whose current-model streamlined cars appeared to advantage against a rich, neutral backdrop.

Unfortunately, the degree of collaboration between Geddes and Saarinen cannot be reconstructed. Saarinen was well paid, receiving the office's second-highest salary. Another draftsman, Garth Huxtable, described him as a "star designer" on the project but cautioned that he worked "closely" with his boss, who was fully responsible for the "end result."[38] Oliver Lundquist, an industrial designer who met Saarinen at the time, had a different opinion. "Few people know," he wrote in 2004, "that Eero designed the General Motors building that contained Norman Bel Geddes's great Futurama at the 1939 Fair."[39]

However, when General Motors asked Eero Saarinen and his father Eliel to design a suburban research facility in 1945, their response suggested Eero had indeed learned much from Geddes. Preliminary renderings showed a close-up of a long marquee rounding a concave curve and, more startling, a long structure like a flying wing, its cross-section revealing an elongated teardrop. It has been customary to explain away these anomalies by blaming them

on the senior partner Eliel—unlikely because his late work contained not a hint of streamlining.[40] It seems more likely these details derived from Geddes's impact on the younger Saarinen. In any case, the project was postponed, and after it was resumed in 1948, Eero provided the General Motors Technical Center with an array of Miesian buildings, thereby proving his respect for current wisdom. However, he also included two gleaming, reflective stainless steel zingers—a tall water tower with a flattened cylindrical bulb at the top and a partial hemisphere sheltering an auditorium where General Motors' design director, Harley Earl, annually unveiled the company's new models. Even the arrangement of structures around a reflecting pool is reminiscent of Geddes's similar idea for the Toledo Scale factory complex, published in *Horizons* and easily accessible to Saarinen (**FIG. 20**).

The case for Geddes's influence on Saarinen also rests on the Trans World Airlines (TWA) terminal at what is now John F. Kennedy International Airport in New York and the main terminal at

FIGURE 21

Eero Saarinen and Associates, Dulles International Airport, Chantilly, Virginia, 1958–62. Digital reproduction, photograph by Balthazar Korab, courtesy of the Library of Congress.

Dulles International Airport outside Washington, D.C., both of which opened in 1962. Both structures evoke flight, with the TWA facility often compared to a butterfly or bird spreading its wings. Its curvilinear interior, composed of scalloped walls, free-form walkways, and curving mezzanines, suggests both the processing flow of Geddes's Futurama and the open sculptural spaces of Copa City.[41]

Dulles International Airport, on the other hand, is reminiscent of one of Mendelsohn's visionary sketches. With a swayback roof suspended from

sionist streamlining in the first place. However, both terminals also rejected the enclosing quality of 1930s streamlining. Ample opportunities for outward views, framed in one case by sensuous curves, and in the other by bold supporting piers, marked a refusal to focus inward. However much Geddes inspired Saarinen, the form and symbolism of the architect's air terminals seemed in fundamental harmony, not with the General Motors building or Copa City but with the exuberant coffee shops and motels in the dominant Googie commercial style.

two rows of sixteen piers, the terminal offered, like Copa City, an open expanse of interior space. By making the curbside row of outwardly canted piers somewhat higher than those of the flight-side row (which also canted outward), Saarinen invited an observer's gaze to flow quickly down and then, gaining momentum, to sweep upward in potentially limitless motion (FIG. 21). Both TWA and Dulles revealed Geddes's influence—and that of Mendelsohn, the architect whose work inspired Geddes to embrace expres-

Had Saarinen not died suddenly in 1961, further projects might have made him a contributor to the "more is more" postmodern movement. His expressionist celebration of modern technology connects backward to Geddes and ultimately to Mendelsohn, and forward to such architects as Frank Gehry and Santiago Calatrava. One of the many buildings in Gehry's signature style, the Walt Disney Concert Hall in Los Angeles, completed in 2003, embodies technological energies exploding into barely controlled chaos (**FIG. 22**). Even more indebted to Saarinen, and ultimately to Geddes's celebratory streamlining, is Calatrava's Milwaukee Art Museum, completed in 2001, with its wing-like *brise soleil* soaring over Lake Michigan in a twenty-first-century expression of the melding of the mechanical and the organic.

Geddes's commercial modernism, more extravagant than the functional modernism whose promoters adopted "less is more" as a slogan, not only appealed to ordinary citizens and consumers of the 1930s and 1940s but also prefigured avant-garde architecture of the late twentieth century and beyond. Although Geddes failed to gain the professional recognition he believed would come through official licensing, his career in architectural design continued to influence those who came after him in ways that are only now being recognized. Geddes was referring to shaping popular opinions about product design when he argued for staying "a few years ahead," but in the final analysis his success as a modern "architecturalist" depended on his insistence that "a dream is an idea to be translated into a reality."

ENDNOTES

1   Geddes penciled this rephrasing of a motto by Le Corbusier in a personal copy of the latter's book *The City of Tomorrow and Its Planning* (New York: Payson & Clarke, n.d.), 139. L. Garth Huxtable offered the Futurama anecdote in a letter to the author, 5 November 1976.

2   Carbon copy of letter from Geddes to Allen D. Albert, assistant to Rufus C. Dawes, president of the Chicago Second World's Fair Centennial Celebration Corporation, 2 July 1929, Theater Box 198, Folder J-4, XH-1, Geddes Papers. On Geddes's involvement with the exposition, see Lisa D. Schrenk, *Building a Century of Progress: The Architecture of Chicago's 1933–34 World's Fair* (Minneapolis: University of Minnesota Press, 2007), 199–212.

3   Letter from Ralph Walker to Geddes, 13 August 1930 (see also Walker to Geddes, 6 August 1930); press release by Hiram Motherwell; all documents in Theater Box 199, Folder J-1-3, XH-2, Geddes Papers.

4   In-house memo from Geddes to R.B., 16 November 1930, Theater Box 199, Folder J-1-3, XH-2, Geddes Papers.

5   Carbon copy of Geddes petition to "Board of Regents—State of New York," January 1931, PA Box 17, Folder 314, Geddes Papers.

6   Carbon copy of letter from Geddes to Carl Austrian, 7 March 1931, PA Box 17, Folder 314, Geddes Papers.

7   Used in a pamphlet published by Standard Gas Equipment Company to announce the kitchen stove Geddes had designed, Oversize Box 7, Folder 267.2, Geddes Papers.

8   Contract, 13 August 1931, Box 11, Folder 237.1, Geddes Papers.

9   F. E. Turneaure and E. R. Maurer, *Principles of Reinforced Concrete Construction* (New York: John Wiley & Sons, 1914), personal copy autographed "Norman Geddes / 1914" on front endpaper.

10 Geddes as quoted in press release by Hiram Motherwell, Theater Box 199, Folder J-1-3, XH-2, Geddes Papers.

11 Geddes typescript, "reading version" of autobiography, ch. 31, p. 7, Theater Box 11, Folder AE-90, Geddes Papers.

12 The signed Einstein Tower sketch is pasted inside the presentation copy of Erich Mendelsohn, *Structures and Sketches*, trans. Herman George Scheffauer (Berlin: Ernst Wasmuth, 1924); sketches and renderings are on 15, 30.

13 Unidentified author, "The Cover," *Industrial Engineering* 88 (July 1930): 390.

14 Geddes's copy of Sheldon Cheney, *The New World Architecture* (New York: Longmans, Green, 1930), 356, 303.

15 Norman Bel Geddes, *Horizons* (Boston: Little, Brown, 1932), 223.

16 Letter from Geddes to Frances Resor Waite, 29 June [1928], Box 96c, Folder 960.31-33, Geddes Papers.

17 "Note for Autobiography," typescript, stamped 12 August 1957, Theater Box 4, Folder AE-39, ch. 35, Geddes Papers.

18 Douglas Haskell, "A Stylist's Prospectus," *Creative Art* 12 (February 1933): 132–33; Frank Lloyd Wright, "On Popular Mechanics," *Saturday Review of Literature* 9 (31 December 1932): 351.

19 One of the few descriptions of the theaters as streamlined is in Schrenk, 204–205.

20 Geddes, *Horizons*, 160.

21 Mendelsohn, "The Laws of Modern Architecture" (lecture, 1924), as quoted by Susan King, *The Drawings of Eric Mendelsohn* (Berkeley: University Art Museum, University of California, 1969), 59.

22 "Specifications for General Motors World's Fair Building," stamped 9 August 1938, Box 19a, Folder 381.4, Geddes Papers. There are many photographic sources for this description. However, most useful for experiencing the mood evoked by this approach to the General Motors building is brief footage in the six-hour collection of color home movies of the entire fair filmed by one Medicus, available in the Prelinger Archive by searching at http://www.archive.org.

23 Douglas Haskell, "Tomorrow and the World's Fair," *Architectural Record* 88 (August 1940): 71.

24 Letter from Geddes to Frances Resor Waite, 16 November 1938, Box 96c, Folder 960.31–33, Geddes Papers.

25 Unidentified author, "Art and Machine," *Architectural Forum* 60 (May 1934): 331.

26 "Minutes of Meeting," 3 October 1941, and "Data for Preparing Estimate and Proposal," 24 March 1941, both in Box 29, Folder

443.1, Geddes Papers.

27 "Report and Recommendations with Reference to the Ambassador Hotel, Los Angeles," stamped 20 August 1948, 13, Oversize Box 10, Folder 592.1, Geddes Papers.

28 John S. Wilson, "New York, N.Y.," *New York Star*, 1 October 1948, clipping, Theater Box 155, Folder I-2–4, TH-11, Geddes Papers; and Gabriel Heatter, "Heatter Hails New Copa City as 'The Impossible Dream Come True,'" *Miami Beach Florida Sun*, 24 December 1948, 32, clipping, Theater Box 155, Folder i.6-9, TH-11, Geddes Papers.

29 "Correspondence—Memos—Telephone Conversations," Geddes's conversations with E. Robert Swartburg and Murray Weinger, 8 June 1948, Theater Box 155, Folder J-1-2, Geddes Papers.

30 "Correspondence—Memos—Telephone Conversations," Geddes's conversation with Weinger, 24 June 1948, Theater Box 155, Folder J-1-2, Geddes Papers. Giller praised Geddes as a "mentor" with a "fearless use of fluid forms" but also took credit for the system of hanging partitions. See Norman M. Giller and Sarah Giller Nelson, *Designing the Good Life: Norman M. Giller and the Development of Miami Modernism* (Gainesville: University Press of Florida, 2007), 45, 47.

31 Unidentified author, "Step Up Night Life," *Detroit Times*, 26 December 1948, Theater Box 155, Folder I-2–4, TH-11; and Dick Lowe, "Show Time: Berle Smash Hit in Copa

Inaugural Show," *Miami Daily News*, 24 December 1948, p. 6A, Theater Box 155, Folder I-6–9, TH-11, Geddes Papers.

32 Barry Gray, "Lush New Miami Copa All Set to Gun for Year-Round Haul," *Billboard* 61 (26 November 1949): 3; and "Guide to After-Dark Miami," *Cabaret Yearbook* 1 (1956): 20, text available at http://cuban-exile.com/doc_176-200/doc0189.html. The building's current incarnation may be viewed at http://publicstorage.com, but for a full range of contemporary exterior views and the building's unmistakable footprint on a map, search Google Maps for 1301 Dade Boulevard, Miami Beach.

33 Carbon copy of letter from Geddes to Austin K. Doyle, 4 March 1949, Box 95a, Folder 957.107, Geddes Papers.

34 "Interview between Gabriel Heatter, Norman Bel Geddes, and Murray Weinger," 22 December 1948, typescript, 2, Box 155, Folder I-1, Geddes Papers.

35 Heatter, "Heatter Hails New Copa City," 32.

36 On this connection see Christopher Innes, *Designing Modern America: Broadway to Main Street* (New Haven: Yale University Press, 2005), 291. More generally see Thomas Hine, *Populuxe* (New York: Alfred A. Knopf, 1986); Alan Hess, *Googie: Fifties Coffee Shop Architecture* (San Francisco: Chronicle Books, 1986); Alan Hess, *Googie Redux: Ultramodern Roadside Architecture* (San Francisco: Chronicle Books, 2004); Martina

Düttmann and Friederike Schneider, eds., *Morris Lapidus: Architect of the American Dream* (Basel and Berlin: Birkhäuser Verlag, 1992); and Alan Hess, *Viva Las Vegas: After-Hours Architecture* (San Francisco: Chronicle Books, 1993).

37 W[orthen] P[axton], "Estimate for General Motors / N. Y. World's Fair Exhibit," 27 April 1938, initialed by Geddes on 29 April 1938, Box 19a, Folder 381.6 (1 of 2), Geddes Papers. Although these lists of subprojects, names of workers assigned to them, and their daily rates were presented as an estimate dated less than a week before Geddes signed a contract with General Motors, it is possible much of the work outlined had already been completed for submission to Goodyear, whose executives had rejected Geddes's proposal. That Geddes appreciated Saarinen's contribution to the General Motors building was suggested by the contents of a file folder I examined during the mid-1970s, at which point the industrial design files, then uncataloged, were housed in Geddes's original metal file cabinets, exactly as received by the Ransom Center. The folder was two inches thick, filled with clippings of hundreds of newspaper and magazine articles about Futurama and the General Motors building—and two clippings devoted to Saarinen's career.

38 L. Garth Huxtable, typed six-page memoir, enclosed in a letter to the author, 5 November 1976.

39 Letter from Oliver Lund-

quist to Robert A. M. Stern, 2004, Eero Saarinen Collection (MS 593), Manuscripts and Archives, Yale University, Series I, Box 3, Folder 27. I am indebted to Laura Tatum, architectural records archivist, for transcribing relevant parts of this letter for me. Saarinen's involvement with the General Motors building was first noted in my doctoral dissertation, "Technological Visions of American Industrial Designers, 1925–1939," University of Texas at Austin, 1977, 657–58, 946–49, and summarized in my *Twentieth Century Limited: Industrial Design in America, 1925–1939* (Philadelphia: Temple University Press, 1979), 201, 230 n.32. More recently it was discussed by Sandy Isenstadt, "Eero Saarinen's Theater of Form," in *Eero Saarinen: Shaping the Future*, eds. Eeva-Liisa Pelkonen and Donald Albrecht (New Haven: Yale University Press, 2006), 103–104, 107–108, 110.

40 For the most recent example of this attribution see Thomas Mellins, "General Motors Technical Center, Warren, Michigan," in Pelkonen and Albrecht, *Eero Saarinen*, 147.

41 This comparison is suggested by Isenstadt, "Eero Saarinen's Theater of Form," 108, 110.

6

THE FUTURE IS HERE:
NORMAN BEL GEDDES AND
THE THEATER OF TIME

Sandy Isenstadt

orman Bel Geddes's understanding of the future took many forms, which varied with the media he worked in and with the stage of his career. A set designer in the late 1910s and 1920s, Geddes described a theater of the future that would enrapture large audiences with ambitious programs. Late in the '20s, when Geddes launched his career in industrial design, he retained his faith in aesthetic democratization, but, increasingly, he imagined a consumer of the future as its agent, one who valued utility over appearance and was prepared to embrace the enlightened candor of modern design. Hoping to facilitate, at least in visual terms, the forthright and faster pace of modern life, Geddes's commercial designs in the 1930s took on a distinct, streamlined character. Toward the end of the decade, addressing himself to a larger scale of design, Geddes envisioned entire cities of the future, culminating in his Futurama exhibition for the General Motors pavilion at the 1939–40 New York World's Fair. Here, daily life harmonized with its architectural setting, bringing aesthetic as well as functional satisfaction to all of society. In addition to creating stage sets, commercial products, and city plans that were, for Geddes, harbingers of the future, he also predicted when such promises would be fulfilled. Over the course of his career, Geddes projected that the future—the moment when then-emerging trends would be fully realized and made part of everyday life—would arrive within a shorter and shorter time frame until, as Futurama suggested, the future was here.[1]

Opinions regarding the future—what it entailed and when present-day predictions would be fulfilled—were quite different when Geddes was young. Just four days before his birth in 1893, the World's Columbian Exposition opened in Chicago. There, the future appeared as the "White City," the exposition's monumental core (**FIG. 1**). An idealized urban vision, its broader realization was presumed to lie as far in the future as ancient Rome, on which it was modeled, lay in the past. Just as historical perspective sharpens understanding of the past, so would the passage of time provide the only possible lens onto the present, whose disorder, as the architect Henry Van Brunt described it in 1886, was an inevitable consequence of the "violent perspective of proximity."[2] Travel through

time became a recurrent trope among writers about the White City, from William Dean Howells's universal protagonist, "A. Homos," for whom "time itself was overcome in this work," to the French novelist Paul Bourget, who called it "a promise" impelling architects "to collaborate with the future," to architecture critic Montgomery Schuyler, who described it as being "ten thousand miles and a thousand years away from the City of Chicago," and even to Henry Adams, writing as a historian: "Here was a breach in continuity—a rupture in historical sequence!"[3] They all imagined themselves "looking backward," the title of Edward Bellamy's 1894 novel, when the future would wring order from the present. The White City was a postcard from the future that flattered American self-representations with the thought that the country was still in its formative years and its errors were those of youth rather than character. Indeed, one of the most moving aspects of such writings is how all shared the certainty that none would live to see the day when the future would actually come.

THE THEATER OF THE FUTURE

Geddes's first major pronouncement regarding the future appeared in a compact essay of 1919 on the "Theatre of the Future." Geddes, barely twenty-six, brought together several elements that would thread through his career: theater, architecture, a distinctly American mentality, and the future. Still a rookie, Geddes reflected on the serendipitous path that led him to scenic design. But theater's complete destiny would be realized only when audiences opened their eyes to the place of art in theater, which, in turn, would fulfill the theater's egalitarian potential.

This future, Geddes asserted, would be realized in America, for it was where European traditions were a gift rather than a heritage, a resource rather than an obligation. Beneath Americans' "drowsy ignorance . . . an unprejudiced freshness predominates," he wrote. His tone rose at the close of the essay, conjuring the vision of a widespread "beautiful, fresh growth of the future theatre" in America, where the seeds had already been sown by developments such as the Little Theatre movement, which he had participated in only a few seasons before in Los Angeles. Geddes likened the situation in his own time to a fourteenth-century map. Current audiences were just now poised to discover genuine theatrical art "with the same éclat that the Europeans 'discovered' an America already inhabited. Discovery is only the awakening of human consciousness to a reality that always exists. . . . Man's horizon has broadened so that he can advance where he pleases." He portrayed the future as a spatial concept, a place on the horizon, proximate but unseen, accessible as much by disclosure as by duration, and determined as much by audience reception as by dramatic art.[4]

As his work on the 1924 play *The Miracle* suggests, Geddes did not believe the future of theater required an image of the future. Rather, it implied a "discovery" of some kind, a sense of participation in, rather than observation of, an event. In *The Miracle*,

"contribute powerfully to the cumulative effect, so that the spectators themselves seem to participate in the play."[5] Its central idea was emotional rather than intellectual. Reliant on gesture rather than language—the play was a pantomime—*The Miracle* worked on a visceral level; physical ambience delivered much of its core message. Appealing to several senses simultaneously and doing away with the proscenium to immerse the audience in the setting, Geddes loosened the self-awareness inherent in spectatorship. The play's critical success—which relied on the audience becoming part of, rather than just witness to, a representation—was in many ways the awakening Geddes anticipated in his 1919 essay on the theater of the future.

produced at the Century Theatre, New York, the setting was a medieval cathedral, with props and backcloths positioned as far back as the theater's last balcony, but the means were cutting-edge: motorized stage elements, an elaborate sound system, and the most advanced stage lighting installation anywhere (**FIG. 2**). With lights from a multitude of sources, incense censers, and an enormous cast filtering through the theater, the play acted on multiple senses. Dramatic elements were orchestrated to

THE CONSUMER OF THE FUTURE

A sense of progress toward the future, in terms both of aesthetic democratization and theatrical techniques, remained on Geddes's mind even after he changed professions. He explained his thinking to former theater colleagues in a 1930 essay, "The Artist in Industry: An Unrepentant Confession by a Famous Scene Designer." He insisted that his move to industrial design was consistent with prior commitments to awaken audiences to art. It was thus "an entirely natural evolution towards what seemed to me one of the most useful functions the artist of to-day can perform." Indeed, the untapped potential of a "utilitarian art" could best be unlocked by someone with a background in theater. His 1927–29 designs for the Fifth Avenue display windows of Franklin Simon & Company succeeded, he said, because he treated the window display as a stage and pictured the merchandise as actors (FIG. 3).[6]

In short, Geddes argued that commercial art, buoyed by theater design skills, had the power to reach the large audiences foundational to theater, architecture, and mass production. Industrial design could achieve the ideal of aesthetic democratization that he earlier believed would signal the theater of the future. Everyone, consumers as well as theater-

goers, would be affected. As a corollary, his time frame for the arrival of that future shifted from the span imagined by earlier visionaries to the time-bound cycles of production and consumption, that is, the schedule by which manufacturers obtain fresh designs, retool factories, mass produce, distribute, and market goods to the consuming public. The future, in other words, was becoming for Geddes less a distant state into which present trends would one day converge than it was a dynamic dialogue of prob-lem and solution, a view he would continue to refine over the years.[7] Time itself, in turn, became less of an objective metric than a technologically conditioned reality of consumer society.

To many observers then, the future approached fastest on the wings of modern design, a loosely

FIGURE 3

Geddes-designed "Smart Hats" display for the Franklin Simon depart-ment store, c. 1927–29. Photograph by Vandamm Studio, 10 x 8 in., 25.4 x 20.3 cm

knit program of simple lines, reduced ornament, new materials, smooth surfaces, and structural and functional expression. The visual impact could be unsettling, a "lurid picture of angular gadgets on box-like furniture in nursery colors," as Geddes said in a 1931 interview. But bad rather than modern design was to blame. He allowed that modernism entailed a degree of experimentation that could go wrong, but it ultimately aimed for a confluence of cost-effective manufacturing, functional ease, and honest form or, as he tersely put it, a congruence of "tasteful appearance and practical construction for efficient operation." American consumers were a practical sort and would come to accept the unfamiliar forms of modern design once they recognized its functional underpinning. Fulfilling goals of efficiency and direct expression, modern forms manifested the convergence of fabrication and use—for Geddes they were visual proof of "reality in everything."[8]

As it developed, Geddes's understanding of the future in relation to industrial design consolidated around this idea of convergence. It is in many ways the primary theme of Geddes's 1932 book, *Horizons,*

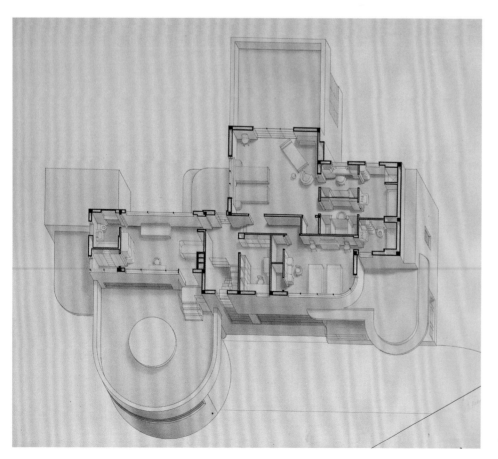

more so than its ostensible subject—streamlining. In the first pages, Geddes described the industrial world as shaped by three perspectives—those of consumers, manufacturers, and designers—and the "viewpoint of each is rapidly changing, developing, fusing. More than that, the economic situation is stimulating a unanimity of emphasis, a merger of viewpoints."[9] Subsequent chapters of *Horizons* treat a range of distinct objects at all scales, including desktop radios, automobiles, kitchens, factories, airports, and cities. But the book's ambition is synthetic, evident in the sum of those chapters and in typically unseen factors, such as steel-frame construction, which led Geddes to link stovetops with skyscrapers. He even anticipated industrial consolidation that, by bringing under one management otherwise competitive corporate programs of design and production, would unify formal directions: "the inauguration of far-seeing plans for economies and efficiency in terms of future developments."[10] As in earlier essays, Geddes posited the future in *Horizons* in spatial terms, suggesting that it is reached not over time but, rather, by connecting current trends with a commonly held ideal, a point of aesthetic convergence. In keeping with the older formula that presumed future perspectives would sort present trends, Geddes wrote: "To-morrow, we will recognize that in many respects progress and combination are synonymous."[11] That is to say, closer and closer relations between manufacturers, and between manufacturers and consumers, would drive industrial society forward.[12]

To be sure, Geddes pictured a consumerist future. Issues of social equity, for example, or labor relations were entirely unaddressed and the very convergence that signaled the future's arrival appears first in the marketplace, where up-to-date objects met a public eager for them. With merchandise and taste thus aligned, the buying public would distribute modern goods throughout the private realm, effectively making an everyday reality of what was just a design sketch a year or two earlier. In this context, Geddes's design method may be described as trend-spotting, that is, identifying a visual trope and recasting it as an about-to-prevail tendency, a vogue just starting to crystallize into a norm. Such an approach is evident in his preparation for House Number 3 (**FIG. 4**), published in *Ladies' Home Journal* in April 1931 as the "House of Tomorrow." Many aspects of the house were drawn from current articles on, for example, "Certain Tendencies in House Planning Today," which were summarized for Geddes by his office staff, as well as from well publicized buildings such as Richard Neutra's 1929 Lovell House in Los Angeles.[13] These aspects included formal elements of the plan, such as its orientation toward the rear yard, its grouping of services toward the front, and its incorporation of an alcove for dining rather than a separate room; mechanical devices, including conveniently located comfort controls; structural innovations like its "curtain wall systems"; even rhetorical claims, such as "scientific planning." While extrapolating from current tendencies was an established strategy for late-nineteenth-century utopian writers, Geddes posited a future scenario as if it were the form that would arise almost naturally from the convergence of functional optimization, the logic of mass production, and, ultimately, public approval. In this, he aligns with a model of technological futurism, where social forms adjust to technological advance.[14] But his specific talent was less his aggregation of the ideas of others than it was his dramatic exaggeration and advocacy of these trends as portents of approaching change. Where the articles he looked at objectively described stylistic differences or new conveniences, Geddes introduced a current of inevitability. He narrated the future, although he was careful to stop short of the stridency of a manifesto. He opens "Ten Years from Now," for instance, with a pronouncement simultaneously assertive and self-effacing—"All the following prophecies will be old-fashioned"—and so substitutes a sense of inescapable evolution for the demanding urgency of avant-garde tracts.

Trend-spotting was at that moment only just emerging as a means of apprehending the future. The term itself does not come into common use until the 1960s, while today's denotation of "trend," to mean a temporally delimited cultural tendency, dates back only as far as the late nineteenth century. As a forecasting device, "trend analysis" was still a novel idea in the 1920s, most rigorously pursued in finance and political economy. The Depression

FIGURE 5 (ABOVE)
Geddes with model City of Tomorrow for Shell Oil advertising campaign, c. 1937. Photograph by unidentified photographer, 8 x 10 in., 20.3 x 25.4 cm

FIGURE 6 (LEFT)
General Electric Monitor Top refrigerator ad, c. 1931, from Geddes's Shell Oil City of Tomorrow research files. The city depicted in this ad bears a striking resemblance to the City of Tomorrow depicted in Geddes's advertisements for Shell Oil.

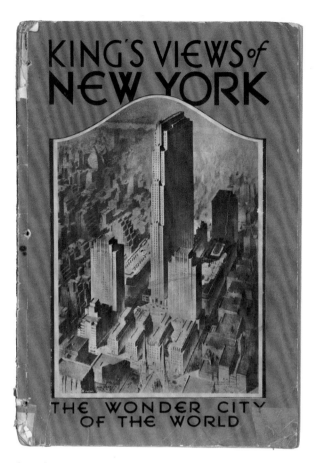

lent forecasting new urgency as financial matters increasingly came within the purview of government rather than individual investors; forecasters focused more on ways to control the future, not just to bet on it. At this point, the future also assumed new prominence in advertising and popular culture, including movies about the future, such as William Cameron Menzies's 1936 *Things to Come*, or promotions like "the floor of the future," as well as numerous cars, trains, homes, and cities of tomorrow.[15] The technocracy movement, which espoused political control by an engineering elite, briefly flowered at this time, too, based on its potential to harness and control current trends. Extrapolating from trends became more of a science with RAND, the first American "think tank," which played out alternative scenarios, usually military, with empirical detail, powerfully influencing research into future trends.[16] By the 1950s, predicting the future had become its own industry, with specialized consultants in the trade.

Geddes's appropriations of the observations of others may thus be seen as contributing to the emerging profession of trend analysis.[17] In this sense, Geddes recast the oftentimes evangelical rhetoric

of avant-garde modernists—he was familiar with Le Corbusier's writings, for instance—as an exercise in pragmatism, a tabulation of trends rather than a polemic. Considering the "House of Tomorrow" as an extrapolation and exaggeration of then current trends explains why such projections appear as caricatures: They inflate features, enlarging their visual importance without necessarily articulating or developing them further.[18] While Geddes was rarely explicit about his trend-spotting, it is evident in his working methods, and occasionally he openly wrote about it. In the conclusion of *Horizons*, for example, Geddes noted design improvements in transportation and manufactured goods and anticipated changes in architecture, too, especially in terms of mass-produced and prefabricated buildings. But, he argued, current plans at the largest scale—city and regional plans—failed to extrapolate trends sufficiently. Recent plans for New York, for instance, "are based too much on present conditions." Instead, he argued, "The intelligent plan will be based upon the extreme of ultimate possible developments a good many years ahead."[19]

VISIONS OF THE FUTURE CITY

In the 1930s Geddes convincingly demonstrated his ability to exaggerate potentialities as a way to invoke future scenarios. For a commission for the 1933–34 Century of Progress International Exposition in Chicago, he designed in rapid succession a number of restaurants and performance venues, each based on still-new structural or architectural principles, including an aerial rotating platform for dining and an underwater eatery. A press release from his office stressed their extraordinary character but insisted their eccentricity would fade with time, as Geddes put it: "... many people find that my projects 'look queer.' All new forms, of course, look queer at first." However inventive, these designs remained isolated one from the other and, in any case, were never built.

With a 1936 commission to design a Shell Oil ad campaign, Geddes widened his scope to include designs for an entire city of the future, although he was only asked initially to visualize ideas of traffic planning. But Geddes quickly expanded the project to encompass questions of urbanism

FIGURE 9

Aerial view of Shell Oil City of Tomorrow model, c. 1936–37. Photograph by Norman Bel Geddes & Co., 19½ x 15 in., 49.5 x 38.1 cm

more generally.[20] He consulted experts in the field, gathered statistics about current trends and extrapolated from them, anticipated continued growth in automobile ownership and more intense use of both city and country roads, and predicted a point at which present roadways would choke on traffic. To avert paralysis, he modeled a city of the future with segregated but coordinated channels for traffic, including pedestrians and local and express vehicles, and laid out bypass roads that avoided city centers altogether in favor of uninterrupted, friction-free motion (**FIG. 5, 6**).[21]

Streamlined movement was a visual theme of 1930s design, but traffic flows in particular had been an ongoing concern in visionary urban schemes since the turn of the century, as urban streets began to swell with private automobiles. In 1910, speaking in his new role as chairman of New York's Public Service Commission, William R. Willcox underscored the "heroic means" necessary to coordinate transportation with further growth in population and commerce. Transportation, including a web of subways and regional rail lines meeting at multilevel exchanges, and moving sidewalks beneath busy commercial corridors, would be the force that shaped New York's future.[22] More than just an expedient, improving traffic flows redressed "congestion," arguably the greatest ill in an age of speed. Congestion did

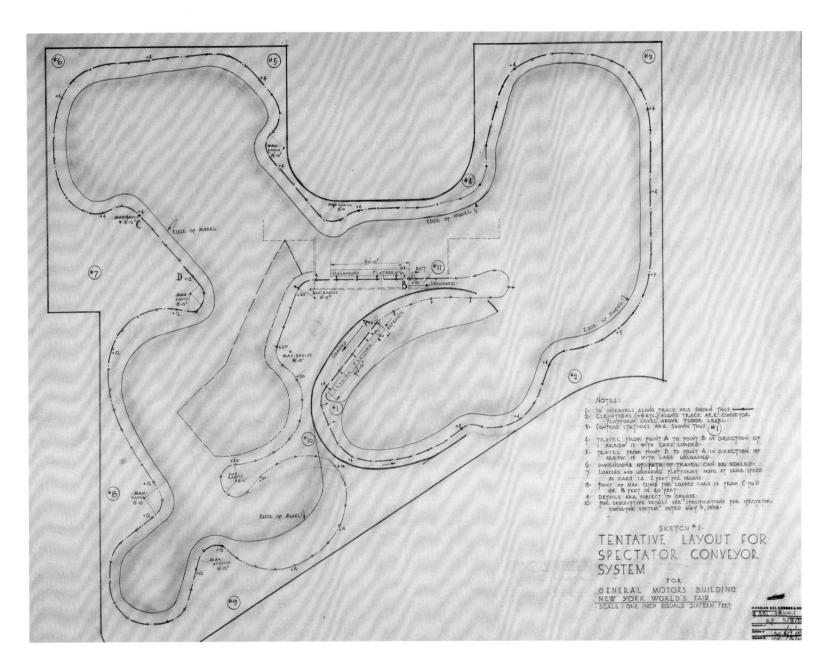

NOTES:
1. 10' INTERVALS ALONG TRACK ARE SHOWN THUS
2. ELEVATIONS (+4 ETC.) ALONG TRACK ARE CONVEYOR PLATFORM LEVEL ABOVE FLOOR LEVEL.
3. CONTROL STATIONS ARE SHOWN THUS (#1)
4. TRAVEL FROM POINT A TO POINT B IN DIRECTION OF ARROW IS WITH CARS LOADED.
5. TRAVEL FROM POINT B TO POINT A IN DIRECTION OF ARROW IS WITH CARS UNLOADED.
6. DIMENSIONS OF PATH OF TRAVEL CAN BE SCALED.
7. LOADING AND UNLOADING PLATFORMS MOVE AT SAME SPEED AS CARS I.E. 2 FEET PER SECOND.
8. POINT OF MAX. CLIMB FOR LOADED CARS IS FROM C TO D OR B FEET IN 40 FEET.
9. DETAILS ARE SUBJECT TO CHANGE.
10. FOR DESCRIPTIVE DETAILS SEE "SPECIFICATIONS FOR SPECTATOR CONVEYOR SYSTEM" DATED MAY 8, 1938.

SKETCH #1.
TENTATIVE LAYOUT FOR SPECTATOR CONVEYOR SYSTEM
FOR
GENERAL MOTORS BUILDING
NEW YORK WORLD'S FAIR
SCALE: ONE INCH EQUALS SIXTEEN FEET.

not simply hamper movement; it was a disorder and a threat to social progress.[23]

The forms of many visionary urban schemes became more assertively modern in the 1920s. No longer exaggerating existing architectural features, schemes instead proffered a new vocabulary of unadorned cubic towers, each rising in ziggurat form in its own open space, while the pattern of multilevel roads segregating rail, automotive, and pedestrian traffic continued. A number of well-publicized projects, such as Le Corbusier's "City for Three Million," "Titan City" (a collaboration between Harvey Wiley Corbett and Hugh Ferriss), and Ferriss's other published schemes, featured stacked roadways and transit lines and often flight corridors for airplanes. Even the film sets for *Just Imagine* (1930) and *Things to Come* (1936), in which engineers restore order to civilization, depict multiple layers of segregated traffic.[24] In Shell City, Geddes rejected the emphatically vertical orientation of transportation hubs in favor of a more horizontal development, aligning his design with Frank Lloyd Wright's continent-wide Broadacres project, which demonstrated the decentralizing potential of transportation. In addition, Geddes proposed architectural and urban forms that evoked the aerodynamic forms of his earlier designs for automobiles, locomotives, ships, and airplanes.

FIGURE 11
Visitors in full-scale intersection of Futurama, c. 1939. Photograph by Richard Garrison, 10 x 8 in., 25.4 x 20.3 cm

To prepare for its publication in magazines, Geddes erected scaffolding around the Shell City model, allowing him to assess multiple viewpoints for photographs, as if he were circling the city in an airplane. The resulting images express what Geddes had envisioned, but they do not transmit the sense he must have felt as he moved over and around the model (**FIG. 8, 9**).[25] While Shell City and the urban schemes to which it is indebted all accommodate and

even accentuate transportation, only cinema could represent the experience of transportation, of actually moving through a city of the future. It is tempting to imagine Geddes thinking that, for another project, he might transmit the excitement of seeing such a place firsthand to a live audience, rather than mediated through still photographs to a readership.

The opportunity to do exactly that arrived swiftly, with Futurama, an enormous model in the

General Motors pavilion at the 1939–40 New York World's Fair. It was an imaginative tour de force where orchestrated transportation technologies were both means and metaphor. Futurama would prove to be Geddes's clearest articulation of the future; it visually and viscerally manifested his longstanding theme of convergence.[26] Highways threaded throughout the model, linking countryside with urban core; distances were compressed as viewers, seated on chairs moving along a balcony, effortlessly traversed diverse forms of settlement (**FIG. 10**). Buildings, vehicles, highways, and even the curving balcony echoed each other, sharing long arcs punctuated by tighter bends. Different kinds of representations were likewise linked up: Visitors consulted a map at the pavilion entrance and then settled into their seats to witness cartography glide into geography; speakers mounted on each seat directed attention to points on the model, close-by whispers correlating with seemingly distant views. The harmonious mesh of the whole delivered a conceptual convergence of experience as well as form.

According to numerous accounts, the tour's final moment was dazzling, even revelatory (**FIG. 11**).[27] An article in *Cue* magazine described a cosmic sense of wonder following the final sequence of urban scenes of increasing scales, with blackouts in between, until arriving "at the identical traffic intersection you have just left, except that the buildings, automobiles, pedestrians, and everything else are full-sized. The effect is a good deal like suddenly becoming Alice Through the Looking Glass. For fifteen minutes you've been so thoroughly imbued with the idea that you're looking at a world of twenty years from now, that when you see it in fact it seems perfectly natural, if just a trifle Einsteinian."[28]

The visionary representation dissolved seamlessly into everyday life in the future, no longer a scaled model but "a full-scale fragment of the new reality."[29] Much as he did with *The Miracle*, Geddes collapsed the otherwise distinct spaces of audience and stage. As with a cinematic match cut, the gliding fairgoer was left to establish the continuity between one close-up and the next, between looking at and walking within. Moving through the sequence of changing perspectives, Geddes had unbound viewers' understanding of place: Place had become situational, fluid rather than fixed. The objectivity of aerial vision flowed directly into the visceral effect of bodily immersion as the shift in scale and spectator position corresponded with a shift from a future conceived in terms of duration—the city predicted to arise in twenty years—to a future apprehended in space—the city directly in front of visitors. Condensing into one moment the distinct shifts from mov-

Geddes had dramatized a long-observed truth about technology's ability to rend the fabric of everyday life, to "annihilate time and space," in a paraphrase of poet Alexander Pope's line that had echoed throughout the nineteenth century. The increasingly common travel by rail, automobile, or air seemed to compress time. Futurama, then, was a spectacle of the technologically conditioned tempos of modern life. But travel here led to a place that was already

ing chairs to moving bodies, from single seat with separate speakers to collective disembarking, from focused gaze to environmental immersion, from the observer's imagination to the participant's "reality," Geddes created by spatial means the impression of a temporal convergence. In turn, the audience, shifting from removed observation to physical participation, became actors in the future scene they had only just been witness to (FIG. 10-12).

familiar, not only from prior views over the model, but also because the ultimate destination was structured by common consumer experiences: Visitors window-shopped their way through automobile showrooms lining the intersection of the future. Where modern cities had been characterized by random and dense encounters between strangers and disparate activities, Geddes saw a fusion of fluid forms, continuous motion, and shared beliefs, a

FIGURE 13

Geddes's "Dreamlining Tomorrow" article in Mademoiselle, *March 1944. Photograph: Gill/ Mademoiselle;* © Condé Nast. *Text: Copyright © 1944. All rights reserved. Originally published in* Mademoiselle. *Reprinted by permission.*

FIGURE 14
Geddes's article, "Your Home of Tomorrow," in The American Weekly, *March 21, 1954.*

carefully choreographed convergence of otherwise incommensurate temporalities.[30] The lubricated locomotion at Futurama suggests that streamlining was less an aerodynamic concept for Geddes than it was a metaphor for the frictionless convergence of buildings and vehicles, bodies and machines, as well as manufacturers' intent, designers' vision, and consumers' desire. To paraphrase Geddes's 1919 essay, "Theatre of the Future," the audience had only to discover a future already inhabited by itself. Whereas the vision of the future presented at the 1893 Columbian Exposition would not be realized for hundreds of years, in the case of Futurama, this took about eighteen minutes.

THE FUTURE OF THE FUTURE

Geddes was only one of many forecasters who felt that the present was catching up to the future, the result of accelerating technologies more generally. In 1929, for example, William B. Stout, an industrial designer himself, observed how the speed with which

new ideas became everyday realities had changed expectations regarding the future: "Our fathers used to talk about what would be done a hundred years in the future. After the war we listened to prophecies of what would happen in ten years. Today the scientific future is but two years ahead, or five at the most."[31] But Geddes was unusual in assuming the rhetorical mode of science fiction, making the future vivid, even palpable, rather than just predicting it. When he addressed members of industry, he did, indeed, lay down principles and portentous imperatives. To consumers, however, he told stories, detailing un-invented technologies as matters of fact **(FIG. 14)**. "Dreamlining Tomorrow," for instance, a piece that ran in *Mademoiselle* magazine in 1944 **(FIG. 13)**, described "one day in your life and times ten years from now." Written in the second person, Geddes's voice was intimate, like one's interior thoughts. He described not only new devices, but also how wonderfully little the homemaker needed to know about them. Despite scientific advances, the homemaker's whimsy and "conventional tastes" would always be accommodated: "One of the most attractive features of this home of yours is that you can have all the familiar things you want, no matter how useless they are."[32] For such essays, Geddes did not outline the future; he rendered it, almost empathetically, from the consumer's point of view. What would consumers want, not from *the* future but from *their* future? This was the key question he insisted that other designers and manufacturers ought always to consider.[33]

In 1952 Geddes wrote a set of twelve essays that were never published. Titled "Today in 1963," they tell the story of the Holden family "living when this very realistic book was written, in 1963."[34] He dramatized the surprises the future would bring by treating them as banalities. He intended that remarkable novelties—a covered all-weather sports stadium, flying automobiles, disposable clothing, powerful businesswomen, three-dimensional television, a cultural "emphasis on the visual," the embrace of solar energy, and more—would all be "referred to in casual conversation." For the Holdens, "the majority of items will be 'old stuff' like TV, radar and the atom bomb is [*sic*] to us." In other words, Geddes treated his predictions as if they were already prosaic—his characters enjoyed a casual fluency with the future that, in a sense, had already happened. The story was less a tale of technology overcoming nature than it was about normalizing innovation. If the present caught up to the future at the end of Futurama, then these stories mark the moment that the present started to pull ahead. From this point forward, optimistic visions of the future seemed to lose their traction in American society, and the best the nation could look forward to would be embalmed in a visualization from the past.

What part did Norman Bel Geddes play in this process of embalming the future in a vision from the past, how did he give it form, and where can we see it manifested in contemporary America? Disneyland, which opened in 1955 in Anaheim, California, was in many ways a permanent World's Fair, with Tomorrowland, in particular, intended to replicate the visionary urbanism that had been a keynote of fairs since 1893. Shortly after its opening, however, Walt Disney himself referred to it as "Todayland,"

and soon after his staff started calling it "Yesterdayland."[35] It was recommissioned in 1998 as a "classic Tomorrowland," an attraction valued more for its light on the past than for any intimation of the future. While Disneyland and other contemporary urban schemes, such as suburban shopping malls, could be cultivated and sheltered within the private sphere, city planners, for their part, began to reconsider the collective, public sphere. They evinced what might be called a new "presentness," driven by the finely detailed observations of Jane Jacobs and Kevin Lynch, who drew attention to existing urban fabric, while architects, such as Louis Kahn, Charles Moore, and Robert Venturi, turned more and more to past buildings to decide what to build next.

It was not that a fascination with the future declined. If anything, groups such as the World Future Society, founded in 1966, and its organ, *The Futurist*, institutionalized proleptic thinking.[36] But the future was considerably less shiny, especially in popular culture. From Stanley Kubrick's *2001: A Space Odyssey* and Roger Vadim's *Barbarella*, both made in 1968, to Ridley Scott's *Blade Runner* (1982), visions of the future went from ambivalent to dystopic. In contrast, the vision of the future on display at Futurama, preserved in photographs, film, and memory, shone all the more brightly. To some extent, 1930s predictions about the future, including those of Geddes, had come true. But the technologies that were envisioned had not brought with them the leisure, social equality, or peace many had predicted. As Hendrik Hertzberg wrote in 1981, following his first return to Disneyland since he was a child, "if Tomorrowland is any guide, the future has seen better days."[37] In retrospect, as a recent essay in *Vanity Fair* magazine argued, "what we're left with is a nostalgia for those space-age, midcentury dreams—the semi-kitsch echoes of Tomorrowland, *The Jetsons*, and the 1939–40 New York World's Fair." By now, Geddes's future is "marketed for its reassuring, old-timey appeal," traveling under the rubric of "retro-futurism."[38] Today, looking backward, it seems that the end of the ride at Futurama remains the most compelling vision of the future we have ever had. More than any single individual, Geddes gave form to the moment when the present caught up with and passed the future.

ENDNOTES

1   I am grateful to Cathy Henderson and Natalie Shivers for their astute editorial comments and happily indebted to Donald Albrecht for his much-needed guidance throughout the preparation of this essay.

2   Henry Van Brunt, "On the Present Condition and Prospects for Architecture," *Atlantic Monthly* 57 (March 1886): 375.

3   Howells, "Letters of an Altrurian Traveller," *The Cosmopolitan* 16:2 (December 1893): 221; Bourget, "A Farewell to the White City," *The Cosmopolitan* 16:2 (December 1893): 138; Schuyler, "Last Words About the Fair," *Architectural Record* 3 (1893–94): 300; Adams, *The Education of Henry Adams* (New York: Oxford University Press, 1999), 286. For more on the Columbian Exposition, see "The White City" in Alan Trachtenberg, *The Incorporation of America: Culture and Society in the Gilded Age* (New York: Hill & Wang, 1982), and Robert Rydell, *All the World's a Fair: Visions of Empire at American International Expositions, 1876–1916* (Chicago: University of Chicago Press, 1984). For more on technologically driven ideas of the future, see Howard P. Segal, "The Technological Utopians," in Joseph Corn, ed., *Imagining Tomorrow: History, Technology, and the American Future* (Cambridge, MA: MIT Press, 1986).

4   Geddes, "Theatre of the Future," *Theatre Arts Magazine* 3:2 (April 1919): 123–24, in Folder WA-17, "Theater of the Future," Geddes Papers. See also "Design Book," Theater Box 152, Folder K-31 SC-4, Job 79, Geddes Papers. Regarding Geddes's views of theater's parallels with architecture, especially in terms of their relations with an audience, see "Lecture Three, November 12th, 1927, Visualizing the Setting," Theater Box 152, Folder K-32 SC-4, Job 79, "Stage Design Course, 1921–31," and "18 Audiences," Folder Y-1 SC-6, "Lecture Notes 1922," Box 153 "Design Course," Job 79, all in Geddes Papers.

5   Michael Monahan, "The Miracle," *New York Times* (17 February 1924): X4. See also John Corbin, "The Miracle," *New York Times* (16 January 1924): 17, and Rudolf Kommer, "The Genesis of 'The Miracle,'" *New York Times* (30 December 1923): X2. See also "Design Book," typescript, Theater Box 152, Folder K-31, SC-4, Job 79, Geddes Papers.

6   Geddes, "The Artist in Industry: An Unrepentant Confession by a Famous Scene Designer," *Theatre Guild Magazine* (January 1930): 23–25, 61. Box 173, Folder WA-1, Job 937, Geddes Papers. Regarding Geddes's ambivalence toward the corrosive threat posed by commercial motivations, see "Laboratory Theatre," 3 March 1924, typescript, Box 153, Folder Y-2 SC-6, Geddes Papers.

7   Geddes identified two streams of change: first, the technical progress of continual improvement that develops along its own course and, second, visual progress, which proceeds from the designer's explicit effort to keep forms commensurate with technological change. See Geddes, "Tomorrow's Consumer," paper presented to the annual meeting of the American Society of Refrigerating Engineers, Philadelphia, 9 December 1943, Box 175, Folder WA-20, Job 937, and "Modern Design: Its Problems and Their Solution. Encyclopaedia Britannica," Box 173, Folder WA-12, Job 937, both in Geddes Papers.

8   "Interview with Norman Bel Geddes," *Product Engineering* (May 1931): 222, and "Built-In Eye Appeal Has Sales Value," *Product Engineering* (October 1930): 476, in Box 173, Folder WA-1, Job 937, Geddes Papers.

9   Norman Bel Geddes, *Horizons* (Boston: Little, Brown, 1932), 5.

10 Ibid., 291. Perhaps the most explicit statement along these lines is R. Buckminster Fuller's call for the "streamlining of society" in his *Nine Chains to the Moon* (Philadelphia: Lippincott, 1938).

11 Ibid., 289.

12 He also published a synopsis of *Horizons* in the *Atlantic*, prompted by the magazine's editor, Ellery Sedgwick, and then mailed 1,200 copies of it to businesses engaged in a variety of industries and services, including government agencies, service stations, and museums. Box 173, Folder WA-14b and WA-14c, Job 937, Geddes Papers.

13 Examples include R. W. Sexton, "The House of Today," *House Beautiful* 67 (May/June 1930): 596–98, 636, 744–45, 788; Richardson Wright and Margaret McElroy, "House and Garden Designs Its Own Modernist House," *House and Garden* 57 (January 1930): 58–65; Howard T. Fisher, "The Country House," *Architectural Record* 68 (November 1930): 363–440, all three in Folder 206.2, "Research Data"; and "Outline Notes and Drafts for Articles, 'Upstairs, Downstairs and in My Lady's Chamber,'" *Ladies' Home Journal*, Folder 206.1. Two publications by Geddes resulted from this study: "Ten Years from Now," *Ladies' Home Journal* 48 (January 1931) (reprinted in *Reader's Digest* [February 1931]) and "House of Tomorrow," *Ladies' Home Journal* 48 (April 1931): 12–13.

14 Richard B. Halley and Harold G. Vatter, "Technology and the Future as History: A Critical Review of Futurism," *Technology and Culture* 19:1 (January 1978): 54–55. An early and classic example is H. G. Wells, *Anticipations of the Reaction of Mechanical and Scientific Progress Upon Human Life and Thought* (London: Chapman & Hall, 1902).

15 Discussed in Joseph Corn and Brian Horrigan, *Yesterday's Tomorrows: Past Visions of the American Future* (New York: Summit Books, 1984), 12–13. For a more recent overview of future visions, see Lawrence R. Samuel, *Future: A Recent History* (Austin: University of Texas Press, 2009), especially chapter 1, "The Shape of Things to Come."

16 David Rejeski and Robert L. Olson, "Has Futurism Failed?" *The Wilson Quarterly* 30:1 (Winter 2006): 14–16.

17 Trend analysis developed largely from efforts to predict the behavior of stock markets. The best known such effort, that of Charles Dow, distinguished three types of market movement, with the longest being only four to six years. For many, a ten-year cycle was the furthest anyone could see into the future. See the "Wall Street's Mysteries" column in the *New York Times*, especially 13 December 1903, F, and 17 January 1904, FS2.

18 H. G. Wells had already noted that "enlarging the present" resulted in "a sort of gigantesque caricature of the existing world." Discussed by Carol Willis, "Skyscraper Utopias: Visionary Urbanism in the 1920s," in Joseph Corn, ed., *Imagining Tomorrow: History, Technology, and the American Future* (Cambridge, MA: MIT Press, 1986), 167.

19 Geddes, *Horizons*, 283–85.

20 Geddes was hired by the J. Walter Thompson advertising agency on behalf of Shell Oil. See the detailed discussion in Jeffrey Meikle, "The City of Tomorrow: Model 1937," *Pentagram Papers* 11.

21 "Pedestrians—Express Traffic—Local Traffic—Each Will Be Given a Clear Path by 1960," in *Life* 3 (5 July 1937): 53.

22 "New York City Twenty Years Hence," *New York Times* (6 February 1910): SM1. Even those schemes driven more by City Beautiful ideals likewise proposed enhanced roadways to keep the expanding

cities knit together. For example: "Finally, the town of the future will be traversed by large radiating thoroughfares, occupied partly by raised platforms continually moving, which will insure rapid communication between the different zones." From a report on a conference in London with Daniel Burnham and other City Beautiful advocates in attendance, "Cities of Future Will Be Beautiful," *New York Times* (16 October 1910): C4. See also Tom McCarthy, "Transportation: The Coming Wonder? Foresight and Early Concerns about the Automobile," *Environmental History* 6:1 (January 2001): 46–74.

23 Lawrence Samuel, *Future: A Recent History* (Austin: University of Texas Press, 2009), 33.

24 Corbett, as chair of the architects subcommittee of The Regional Plan of New York and Its Environs, had been promoting separate channels for traffic since 1923. See Harvey Wiley Corbett, "Different Levels for Foot, Wheel, and Rail," *American City* 31 (July 1924): 2–6, and Thomas Adams, et.al., *Regional Plan of New York and Its Environs*, v. 2, The Building of the City (New York: 1931). Both works are discussed in Carol Willis, "Drawing Towards Metropolis," in Hugh Ferriss, *The Metropolis of Tomorrow* (Princeton: Princeton Architectural Press, 1986), 158–62. Ferriss himself thought stacked roadways would degrade air and light quality around skyscrapers but thought some degree of layering was inevitable. In Ferriss, *Metropolis*, 64–67.

Geddes owned a number of titles on city planning and traffic, such as Fritz Malcher, *The Steadyflow Traffic System* (Cambridge, MA: Harvard University Press, 1935), as well as those by Ferriss and Le Corbusier. See also "New York of the Future: A Titan City," *New York Times* (2 November 1924): XX7; Carol Willis, "Skyscraper Utopias: Visionary Urbanism in the 1920s," in Joseph Corn, ed., *Imagining Tomorrow: History, Technology, and the American Future* (Cambridge, MA: MIT Press, 1986), 164–87, and her "The Titan City," *American Heritage of Invention and Technology* 2:2 (Fall 1986): 44–49.

25 Unidentified author, "City 1960: Norman Bel Geddes, Designer," *Architectural Forum* 67 (July 1937). Archival files may be found in Job No. 356, "Shell Oil Advertising Campaign," Geddes Papers.

26 Futurama has been carefully studied in Jeffrey Meikle, *Twentieth Century Limited: Industrial Design in America, 1925–1939* (Philadelphia: Temple University Press, 1979), 200–209; Roland Marchand, "The Designers Go to the Fair II: Norman Bel Geddes, The General Motors 'Futurama,' and the Visit to the Factory Transformed," *Design Issues* 8:2 (Spring 1992): 22–40; Adnan Morshed, "The Aesthetics of Ascension in Norman Bel Geddes's Futurama," *Journal of the Society of Architectural Historians* 63:1 (March 2004): 74–99; and Christopher Innes, "Riding into the Future," in *Designing Modern America: Broad-*

way to Main Street (New Haven, CT: Yale University Press, 2005), 120–43; Christina Cogdell, "The Futurama Recontextualized: Norman Bel Geddes's Eugenic 'World of Tomorrow,'" *American Quarterly* 52:2 (2000): 193–245. The fullest documents of the exhibit are *Highways and Horizons* (General Motors, n.d.), n.p., Box 19e, Folder 381.49 "Publicity," Job 381, Geddes Papers; and the film *To New Horizons*, Jam Handy Organization and General Motors, 1940.

27 A reviewer of Futurama in *Pencil Points* was moved to speculate: "Does this not suggest a fourth dimensional to strive for, a new step in the integration of art with nature, with life, with the universe?" Robert Henri Mutrux, "The World's Largest Rendering," *Pencil Points* (18 May 1939): 4. See also George Herrick, typescript for *Automotive Industries*, Box 19e, Folder 381.48, Job 381, Geddes Papers.

28 "How to See the World's Fair," *Cue* (6 May 1939): 56–57, Folder 381.65, Box 19e, Job 381, Geddes Papers.

29 Folke Kihlstedt, "Utopia Realized: The World's Fairs of the 1930s," in Joseph Corn, ed., *Imagining Tomorrow: History, Technology, and the American Future* (Cambridge, MA: MIT Press, 1986), 108, and discussed in Marchand, 34.

30 Geddes recognized the importance of the intersection of the future in his own body of work and tried in subsequent years to have some version of it actually built, researching and writing articles and proposing designs

for traffic control, always careful to join them to the forward-looking American disposition he believed in. Geddes implored William Randolph Hearst, for example, to sponsor a national highway system to fulfill this vision, which rested on a national character trait: "This characteristic of the American people is an infinite capacity of hope and confidence in the future." By appealing to such native optimism, Franklin D. Roosevelt had risen to the presidency, as had Dwight Eisenhower, Geddes wrote. The same spirit had made Futurama a great success, he continued. See letter to Hearst, 11 February 1953, Box 48, Folder 619.5, Geddes Papers. See also Robert Moses, "The Highway Maze," *New York Times Magazine* (11 November 1945), and other clippings in Box 48, Folder 619.1, and Box 19e, Folder 381.55, Geddes Papers.

31 William Bushnell Stout, as told to John B. Kennedy, "There's a Great Day Coming," *Collier's* (27 July 1929): 9.

32 Geddes, "Dreamlining Tomorrow: One Day in Your Life and Times Ten Years from Now, Prognosticated," *Mademoiselle* (March 1944): 148–50, 202–204.

33 Geddes, "Tomorrow's Consumer."

34 "Today in 1963," 4, Box 54, Folder 671.3, Job 671, Geddes Papers.

35 Beth Dunlop, *The Art of Disney Architecture* (New York: Abrams, 1996), 131. The monorail, completed in 1959, is surely indebted to Geddes's moving chairs at Futurama.

36 The idea of a shared future was also used to approach

issues of globalization in, for example, Margaret Mead, "The Future as the Basis for Establishing a Shared Culture," *Daedalus* 94:1 (Winter 1965): 135–55, and Anthony Blake, "Future Human Society: Continuities in Cultural Evolution," *Systematics* 2:3 (December 1964): 242–52.

37 Hendrik Hertzberg, "Fun Factories," *The New Republic* (25 April 1982): 43.

38 Bruce Handy, "Tomorrowland Never Dies," *Vanity Fair* 475 (March 2000): 114. Handy argues that *Star Wars* (George Lucas, 1977) is the "first retrofuturist film." Successors include *The Rocketeer* (Joe Johnston, 1991) and *Sky Captain and the World of Tomorrow* (Kerry Conran, 2004), both depicting the future from the late 1930s.

7

THEATER PRODUCTIONS

Christin Essin

Norman Bel Geddes first gained public recognition as a modern visionary and innovator during his early years as a theater artist. Even as a youth building toy theaters and producing performances for neighborhood friends, Geddes envisioned the stage as a space to experiment and reimagine the everyday. From his initial experiences in art theaters to large-scale Broadway productions, he amazed audiences with designs that captured the essence of the dramatic text and enveloped them within its story. A survey of Geddes's designs for theater productions suggests his dedication to creating performances that not only entertained contemporary audiences, but also helped them to understand their modern world and their role as modern citizens and to recognize the significant function that theater could play in American culture.

Geddes's desire to reform the American theater from a largely commercial enterprise to a forum for artistic expression reflected the broader goals of the art theater movement during the early decades of the twentieth century. Critics quickly associated Geddes with the New Stagecraft, an experimental style of staging practiced by young artists who drew inspiration from the avant-garde aesthetics of modern painters—minimalist shapes and abstract figures, expressive color choices, and techniques that acknowledged the material reality of a canvas rather than treating it as a window on the world. Likewise, New Stagecraft artists embraced the inherent beauty of the stage, a three-dimensional canvas with the potential to represent infinite locations. In particular, they found motivation from European theater artists such as Edward Gordon Craig and Adolphe Appia, who rejected the "old" stagecraft of elaborately painted backdrops or excessively decorated, realistic three-sided rooms for a new, more austere style of simplified staging. A neutral, architectural space, they argued, drew more focus to the actor who, as the conveyor of the text, revealed the play's central themes. Furthermore, they preferred color applied through light rather than paint to allow more flexibility in suggesting locations and quickly shifting scenes. As practiced by Geddes and other contemporaries, such as Robert Edmond Jones and Lee Simonson, the New Stagecraft was more than a set of techniques for creating scenery, but a holistic design philosophy that envisioned the spatial and visual components of performances as vital to the interpretation of dramatic texts and the creation of vibrant and meaningful theatrical events.

While many New Stagecraft designers gained their appreciation for modern aesthetics in Ivy League schools such as Harvard or artistic enclaves such as Greenwich Village, Geddes, a midwesterner with an intermittent education, forged his artistic perspective through practical experience and hands-on experimentation. While still working in Detroit as a poster illustrator, he created a small-scale model theater to illustrate scenic and lighting plans for *Thunderbird,* a play he wrote with his first wife, Belle Sneider, based on a Native American legend. When progressive arts patron Aline Barnsdall saw the model, she invited him to Los Angeles to help her develop a new art theater. Although Barnsdall's full vision never materialized, Geddes's work on her productions in Los Angeles allowed him to explore scenic theories and techniques.[1] His New Stagecraft interpretation of Ossip Dymow's *Nju* (1916), subtitled "an everyday tragedy," conveyed the emotional landscape beneath the surface of daily life, rather than a realistic depiction of the play's domestic settings. Critics celebrated his "impressionistic" lighting, accomplished by the elimination of footlights and careful placement of overhead lamps, and scenery that translated everyday interiors into modern expressions of abstract lines and symbolic colors (FIG. 1–4).[2]

Nju also gave Geddes the opportunity to learn from director Richard Ordynski, an ensemble member from Max Reinhardt's Deutsches Theater in Berlin. Reinhardt, Geddes's future collaborator, had gained an international reputation for his innovative, visually stunning productions that offered an imaginative alternative to the realistic dramas that dominated most commercial theaters. During an earlier trip to New York, Geddes had marveled at Reinhardt's touring production of *Sumurun* (1912), designed by Ernest Stern and considered the first appearance of the New Stagecraft on an American stage. Geddes left Los Angeles for New York in 1917, determined to break into the professional theater. Within a few years he secured a number of high-

Scenic renderings for Nju, *illustrating Geddes's New Stagecraft interpretation of the set, c. 1916.*

FIGURE 1 (TOP)

Private room in café. Pastel on board, 11¼ x 4⅝ in., 28.6 x 11.7 cm

FIGURE 2 (MIDDLE)

Husband's home. Pastel on board, 11¼ x 4⅝ in., 28.6 x 11.7 cm

FIGURE 3 (BOTTOM)

Furnished room. Pastel on board, 11¼ x 4⅝ in., 28.6 x 11.7 cm

FIGURE 4 (LEFT)

Players Producing Company program for Nju, *1916.*

FIGURE 5 (LEFT)

Geddes rendering of a scene ("A winged Figure jumps over his head") from The Divine Comedy, *c. 1920. Watercolor on paper, 23 x 20 in., 58.4 x 50.8 cm*

FIGURE 6 (RIGHT)

Image of Geddes's model ("winged Figures" scene) for The Divine Comedy, *c. 1920. Photograph by Francis Bruguière, 13¼ x 9⅝ in., 33.7 x 24.4 cm*

profile commissions, including designs for the Metropolitan Opera Company and the Broadway musical *Erminie* (1920). He gained the most critical acclaim, however, from a design that was never produced before a live audience.

Geddes's proposed adaptation of Dante's epic poem *The Divine Comedy* into a large-scale pageant exemplified his fundamental beliefs about devising theater for modern audiences. Created on a drafting board without budget restrictions or spatial limitations, the project represented an ideal expression of his New Stagecraft philosophy. Rather than merely create scenic elements for an existing space, Geddes

Francis Bruguière to capture stills of each scene **(FIG. 5, 6)**.[3] Critic Kenneth Macgowan described the design as a "gigantic and adroitly curving diabolical pit of many levels," which could represent the varying depths of Dante's paradise, purgatory, and hell.[4] Geddes himself compared it to ancient Greek theaters, intending his circular space to echo classical performances that had inspired past actors and audiences.[5]

Geddes's *Divine Comedy* design gained significant public exposure through publication and exhibition. Macgowan featured Geddes's design sketches in the 1921 issue of *Theatre Arts Magazine*, promoting it as an architectural alternative to the

FIGURE 7 (OPPOSITE)

Geddes rendering of a stained glass window for the set of The Miracle, *c. 1924. This is one of thirty-six windows designed to be 86 feet high at the sides of the chancel. Watercolor on paper, 16 x 45 in., 40.6 x 114.3 cm*

used modern design principles to envision the whole production. He designed an original space to house a cast of more than five hundred performers; arranged scenic, lighting, and costume elements; and adapted the text and sound orchestration into a "score" divided into quarter-minute increments. The colossal stage contained a series of steps encircled on three sides by a massive auditorium; behind the stage, a curved backdrop provided a neutral surface to reflect his lighting effects. To illustrate the performance sequentially, Geddes painted a series of renderings; constructed an elaborate model, complete with lighting; and commissioned renowned photographer

proscenium playhouse that might liberate artists to imagine a truly modern theater.[6] Critic Sheldon Cheney featured Bruguière's model photographs in the American entry for the 1922 International Theatre Exhibition in Amsterdam, launching Geddes into international prominence. *The Divine Comedy*, in essence, became Geddes's manifesto: Theater designers should not merely create scenery for preexisting stages, but should use design to motivate the development of a truly modern theater that fully engages spectators' modern sensibilities.

Geddes attempted for many years to find a producer for *The Divine Comedy*, but none emerged: The extravagant design never convinced producers of its viability. While many labeled the project a failure and branded Geddes a visionary whose ideas were better suited to the drafting board than an actual stage, the design did materialize as a significant expression of the New Stagecraft movement in America. Published throughout the 1920s, *The Divine Comedy* design prompted many theater artists to reimagine the possibilities of modern performance space. Geddes's use of design as a conceptual force behind performance, as well as his experimentation with models, foreshadowed the theoretical and stylistic approach he later brought to his industrial design projects.

The exhibition photographs of *The Divine Comedy* drew Max Reinhardt's attention, and he asked Geddes to design his upcoming production of *The Miracle* at New York's Century Theatre. A pantomime written by Karl Vollmoeller, *The Miracle* told the story of a Catholic nun's wayward journey and miraculous return to salvation. Reinhardt had staged previous productions in large arena-like venues, so Geddes's first challenge was to adapt the sizeable visual spectacle for a conventional proscenium theatre. His solution, however, was far from conventional.

Geddes encased the existing proscenium architecture with the semblance of a medieval cathedral, concealing the structure behind simulated stone walls, Gothic arches, and stained-glass windows (**FIG. 7**). Geddes oversaw myriad details to re-create the atmosphere of a twelfth-century cathedral: Church pews replaced theater seating, colored light streamed through the windows, church bells and organ music rang through the auditorium, and even ushers wore costumes to resemble Catholic nuns.[7] The design not only reinforced the characters' story, but also cast audience members as churchgoers, establishing an atmosphere of solemnity and awe even before the performance began.

Geddes insisted that *The Miracle*'s large-scale staging evolved organically from pantomime's spectacular nature, but New Stagecraft colleagues decried its overwrought decoration and excessively realistic details, restating their preference toward a more simplified modern design aesthetic. *The*

Miracle was immensely popular with the public, however. After opening in 1924, it ran two seasons and produced a national tour. Critics hailed it as a remarkable theatrical event. While praise for Reinhardt was generally unanimous, many also recognized Geddes's fresh talent and innovative spirit. Articles in the *Architectural Record* and *Scientific American* featured his technical achievements and the sheer number of resources needed for the design's construction and installation.[8] Reviewers also remarked on the powerful feelings of spirituality produced by the cathedral-like setting and relayed reports of spectators "chipping pieces of wood from pews and walls" to take home as souvenirs.[9] Seated within the scenic environment, audiences more readily suspended their disbelief and felt actively involved as participants. Geddes's transformation of the theater aisle into a cathedral nave and stage into an altar reminded them that centuries of spectators had situated themselves similarly in Roman Catholic churches. As with *The Divine Comedy*'s homage to the Greek theater, Geddes's *Miracle* design referenced an architectural structure of historical and cultural significance, signaling the audience to regard the performance as an event laden with religious and civic meaning.

Because Geddes established his professional credentials with such large-scale, spectacular projects, he quickly gained a reputation as innovative but impractical, an accusation that followed him into his industrial design career. He claimed that his career shift toward industrial design in 1927 stemmed from his frustration at the slow pace of modern theater reform. Industry and corporate executives, he hoped, would have more motivation and financial resources to bring about the modern design revolution that he envisioned.

Geddes, however, never fully left the theater. He continued to return with projects that implemented his modernizing mission. One of his more high-profile and controversial projects was a 1931 production of *Hamlet* at New York's Broadhurst Theatre. He served as both designer and director and collaborated with literary advisor Clayton Hamilton to edit the Shakespearean tragedy. Rather than treat *Hamlet* as a classical masterpiece, Geddes significantly abridged the play to emphasize the characters' actions. Geddes's *Hamlet* was more melodramatic than tragic, and the title character more "nervously agile" than indecisive, a choice decried by many critics and stalwart fans of Shakespeare.[10] But, as Hamilton argued, Geddes's intent was to purge the play of its literary stuffiness and "produce upon a modern audience an emotional response as similar as possible to that which Shakespeare himself produced upon his Elizabethan audience."[11] Reenvisioned as a dynamic story for the contemporary spectator, replete with psychoses befitting the complex theories of modern psychology, Geddes's *Hamlet* continued to assert his faith in a theater that drew from the past but through modern idioms that would inspire the current generation.

Geddes based the design's spatial arrangement on his interpretation of the dramatic text, developing a ground plan derived from the characters' actions. Steps and platforms of varying shapes and heights populated the stage, all positioned on a diagonal so that the furthest downstage angle jutted out into the audience (FIG. 8). Geddes's experimentation with lighting effects achieved a new level in *Hamlet*. Through concentrated area lighting, actors could play a scene on one platform while stagehands on an adjacent platform set the next scene in darkness; transitions between scenes, therefore, could happen rapidly and seamlessly (FIG. 9). While a common practice today, Geddes's innovation was a revelation in 1931, and critics collectively noted the production's swift, cinematic quality. With each of Geddes's choices—the abridgement of text, architectural stage, sharply focused lighting, and minimal scenic elements—he created a fluidity of movement, unifying the production elements to tell the story at the rapid pace of modern life.

One of Geddes's significant technical innovations was the development of recorded sound for theatrical productions, first implemented on *Hamlet* but later used to great effect on Sidney Kingsley's *Dead End*, which opened in 1935 at the Belasco Theatre.[12] In addition to his scenic and lighting contributions, Geddes undertook responsibility for sound design, recording the various sounds one might hear from a pier on New York's East River—water lapping against the dock, boats whistling offshore, and street traffic bustling from the opposite direction—in an effort to bring an additional layer of realism to this play about the harmful social consequences of the city's slum housing. Critics largely dismissed Kingsley's drama as an overly melodramatic depiction of neglected children living in dead-end slums while wealthy New Yorkers on the same block looked the other way. They praised Geddes's design, however, as a fitting environment for the street urchins' violent tendencies, scatological language, and allegiance to corrupt gangsters like Baby Face Martin.[13]

Geddes spent many hours on the East River docks, recording waterfront sounds and photo-

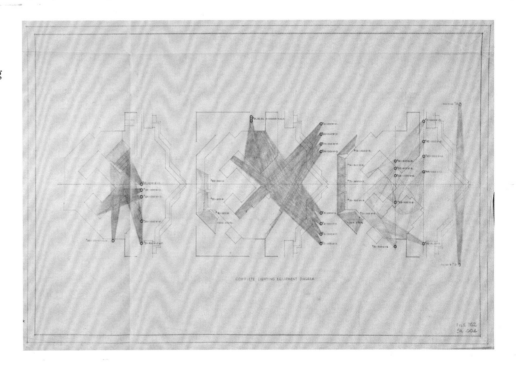

graphing dingy tenements. His resulting design was distinctly realistic, thus drastically different from his modern aesthetics in *Hamlet* or *The Divine Comedy*. He argued for the design's appropriateness, however, because it so thoroughly communicated the play's social message of the city's abandonment of its underprivileged youth. A ramshackle tenement of red bricks and rotting wooden boards stood on stage left while the rear side of a well-appointed apartment building stood stage right, its solid stone fence topped with iron spikes warding off the neighborhood gangs. Weathered pylons coiled with rope sat on the front of the stage, positioning the audience

FIGURE 8 (OPPOSITE)
Raymond Massey (Hamlet) and Colin Keith-Johnston (Laertes) performing the duel scene with producers observing at rehearsals of Hamlet, *c. 1929. Photograph by unidentified photographer, 7½ x 13½ in., 19 x 34.2 cm*

FIGURE 9 (BELOW)
Geddes's "Complete Lighting Equipment Diagram" for Hamlet, *1929. Pencil on paper, 31 x 21 in., 78.7 x 53.3 cm*

FIGURE 10

*Geddes scene design
with source photographs
for* Dead End, *c. 1935.
Photographs by unidenti-
fied photographer and
gouache on board, 29½ x
18¼ in., 74.9 x 46.35 cm*

TERRACE FLOOR

APARTMENT
TO LET
CHARLES B. BROWN

UNITED SCENIC ARTISTS
ASA
34
LOCAL 829

Signature

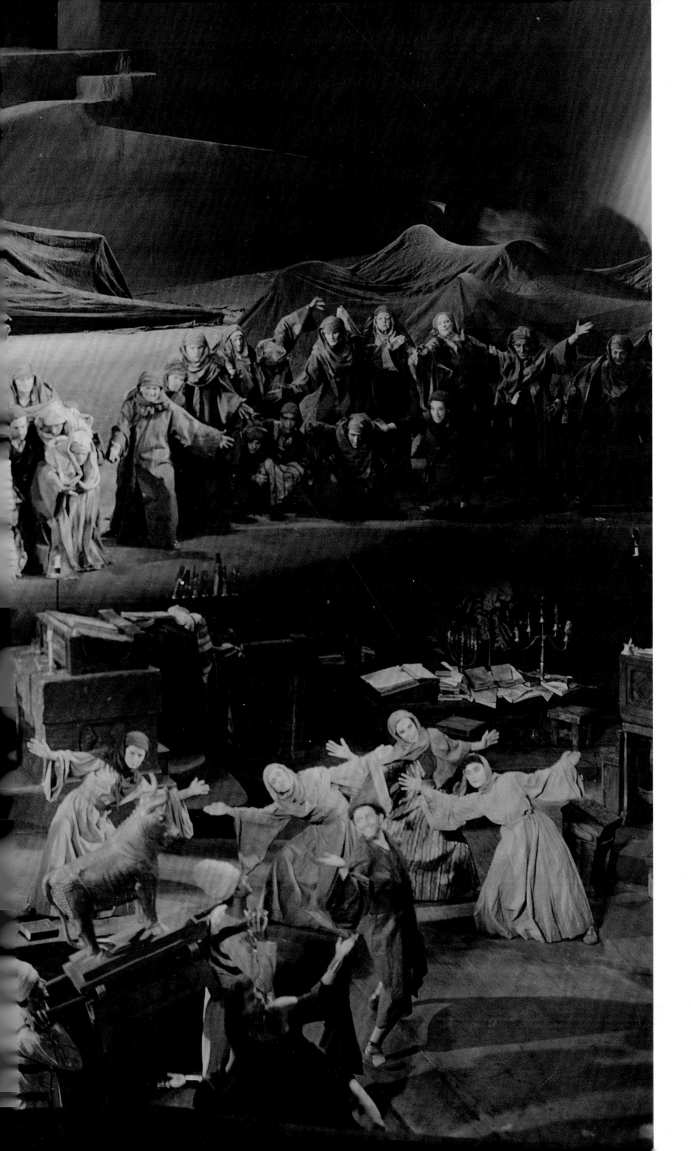

THE ETERNAL ROAD

just offshore, looking inward toward the dense city. Much to the spectators' delight, the boys regularly jumped off the pier (into the orchestra pit) to swim in the dirty river. Though approximating the reality of many dead-end streets in New York, Geddes's setting demonstrated artistic flair in its use of angles and perspective, accentuating the disparities between the wealthy and poor inhabitants and symbolizing the overwhelming obstacles facing these boys. Thus, through an integration of scenic, lighting, and sound elements, Geddes encouraged a New York audience to look beyond their busy, everyday streets to see the perspective of their less fortunate neighbors, the city dwellers trapped by their "dead-end" circumstances (FIG. 10).

During this same period, Geddes revisited his collaboration with Reinhardt on another spectacular pageant production, *The Eternal Road* (1937), written by Franz Werfel with music by Kurt Weill. Regularly compared to *The Miracle* due to its spectacular scale and religious subject matter, *The Eternal Road* featured a cast of nearly 250 performers portraying Old Testament scenes on gently sloping ramps and platforms that gradually rose fifty-nine feet with nine alternating levels (FIG. 11, 12). Geddes's vast design required the removal of the proscenium at the Manhattan Opera House and an extension of the stage thirty feet into the orchestra. Combined with his characteristic direct-focus lighting and amplified sound effects, the design overwhelmed critics and audiences with its majestic splendor. On the lower level, a rabbi in a Spanish synagogue reassured his persecuted congregation by reading from the Torah scrolls; the biblical stories of Abraham, Joseph, David, and Solomon played out on the stages above, with the highest levels reserved for scenes of divine revelation.

Critics largely praised Geddes's modern stagecraft in presenting the epic story in such a "magnificent," "magical," and "wondrous" manner, and the press regularly cited the design's construction details and costs, particularly since they contributed to the production's half-million dollar loss.[14] Many felt the expense was justified, however. A number of wealthy New Yorkers had contributed funding, hoping the event would unite the city's Jewish community and bring awareness to the current

injustices perpetrated against German Jews. *New York Times* critic Brooks Atkinson remarked that the production's ten postponements were "understood and forgiven," and while "the event may have had a political motive originally; it was now the story of the ages, told with great dignity, power and beauty."[15] Geddes's design, once again, enthralled audiences with a powerful theatrical experience, connecting them to the dramatic story regardless of religious or political affiliation.

The Eternal Road was Geddes's last significant theatrical production, after which he shifted more exclusively toward industrial design. Appreciating Geddes's ability to turn theater productions into must-see public events, industry executives and corporations increasingly commissioned his design expertise to provoke consumers' interest in their products and services. His theatrical experiences undoubtedly shaped his approach toward product design and advertising, and while many historians cite his theater career as key to his industry success, the productions examined in this essay are significant themselves as milestones in the history of the American stage. Geddes's innovations not only prompted theater producers to reassess the value of designers' contributions, but also to reenvision the possibilities of the modern theater and its cultural impact.

FIGURE 12
Program cover for The Eternal Road *mirroring Geddes's set design, 1937.*

FIGURE 13 (ABOVE)
Geddes sketch of the grave-
yard scene in Hamlet,
c. 1929. Pen and ink on
board, 16¼ x 7⅛ in.,
41.3 x 18 cm

FIGURE 14 (RIGHT)
The graveyard scene
in Hamlet, *c. 1929.*
Photograph by unidenti-
fied photographer,
9½ x 7½ in., 24.1 x 19 cm

FIGURE 15 (OPPOSITE)
Mary Servoss as Gertrude
in Geddes's production
of Shakespeare's Hamlet,
1931. Photograph by
Maurice Goldberg, 10⅜ x
13⅜ in., 26.4 x 34 cm

ENDNOTES

1   Norman Bel Geddes, *Miracle in the Evening,* ed. William Kelley (Garden City, NY: Doubleday, 1960), 166. A primary reason for the failure of Barnsdall's theater was the resignation of architect Frank Lloyd Wright from the project.

2   Geddes would later hire a clipping service to collect reviews of his productions. He collected the reviews from *Nju* himself and edited them into captions to publicize his success. "From the Press Notices of Nju—1916," typewritten notes, Box 70, Job 22, Geddes Papers.

3   Fredrick J. Hunter, "Norman Bel Geddes' Conception of Dante's 'Divine Comedy,'" *Educational Theatre Journal* 18 (1966): 240–46. Also see Geddes's own *A Project for a Theatrical Presentation of The Divine Comedy of Dante Alighieri* (New York: Theatre Arts, 1924).

4   Kenneth Macgowan, "The Next Theatre," *Theatre Arts Magazine* 5 (1921): 310.

5   Norman Bel Geddes, *Horizons* (Boston: Little, Brown, 1932), 156.

6   Macgowan, "The Next Theatre": 300.

7   Christopher Innes, *Designing Modern America: Broadway to Main Street* (New Haven: Yale University Press, 2005), 68.

8   See Claude Bragdon, "A Theatre Transformed: Being a Description of the Permanent Setting by Norman-Bel Geddes for Max Reinhardt's Spectacle, *The Miracle,*" *Architectural Record* (April 1924): 393; Albert A. Hopkins, "A Theatre without a Stage," *Scientific American* (April 1924): n.p. Included in clippings from Box 94, Folder I-2–3, Job 85, Geddes Papers.

9   Jennifer Davis Roberts, *Norman Bel Geddes: An Exhibition of Theatrical and Industrial Designs*, exhibition catalog (Michener Galleries, Humanities Research Center, University of Texas at Austin, 10 June 1979 to 22 July 1979), 12.

10 Brooks Atkinson, the *New York Times* theater critic, criticized Geddes's choice to produce *Hamlet* as a "play of action, to be interpreted with the nervous agility of contemporary life." Reviews are gathered in the Geddes Papers, Job 162, Oversize Box 19, Folder I-9.

11 Clayton Hamilton, "Hamlet for Its Own Sake," *Philadelphia Forum* (October 1931): n.p. Oversize Box 19, Folder I-9, Job 162, Geddes Papers.

12 Geddes also functioned as a producer of *Dead End*. His innovations in sound recording and amplification were reported by *Scientific American* in the March 1932 issue. Oversize Box 19, Folder I-11, Job 162, Geddes Papers.

13 Many of these actors would later reprise their roles in the film version of *Dead End* (1937), adapted by Lillian Hellman and produced by Metro Goldwyn Mayer, or one of the film sequels that followed.

14 See clippings from the *New York Times*, *Women's Wear Daily*, *New York Sun*, *New York Herald Tribune*, and other publications gathered in Box 87, Folder G-12, Job 346, Geddes Papers.

15 Brooks Atkinson, "The Eternal Road, Produced by Max Reinhardt, at the Manhattan Opera House," *New York Times* (8 January 1937): 14.

FIGURE 16
Raymond Massey as Hamlet in the soliloquy scene in Geddes's production of Shakespeare's Hamlet, *1931. Photograph by Maurice Goldberg, 10⅜ x 13⅜ in., 26.4 x 34 cm*

THEATERS

Laura McGuire

In a 1925 critique of the contemporary theater, the Viennese architect Adolf Loos wrote that in the theater of the future, the auditorium would become more important than the stage. Novel uses of space, light, time, and sound magnified to capture the whole interior of a theater would foster new sensory experiences. Modern theater architecture would inspire the growth of a unified creative consciousness, which would connect theatergoers both to the action on stage and to one another.[1] Loos was not alone in his call to make theatrical architecture more conducive to interaction between the audience and performance. Indeed, this concern preoccupied European avant-garde architects, designers, and artists throughout the first quarter of the twentieth century.

From 1915 through the 1920s, American architects began to draw on the progressive ideas of European theatrical designers and theorists (particularly the Swiss designer Adolphe Appia and London designer Edward Gordon Craig) inspiring the development of the New Stagecraft movement.[2] Both Appia and Craig (whose works were promoted by the influential American architectural and theatrical critics Sheldon Cheney and Hiram Kelley Moderwell) advocated a holistic theater that simplified stage scenery and employed inventive lighting to focus attention on the actor.[3]

Along with designers Joseph Urban and Livingston Platt, Norman Bel Geddes was one of the new theatrical movement's leading practitioners in the United States. He produced a series of visionary projects to reform the theater from the mid-teens until the 1930s, when he shifted into industrial design. His work included Theater Number 6, the Repertory Theater, the Divine Comedy Theater, the Ukrainian State Theater, and the Island Dance Restaurant, among other projects, none of which were built. In these designs, Geddes sought to dissolve the boundary between stage and audience. He dispensed with conventional proscenium-based interiors and introduced configurations that looked back to classical models. Exteriors were monumental in scale and delineated into distinct units, their forms derived from their uses and from various stylistic vocabularies of European avant-garde modernism.

To decorate smooth and unornamented interior surfaces, he would use dramatic displays of light and sound designed to transport the audience into the drama before them. His buildings also demonstrated his acute sensitivity to practical organization. In an attempt to reconcile the sublime with the scientific, Geddes reenvisioned the theater as a performance vessel simultaneously functional and exalted.

THEATER NUMBER 6

Although he had no formal training in architecture or license to practice professionally, Geddes tackled the architectural configuration of theaters in convergence with his early interest, about 1914 to 1915, in designing theatrical settings. One of these projects, Theater Number 6, set a defining precedent for his mature works of the later 1920s and 1930s.[4] Inspired by Greek theaters in the round, Theater Number 6 was novel in configuration and eschewed an ornate proscenium stage, which was increasingly detested by the theatrical avant-garde. Instead, Geddes envisioned a flexible space, free of physical barriers between the play and the audience.

In a short 1914 essay titled "Main Features of a Theatre for a More Plastic Style of Drama," Geddes described the innovative characteristics of the 3,604-seat Theater Number 6. Square in plan, the auditorium would be set along the diagonal, with the stage at one corner of the square. The entire space would be surmounted by a vast dome, which spanned the stage and seating area simultaneously (**FIG. 2**). Eight years later, in 1922, Geddes publicly presented his drawings of Theater Number 6 at an address to the Architectural League of New York.[5]

In the auditorium, Geddes arranged eight tiers of seats around the stage in a wide arc (**FIG. 1**). To better fuse the audience together, he eliminated transverse aisles as well as all balconies and galleries. Patrons would enter the auditorium through one of eight arched doorways positioned at each tier and walk along wide aisles, which also functioned as rows of seating. This arrangement provided each seat with nearly twice the legroom typical of other theaters and reduced jostling if one had to exit the theater in the middle of a performance. Spectators were brought together in one cohesive space,

FIGURE I (RIGHT)
Cross-section of
Theater Number 6 audi-
torium, c. 1922. Ink on
paper, 17½ x 16½ in.,
44.5 x 41.9 cm

FIGURE 2 (BOTTOM LEFT)
Geddes preliminary sketch
for Theater Number 6, not
dated. Pencil on paper,
11 x 8¼ in., 27.9 x 21 cm

FIGURE 3 (BOTTOM RIGHT)
Cross-section of Theater
Number 6 for the Chicago
World's Fair, c. 1929. Ink
on paper.

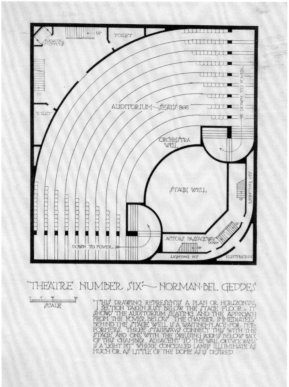

In order to remove all barriers between the audience and the actors on stage, Geddes submerged the orchestra under a ceiling that was level with the auditorium floor. Through perforations in the covering, music would float mysteriously upward from an invisible source. The conductor would be able to watch the stage through a periscope, as if he were in a submarine. Furthermore, no footlights, no curtain, and no proscenium arch interrupted a feeling of unity under the great dome above.[8]

The dome was to function as a continuation of the stage set, expanding outward into the zone of the audience. Light wells positioned along the inner edges of the stage would illuminate the bare space above, creating an illusion of the sky and bathing the

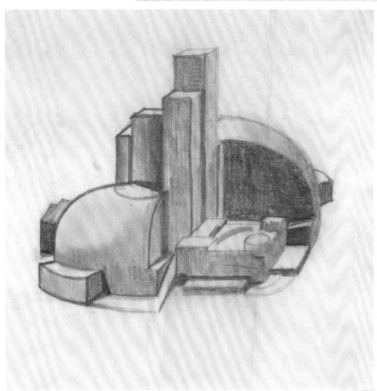

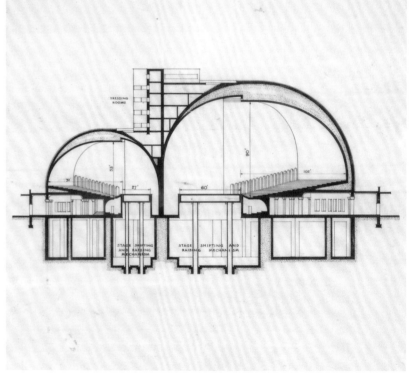

reducing distinctions between social classes. In order to emphasize unity between audience members and the drama, Geddes claimed that there would not be one bad seat in the house.[6] This reflected his tendency to view design as a democratizing force in American culture, an architectural tradition following the ideas of both Louis Sullivan and the architect Claude Bragdon, who enthusiastically supported Geddes's work.[7]

spectators below in variously colored lights.[9] Indeed, light provided the primary scenographic architecture of the performance and could even eliminate the need for conventional scenery.[10] Geddes intended plays of illumination across the vast domed stage to inspire wonder and awe. The dome would heighten dramatic experience through the creation of a scenography of pure light, both powerful and mutable. Lighted domes became a central feature of many of his later projects, including the Repertory Theater and the Divine Comedy Theater.[11]

By placing the stage at an angle in the corner of the auditorium and projecting it outward in an arc concentric with the curve of the seats, Geddes created a deeper stage. The actors would move freely about the space, giving performances a more three-dimensional quality than those set behind a diorama-like proscenium arch. A low set of stairs at the front of the stage pushed the action out into the audience. Actors could step off the stage and perform at the same level as the audience.

The stage itself consisted of two hydraulic platforms, which could be lowered into the basement for scene changes. All scenery and props could be stored in a spacious basement next to the shops without being carried upstairs to the stage, substantially streamlining stagehands' jobs. At the same time, actors could descend a staircase from their dressing rooms positioned along the sidewalls of the stage to take their places at the start of a scene. The moving platforms created seamless transitions between acts without the spatial disruption of a descending curtain (**FIG. 3**).

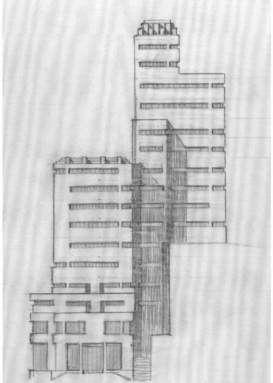

FIGURE 4 (FAR LEFT)
Repertory Theater (diagonal axis) plan and elevation, c. 1929. The Repertory Theater is difficult to distinguish from Geddes's Theater Number 6. Charcoal on paper, 13 x 21 in., 33 x 53.3 cm

FIGURE 5 (LEFT)
Geddes preliminary sketch for the Repertory Theater, c. 1929–30. Charcoal on paper, 8⅜ x 10⅞ in., 21.3 x 27.6 cm

FIGURE 6 (BELOW)
Geddes model of the Repertory Theater, c. 1929. Photograph by Maurice Goldberg, 9⅝ x 7⅝ in., 53.3 x 19.4 cm

OFFICE TOWER

STAGE SET No.1 IN POSITION

STAGE SET No.2 READY TO BE ROLLED ON ELEVATOR PLATFORM

TRACKS

HYDRAULIC PLUNGERS OF STAGE ELEVATOR

FIGURE 7 (LEFT)
Side elevation of Geddes's model of the Divine Comedy Theater, c. 1929–30. Photograph by Maurice Goldberg, 9½ x 7½ in., 24.1 x 19 cm

FIGURE 8 (RIGHT)
Geddes model of the Divine Comedy Theater, c. 1929–30. Photograph by Maurice Goldberg, 9⅛ x 7 in., 23.1 x 17.8 cm

Geddes's architectural ideas were not entirely new. Otto Brückwald's Festspeilhaus, designed for Richard Wagner (Bayreuth, 1872–76), was also based on antique models, eschewed balconies, and used a hood to hide the orchestra from view. Similarly, Max Littman's Prinzregenten Theater (Munich, 1900–01) had a submerged orchestra pit and a stage that projected outward into a shallow arc of seating. In his dramatic Großes Schauspielhaus (Berlin, 1919), Hans Poelzig remodeled a circus into an Expressionist theater with an extraordinary dome of red-painted stalactites and a semicircular stage thrust into a fan-shaped auditorium. Nevertheless, Geddes's Theater Number 6 pushed beyond many European precedents, presaging even more ambitious avant-garde projects,

without a professional architectural license.) Geddes was put in charge of designing entertainment venues for the exposition, including theaters, cabarets, and restaurants. Initially, he envisioned at least ten theaters for the fairgrounds, each for different styles of performance.[13] In late 1929, he sent a letter to a variety of internationally known architects, directors, playwrights, and artists soliciting architectural ideas and asking them to send him potential plans for the theater buildings.[14] But by 1930, Geddes had made himself solely responsible for the projects.

REPERTORY THEATER

Geddes's design for the main auditorium of the exposition's Repertory Theater was identical to

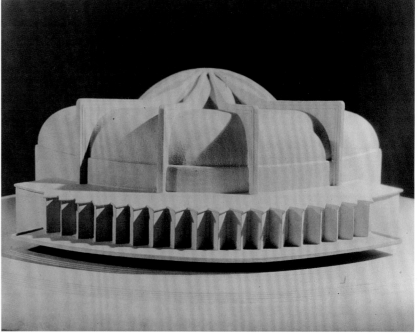

such as Frederick Kiesler's early 1920s designs for his enormous, spheroid Endless Theater and Walter Gropius's Totaltheater of 1927.

1933–34 CENTURY OF PROGRESS INTERNATIONAL EXPOSITION

In 1929, Geddes joined well-known architects, including Harvey Wiley Corbett, Raymond Hood, and Paul Cret, to form the architectural advisory commission for the 1933–34 Century of Progress International Exposition in Chicago.[12] (Geddes was the youngest member of the group and the only one

Theater Number 6, with a thrust stage surrounded by concentric quarter circles of seats and topped by a dome. In addition, a smaller theater to seat six hundred people, a theater for children, a cabaret, roof garden, and a nineteen-story tower to house rehearsal rooms, offices, dressing rooms, and storage joined the main auditorium. By positioning the auditorium on the diagonal axis of a square, Geddes could replicate its plan into a series of interlocking fan-shapes, creating a multifunctional performance building (FIG. 4).

His numerous sketches of dynamic, asymmetrical geometries of circles intersecting rectangles show that Geddes initially conceived of the Repertory Theater in plan.[15] He then projected it upward into three-dimensional space to form the theater's exterior organization. A model of the design shows an agglomeration of broad, sliced domes and boxy, stepped towers nestled together in a balanced composition (FIG. 6). The towers, similar to William Lescaze and George Howe's pioneering Philadelphia Saving Fund Society skyscraper (1929–32), were punctuated with setbacks and ribbon windows derived from European modernism (FIG. 5). The building's asymmetrical intersections of rounded and rectangular forms also recalled Constructivist stage settings by Varvara Stepanova and Liubov Popova, as well as the paintings

produce theater for education and recreation as if it were an industrial activity. Geddes argued that the success of a theater depended on a rational configuration of parts within the whole. In the Repertory Theater, he set each performance space around an axis and made each section clearly legible on the exterior. By positioning a small tower (reserved for the mechanical organization and theater business) at the center of a small city of performers and patrons, he referenced the function of commercial urban skyscrapers.

DIVINE COMEDY THEATER

Geddes's most ambitious and holistically conceived theater for the Century of Progress

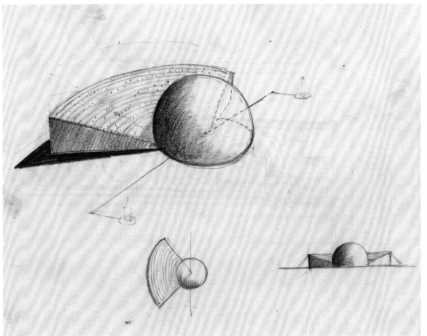
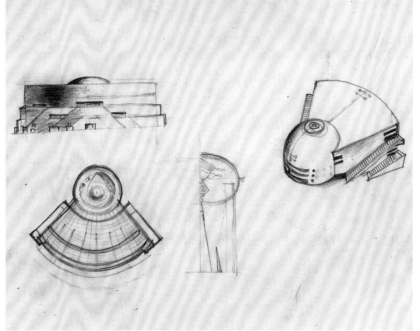

of Alexandra Exter, which Geddes would have seen at the International Theatre Exhibition in New York in 1926. His design thus represents an early example of interest in European avant-garde forms in the United States.

Modernist forms were not his only interest in the Repertory Theater. In the essay "Industrializing the Theater" in *Horizons* (1932), Geddes explained that the problem with American theater was that it was not sufficiently organized around principles of efficiency and scientific management. He lauded efforts undertaken by the Soviet government to

International Exposition was a five-thousand-seat structure designed specifically for performances of his own production of Dante's *The Divine Comedy*.[16] The Divine Comedy Theater reiterated the principal ideas of Theater Number 6 and the Repertory Theater, but amplified the building to an enormous size and distilled it into its most basic geometries (FIG. 7, 8). As in his previous projects, Geddes planned a semicircular stage surrounded by seating with no balconies, proscenium, or curtain. The plan consisted simply of a circle pierced by a fan-shaped auditorium, promenade,

FIGURE 9, 10

Geddes's preliminary sketches of the Divine Comedy Theater, c. 1929–30. Charcoal on paper, 10⅞ x 8⅜ in., 27.6 x 21.3 cm

FIGURE II (TOP LEFT)
Film set for Feet of
Clay, *1924. Photograph
by Eugene Robert
Richee (for Paramount
Pictures), 9 x 6¼ in.,
22.9 x 15.9 cm*

FIGURE 12 (TOP RIGHT)
*Geddes model of the
Island Dance Restaurant,
c. 1929–1930. Photograph
by Maurice Goldberg,
9½ x 7½ in., 24.1 x 19 cm*

FIGURE 13 (BOTTOM)
*Isometric drawing of
Island Dance Restaurant,
c. 1929–1930. Charcoal
on paper, 27½ x 19½ in.,
69.8 x 49.5 cm*

NORMAN BEL GEDDES DESIGNS AMERICA

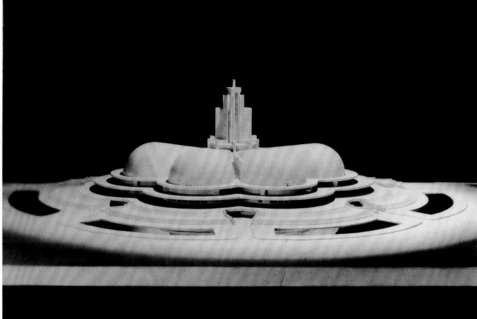

and terrace. Geddes transformed the traditional level surface of the stage into a series of steps: Because the actors could perform the play at multiple levels, the audience in upper seats would often be positioned eye-to-eye. In this project, the dome did not span the entire auditorium; instead, the seating was covered by a second, curving vault. Geddes positioned all auxiliary and work spaces underneath the stage so that their forms would not interfere with the purity of his plan.

Geddes's use of basic geometry at a massive scale resonated with Enlightenment-era efforts to express the sublime in works of architecture. Many of his early sketches for the project bear a striking similarity to Étienne-Louis Boullée's cenotaph for Isaac Newton (1784) (FIG. 9, 10). In the final model for the theater, Geddes left the basic forms and structural supports of the dome and the auditorium exposed. The terrace was a smooth, rounded platform cantilevering out from a curving wall of zigzag cutouts. The design simultaneously evoked a streamlined modernism and ordered Classical monumentality.

ISLAND DANCE RESTAURANT

Impressive and otherworldly displays of light also played a central role in Geddes's design for the exposition's Island Dance Restaurant, which was intended to be a center of both dining and entertainment. His restaurant design was repurposed from his set design for the 1924 motion picture *Feet of Clay*, produced by Famous Players Lasky Corporation and directed by Cecil B. DeMille (FIG. 11). Applying his vision for the theater as a place where an audience could become a part of the drama, Geddes envisioned a giant floating lagoon in which patrons took on the role of performers as they danced (FIG. 13). The circular, 500,000-square-foot space was organized as a group of four islands: The central platform was for the orchestra and main dance floor; the other three platforms were for dining. Like Geddes's theater auditoriums, the terraces were organized into concentric rings so that the dance floor would be visible from every table (FIG. 12).[17]

FIGURE 14 (TOP LEFT)
Geddes model of the Water Pageant Theater, c. 1929. Photograph by Maurice Goldberg, 9½ x 7½ in., 24.1 x 19 cm

FIGURE 15 (TOP RIGHT)
Geddes model of the Temple of Music, c. 1929. Photograph by Maurice Goldberg, 9½ x 7½ in., 24.1 x 19 cm

FIGURE 16 (BOTTOM)
Geddes model of the Aquarium Restaurant, c. 1929. Photograph by Maurice Goldberg, 9½ x 7½ in., 24.1 x 19 cm

Surrounding the orchestra and dancers in a flood of light, thirty-six neon tubes sprang from the orchestra floor, forming a series of latticed arches overhead. Geddes predicted that the tubes would produce enough light to illuminate the central portion of the exposition grounds and would be observable from a substantial distance as the "largest beacon in the world."[18] His luminous design had significance in a world where the bird's-eye view afforded by air travel was a vivid symbol of progress and modernity. The Island Dance Restaurant rep-

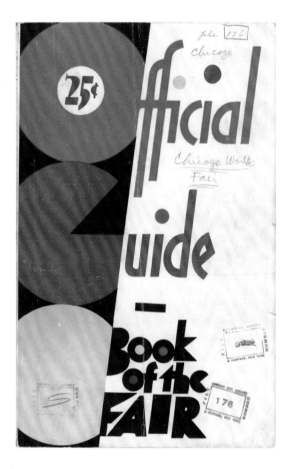

resented a theatrical spectacle not only at the level of daily use, but in an aerial play of light designed to captivate and inspire. In a dramatic reversal of Greek drama, which brought the gods into the realm of mankind, Geddes projected man's technological achievements outward in transcendent illumination.

UKRAINIAN STATE THEATER AND OPERA HOUSE

Geddes's most ambitious project of the early 1930s was a competition entry for a Ukrainian State Theater and Opera House, sponsored by the Soviet government in 1931. In this project, Geddes drew on previous designs to create several performance spaces for professional dramatics as well as for political gatherings. Monumental in scale and organized along a longitudinal axis similar to Le Corbusier's design the same year for the Palace of the Soviets, the Ukrainian State Theater was divided into zones containing three complete theaters, as well as auxiliary workspaces (**FIG. 19**).[19]

The main indoor theater would seat four thousand people in a wide semicircle (**FIG. 20**). The movable stage would allow scenery to be changed easily, and actors and audience could circulate between the auditorium and the stage via a mechanical apron, which would project outwards to a variety of distances. An open-air theater, located at the rear of the main building and accessed directly from the street, would seat an additional two thousand people.

In a plaza behind both the indoor and outdoor theaters, Geddes positioned a second outdoor theater to accommodate sixty thousand people for performances and political gatherings. Remarkably, Geddes envisioned the entire space as an enormous stage. Great floodlights and amplifiers positioned like columns surrounding the seating area could illuminate up to five thousand actors who would perform along the structure's rear facade. The political implications of these flexible spaces—which highlighted theatrical performance as a public and everyday act—were not lost on Geddes. Indeed, he admired the Soviet government for its efforts to treat the theater as a centralized industry for public education and amusement.[20]

It is remarkable that an American designer— relatively isolated from his European and Soviet colleagues—was able to give architectural form and functionality to many of the theories developed by the theatrical avant-garde in the teens and 1920s. Geddes's theater designs are not necessarily remarkable for his desire to integrate audience and performer through means of space and light, but because few other American architects—at least those with any commercial success—had yet put forth such forward-thinking, comprehensive, and structurally feasible theater projects.

FIGURE 19 (TOP)
Geddes's model of his design for the Ukrainian State Theater and Opera House at Kharkov, Russia, submitted to the U.S.S.R. Competition, 1931. Photograph by Maurice Goldberg, 8⅜ x 8⅞ in., 21.3 x 22.5 cm

FIGURE 20 (BOTTOM)
Geddes rendering of the interior of the Ukrainian State Theater and Opera House indoor theater, c. 1931. Charcoal on board, 38 x 27 in., 96.5 x 68.6 cm

ENDNOTES

1 Adolf Loos, introduction to the *International Theatre Exposition New York 1926* (New York: The Little Review, 1926).

2 Craig's ideas were pervasive in progressive theatrical circles in the United States. His monthly magazine, *The Mask*, was available in New York bookstores, and his *On the Art of the Theatre* (Chicago: Brown's Bookstore, 1911) went through nine editions between 1911 and 1914.

3 Moderwell's *The Theatre of Today* (New York: Dodd, Mead & Co., 1914) provided an early, comprehensive discussion of new developments in European stage design. Sheldon Cheney's *The Art Theatre: A Discussion of Its Ideals, Its Organization, and Its Promise As a Corrective for the Present Evils in the Commercial Theatre* (New York: Knopf, 1917) gave an account of avant-garde theatrical theories in Europe and suggestions for adapting these ideas in the American theater. For a comprehensive account of the New Stagecraft movement in the United States, see Orville Kurth Larson, *Scene Design in the American Theatre from 1915 to 1960* (Fayetteville: University of Arkansas Press, 1989).

4 The origin of the name Theater Number 6 is unclear but indicates that Geddes had prepared several earlier designs— he called a much later project from 1929 "Theater Number 14." There are no extant records of designs prior to Theater Number 6 or intervening projects before Theater Number 14.

5 "Main Features of a Theatre for a More Plastic Style of Drama," 1914, Box 161, Folder 3, Geddes Papers; manuscript notes for lecture to Architectural League of New York, 1922, Box 161, Folder Y-1, Geddes Papers.

6 Claude Bragdon, "Towards a New Theatre," *Architectural Record* 52 (September 1922): 172–73, 182; Norman Bel Geddes, *Horizons* (Boston: Little, Brown, 1932), 150.

7 Claude Bragdon wrote the first comprehensive analysis of Geddes's Theater Number 6 in 1922, "Towards a New Theatre," 172–73.

8 Ibid., 174.

9 Ibid.

10 Geddes, *Horizons*, 152. See also Sheldon Cheney, "The Architectural Stage," *Theatre Arts* (July 1927): 24–25, and Bragdon, "Towards a New Theatre": 182.

11 Geddes's contemporary, the Italian Futurist painter and scenographer Enrico Prampolini, was perhaps the most vocal advocate of light as the basis of scenic design. In his 1915 manifesto, *Futurist Scenography*, he called for the creation of an "illuminating stage" in which "the luminous dynamic architecture of the stage emanate [*sic*] from chromatic incandescences that, climbing tragically or showing themselves voluptuously, will inevitably arouse new sensations and emotional values in the spectator." Enrico Prampolini, "Futurist Scenography" (first published in Italian, 1915). In *Futurist Performance*, by Michael Kirby, trans. Victoria Nes Kirby (New York: Dutton, 1971), 204–205.

12 Other architects on the commission included Ralph T. Walker, John Holabird, Arthur Brown Jr., Edward Bennett, and Daniel Burnham Jr.

13 "World's Fair Notes," Franklin Park Leydenite, 21 June 1929, n.p., Box 198, Folder I-1–2, Geddes Papers.

14 Letter from Geddes to various, 23 October 1929, Box 198, Folder J-3.5, Geddes Papers.

15 Sketches of Repertory Theater, Box 161, Folder E-1–4, Geddes Papers.

16 Specifications and building description for the Divine Comedy Theater, Box 157, Folder P-1, Geddes Papers.

17 Geddes, *Horizons*, 191–93.

18 Ibid., 191.

19 Ukrainian State Theater specifications, Box 162, Folder P-1, Geddes Papers.

20 Geddes, *Horizons*, 140–41.

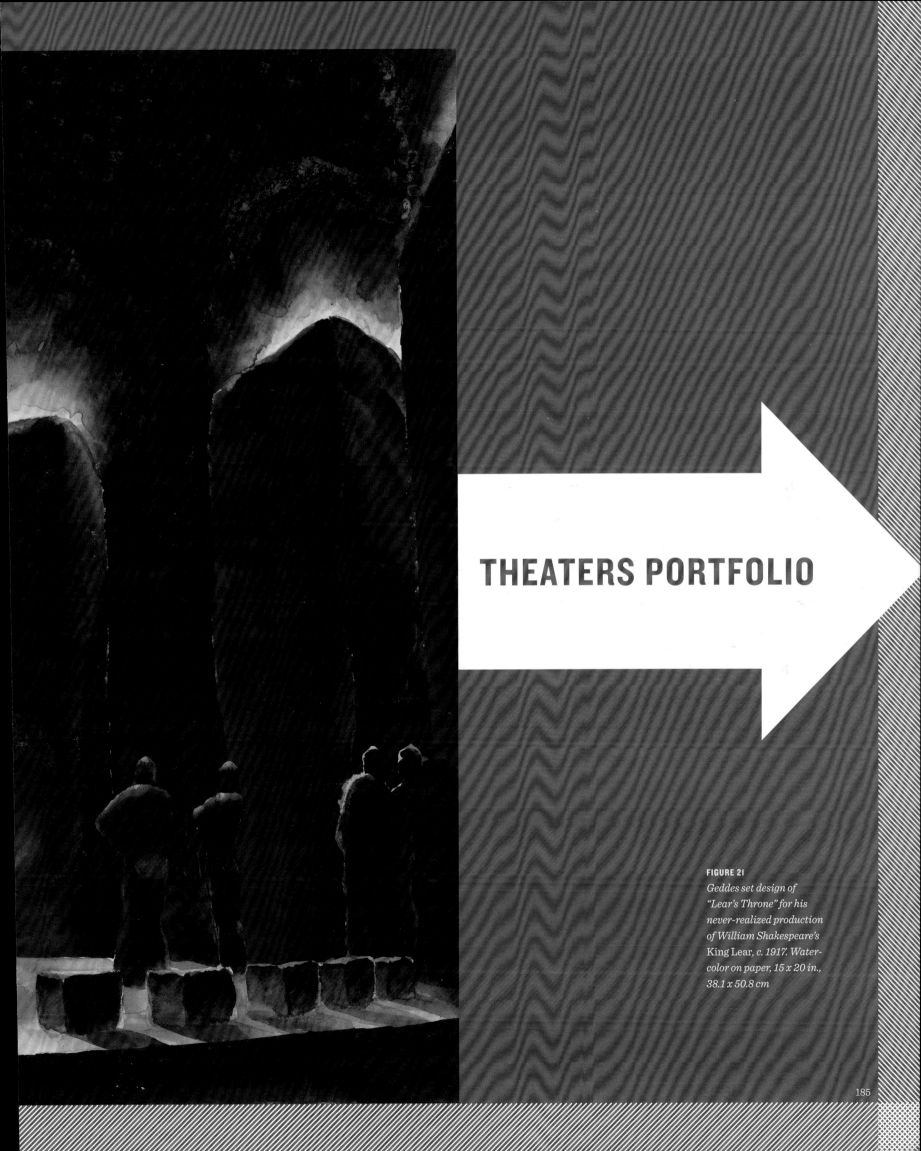

THEATERS PORTFOLIO

FIGURE 22 (OPPOSITE)
Geddes costume design for Albany in his never-realized production of William Shakespeare's King Lear, *c. 1917. Charcoal on paper, 9 x 12 in., 22.9 x 30.5 cm*

FIGURE 23 (TOP)
Geddes design for an Angular-Garden Theater built for Carolyn B. Hastings of Santa Barbara, California, 1917. Watercolor on board, 11⁵/₁₆ x 9³/₈ in., 28.7 x 23.8 cm

FIGURE 24 (MIDDLE)
Geddes set design of the "Hut on the Heath" for King Lear, *c. 1917. Pastel on paper, 19¹/₂ x 14³/₄ in., 49.5 x 37.5 cm*

FIGURE 25 (BOTTOM)
Geddes set design of "Hilltop Near Dover" for his never-realized production of William Shakespeare's King Lear, *c. 1917. Watercolor on paper, 18⁷/₈ x 12 in., 47.9 x 30.5 cm*

Geddes scene renderings for his never-realized production of Dante Alighieri's The Divine Comedy, 1920–24.

FIGURE 26 (TOP LEFT)
"The earth opens and in the sulphurous green of the inferno Dante and Virgil descend." Sanguine on paper, 23 x 20 in., 58.4 x 50.8 cm

FIGURE 27 (TOP RIGHT)
"At the beginning of his search for infinity. Dante is stopped by the three beasts." Sanguine on paper, 23 x 20 in., 58.4 x 50.8 cm

FIGURE 28 (MIDDLE LEFT)
"Above Dante and Virgil winged creatures in yellow light, and in the shadows the damned emerge." Sanguine on paper, 23 x 20 in., 58.4 x 50.8 cm

FIGURE 29 (MIDDLE RIGHT)
"Circles of agonizing souls and immense wavering shadows in a glare of crimson." Sanguine on paper, 23 x 20 in., 58.4 x 50.8 cm

FIGURE 30 (BOTTOM LEFT)
"In a path of blue-white light Beatrice steps down from her chariot to meet Dante." Sanguine on paper, 23 x 20 in., 58.4 x 50.8 cm

FIGURE 31 (BOTTOM RIGHT)
"The eyes of the beast divide and sub-divide." Sanguine on paper, 23 x 20 in., 58.4 x 50.8 cm

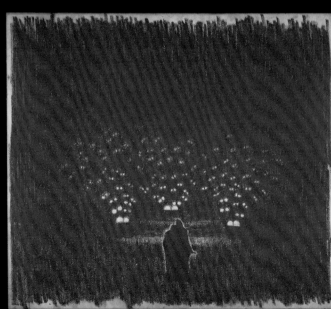

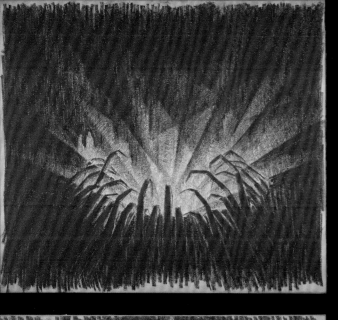

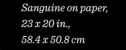

FIGURE 32 (TOP LEFT)
"The forms droop, crumble and collapse into the chasm." Sanguine on paper, 23 x 20 in., 58.4 x 50.8 cm

FIGURE 33 (TOP RIGHT)
"The movement is the convulsion of decayed humanity." Sanguine on paper, 23 x 20 in., 58.4 x 50.8 cm

FIGURE 34 (MIDDLE LEFT)
"Beatrice appears in a bolt of light." Sanguine on paper, 23 x 20 in., 58.4 x 50.8 cm

FIGURE 35 (MIDDLE RIGHT)
"The light has risen and divided itself more, revealing towers." Sanguine on paper, 23 x 20 in., 58.4 x 50.8 cm

FIGURE 36 (BOTTOM LEFT)
"Dante meets Beatrice." Sanguine on paper, 23 x 20 in., 58.4 x 50.8 cm

FIGURE 37 (BOTTOM RIGHT)
Geddes model stage set for The Divine Comedy *with lighting and figures, 1921–24. Photograph by Francis Bruguière, 9¼ x 6½ in., 23.5 x 16.5 cm*

NORMAN BEL GEDDES DESIGNS AMERICA

More Geddes scene renderings for his never-realized production of Dante Alighieri's The Divine Comedy, *1920–24.*

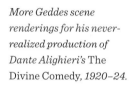

FIGURE 38 (OPPOSITE)
"Dante meets Beatrice." Watercolor on paper, 23 x 20 in., 58.4 x 50.8 cm

FIGURE 39 (TOP)
"The earth-forms rise in groups and divide." Watercolor on paper, 23 x 20 in., 58.4 x 50.8 cm

FIGURE 40 (BOTTOM)
"Two winged guardians of Purgatory." Watercolor on paper, 23 x 20 in., 58.4 x 50.8 cm

Jessie Tarbox Beals

FIGURE 41 (LEFT)
Norman Bel Geddes
working on costume sketch
for The Miracle, *c. 1924.*
Photograph by Jessie
Tarbox Beals, 7¼ x 9 in.,
18.4 x 22.9 cm

OPPOSITE
Geddes costume designs
for The Miracle, *c. 1924.*

FIGURE 42 (TOP LEFT)
Gypsy Woman.
Watercolor on paper,
10½ x 14 in., 26.7 x 35.6 cm

FIGURE 43 (TOP RIGHT)
Falcon Keeper. Watercolor
on paper, 10½ x 14 in.,
26.7 x 35.6 cm

FIGURE 44 (BOTTOM RIGHT)
Grooms' Man. Watercolor
on paper, 10 x 15 in.,
25.4 x 38 cm

FIGURE 45 (BOTTOM LEFT)
Chief Gypsy or Jester.
Watercolor on paper,
11¾ x 13½ in., 29.8 x 34.3 cm

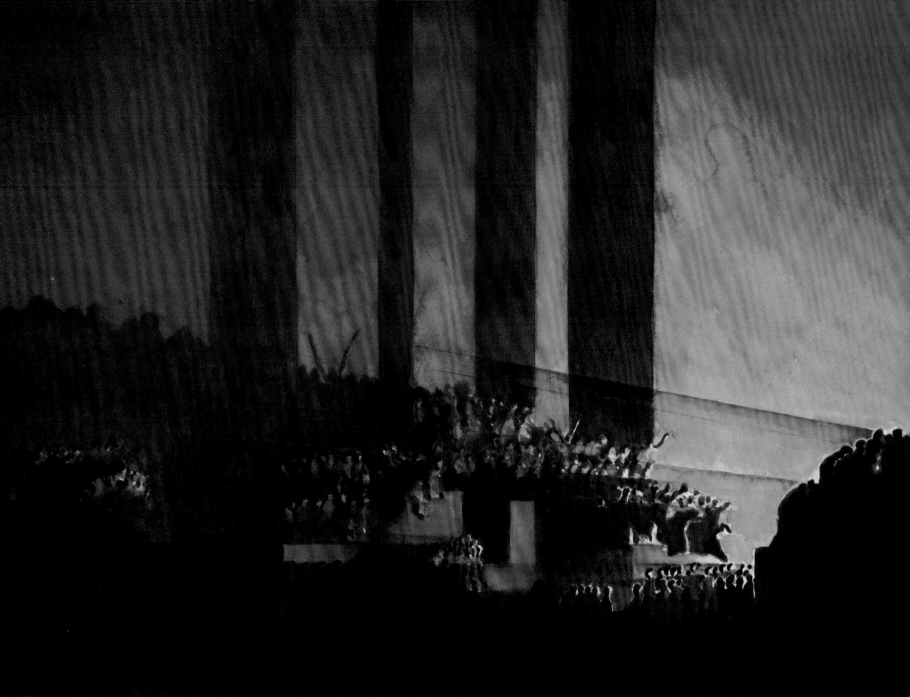

FIGURE 54 (ABOVE)
Geddes scene render-ing ("The Burning") for Jeanne d'Arc, c. 1925. Watercolor on paper, 19¾ x 15¾ in., 50.1 x 40 cm

FIGURE 55, 56 (RIGHT)
Geddes sketches of masks for a never-realized production of Eugene O'Neill's Lazarus Laughed, 1927. Pencil on board, 6¼ x 10½ in., 17 x 26 cm each

FIGURE 57 (ABOVE)
*Geddes scene rendering
("The Crowning") for
Jeanne d'Arc, c. 1925.
Watercolor on paper,
19½ x 14¾ in.,
49.5 x 37.46 cm*

FIGURE 58 (LEFT)
*Geddes scene render-
ing ("The Capture") for
Jeanne d'Arc, c. 1925.
Watercolor on paper,
20 x 16 in., 50.8 x 40.6*

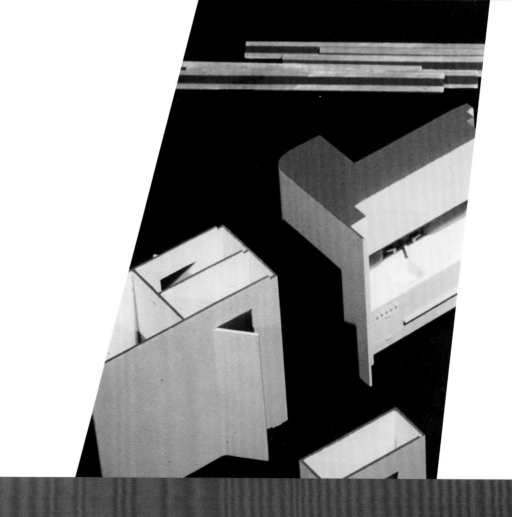

9

MODULAR AND MOBILE

Christopher Innes

Many aspects of Norman Bel Geddes's industrial and architectural designs can be traced to his theatrical perspective and experience. This is particularly obvious with respect to the mobile and modular construction systems that Geddes pioneered in Broadway productions and then carried through to his designs for kitchen equipment and houses. However, the link between Geddes's theatrical and industrial design work was mediated by his 1932 book on design, *Horizons*. This was the first work to attempt a holistic design approach covering every aspect from reconceptualizing the theater as a factory for play-production through all sorts of home equipment and every form of transport (ships, airplanes, trains, cars, as well as a combined airport, bus, and rail hub) to streamlined designs for factories. While the Standard Gas Equipment Company (SGE), featured in *Horizons*, had engaged Geddes to redesign their stoves before the book's publication, the fact that he was sought out subsequently by such firms as Frigidaire and Electrolux, as well as automobile manufacturers like General Motors, was due to the impact of this publication on the popularization of streamlining, effectively setting the style of the 1930s and beyond through its highly effective promotion of this stylistic trend.[1] In numerous interviews, Geddes himself seldom referred directly to the connection between his architectural, industrial, and theatrical design work, instead always referencing *Horizons*. One visual example of this is a publicity photograph for the streamlined 1934 Chrysler Airflow car Geddes designed in which Geddes staged Byron Foy, the president of the DeSoto Motor Corporation, next to the chairman of Chrysler, holding up a scale model of the "Flying Wing" aircraft from *Horizons*.

The most compelling elements that illustrate Geddes's argument for a unified modern industrial design in *Horizons* are the pairs of "Before and After" photographs: the upright 1932 Packard and the 1929 marbleized imitation-cabinet Magic Chef gas stove set side-by-side with his own ultra-modernistic streamlined designs (**FIG. 1, 2**). Although the old and the new fulfill exactly the same function, the difference in image and aesthetic was crucial for Geddes's wider aims to promote a quintessentially modern lifestyle for America. As in the theater, Geddes's promotion of streamlining in his industrial designs relied on image for its impact; yet this was underpinned by the engineering innovations Geddes introduced in the construction of stoves and refrigerators, as well as the homes they were intended to be set in, which also derived from his work in theater. Indeed, the stage could be seen as a relatively free space for experimentation through which Geddes evolved the design concepts and mechanical principles that he carried into his industrial and architectural work.

His development of technological innovations for mobile and modular sets to enable rapid theatrical set changes led directly to his development of modular appliances and to his concept for mobile walls in houses. Equally, it was the extensive mechanical and architectural expertise gained during his career in theater that formed the basis for his home and kitchen designs, and helped to define a specifically modern domestic lifestyle.

Two particular Broadway productions offer examples of the complex relationship between Geddes's theater designs and his industrial and architectural work. Geddes's 1936 staging of his own script for *Iron Men* showcases his architectural designs as well as his industrialization of the theater. It illustrates the way in which he transferred concepts from his design work for industry back into the theater. The production also demonstrates his typical focus on contemporary social issues. The second production discussed here, his 1928 scenic designs for Ashley Dukes's adaptation of Alfred Neumann's *The Patriot*, conversely shows how Geddes subsequently adapted staging techniques to both industrial design and domestic architecture.[2]

Geddes explicitly adopted industrial standards and imagery for the theater in the setting for *Iron Men*. The whole play (originally conceived by Geddes in 1924–25 as a film script titled "The Steel Story") was organized around the construction of a skyscraper frame that was bolted together on stage, piece by piece, during the performance. Geddes's set designs were actual engineering blueprints (**FIG. 3, 4**). Steel posts and girders formed the acting area, each labeled by numbers (C1-60 or S4-59, etc.) with notes

NORMAN BEL GEDDES DESIGNS AMERICA

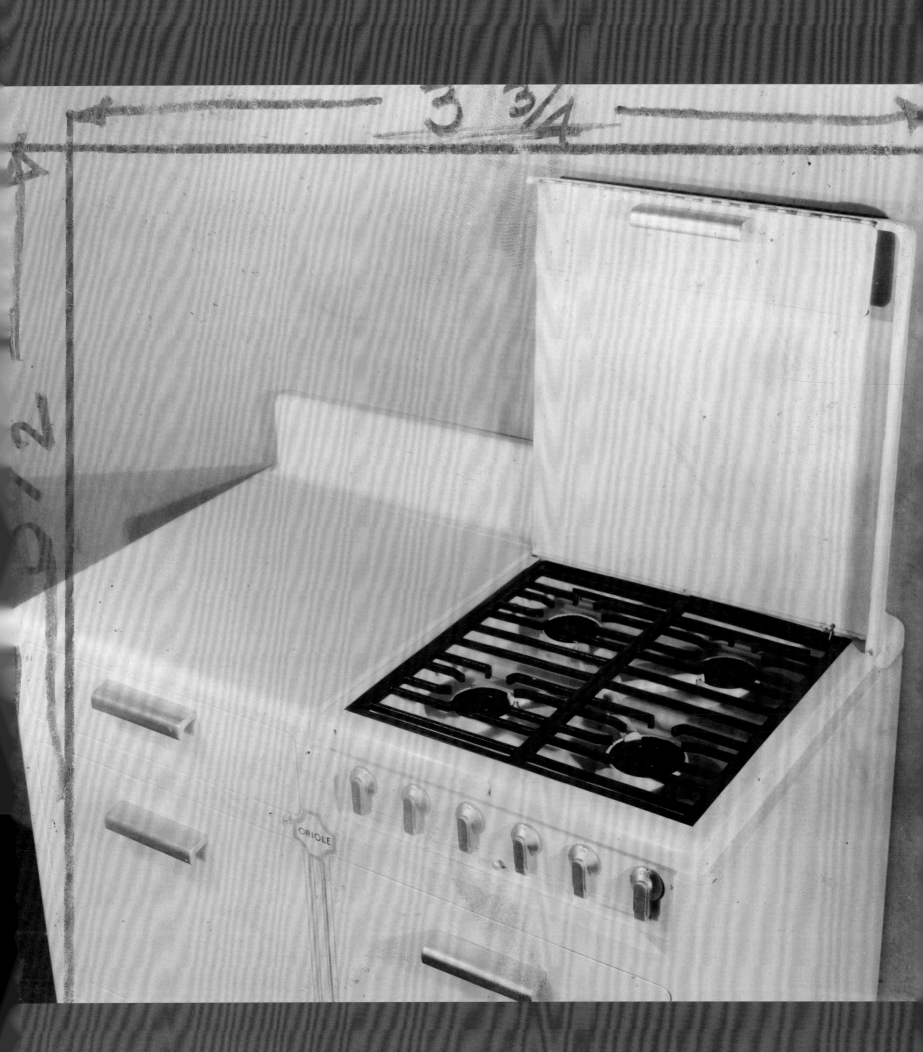

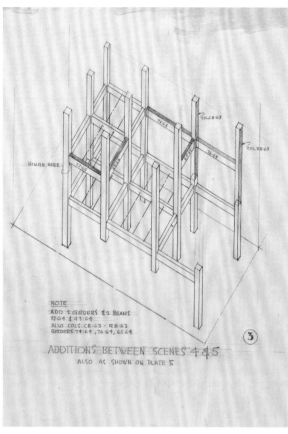

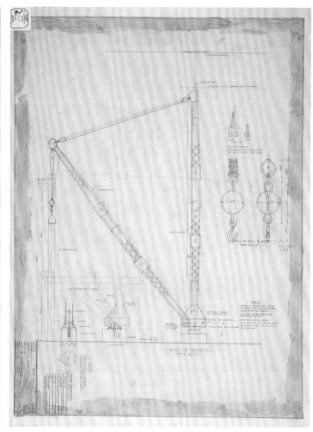

not, as one would expect, on the visual effect, but solely on technical structural requirements such as "Girder D must be designed to take LL [live load] of 3,000 lbs."[3] The top section of a crane which swung the girders into position appeared diagonally through the middle of this rising steel frame. Indeed, the main dramatic action was the actual construction, in full view of the audience, of a massive steel scaffold, representing the fifty-ninth to sixty-first floors of a midtown Manhattan office tower (**FIG. 5**). This corresponded with Geddes's aim of industrializing the stage, applying engineering principles to scenic techniques, discussed at length in chapter 7 of *Horizons*, "Industrializing the Theater."[4] This goal also led to his designs for "Factory Theater" buildings, where a repertoire of plays could be mounted on production-line principles: entertainment appropriate to the modern age he was intent on promoting. But the aim of the *Iron Men* show was also to expose audiences to an up-to-the-minute, in-depth view of the most modern, urban life that was literally rising around the theater in which they were sitting.

The 1930 competition between the builders of the art deco Chrysler Building and the bank tower at 40 Wall Street to construct the tallest building in the world was still, just about four years after the fact, very much in the public consciousness. (This was won, briefly and suspensefully, by Chrysler architect William Van Alen, who had the 185-foot-high spire fabricated inside the gleaming steel ellipses of the crown and, as soon as the bank tower had been topped out, pushed up through the peak to make the Chrysler Building the tallest in the world—only to be out-topped by the even taller Empire State Building just a year later.) The romance of this battle for the heights was intensified by dramatic newspaper photographs of steelworkers laboring on these and other skyscrapers, high above the structures below, nonchalantly balancing on thin girders without safety lines or hard hats. [5]

The characters in Geddes's play, all steelworkers, reflected these events and reinforced the interconnections between Geddes's theater and contemporary life, while simultaneously expressing his socialist politics.[6] The actors functioned as real roustabouts and welders, while (according to a carefully orchestrated pre-performance publicity leak) an actual steelworker, who had never before acted professionally, played the lead role (**FIG. 6**). This casting method had become an established practice in Geddes's search for realism. In 1935's *Dead End*, too, none of the children in the cast were trained actors, but were cast, as Geddes's advertising emphasized, from the Madison Square Boys Club, a charitable youth center in Manhattan. Though the mean streets depicted in *Dead End* were different from the architectural aspirations and hardy laborers of *Iron Men*, both speak to Geddes's political aims, and appealed to contemporary social concerns (**FIG. 7**). A performance of *Dead End* was broadcast as part of the 1936 "Mobilization for Human Needs" radio campaign, motivating the New York Police Department to open a Community Youth Center. Even the White House became involved, as Eleanor Roosevelt hosted a group of the child actors and showcased them in her radio and newspaper charity appeals.[7]

While these two productions are indicative of the social and thematic links between Geddes's theater interests and contemporary American life, *The Patriot*, more importantly, demonstrates Geddes's development of particular theatrical elements that became the basis for several of his industrial and architectural designs. At first glance the play's theme might make it seem an unlikely project for Geddes, but its production offered a significant challenge in terms of stage design (**FIG. 8**). However, this fast-moving epic about the assassination of the son of Catherine the Great, Tsar Paul I, whose plans for social reform aroused aristocratic opposition, posed a compelling technical challenge for Geddes that

FIGURE 5
Derrick construction during a performance of Francis Gallagher's Iron Men*, 1936. Contact prints by Lucas-Pritchard Studio, each 10 x 1½ in., 25.4 x 3.8 cm*

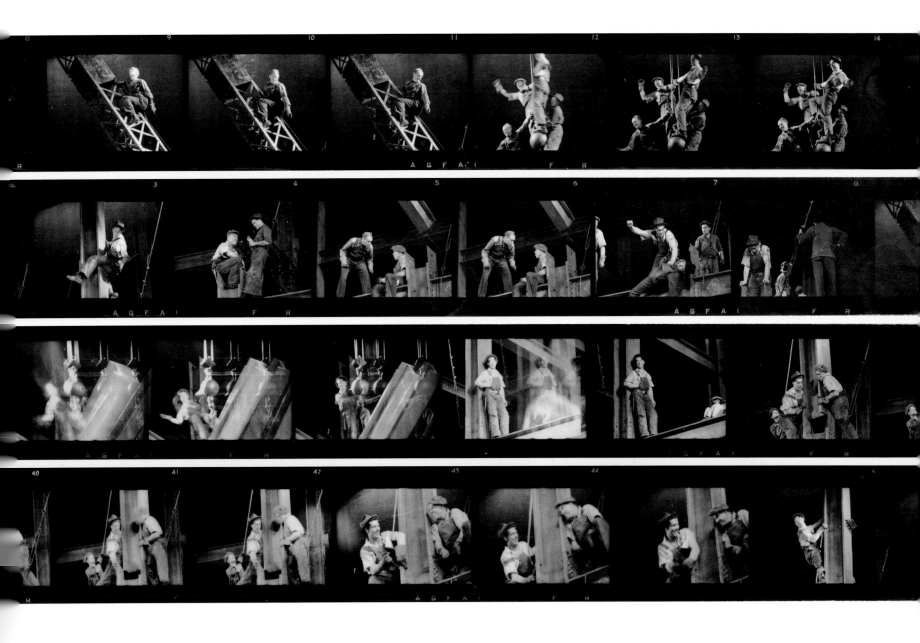

produced some of his most significant concepts for the modern American home.

The play called for elaborate settings and numerous, almost instantaneous, scene changes. The action shifted between five different locales, and in several scenes characters exited from one place carrying on a dialogue that was resumed, almost uninterrupted, in the next. The standard solution would have been to set scenes on a revolving stage,

the room for the next scene, already fully constructed, were swung down onto the platform from above, while a ceiling, hinged to the back of the proscenium, was lowered to hide the other pieces of scenery hanging overhead (**FIG. 9**). More significantly, even though this was not mentioned in the reviews and commentary on the production, the mechanics of this type of scene change required all the various rooms to be designed as interchangeable modules.

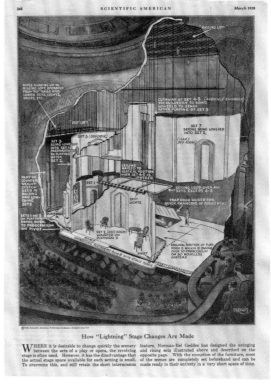

as had been done in European productions of the play. Yet, mounting just two scenes on a circular floor cut the acting area of the stage in half, and each additional scene made the stage even smaller and more cramped. The challenge was to create palatial spaces that the historical grandeur depicted in the play demanded. In response, Geddes developed a novel mechanism that made extremely rapid scene changes possible, while still allowing the actors to use the whole stage in each scene. His solution was to lower complete scenes on wires from the flies, while two platforms, each holding half of a complete set, pivoted out of each side wing on silent castors to meet in the center of the stage. Each setting was changed out of sight in the wings. The walls forming

Geddes's solution was innovative enough to be discussed at length by *Scientific American* (**FIG. 8**). (In the 1920s and 1930s, articles on Geddes's set designs were frequently featured in *Scientific American*, demonstrating the crossing of theatrical and industrial boundaries that characterized his work.)

Geddes's designs for Standard Gas Equipment Corporation (SGE) stoves came directly from the use of interchangeable modules in *The Patriot*. By 1930, less than two years after the opening of *The Patriot*, Geddes was sketching out a schema for cooking ranges that made stove parts interchangeable. SGE had been manufacturing about a hundred models in various sizes and configurations, each with different sizes of broilers and ovens. Geddes simplified their

FIGURE 7 (LEFT)
Geddes model of the stage set for Dead End, *c. 1935. Child actors climbed out of the "river" in* Dead End *using the ladder in the middle foreground. Mixed media, 32 x 20 x 29 in., 81.3 x 50.8 x 73.7 cm*

FIGURE 8 (RIGHT)
Oliver M. Saylor illustration of the stage mechanism for The Patriot *in* Scientific American, *March 1928.*

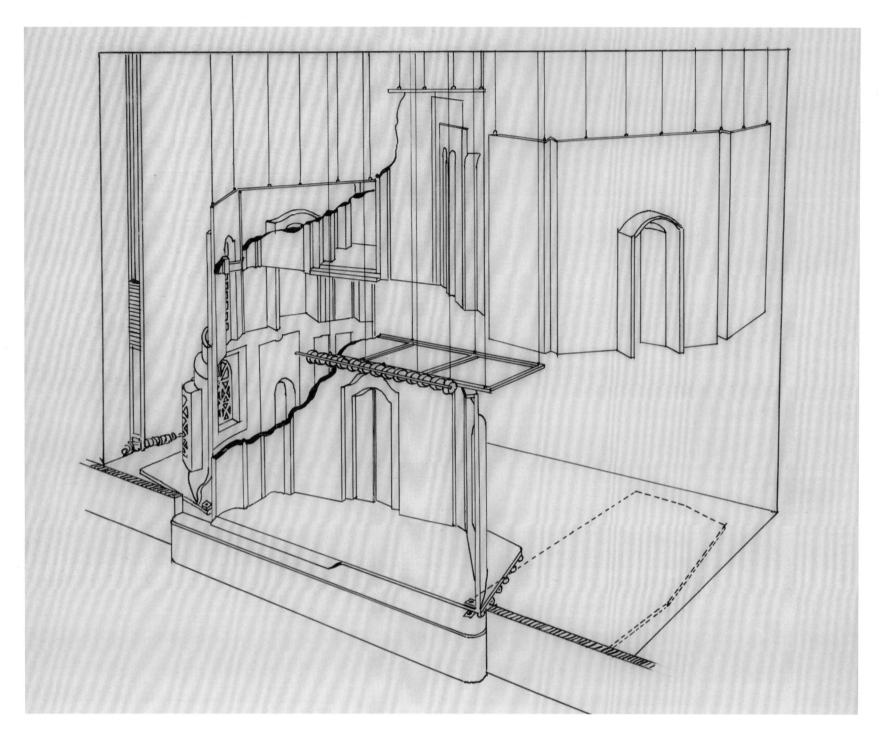

production by devising standard modules: three sizes of broilers, five sizes of utility drawers, a single oven, etc. The result was a cooking machine. Since their proportionate sizes allowed broilers, utilities, and cook tops to be arranged around an oven in a variety of configurations to suit the individual consumer, this system represented an unusually democratic form of manufacturing. In addition, Geddes's design streamlined the production process and introduced revolutionary new engineering principles, hiding all the mechanics. To gain the new, clean lines he envisaged, Geddes came up with a completely new type of construction, patented in

1933, which he compared to a skyscraper in miniature: an independent steel frame onto which the thin enamel skin was attached with hooked clips **(FIG. 10–11C)**. Geddes used the same principles for the refrigerators he designed for Electrolux. The system became standard for kitchen appliances and remained the typical method of construction into the 1970s. Indeed, the average stove maintains much the same shape and structure today.

At the end of World War II, Geddes turned to designing standardized, low-cost suburban houses for mass production by the Housing Corporation of America. Fifteen years after producing his SGE stove

FIGURE 10 (TOP LEFT)
Patent drawing of SGE Gas Stove Casing; patent awarded to Geddes June 13, 1933.

FIGURE 11A, 11B, 11C
Philadelphia Gas Works publicity piece for "The Modern Acorn Gas Range," c. 1930s.

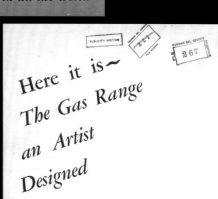

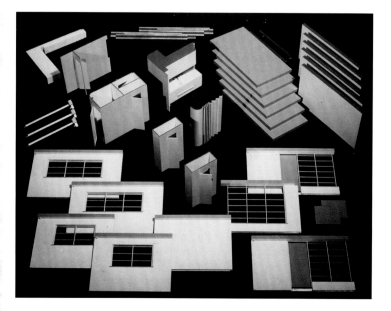

designs, Geddes developed an architectural model based on the same principle as the SGE stoves and, fundamentally, his modular theater sets. All elements of the homes Geddes designed were modules that could be fitted together in different ways for a variety of living arrangements. The exterior walls and flat roof sections were pre-manufactured in a "sandwich construction" of thin concrete sheets with an expanded steel core (to be filled with pipes, wiring, and insulation)—an equivalent to the canvas-covered "flats" that were lashed together to form a scene in a conventional theater set—while internal support was provided by the built-in cupboards that came as self-standing units (FIG. 13, 14). Geddes partnered with the Revere company (for whom he had designed a line of metal giftwares in 1934) and wrote specifications that were published in an illustrated booklet titled "For us the living... better homes" or

"Tomorrow's Homes for the Many" but commonly referred to as *Better Living* (FIG. 12). Since Revere was primarily a manufacturer of decorative brass and copper household items, Geddes's unified housing designs formed the basis of a national advertising campaign for the company's products, giving Geddes's ideas wide coverage. (By 1945, the company had distributed more than 800,000 copies of the "Better Living" booklet.)

In fact, all the houses Geddes designed had features derived from the theater. His "House of Tomorrow" (designed for the *Ladies' Home Journal* in 1931 and republished in *Reader's Digest* [8] and in *Horizons*) had a circular garage equipped with a revolving floor—in effect a miniature stage revolve—that allowed cars to be driven straight in and automatically turned around so they could be driven straight out again with no need to reverse (FIG. 15, 16). The interior walls of the house were movable—like the flats of stage scenery—and could be reconfigured almost at will, while the variable-intensity electric lighting supplying the rooms was unique in ordinary homes but standard in the theater. Striking in its "rejection of the traditional styles and conventions of the past," as Geddes wrote in the *Ladies' Home Journal*, this house represented a veritable machine for living. Designed specifically to reflect the spirit of the age, with its curving corners, flat roof, and absolutely plain walls with built-in closets and furniture, the house presented an image of streamlining that became widely popular.

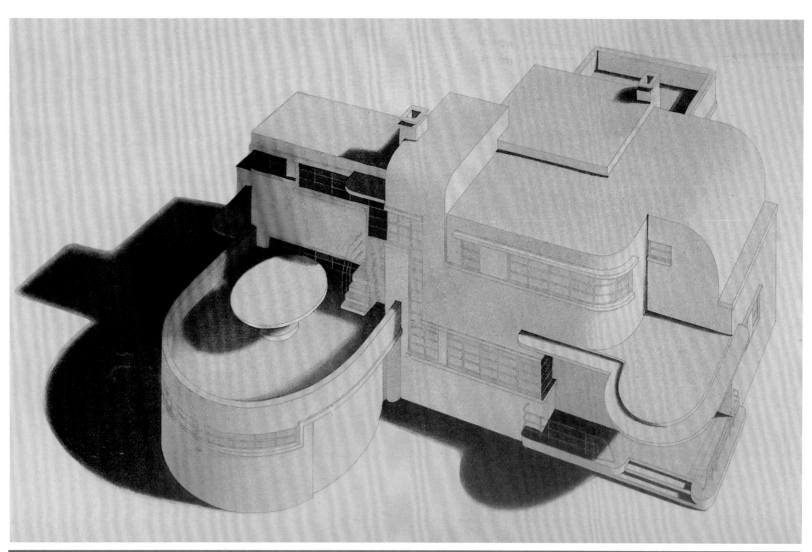

Theater also played a role in Geddes's concept of the way these houses should be decorated, at least in terms of the kitchen, which (given the emphasis on women's status that came from his socialist principles) was for Geddes the center of a household. The color white, for instance, had much significance for Geddes: As he noted in *Horizons*, it is universally accepted as the most sanitary color. But it also had strong theatrical connotations, since in both his sketched production of *The Divine Comedy* and in his designs for *The Miracle*, white clothing for Dante's Beatrice and for the repentant nun represented spiritual purity and moral cleansing, standing out against the dark shades of hell or the earthy colors of ordinary people. Geddes's concern for unity in design expanded from the glossy white enamel that he introduced in stoves and refrigerators to kitchens as a whole. Geddes insisted that the kitchen cupboards should be white and in modules echoing the proportions of the appliances. The result was a clean, high-tech center, which, as *Fortune* magazine noted, would be as antiseptic as a hospital in its "porcelain and surgical white."[9]

What is striking is the extent to which Geddes carried his work on Broadway over into these architectural and home appliance designs, using the theater as a source and (in a sense) testing ground for his industrial concepts. The designs were consciously intended to promote a specifically modern domestic lifestyle, and Geddes promoted them for industry solely in terms of images and their subliminal messages. While functionality had been a major focus in *Horizons*, subsequently it was the styling and color of his refrigerators and stoves—the visual impression and its symbolic connotations—that became Geddes's focus. Indeed, Geddes tended to downplay the mechanical and structural innovations he had introduced to the home appliance industry; his extensive publicity campaign for his stove and refrigerator designs, through interviews and journal articles, focused on impression. Thus, he stated that his kitchen appliances were all designed on the principles of "simplicity, freedom from intricate decoration, reliance upon the beauty of form" and were "in tune with our ever progressing civilization."[10] Yet in a very real sense it is the technical principles carried over from theater that have been one of Geddes's most compelling contributions to contemporary lifestyles. From the 1930s to today, mobility characterizes our society, while modules have become an accepted way of viewing experience.

ENDNOTES

1   See Jeffrey L. Meikle, *Twentieth Century Limited: Industrial Design in America, 1925–1939 2nd Ed.* (Philadelphia: Temple University Press, 2001), 48.

2   *The Patriot,* by Alfred Neumann, was originally performed in Berlin, directed by Karl Heinz Martin, in 1927. The Broadway show was subsequently turned into a movie by Ernst Lubitsch, starring Emil Jannings as Czar Paul I and Neil Hamilton as Crown Prince Alexander—a role played on Broadway by Sir John Gielgud—in the last silent movie to win an Oscar.

3   These plans and elevations, forming the set design for *Iron Men*, are preserved in Job 353, Flat File, Folders 1–10, Geddes Papers.

4   Norman Bel Geddes, *Horizons* (Boston: Little, Brown, 1932), 140f (see in particular 146–50).

5   For example, see untitled article in the *New York Times*, 2 August 1926: n.p., Job 353, DR-19, Geddes Papers.

6   While there is no record of Geddes directly involving himself in any political campaign, his concern for urban poverty is implicit in stage productions like *Dead End*, just as his support for the condition of the working class is clear in his chapter in *Horizons* on "What Price Factory Ugliness" (200f)—and his praise for Soviet Russia as "one of the greatest experiments the world has ever known," because they "look ahead and see where they are going." *Horizons*, 289–90.

7   See Eleanor Roosevelt, *New York World Telegram*, 17 February 1927: n.p. Other articles on the social importance of *Dead End* appeared in *Commonweal* (8 November 1935), *America* (30 November 1935), and *Catholic World* (2 December 1935).

8   April 1931 issue of *Ladies' Home Journal* and (in a compressed form) May 1931 issue of *Reader's Digest*.

9   "Color in Industry," unidentified publication, 1 February 1930: n.p.

10   Geddes interview, *Ladies' Home Journal* 48 (January 1931).

10

DERN

by

FURNITURE

Christopher Long

EET

MPETITION

ver the course of his career, Norman Bel Geddes repeatedly engaged the problem of designing furniture for the modern age. It was never a sustained inquiry for him, however; he accepted jobs when they came to him, and he "solved" these problems with his usual efficiency and well-sharpened design logic. The result was a sundry collection of pieces, some good, some less so, some at the cutting edge, some decidedly *retardataire*, or at least unambitious. But Geddes's furniture designs offer a chronicle of his shifting approaches to fashioning the modern environment, and even more, they reveal some of his attitudes and his aesthetic assumptions about living in the new industrial age.

One of Geddes's first commissions for furniture came in 1928, not long after he opened his industrial design office, when he was asked to create a line of modern bedroom furniture for the Simmons Company of Chicago.[1] He responded with a group of steel pieces sporting simple, right-angled lines and smooth surfaces (**FIG. 1**). Their overall cast was remarkable for the time. They were unquestionably the most "modern" American designs of the 1920s, far more hard-edged and spartan than anything else being made in the country at the time. In 1928, most American designers were still wedded to the modernized classicism of the French; what Geddes produced for Simmons was closer in form and spirit to works of the leading designers at the German Bauhaus or of the Dutch De Stijl movement. And Geddes not only made individual pieces with the new look but entire ensembles. The Simmons Company previously had only offered beds and nightstands; Geddes convinced Z. G. Simmons Jr., the company's owner, to add dressing tables, a highboy, and various chairs to complete the suite (**FIG. 3**).

But if the elemental cast of the pieces reflected the crisp-edged, geometric aesthetic of the European avant-garde, Geddes's approach had at least as much to do with his belief in the importance of matching material and form. He had sought, he told one reporter, to use metal in a way that was true to its fundamental properties: "Metal furniture had previously imitated wood. This not only involves needless expense but is also poor sales psychology, bringing about an undesirable reaction when touch discloses

that the furniture is of metal. Materials should be permitted to be themselves, honestly and openly, in order that the best effects be obtained."[2]

Yet Geddes's "material honesty" had its limits. Although the designs imitated neither wood nor traditional forms, most of their surfaces were painted, either "black and burnished," so that they reflected "light like black glass," or one of several other color combinations, "veridian green and brass, blue and ivory, and maroon lacquer and ivory."[3]

The new line, which premiered at the Hale Bedding Company in New York City in mid-October 1929, was a great success—at least according to the publicity materials Geddes's office sent out to the media. As a prepared write-up in *Retailing* described it, the pieces prompted so much attention from retailers and consumers that the store was reportedly "obliged to remove the suite from display because of the inability to supply the demand."[4] Given their keenly honed rectilinearity, it is difficult to imagine, in a period when Americans were just beginning to embrace modernism, that they were really so much in demand: The statement smacks instead of Geddes's skill as a promoter for his own work. But the fact that the Simmons Company continued to produce the designs in relatively large numbers through the mid-1930s is a testament to Geddes's capacity for finding a modern expression that many could accept—and would willingly purchase.

Geddes, though, was ever the pragmatist when it came to dealing with his clients. Immediately before he began working for Simmons, he had created a series of much less challenging designs—all for beds—for the Warren Rome Metallic Bed Company of Rome, New York. The beds, most executed in wood, drew from the standard language of the French-inspired "modernistic" style in America, with stair-stepped massing and classicized details (**FIG. 2**). They were much less expressive of the new functionalism than the Simmons pieces and also much less refined—undoubtedly a reflection of the client's more conservative tastes and a testament to Geddes's willingness to adapt his work to different needs.

Geddes's desire to meet his clients' requirements, rather than to proffer a more extreme design statement, seems also to have driven his

OVERLEAF

FIGURE 1 (TOP LEFT)
Simmons Company twin day bed designed by Geddes, c. 1928–29. Photograph by unidentified photographer, 10 x 8 in., 25.4 x 20.3 cm

FIGURE 2 (TOP RIGHT)
Geddes-designed beds for the Warren Rome Metallic Bed Company, c. 1933–34. Publicity photograph, 10 x 7¾ in., 25.4 x 19.7 cm

FIGURE 3 (BOTTOM)
Model room showing bedroom furniture for the Simmons Company, c. 1929. Photograph by unidentified photographer, 10 x 8 in., 25.4 x 20.3 cm

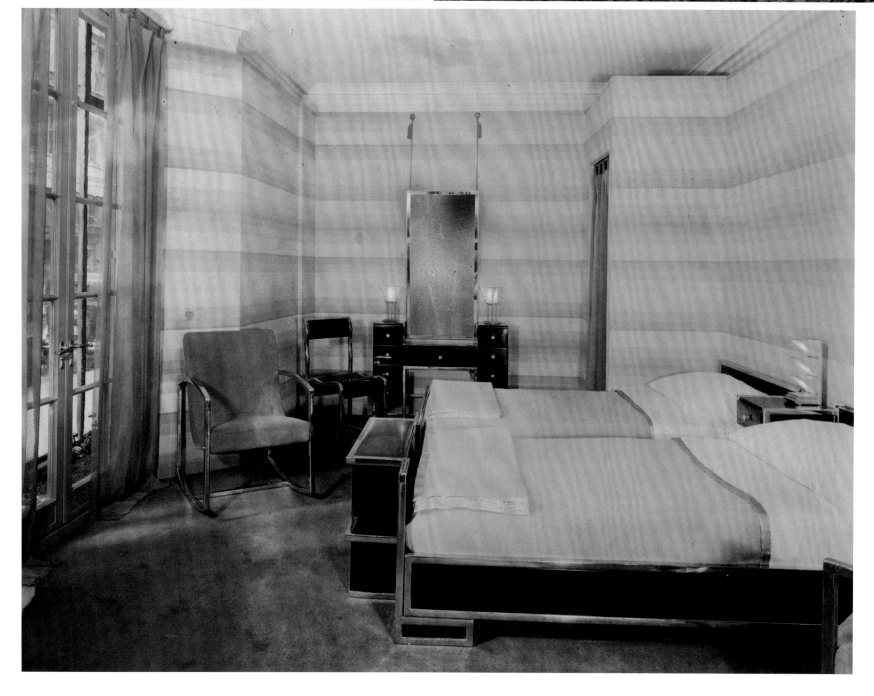

installation in the offices of the J. Walter Thompson advertising agency in the new Graybar Building in New York City in 1929. The company hired him to design an unfinished two-story room to serve as a small auditorium and meeting space (FIG. 6–8).[5] The lobby area and auditorium, which seated approximately forty people, featured several of Geddes's designs for furnishings, among them black lacquer "box" chairs with green upholstery and an upholstered bench with a wooden base (FIG. 4, 5). Although his straightforward presentation of the spaces ("carried out appropriately lacking in meaningless ornament," as one reporter noted) was unquestionably modern, it was a mitigated modernism, with softened contours and materials chosen specifically for an upscale environment.[6] The upholstery had the effect of "blotting" the edges of what were otherwise very simple forms, and the fluting in the base of the stool—an unmistakable reference to the columns and pilasters in classical architecture—suggested a linkage with the past that was mostly

absent in Geddes's designs of the 1930s. Once more, he had adapted his work to suit the client.

This is even more apparent when one recalls that Geddes was already at work at the time on a number of the visionary designs that would form the substance of *Horizons* when it was published a little more than two years later. More inspired than the Thompson conference room were the drawings of interiors he prepared for House Number 3, executed in 1930, which formed one of the central chapters of his book.[7] His design for the piano in the house's living room, for example, relied on smooth contours and unembellished surfaces, employing the streamlined forms that would become his stock-in-trade (FIG. 9). Especially noteworthy is the large, L-shaped desk he created for the study (FIG. 10). Here, he melded the planar surfaces and crisp detailing of his Simmons designs with a streamlined leg and rounded chair, producing a look that was at once distinctive and novel.

Geddes wrote in *Horizons* that the house would feature "built-in furniture and other built-in equip-

ment," including "bathroom, kitchen, nursery furnishings and cabinets, bookshelves, desks, and sofas."[8] But the manifest differences between the pieces he conceived of as furniture and those he regarded as appliances are among the house's most arresting features. Geddes's design for the sleek, updated kitchen underscored his newfound interest in modularity. The idea that products like stoves were composed of a group of basic, functional forms that could be shifted around to make up an almost endless series of configurations would soon become a driving concept of a number of his designs.

... a plain out-and-out cooking machine with no frills, no gadgets, no decoration to dress it up. Its attractive appearance, its efficient operation and ease to clean and its economy of manufacture by mass production methods, combine to make it an almost ideal example of what a good industrial designer can and does do to improve living standards.[9]

It was not only the utilitarian look of the stove design that made it stand out, however. Geddes had sought from the outset to rationalize both its functions and the way in which it could be manufactured. He wrote,

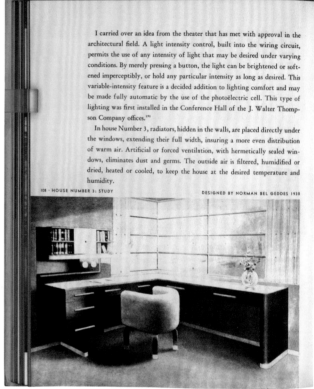

He used this idea in a particularly effective way for his Oriole stove for the Standard Gas Equipment Company, one of several designs he made for the company in the early 1930s (**FIG. 11**). Among its innovative features was the introduction of lightweight enameled sheet metal in place of cast iron and a solid base that replaced open legs and eliminated the necessity of cleaning underneath. He also employed insulated Bakelite handles and an automatic shut-off to the gas-cocks, which was activated when the lid was closed. For Geddes, the stove was:

*One of our aims is to standardize the different parts so that, without alteration, the same part, the oven for instance, could be used in all models. A series of blocks was made, painted in different colors to represent different classes of units, and various combinations tried. Eventually, after determining the proper sizes, it was found that the equivalent of most of the hundred stoves the client was then making could be made in four models, using only twelve different standardized units in various combinations (**FIG. 12A, 12B, 14**).[10]*

HERE IS THE MODERN
GAS RANGE

Designed by

NORMAN BEL GEDDES

TO MEET
TODAY'S COMPETITION

STANDARD GAS EQUIPMENT CORPORATION
IS BUILDING IT IN A SHORT LINE
...PRICED RIGHT FOR THE TIMES...

When Norman Bel Geddes sets his genius and the wheels of his busy organization to work to increase the utility and salability of an industrial product through modern design...the result is something for the trade that will meet the stiffest competition.

Standard Gas Equipment Corporation commissioned Norman Bel Geddes to design a range that would revitalize the gas industry.

The designer asked himself, "What is the most satisfactory gas range that can be imagined?" From there on he worked to create it.

He saw this: salesmen had been employed to get results...statisticians to compile results... economists to ponder results. Unquestionably, gas ranges had been sold by this policy. But those sales were more costly to both manufacturer and retailer than as if inherent salability had been built into the product.

Unquestionably the gas range had gone through an evolution. Improvements had been added from time to time to keep pace with or ahead of competition. But the business aspects of fresh new charm and effectiveness that would grow out of a design built up from the basic utility and

purpose of a gas range had never, as yet, been taken advantage of.

Into the field went Norman Bel Geddes men. They visited industry, trade and market. They interviewed 1,200 representative women users. They reported their findings.

The Norman Bel Geddes design for the Modern SGE Gas Range has no extraneous detail. Unnecessary outer appendages have been eliminated. It is easy to use and to keep clean. It has new improvements for better cooking results. Exterior revolution brought about internal improvements that make it superior in operation. All holdovers and gadgets from the dark ages of the industry have gone. In their place have come amazing beauty and greater salability. Yet this range cannot be mistaken. It looks like what it is and, still, it is more than it ever was before. Its manufacture presents possible economies in production that will make its cost to the consumer most attractive. Laboratory standardization has made it possible to manufacture it as a short line but a complete one. *The features of the basic model of this Modern SGE Gas Range line will be described in the next folder of this series.*

STANDARD GAS EQUIPMENT CORPORATION, 18 E. 41st Street, New York, N.Y.

THE MODERN SGE RANGE WILL MEET TODAY'S STIFFEST COMPETITION

FIGURE 13

The sitting areas in the Norman Bel Geddes & Co. offices, Rockefeller Center, June 27, 1940. Photograph by Richard Garrison, 10 x 8 in., 25.4 x 20.3 cm

The idea of rigorous standardization suggested a new image of modernity, although, as it turned out after the company explored the concept, it yielded little in the way of true cost savings.[11] The Oriole stove as it was mass-produced came in only a small number of configurations. Geddes nonetheless would go on to employ the same principles of functionality and a fluid language of form in his many designs for the Toledo Scale Company, Philco, Walter Kidde Sales Company, and other clients. What is most striking, though, is that he never applied the same logic to furniture design. In 1934, even after the publication of *Horizons*, Geddes's approach to furniture remained largely traditional, rooted in an

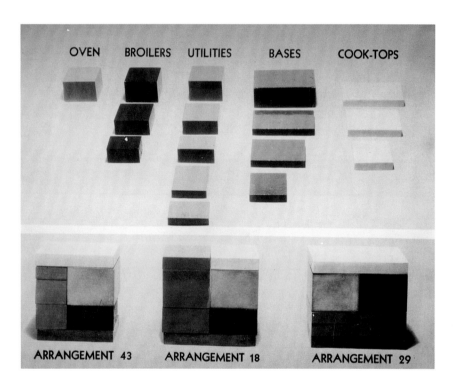

FIGURE 14
Massing study for Oriole stove for the Standard Gas Equipment Corporation, c. 1932. Photograph by Norman Bel Geddes & Co., 10 x 8 in., 25.4 x 20.3 cm

exploration of pure style rather than the possibilities of how his designs might be used or made. In that year, he began work on a wide array of pieces for a new suite of offices for his rapidly expanding firm, housed on the eighth floor of the Associated Press Building in Rockefeller Center.

Ever aware of the importance of imagery for marketing (in this instance, for his own firm), Geddes lavished attention on the project, generating a broad assortment of designs. The challenge of coming up with a magazine rack for the reception room, for example, gave rise to several different types, including

one with simple curves and straight lines, with semi-cylindrical supports and a square top, and another with a round base and two round shelves supported by a central rounded column (**FIG. 15**). The drawings display his penchant and skill for formal inventiveness, but they lack the rigor of his other product designs. They are the outcome of his imagination, not a sustained search for the practical or the good.

For a few of these designs, Geddes even resorted to older forms. A table he designed in Circassian walnut, with a square top and base, round apron, and curving, classical legs, was reminiscent of Neoclassical tables of the late eighteenth and early nineteenth centuries—an homage to the time of the French Empire and the Central European Biedermeier (**FIG. 16**). It was a conspicuous return to history and oddly unmodern for a designer who had so loudly trumpeted the idea of recasting the very morphology of design. The offices, as they were eventually completed, adopted a much cleaner and simpler form-language, at once relaxed and manifestly elegant (**FIG. 13**). But they were hardly revolutionary.

The question, then, with Geddes's furniture, is why his designs were not more assertively new, that is, more in line with his designs for automobiles, exhibitions, or commercial products. Aside from his pieces for Simmons, Geddes offered little that was important or memorable. Unlike many of his American contemporaries—Donald Deskey, Paul T. Frankl, Richard Neutra, Gilbert Rohde, R. M. Schindler, Kem Weber, or Russel Wright—he created no iconic furniture designs, nothing that stood apart from the modernists' usual efforts. Even later, after World War II, when he undertook a small number of designs for the Valley Upholstery Company, he offered pieces very much in the mainstream, derived in large measure, it seems, from the earlier works of Bruno Mathsson and other Scandinavian modernists.

Part of the explanation, no doubt, rests with the fact that furniture never had a central place in his program. When he opened his industrial design practice in the late 1920s, he was preoccupied with other issues—with the problems of commerce and display, and later with transportation, speed, and movement. The intimate scale of furniture appeared to hold little interest for him. But perhaps more important is that

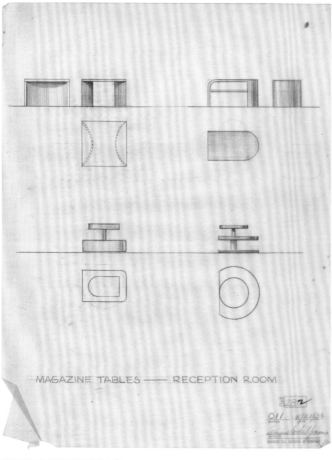

MAGAZINE TABLES —— RECEPTION ROOM

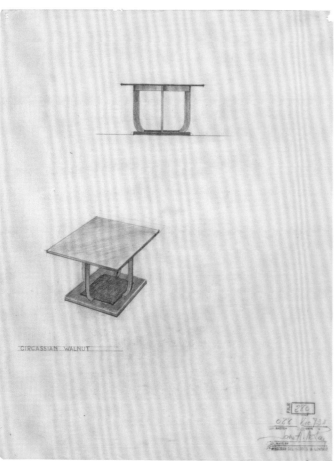

CIRCASSIAN WALNUT

he never fully addressed the concept of furniture as an industrial product. With the notable exception of his brief stint working for the Simmons Company, he expended little time examining either the possibilities of new materials in furniture or how they might be mass-manufactured. Most of his designs were quite conventional in terms of material and fabrication. He simply did not devote the same attention to furniture that he gave to stoves or clocks or automobiles. Perhaps, in the end, he thought of furniture as passé, a dead end. Perhaps he deemed the field of furnishings too static, too closely tied to traditional modes of living. It represented an end for him, it seems, when he was searching for a new beginning.

ENDNOTES

1 Geddes signed the contract with Zalman G. Simmons Jr. in October 1928, Box 7, Folder 136.1, Geddes Papers.

2 "Simmons Co. Offers Suite by Bel Geddes," *Retailing*, 19 October 1929.

3 Ibid.

4 Ibid. See also "Manufacturers Use Ensemble Displays," *New York Journal of Commerce*, 18 November 1929; "Modern Metal Furniture Opens Way to New Bed Covering Ensembles," *Retailing*, 2 November 1929; "Steel Furniture for the Modern Bedroom," *Retailing*, 2 November 1929.

5 The total cost for the project was $10,000, a very large sum at the time for an office space. Letter from Geddes to Mr. Stanley Resor, 4 June 1928, J. Walter Thompson Correspondence, Box 6, Folder 133.1, Geddes Papers.

6 "A Modern Room for a Modern Purpose," *American Architect* (20 July 1929): 99–102.

7 See Norman Bel Geddes, *Horizons* (Boston: Little, Brown, 1932), esp. 135–36.

8 Ibid., 138.

9 Caption for a publicity photograph of the Oriole stove, Photo Box 5, Folder 267.2, Geddes Papers.

10 Publicity copy for the Oriole stove, Box 13, Folder 267.3, Geddes Papers.

11 Letters from W. Frank Roberts to Geddes, 1 and 5 September 1933, Box 13, Folder 267.1, Geddes Papers.

FIGURE 15 (TOP)
Consuelo de Yoama sketch of magazine tables for the reception room, Norman Bel Geddes & Co. offices, Rockefeller Center, 1939; designed November 21, 1934. Pencil on paper, 8½ x 11 in., 21.6 x 28 cm

FIGURE 16 (BOTTOM)
Jane A. McKay sketch of Circassian walnut table for the Norman Bel Geddes & Co. offices, Rockefeller Center, 1939; designed December 7, 1934. Pencil on paper, 8½ x 11 in., 21.6 x 28 cm

11

DOMESTIC MEDIA DESIGNS

Nick Muntean

orman Bel Geddes's involvement in the consumer electronics industry began in 1930, just as radio was achieving widespread consumer adoption and cultural influence, and ended shortly after World War II, when the industry began to shift its focus to television. Due to the changing needs of the market over the fifteen years he worked in the electronics industry, and the various constraints imposed upon him by manufacturers (who often required Geddes to base his designs on their existing chassis), Geddes's contributions to radio cannot be distilled to one particular aesthetic style or design innovation. However, taken as a whole, Geddes's work played a crucial role in domesticating the radio. His designs helped to jettison the hobbyist and industrial vestiges of radio's origins and allowed it to emerge, in Geddes's words, "as a unified whole . . . [that] would blend with the furnishings of any home of decent taste."[1]

Prior to World War I, radios were two-way communication devices sold as kits through mail-order, which users assembled at home. At the time, this piecemeal approach was necessary because the key patents of radio technology were held by a number of competing companies. Upon the United States entry into the war, the federal government consolidated this market by creating a new company, the Radio Corporation of America (RCA), to serve as a patent pool and radio manufacturer and to license radio patents to other manufacturers. After the war ended, RCA's legal structure remained intact, but its government contracts did not.

To offset diminished government demand, RCA, along with other manufacturers, sought to create a consumer market for radios. By 1923, the broadcast model of one-to-many communications emerged, and full-time radio stations developed in America's larger metropolitan areas. Early radio receivers were housed in rectangular wooden cabinets that users placed on a table and listened to via earpieces. (By 1927, the falling cost of amplification circuitry allowed for the addition of integrated loudspeakers.) These sets featured a bewildering array of knobs and dials that made them appear as though they had been pulled from a battleship's control room. In fact, this was often the case, as radio manufacturers frequently repurposed their surplus military inventory for the consumer market with little more than the addition of exterior wooden cladding.

After manufacturers exhausted their excess wartime stock, tabletop radios were replaced by "console" units, which integrated the radio receiver and loudspeaker in a freestanding cabinet. This cabinet style was first introduced in the late nineteenth century as a means for consumers to store sheet music. As phonographs replaced pianos in American homes, the cabinet was repurposed to house record players, with the additional space used to store record albums. Similarly, as radio receivers began to vastly outsell phonographs, these cabinets were then used to house radios.

Although this cabinet style provided far more space than was needed for the radio mechanism, the components were readily available at low cost to electronics manufacturers, and the public had already learned to integrate the cabinet design into their homes. For radio manufacturers in the 1920s, the physical appearance of their devices was a secondary concern, as they were relentlessly engaged in technological one-upmanship with their competitors, knowing that significant improvements in sound quality and reliability would attract the most customers. By the early 1930s, however, radio technology had become fairly refined, and manufacturers' offerings were more or less equal. Any further technological breakthroughs would require enormous capital investments in research and development, which seemed foolhardy amidst the economic uncertainty of the Great Depression. To set their products apart in the marketplace, manufacturers chose to focus instead on their devices' aesthetic qualities, a strategy that usually entailed adorning cabinets with ornate grilles and elaborately detailed woodwork.

Geddes viewed this approach as misguided: The form of radio cabinets was mired in the trappings of earlier eras and unrelated technologies. During the course of his work for Philco, Majestic, Emerson, RCA, and Federal, he sought to create a new form for radio, one uniquely tailored to the ways in which people actually used the technology. Such an ambitious goal was outside the control of any one person, but Geddes nevertheless managed to persistently work toward his vision for more than fifteen years.

PHILCO

While most radio manufacturers struggled in the wake of the Great Depression, Philco Radio thrived, largely due to the success of its Model 20 "Midget" radio introduced in August 1930. The Model 20 was a wholesale departure from the then-dominant console style, as it reintroduced the tabletop style used in the early 1920s. Unlike those earlier sets, however, it offered a built-in loudspeaker and no superfluous dials or knobs. It was sold at an aggressively low price of $49.95, and cash-strapped consumers bought more than 343,000 Model 20s in its first year of production.

The Model 20's massive sales caught Philco executives by surprise, but elation quickly turned to concern with the realization that they had no encore for the radio's category-defining performance. Knowing that other manufacturers would soon introduce their own versions of the Model 20, Philco offered Geddes an exclusive five-year contract, hop-

ing that his reputation for creativity would produce worthy successors to the Model 20.

Before embarking on the design process, Geddes conducted a consumer survey to discern the qualities consumers looked for when buying a radio set and to assess the overall health of the radio market. Geddes found that, despite the dismal economy, "1931 could be a record year in radio sales; design and price were the determining factors; 22,000,000 more radios could be sold before the market became saturated."[2]

Although Philco initially had grand ambitions for its partnership with Geddes, the worsening economy found the company unwilling to allocate the capital needed to produce radically new cabinet designs. Geddes developed a number of designs for the company's 1931 product line, and Philco produced a "Geddes Signature Series" of sorts, with each unit featuring a decal reading "This cabinet designed by Norman Bel Geddes," accompanied by a stylized facsimile of the designer's initials (FIG. 1). The company's management, however, approved the production of only one genuinely innovative Geddes

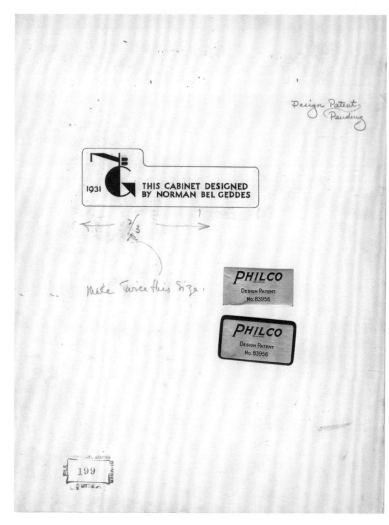

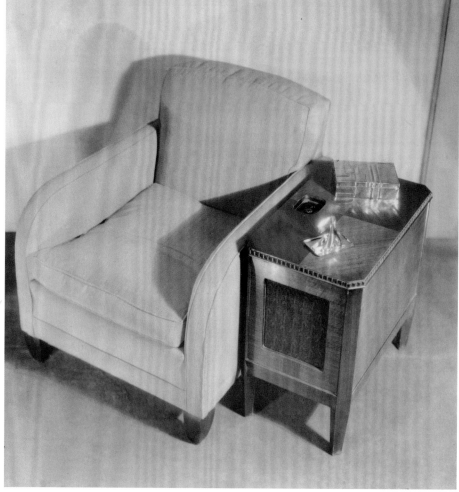

ELD

design, the Model 270 Lazyboy (**FIG. 2**). The three other Geddes-designed consoles that were released alongside the Lazyboy—the Model 112 Lowboy (**FIG. 3, 4**), the Model 112 Highboy (**FIG. 5, 6**), and the Model 212 Combination console—were little more than cosmetic variations of existing Philco cabinets. Geddes's Lazyboy, however, was an entirely new product and holds the distinction of being the first commercial radio expressly tailored to facilitate the

radio client, Majestic Radio, hoped he could bring the business back from the edge of ruin. Majestic had risen to prominence in 1928 by introducing the first radio to feature an electrodynamic loudspeaker, which provided unmatched clarity and tone. Other manufacturers soon copied Majestic's innovation, and as the Depression wore on, Majestic's sales stagnated, with the company losing more than $250,000 a year during the late 1930s.

FIGURE 4 (OPPOSITE)
Geddes original design drawing of the Philco Radio Model 112 Lowboy, c. 1931. Pencil on paper, 8½ x 11 in., 21.6 x 28 cm

FIGURE 5 (LEFT)
Geddes original design drawing of the Philco Radio Model 112 Highboy, c. 1931. Pencil on paper, 8½ x 11 in., 21.6 x 28 cm

user's listening habits. The top-mounted control panel allowed listeners to change stations without leaving their chairs, and, because the Lazyboy's cabinet was finished on all sides, it could be positioned anywhere in the room.

The Lazyboy proved to be a strong seller for Philco and firmly established Geddes's reputation in the consumer electronics industry (**FIG. 7**). Throughout the remainder of his contract, Geddes continued to provide Philco with new and innovative designs, but the company's growing fiscal conservatism kept those designs from entering production.

MAJESTIC

While Philco had enlisted Geddes's services to secure its dominant market position, Geddes's second

Majestic hired Geddes when his public profile was nearing its peak, just before the opening of his Futurama exhibit at the 1939–40 New York World's Fair. Seeking to capitalize on Geddes's prominent reputation, Majestic commissioned him to design two tabletop radios and one combination console. Because Majestic's biggest sales in the late 1930s had come from a tabletop radio adorned with the likeness of Charlie McCarthy (ventriloquist Edgar Bergen's famous sidekick), the manufacturer stipulated that each design include a similar "novelty" feature.

Like Philco, Majestic required Geddes to utilize the company's existing chassis as the basis for his designs. Though the chassis from the Charlie McCarthy model served as the frame for Geddes's

FIGURE 6 (MIDDLE)
The Philco Radio Model 112 Highboy sold for $169.50. The divoted half-round molding along the top of the console was a design touch featured on all of Geddes's Philco sets. The Highboy featured retractable doors that could be slid into place when the radio was not in use. Photograph by unidentified photographer, 9⅝ x 7⅝ in., 24.4 x 19.4 cm

FIGURE 7 (RIGHT)
Advertisement for Geddes-designed Philco Radios in the Saturday Evening Post, August 29, 1931. Courtesy of Royal Phillips Electronics.

Model 651 radio, this comical heritage was nowhere evident in Geddes's sleek, well-proportioned final product, his first manufactured Bakelite tabletop radio (**FIG. 9**). (He had designed one for Philco, but the company, unfamiliar with the material, shelved the design.) An alternative prototype for the Model 651 did include a "No-Grille" novelty feature; a wavy white plastic facade was suspended in front of the speaker location (**FIG. 10**). Geddes's Model 2A50 tabletop ra-

to have the "gadgetry" of entertainment consoles hidden out of sight. They were so impressed by the finished design, however, that they set aside their reservations and put the design into production.

Geddes's Majestic efforts sold well, but they constituted only three of the manufacturer's forty products for the 1940 model year and could do little to rescue the manufacturer from insolvency. Several months after the Geddes-designed units reached

FIGURE 8 (OPPOSITE)
The Majestic Radio model 2A50, c. 1939, featured a standard tuning dial, as well as push buttons for tuning to favorite stations (the push-button feature was first introduced in 1936 and was extremely popular with consumers). Photograph by unidentified photographer, 5⅛ x 4 in., 13 x 10.2 cm

dio (**FIG. 8**) offered an innovative, technical novelty feature, as the loudspeaker was internally mounted to a universal joint, which allowed users to direct the sound without moving the cabinet itself. (This feature was a cost-saving version of Geddes's original proposal, which had called for the speaker to be housed in its own cabinet, separate from the receiver.) [3]

Prefiguring his later designs for combination radio-phonograph consoles, Geddes provided Majestic with an angular, unornamented combination cabinet made of light wood and topped with a transparent plastic lid, which allowed users to view the phonograph mechanism in operation. Majestic's executives initially opposed the clear lid, arguing that seventy-five percent of radio buyers were women, and this important demographic preferred

stores, the company fell into receivership, and retailers soon began liquidating their Majestic inventories.

EMERSON

In the summer of 1940, Emerson Radio, the leading manufacturer of portable and tabletop radios, offered Geddes the opportunity to create what became his most iconic radio design.[4] With America already providing material support to the Allied nations, the country readied for war, and Emerson sought to capitalize on America's invigorated national pride by releasing a patriotically themed portable radio. Emerson's internal design team had been tasked with the assignment, but they had failed to produce an appropriate design. With production scheduled to begin in less than a month, Emerson's president turned to Geddes for an eleventh-hour solution.

FIGURE 9 (LEFT)
The Majestic Radio Model 651, 1939, Geddes's first Bakelite tabletop radio, retailed for $12.95. Photograph by Norman Bel Geddes & Co., 9½ x 7⅝ in., 24.1 x 19.4 cm

FIGURE 10 (RIGHT)
A never-produced, alternative prototype of the Majestic Radio Model 651 tabletop radio, c. 1939. Photograph by unidentified photographer, 8⅛ x 10 in., 20. 6 x 25.4 cm

FIGURE II

Geddes's most iconic radio design, the FC-400 Emerson Patriot Radio, c. 1940–41. Plastic, 11 x 6 x 9 in., 27.9 x 15.2 x 22.9 cm

Geddes had only one week to produce a final design. Because there was neither time nor money for creating elaborate new molds or dies, Geddes had to craft his design from Emerson's existing parts bin. Geddes designed a new tuning dial and star-engraved control knobs to complement his admixture of components selected from older Emerson portable models. The cabinet was cast from Monsanto's "Opalon" plastic, a variation of cast phenolic resin, and was adorned with a red, white, and blue color scheme. Buyers could choose from three versions of the set, each with a different patriotic color as the dominant theme (**FIG. II-12**). The Model FC-400 Patriot Radio hit retailers' shelves in the fall of 1940 and was an immediate success, with one

store reporting first-day sales of more than seven hundred units. The Patriot's popularity led Emerson to release a non-flag-inspired variation of the unit, dubbed "The Aristocrat," which became a perennial best-seller.

Little more than a year after the Patriot was introduced, the United States formally entered World War II, and the entire electronics industry ceased consumer production to devote their facilities to the manufacture of military hardware.[5] Despite the industry's disruption, most manufacturers breathed a sigh of relief, as their factories were running at capacity for the first time in over a decade, and financial analysts forecast a profoundly rehabilitated postwar economy.

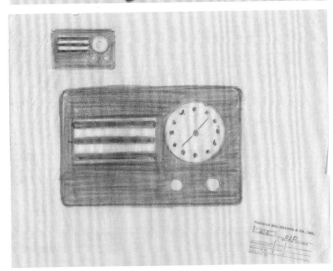

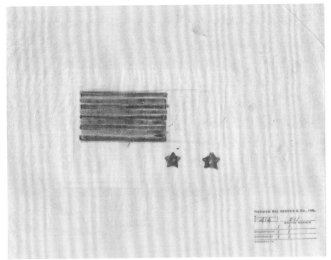

RCA

For RCA, the effects of the World War II production hiatus were mixed. Though they had unveiled a prototype television console at the 1939–40 World's Fair, just a short distance from Geddes's Futurama exhibit, the system required considerable work before it could be commercially viable. With all of the company's research and development resources committed to the war effort, television—which they hoped would become their new golden goose—was postponed indefinitely. In the interim, RCA executives decided to focus their attention on totally revamping their existing domestic entertainment offerings, a strategy described by one RCA executive as intended to "counteract the pre-war impression of RCA instrument mediocrity."[6]

FIGURE 11A–11D (LEFT)
Four preliminary drawings for the Emerson Patriot radio, c. 1940–41. Color pencil or crayon on paper, 11 x 8½ in., 28 x 21.6 cm

FIGURE 12 (ABOVE)
Davega City Radio advertisement for the Emerson Patriot radio, Sunday News, October 20, 1940.

Rebecca Hamilton, one of Geddes's senior employees, learned of RCA's planned redesign through some of her business acquaintances. With Geddes's approval, she met with RCA president David Sarnoff in October 1942, and—based largely on the strength of Geddes's recent work for Nash-Kelvinator—secured a contract to conduct a market forecast and analysis of the postwar consumer electronics landscape. With business at Geddes's office slow due to the war, Hamilton and Geddes entered the relationship with RCA in the hopes that it would eventually yield a full-blown design contract.

Their hopes were soon realized, for almost as soon as the market study began, RCA executives asked Geddes to analyze their "Insurance Line," which comprised the radio and phonograph devices designed before the war and which could be put into production days after an armistice was signed. Within a few months the scope of Geddes's work for RCA expanded to include an entirely new postwar product line, centered around RCA's highly secretive "Model X" project (**FIG. 13**), which in 1949 would be publicly introduced as the 45 rpm record format.

Much of Geddes's market study was, in fact, a design interface study, which identified the cabinet dimensions and control panel configurations best suited to users' needs and behavior (**FIG. 15**). Geddes presented RCA with a number of variations on a basic design. In one, compartments for record storage would fold out from either side of the console, the drawer directly above the grille would pull out to reveal the radio control knobs, and the top panel on the left side of the console would flip up to reveal the phonograph mechanism. This notion of user-oriented design greatly impressed the RCA executives, who admitted that previously only the needs of their retailers were taken into account during the design process.

Though RCA was quite willing to adopt Geddes's user-oriented design ethos, they still had corporate priorities of their own: Specifically, RCA's commitment to broadening the adoption of phonographs in the postwar era meant that all of their console offerings would be "combination" units. Following the style he first introduced in his combination design for Majestic, Geddes's RCA consoles possessed a balance and understated sophistication that made the entertainment consoles of the 1930s—crowded with pediments and pilasters—appear turgid and somber by comparison (**FIG. 14**).

While Geddes's RCA console designs refined and improved upon the industry's earlier console offerings, it was his portable radio designs for RCA that offered a wholesale reimagining of the design and potential functionality of an entire product category. Throughout the 1930s, portable radios had become an increasingly popular product category, but their size and form had been dictated by the large vacuum tubes and batteries then in use.[7] RCA was confident that its wartime research in micro-tubes would do away with those limitations and encouraged Geddes to be radically experimental in his portable radio designs.

Of the many designs Geddes produced for RCA, a proposal for a two-piece shoulder radio was advanced into the prototype stage of production. The design had two parts: an upper (all-black) portion that housed the receiver and earpiece plug, and a detachable lower speaker section. Extensive user testing showed that the optimal shape was a subtle "C" curvature, much like a pocket flask, as this was the only design found to fit both men's and women's

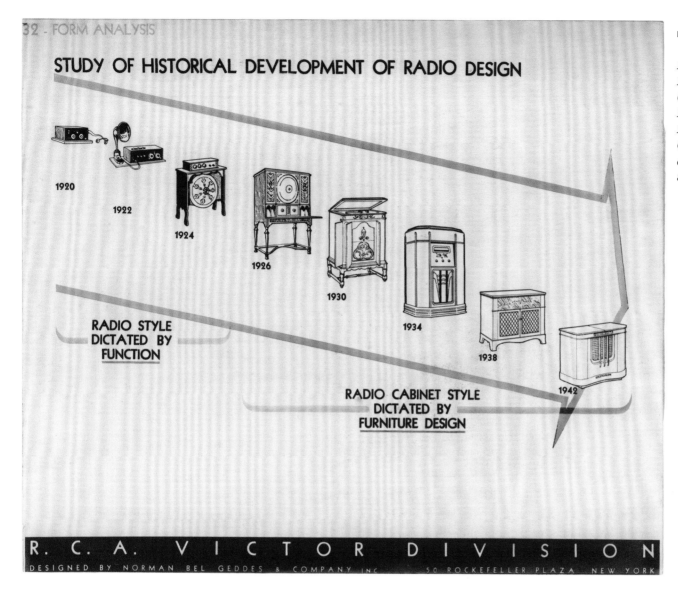

STUDY OF HISTORICAL DEVELOPMENT OF RADIO DESIGN

1920
1922
1924
1926
1930
1934
1938
1942

RADIO STYLE
DICTATED BY
FUNCTION

RADIO CABINET STYLE
DICTATED BY
FURNITURE DESIGN

R. C. A. VICTOR DIVISION
DESIGNED BY NORMAN BEL GEDDES & COMPANY INC   50 ROCKEFELLER PLAZA NEW YORK

FIGURE 14
"Study of Historical Development of Radio Design" in Norman Bel Geddes & Co. "Quarterly Report to R.C.A. Victor Division, Stationary Combinations—Stage 1," c. 1942–44. Photostat, 8¼ x 7 in., 21 x 17.8 cm

pockets without causing unsightly bulges or wrinkles (**FIG. 16, 17**). Though the RCA executives professed great admiration for the design, they shelved the project, claiming that consumers regarded earpieces as too physically intrusive and would be unwilling to use them.[8] Geddes's design would be vindicated a decade later when consumers flocked to buy transistor radios that featured an earpiece, built-in speaker, and overall form uncannily similar to that of Geddes's shoulder radio design.

FEDERAL

RCA was not the only electronics manufacturer who sought Geddes's help in developing postwar product lines. In 1946, after nearly forty years of manufacturing commercial radio and telegraph equipment, Federal Telephone and Radio decided to enter the

consumer market and hired Geddes to provide "the sex appeal" they wanted for their inaugural product line.[9] Unlike Geddes's earlier radio commissions, where his designs had to conform to an existing chassis, Federal offered Geddes the opportunity to exercise near complete creative control over the design process. Because of significant wartime advances in industrial manufacturing processes, Federal first hired Geddes to conduct an exhaustive survey of the state of the art in materials technology, after which Geddes began the formal design process.

The fruits of this research into new plastics and laminates can be seen in nearly every one of the eleven Geddes-designed models that Federal put into production. The 1510-T tabletop radio (**FIG. 20**), for instance, offered a molded plywood cabinet, alumi-

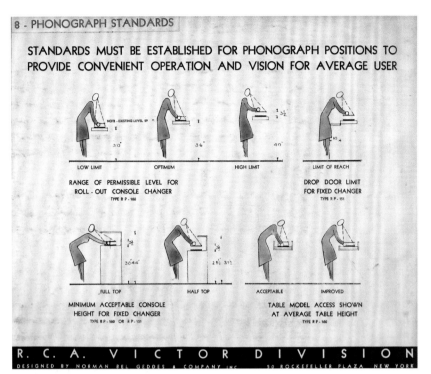

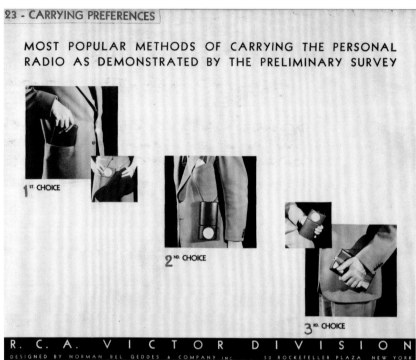

FIGURE 15 (LEFT)

Geddes motion study conducted to determine optional phonograph position standards, c. 1942–44. Photostat, 8½ x 7 in., 21.6 x 17.8 cm

FIGURE 16 (RIGHT)

Norman Bel Geddes & Co. "Quarterly Report to R.C.A. Victor Division, Personal Radio Study—Stage 1, Chart 23—Carrying Preferences," c. 1942–44. An experimental prototype for a new style of portable radio. These images demonstrate the three most popular methods for carrying the device, based on user studies conducted with Geddes's employees. Geddes had initially sought to conduct the study using members of the general public, but RCA refused to grant him permission, out of fear that a competitor might steal the design. Photograph of presentation book, 8⅜ x 7 in., 21.3 x 17.8 cm

num grille, and Plexiglas control knobs, at a competitive retail price of $35. Taking full advantage of then recent advances in plastics manufacturing, the 1031-TB tabletop radio achieved a unique hoodlike effect (**FIG. 21**). While the cabinet design of the all-wood 5000-CP combination console (**FIG. 19**) echoed Geddes's earlier combination consoles, Geddes's 2600-TP combination console (**FIG. 18**) was perhaps his most audacious design since the Lazyboy: It featured a clear Lucite grille trimmed in gold that provided a stark visual and textural contrast with the cabinet's dark stained wood.

Despite more than fifteen years of pioneering and successful work in the industry, Geddes's designs for Federal would be his last consumer electronics products. With the commercial arrival of television, the industry shifted its focus to the new medium, and radio lost its privileged status in both manufacturers' product lines and consumers' living rooms. Much like the early days of radio, early television producers were most concerned with refining their manufacturing processes and increasing product reliability, with the sets' aesthetic qualities little more than a dim afterthought. Although Geddes played a role in the early history of television, it was as a designer of television studios, rather than of the television sets themselves.

Throughout his career in the consumer electronics industry, Geddes's efforts were shaped and directed by a number of forces—manufacturers' requirements, consumer trends, technological limitations, and economic depression, to name but a few (**FIG. 22**). Nonetheless, he managed to create many truly innovative designs—the Lazyboy, the streamlined combination console, the shoulder radio—that profoundly affected the industry's design trajectory. The success of the Lazyboy and Geddes's unyielding commitment to user-oriented design had a profound influence on the industry's design ethos, as it caused manufacturers to assess their products in terms of usability, as well as profitability.

FIGURE 17

*Recognizing that his
shoulder radio design
might be deemed too
radical for the commercial
marketplace, Geddes also
designed more traditional
portable radio prototypes*

*for RCA. This compact set
featured a sliding cover
made of metal, with wood
trim cladding its sides.
Photograph by unidenti-
fied photographer,
10 x 8 in., 25.4 x 20.3 cm*

FIGURE 18 (TOP LEFT)

The Federal Telephone and Radio Corporation Model 2600-TP combination radio-phonograph console retailed for $100. The AM/short-wave frequency radio sound was projected through a six-inch speaker hidden behind the front grille, which was made of clear Lucite and golden trim. The radio tuning knobs were hidden under a hinged wooden cover. The top flipped up to reveal the phonograph mechanism. Photograph by unidentified photographer, 8½ x 10 in., 21.6 x 25.4 cm

FIGURE 19 (BOTTOM LEFT)

The Federal Telephone and Radio Corporation Model 5000-CP combination radio-phonograph retailed for $135. The radio controls, located on the right of this modern-style unit, folded out vertically and sat above the inconspicuously mounted speaker, hidden behind wooden grille slats. The left drawer opened to reveal the turntable, which slid out during use. Record storage was located underneath. Photograph by unidentified photographer, 10 x 8¼ in., 25.4 x 21 cm

FIGURE 20 (TOP RIGHT)

The Federal Telephone and Radio Corporation Model 1510-T, with molded plywood cabinet, metal grille, and Plexiglas control knobs, was powered by six vacuum tubes and featured a two-band tuner—AM and shortwave. Photograph by unidentified photographer, 10 x 8 in., 25.4 x 20.3 cm

FIGURE 21 (BOTTOM RIGHT)

The Federal Telephone and Radio Corporation Model 1031-TB tabletop radio was made of white plastic and sold for $32.50, in the "mid-tier" segment of radio receivers. Photograph by unidentified photographer, 10 x 8 in., 25.4 x 20.3 cm

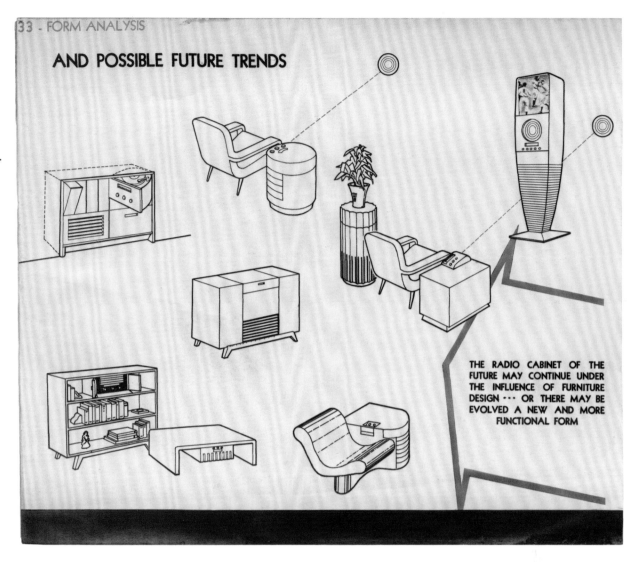

33 - FORM ANALYSIS

AND POSSIBLE FUTURE TRENDS

THE RADIO CABINET OF THE FUTURE MAY CONTINUE UNDER THE INFLUENCE OF FURNITURE DESIGN ··· OR THERE MAY BE EVOLVED A NEW AND MORE FUNCTIONAL FORM

FIGURE 22 (ABOVE)

"Possible Future Trends" for radio and phonograph cabinet design, in Norman Bel Geddes & Co. "Quarterly Report to R.C.A. Victor Division, Stationary Combinations—Stage 1," c. 1942–44. Photograph, 8¼ x 7 in., 21 x 17.8 cm

ENDNOTES

1 Philco Job Diary, 23 January 1946, Box 10, Folder 199.2, Geddes Papers.

2 Ibid.

3 It was not until after the end of World War II, with the rise of "high-fidelity" home stereos, that speakers would commonly be housed in their own cabinets, separate from the receiver and amplifier.

4 As part of its 2011 "Pioneers of American Industrial Design" stamp series, the United States Postal Service selected the Patriot Radio as the image for the Geddes stamp.

5 "War Clouds Fall on Showbiz; Radio-TV Faces 20% Setback; Broadcasters Map Defenses," *Billboard* (22 July 1950): 4, 8, 38.

6 Meeting minutes, 28 February 1944, Box 33, Folder 481.3, Geddes Papers.

7 The Patriot Radio is illustrative of the typical size and shape of 1930s-era portable radios.

8 Well aware of radio manufacturers' tendency toward such conservatism, Geddes also produced several more traditionally styled portable radios.

9 Meeting minutes, 6 February 1946, Box 17, Folder 551.1, Geddes Papers.

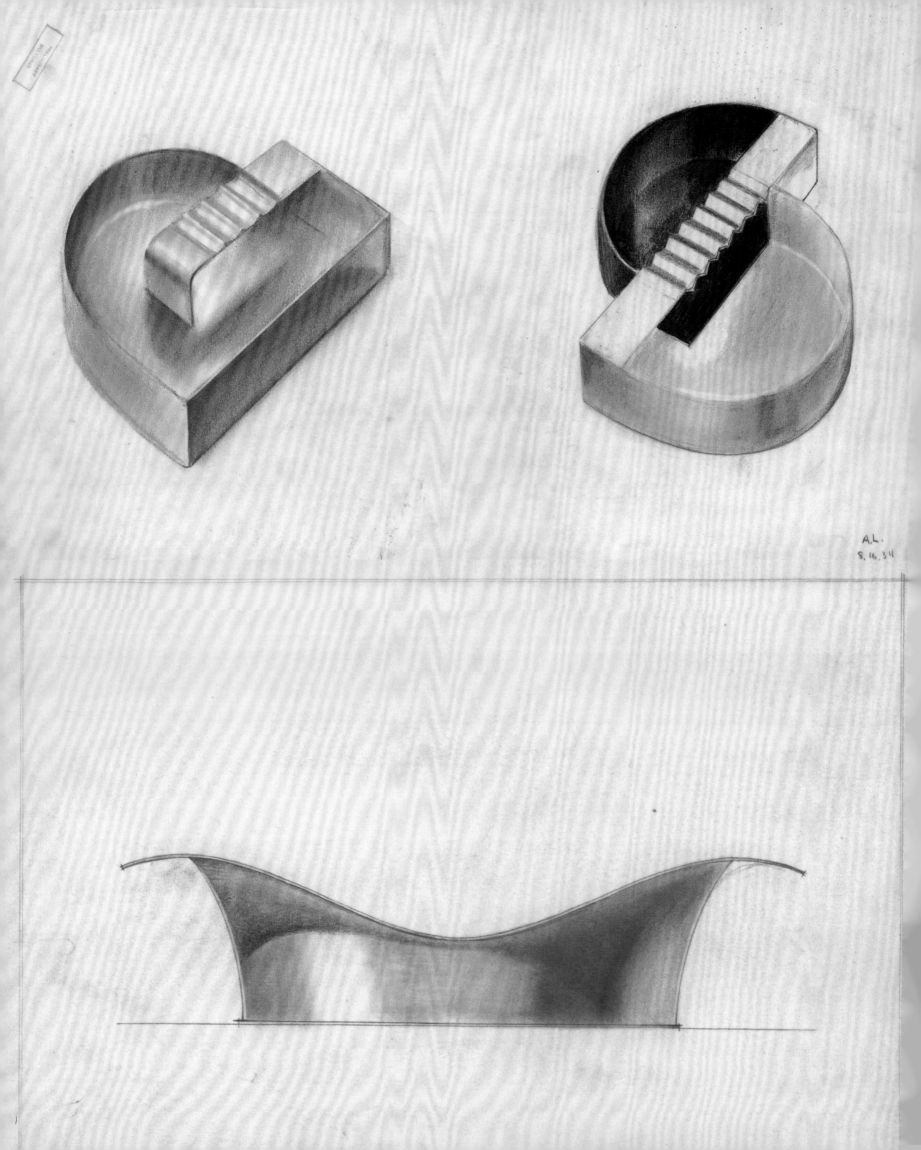

A.L.
8.16.34

PRICE LIST NO. 1

GIFTS

BY

REVERE

Revere Copper and Brass Incorporated
ROME MANUFACTURING COMPANY DIVISION
Rome, N. Y.

Sales Offices

Boston, Mass.
Casey Foster Co.
75 Northampton St.

New York, N. Y.
New York Central Bldg.
75 East 45th St.

Philadelphia, Pa.
1200 Architects Bldg.
17th and Sansom Sts.

Seattle, Wash.
317 Pioneer Bldg.

San Francisco, Calif.
562 Russ Bldg.

Los Angeles, Calif.
124 West 4th St.

Chicago, Ill., 1488 Merchandise Mart

FOUNDED BY PAUL REVERE—1801

(L)

PRODUCTS PORTFOLIO

OPPOSITE
FIGURE 23 (TOP LEFT)
*Geddes-designed ashtray
for Revere Copper and Brass,
c. 1935. Pencil on paper,
8¼ x 10½ in., 46.3 x 26.6 cm*

FIGURE 24 (TOP RIGHT)
*Geddes-designed ashtray
for Revere Copper and Brass,
c. 1934. Pencil on paper,
8¼ x 10½ in., 46.3 x 26.6 cm*

FIGURE 25 (BOTTOM)
*Geddes-designed candy dish
for Revere Copper and Brass,
c. 1935. Pencil on paper,
10 x 7¾ in., 25.4 x 19.6 cm*

FIGURE 26 (ABOVE)
*Price list for the Norman
Bel Geddes line for Revere
Copper and Brass, for 1935
catalog.*

FIGURE 27 (TOP)
Geddes-designed Electrolux vacuum cleaner, c. 1934–35. Photograph by Richard Garrison, 8 x 10 in., 20.3 x 25.4 cm

FIGURE 28 (BOTTOM)
Advertisement featuring Geddes-designed Coca-Cola™ cup vending machine for Mills Industries, 1944.

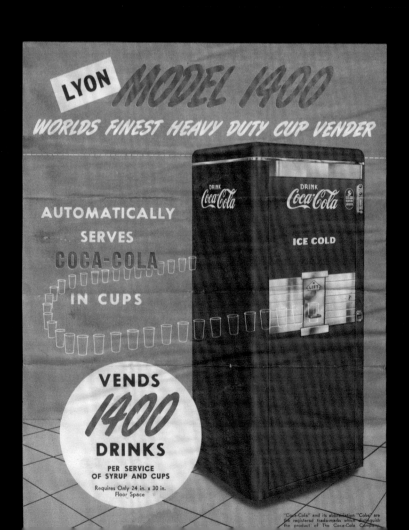

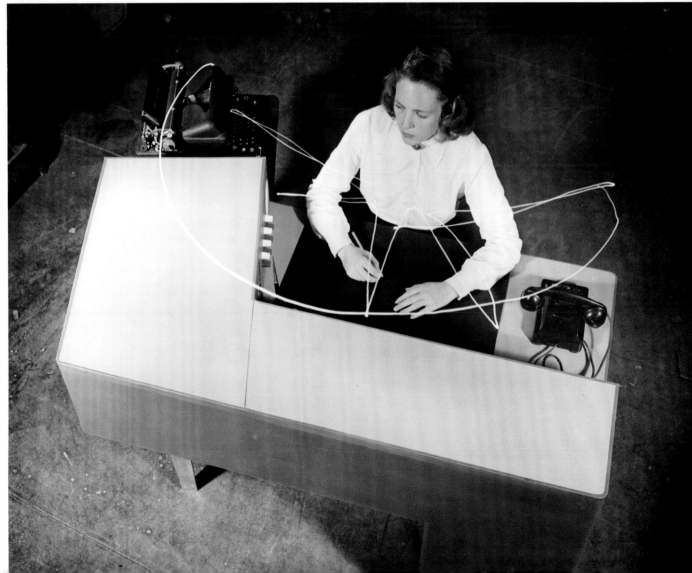

FIGURE 29 (TOP)
Ergonomic motion study at existing IBM office desk, c. 1943–48. Photograph by Norman Bel Geddes & Co., 10 x 8 in., 25.4 x 20.3 cm

FIGURE 30 (BOTTOM)
Ergonomic motion study at redesigned IBM office desk illustrating fewer number of movements needed, c. 1943–48. Photograph by Norman Bel Geddes & Co., 10 x 8 in., 25.4 x 20.3 cm

FIGURE 31 (BELOW)
*Present and proposed dimensions for
redesigned IBM Electromatic typewriter,
September 30, 1946. Photograph with ink
by Norman Bel Geddes & Co., 10 x 8 in.,
25.4 x 20.3 cm*

FIGURE 32 (OPPOSITE)
*"Perfect Impression!" advertisement for IBM
Electric Executive typewriters, annotated "NBG
Design," not dated. The patent for the typewriter
lists Geddes and Eliot Noyes as co-inventors.*

"Perfect Impression!"

INTERNATIONAL BUSINESS MACHINES CORPORATION
590 MADISON AVENUE
NEW YORK 22, N. Y.

Dear Sir:

The letters you send are important.
They should look important, too.

The distinctive typing and the even,
clear impressions of an Executive* model IBM
Electric Typewriter command attention, lend
grace and dignity to all typewritten work.

Public acceptance proves the IBM
Electric is the world's finest typewriter.
Surely, you'll want to investigate its many
advantages -- almost effortless typing, greater speed, economy, outstanding results, and
perfect impressions wherever your letters go.

Sincerely yours,

NBG - Design

Only one typewriter in the world could have been used
to type the letter reproduced above—the IBM Electric Typewriter,
Executive model. Both this model and the Standard model are
available in a wide choice of colors and type faces.

IBM *Electric Typewriters*

249

FIGURE 33 (ABOVE)

Worker creating a model of a corporate bus for IBM, c. 1943–48. Photograph by Norman Bel Geddes & Co., 10 x 8 in., 25.4 x 20.3 cm

FIGURE 34 (OPPOSITE)

Model of a corporate bus with cockpit windshield for IBM, c. 1943–48. Photograph by Norman Bel Geddes & Co., 10 x 8 in., 25.4 x 20.3 cm

NORMAN BEL GEDDES DESIGNS AMERICA

OVERLEAF

FIGURE 35 (LEFT)

"Norman Bel Geddes says..."
endorsement ad for the Bakelite
Corporation, featuring his redesigned
Bates Telephone Index, c. 1933.

FIGURE 36 (RIGHT)

Promotional flyer for Geddes's
designs for Columbus Coated Fabrics
Corporation, 1941.

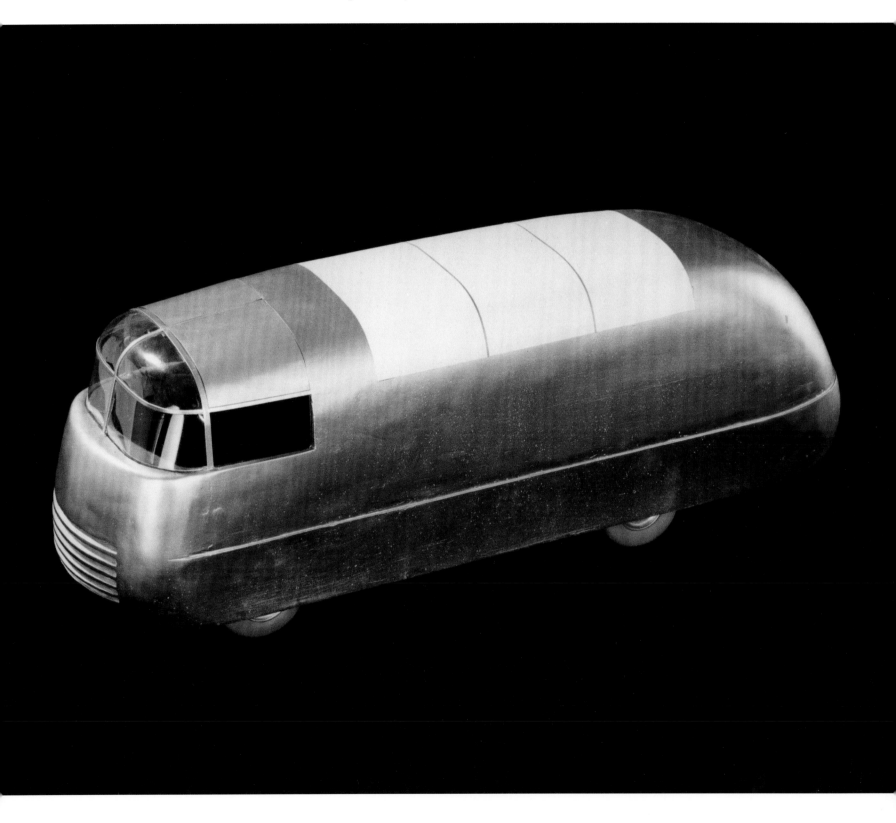

Norman Bel Geddes says...

"...Since public demand now is for quality in appearance as well as for quality in service, artists and industry will still further unite their efforts to win the confidence of the public."

IT IS TRUE that each year the public becomes critical of appearance. "I don't like its looks" more often than not is an insurmountable barrier to the sale of many meritorious products. An excellent example is provided by the Bates Telephone Index, a device widely used by telephone operators in offices and shops for a number of years, but barred from the large home-market because of its commonplace design.

Redesigned by Mr. Bel Geddes this index became a thing of beauty, appropriate for use in the most lavishly furnished home or office. Instead of an unattractive, angular metal case finished with bronze paint, the device has a case formed of lustrous Bakelite Molded, interestingly designed with graceful curves. Here is a typical instance where, through redesign, a potential market of large size was opened up.

Redesigning for more pleasing appearance will be a leading factor in increasing sales during 1934, and, because of their beauty, durability, variety and adaptability, Bakelite Materials are destined to play a more important part in this work than ever before. We welcome inquiries about redesigning and modernizing products through the use of Bakelite Materials, and offer helpful cooperation. We also invite you to write for copies of our booklets **5 M**, "Bakelite Molded" and **5 L**, "Bakelite Laminated."

★ *Before entering the field of industrial art, Norman Bel Geddes enjoyed a notable reputation for theatrical and scenic design. He has been equally successful in product design, and has added beauty to utility in products of every kind from those of simplest type to automobiles, locomotives and steamships.*

BAKELITE CORPORATION, 247 Park Avenue, New York, N.Y.....43 East Ohio Street, Chicago, Ill.
BAKELITE CORPORATION OF CANADA, LIMITED, 163 Dufferin Street, Toronto, Ontario, Canada

REGISTERED · U.S. PAT. OFF.

"The registered trade marks shown above distinguish materials manufactured by Bakelite Corporation. Under the capital "B" is the numerical sign for infinity, or unlimited quantity. It symbolizes the infinite number of present and future uses of Bakelite Corporation's products"

THE MATERIAL OF A THOUSAND USES

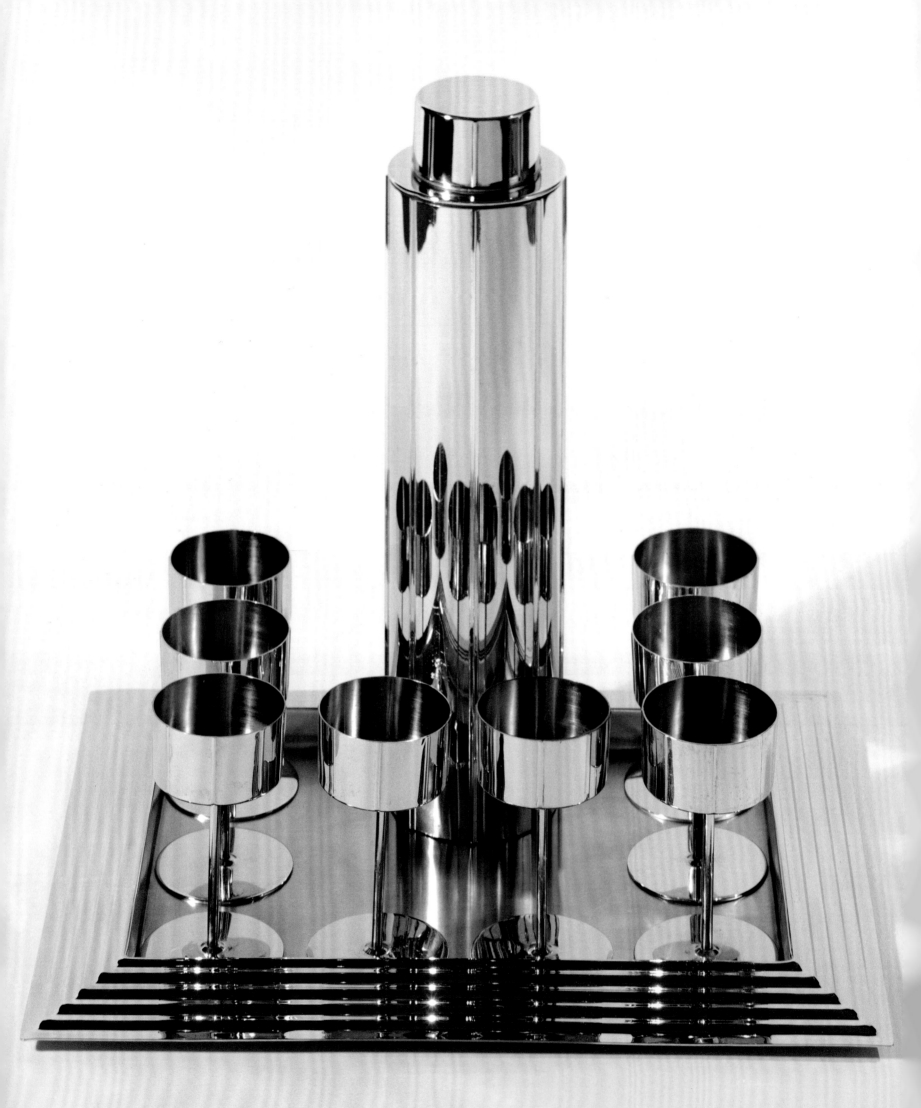

FIGURE 37 (OPPOSITE)

Geddes-designed cocktail set manufactured by the Revere Copper and Brass company, 1937. Chrome-plated metal. "Skyscraper" shaker, 12¾ x 3⁵⁄₁₆ x 3⁵⁄₁₆ in., 32.4 x 8.4 x 8.4 cm; cocktail glass, 4⁵⁄₁₆ x 2½ x 2½ in., 11 x 6.4 x 6.4 cm; "Manhattan" serving tray, ¾ x 14½ x 11⁵⁄₈ in., 1.9 x 36.8 x 29.5 cm. Brooklyn Museum, gift of Paul F. Walter, 83.108.5a–c.

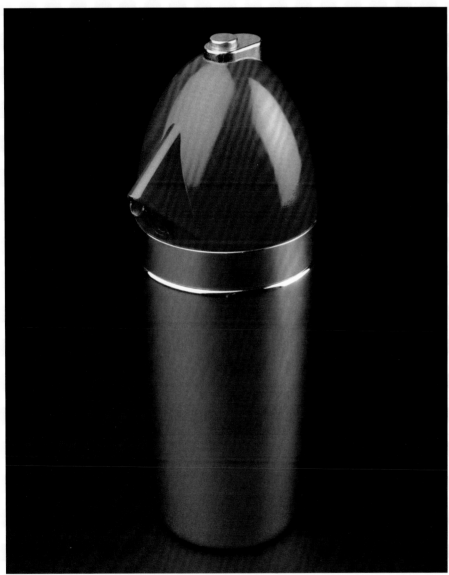

FIGURE 38 (LEFT)

Geddes-designed seltzer bottle manufactured by Walter Kidde Sales Co., c. 1935. Chromed and enameled metal with rubber fittings, 10 x 4¼ x 4¼ in., 25.4 x 10.8 x 10.8 cm. Brooklyn Museum, H. Randolph Lever Fund, 82.168.2a–b.

FIGURE 39 (RIGHT)

Geddes-designed vanity and mirror manufactured by the Simmons Company, 1929–1932. Enameled steel, chrome-plated metal, brass, wood. Vanity, 30 x 40 x 20 in., 76.2 x 111.8 x 50.8 cm; stand, 13 x 27 x 6½ in., 33 x 69.9 x 16.5 cm. Brooklyn Museum, anonymous gift in memory of Benjamin Linder, 87.221.4a–c.

Teetertotter

NORMAN BEL GEDDES & CO.

409 | 055

WG | 7/8/40

ORIGINATED BY

SKETCHED BY

EXPLAINED TO

FIGURE 40

*Geddes & Co. sketch for playground
equipment (teeter-totter) prototyped for Central Park, July 8,
1940. Pencil and colored pencil on
paper, 11 x 8½ in., 27.3 x 27.9 cm*

FIGURE 41 (LEFT)

Norman Bel Geddes & Co. sketch for playground equipment (double pipe swings) prototyped for New York's Central Park, July 3, 1940. Pencil and colored pencil on paper, 8½ x 10¾ in., 21.6 x 27.3 cm

FIGURE 42 (RIGHT)

Geddes & Co. sketch for playground equipment (slide) prototyped for Central Park, June 26, 1940. Pencil and colored pencil on paper, 8½ x 10¾ in., 21.6 x 27.3 cm

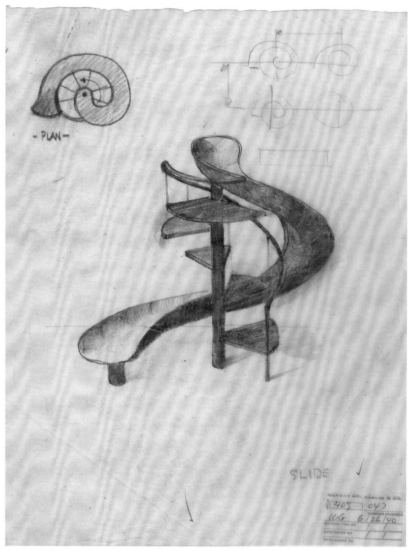

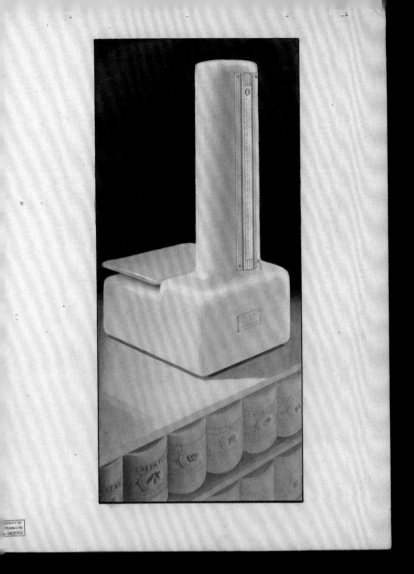

FIGURE 43 (TOP LEFT)
Unidentified Geddes office artist's sketch of counter scale for Toledo Scale Company, c. 1930. Pencil on paper, 8½ x 11¾ in., 21.6 x 29.8 cm

FIGURE 44 (TOP RIGHT)
Sketch by "M.S." of the Geddes office, of a counter scale for Toledo Scale Company, c. 1930. Pencil on paper, 8½ x 10¾ in., 21.6 x 27.3 cm

FIGURE 45 (BOTTOM)
Sketch by "W.H." of the Geddes office, of a counter scale for Toledo Scale Company, c. 1930. Pencil on paper, 8½ x 10¾ in., 21.6 x 27.3 cm

FIGURE 46 (OPPOSITE)
Sketch by "A.L." [Alexander Leidenfrost] of the Geddes office, of a counter scale for Toledo Scale Company, c. 1930. Pencil on paper, 8¼ x 10¾ in., 20.9 x 27.3 cm

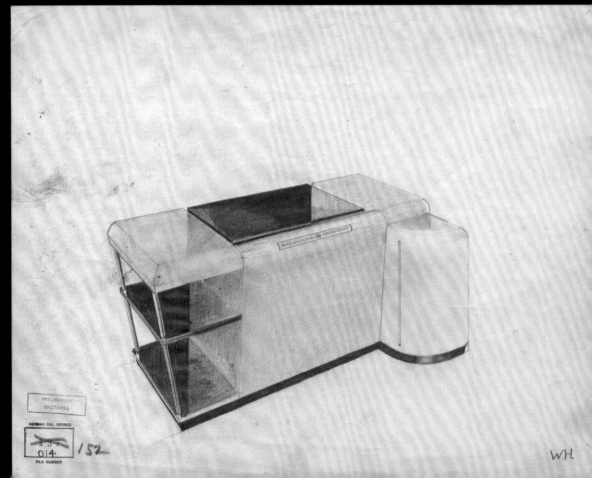

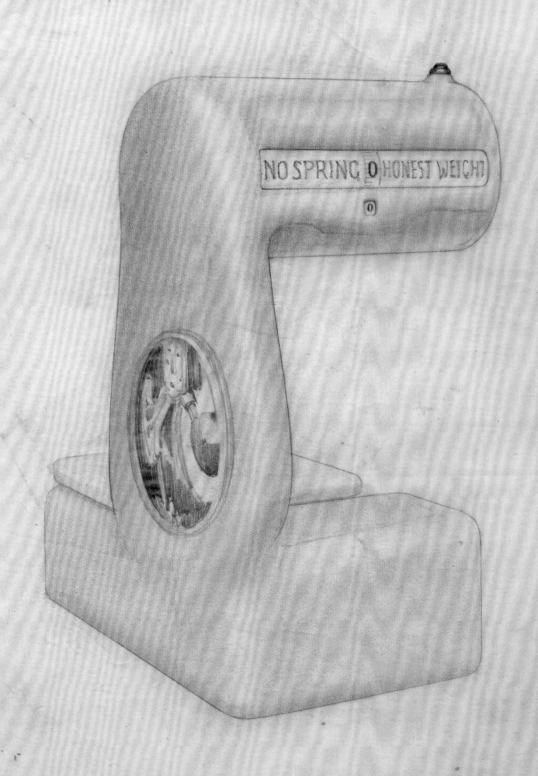

NO SPRING 0 HONEST WEIGHT

PRELIMINARY
SKETCHES

NORMAN BEL GEDDES

152

015

FILE NUMBER

W.H.

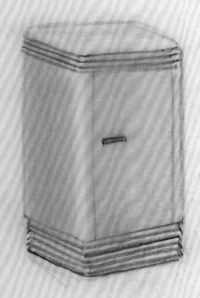
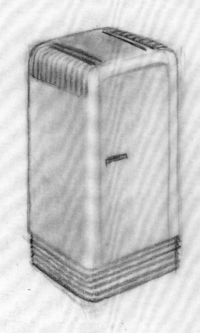
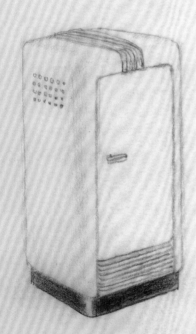
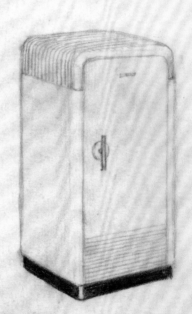

12

HOUSING

Monica Penick

Like many architects and designers of his generation, Norman Bel Geddes recognized the dawning of a new age in which people were no longer "interested in mere living but in living the way they would *like* to live."[1] These changing demands in housing provided a historic opportunity—and presented a series of challenges—that intrigued Geddes as a designer, a promoter, and a salesman. In the beginning years of the Depression, long before the housing crisis of the postwar decades spurred the construction of new suburbs for returning veterans and their families, Geddes recognized that the masses—and designers—stood on a threshold between an outmoded domesticity and the potential for "architectural beauty which reflects the spirit of the age."[2] It was precisely this spirit, this zeitgeist, that Geddes aimed to capture in his domestic experiments.

As Geddes turned his attention to dwelling design, he recognized a significant and complex problem. By the end of the 1930s, Americans faced an unprecedented housing shortage, substandard (and overpriced) living conditions, and mediocre design solutions. Geddes believed that architects had been negligent: More concerned with "big building" than good living, they had forced consumers to "buy below their taste."[3] The decade between 1930 and 1940 was generally marked by the economic depression and impending world war, and for many designers a culture of "criticism, unrest, and dissatisfaction to the point of disillusion."[4] This was a moment of crisis. Geddes, writing in *Horizons* in 1932, seemed ever the optimist; he viewed this moment as one of rich prospect, as a chance for "new beginnings."[5] For him, this was indeed the moment to redefine the horizon of domestic architecture.

Geddes approached house design in much the same way that he approached the design of everyday objects: His purpose was to solve a problem. The particular concern with both the "house of to-day" and the "house of to-morrow" was inefficient (and therefore ineffective) design. For Geddes, this was an issue of waste: wasted space, wasted effort, and wasted opportunities. Geddes aimed to solve these problems, particularly those created by inefficient space planning, poor ventilation, improper lighting, and inadequate attention to the needs of inhabitants in the

categories of rest, eat, and play.[6] The goal, then, was to design a house of tomorrow that would "reduce to a minimum the burdensome features of living and to enable the family to have an economical and relaxing home life."[7] With apt attention, the house could easily become "economical, durable, convenient, congenial to every one."[8] His main goal was to maximize what he termed the "ratio of expense to living value."[9]

Geddes published one of his first designs for the twentieth-century dwelling in *Ladies' Home Journal* in April 1931 (**FIG. 1**).[10] Like many contemporary architects and designers, Geddes had identified both an aesthetic shift (in designers' creations and consumers' taste) and a change in domestic needs; his House of Tomorrow offered a glimpse of what he described as "the threshold of what in a few years will undoubtedly be the universal architecture."[11] For this design, later published in *Horizons* as House Number 3, Geddes emphasized functional values and scientific planning (**FIG. 2**).[12] He was guided by a desire for simplification, a process he described as "starting from the bottom, with our minds clear of the traditional styles and conventions of the past, and, starting from a purely utilitarian basis, trying to create a type of architectural beauty which reflects the spirit of the age. . . . "[13] In his rejection of the past and search for new forms, Geddes was among a small group of Americans to follow their European contemporaries, modernists such as Le Corbusier, Walter Gropius, Ludwig Mies van der Rohe, J. J. P. Oud, and Richard Neutra. While The Museum of Modern Art was still a few months away from exhibiting the work of these masters and codifying it as the uniform (if not universal) International Style, Geddes was clearly familiar with and enamored of the same design principles.[14]

The influence of contemporary European modernism on Geddes's work can be seen in his images and writings. In *Horizons*, he specifically acknowledges the impact of Le Corbusier and Oud (alongside a reference to Frank Lloyd Wright's pioneering efforts in the United States).[15] His illustrations (in *Horizons* and elsewhere) recall the massing, surface treatment, fenestration patterns, and detailing present in the work of Le Corbusier, the Bauhaus masters, and designs from the 1927 Weißenhofsiedlung.

Geddes's House Number 3 shared with this European design a form language of interlocking cubic volumes contained by flat planes, with the occasional relief of a curved elevation (limited to geometrically rigorous semicircles). Showing a particular allegiance to Le Corbusier's Five Points of Architecture, Geddes's House Number 3 is defined by its flat roof, free facade (made possible by a steel and concrete curtain wall system), strip windows, and roof terraces.[16]

Geddes departs from his contemporary modernists, however, in his approach to space planning. He advocated for simplicity and efficiency of plan, though these objectives did not directly translate into

Geddes explored efficient space planning through the reduction of "passages of communication," or hallways.[17] Each room opens onto the next, thereby reducing "wasted" hallway space to one short passage on both floors.

Though Geddes's House Number 3 was neither stylistically surprising nor materially innovative, it was forward-looking in several significant ways. Geddes was interested in accommodating—if not advancing—the technological interests of the twentieth century. He hoped to incorporate industrial inventions that could simultaneously maximize space planning and provide ease of living. One such innovation was his two-car garage with a "turntable

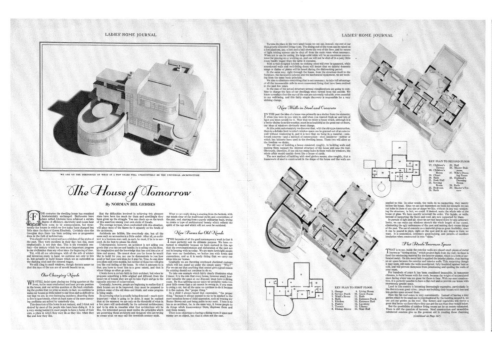

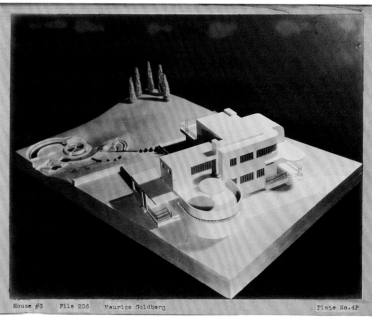

the modernist open plan. The House Number 3 plan is traditional in many regards. Geddes did little to reimagine the social constructs of everyday living (the house had labor-saving devices, yet was designed around a staff of servants), and the two-story house is zoned according to function and privacy. The first floor contains a grouped arrangement of public spaces (living, dining) and servants' spaces (sleeping quarters, kitchen); the second floor contains family sleeping quarters, with parents' and children's units (Geddes's term) separated by a central stair hall. Though this house is compartmentalized and arranged in a fairly typical manner,

[that] eliminates the space of a turning place in the drive."[18] Geddes's efforts to increase interior comfort by mechanically varying the quality of light further set him apart from his contemporaries. With his theater background, Geddes was particularly conscious of the benefit of diffused lighting, localized lighting sources (for specific activities such as reading), and intensity control, which allowed users to brighten or dim lights by push buttons. The house also featured hermetically sealed windows that ensured germ-free living and mechanized and standardized one-piece bath units. With the publication of this house design—notably in a popular women's magazine—

Geddes positioned himself well for the imminent postwar revolution in domesticity.

As the economic depression worsened and global war loomed, Geddes, like many of his design contemporaries, glimpsed a moment of new opportunity. With House Number 3, Geddes had proposed essentially what he had criticized in *Horizons*: an expensive (though neither monumental nor historicist) home. By 1939, however, he began to explore alternatives for low-cost and prefabricated dwellings. Alongside Walter Gropius's and Konrad Wachsmann's Packaged House (1941), Buckminster Fuller's Wichita House (1944–46), and the Lustron Corporation's prefabricated enameled steel house (1947), Geddes proposed a prefabricated dwelling system that he felt could alleviate the growing housing crisis. With his Prefabricated House project fully developed by 1941, Geddes participated in the midcentury discourse on the economics of housing. His project, with the inclusion of one-piece kitchen and bathroom modules adapted from House Number 3, offered a mass-produced panel system house as a cost-effective alternative to traditional building (FIG. 3).

The significance of Geddes's work lies not in the mechanics of his prefabricated system, but in his marketing and sales strategies. Geddes proposed to sell the Prefabricated House through the newly formed Housing Corporation of America (HCA), a cooperative corporation that would provide both shareholder status and salaries to its owner-employees. Geddes, who presumably devised the plan for the HCA, stipulated that employees would be former Works Progress Administration (WPA) workers, thus providing the United States with a means to release approximately 10,000 workers from government assistance. Like other contemporary developers such as Levitt and Sons, Geddes hoped to modernize both the process of building the postwar house and the process of selling it.

With this project, Geddes launched two significant, though ultimately ineffective, promotional strategies. He not only packaged his Prefabricated House in an illustrated presentation book (the first of many used to promote his work), but partnered with Revere Copper and Brass to feature his low-cost

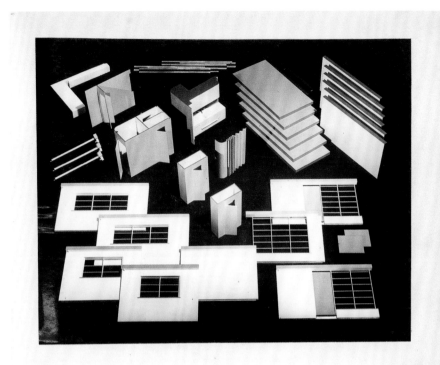

THE HOUSE IS ASSEMBLED FROM 27 BASIC UNITS CONSISTING OF 5 DIFFERENT WALL SECTIONS. COMPLETE WITH INTERIOR AND EXTERIOR FINISH, DOORS, WINDOWS, FLOOR AND ROOF SECTIONS, A UTILITY UNIT CONSISTING OF ALL PLUMBING, HEATING, REFRIGERATION, COOKING, SEWAGE AND CLOSETS FORMING BOTH THE KITCHEN AND BATHROOM, READY FOR CONNECTION TO SERVICE LINES.

housing designs as part of their "Better Living" campaign of 1941. Revere, like Geddes, was interested in promoting ideas that could lead to "better homes and better living"—particularly in peacetime. The company ran full-page advertisements in the *Saturday Evening Post* and published Geddes's designs in its "Better Living" booklet series.[19]

Although Geddes soon abandoned his interest in prefabrication, he continued to develop concepts for low-cost housing. In his Low-Cost House of 1950, Geddes directly campaigned as a competitor to Levitt and Sons, offering promotional materials that underscored the unique value of his designs. As with his earlier models, Geddes employed a stylistic

FIGURE 3

Unassembled model of Geddes's Prefabricated House, c. 1941–42. Photograph by unidentified photographer, 9½ x 7½ in., 24.1 x 19 cm

FRONT ELEVATION

FLOOR LEVEL   BALUSTRADE LEVEL
        TERRACE LEVEL

CEILING LEVEL

FLOOR LEVEL
GRADE LEVEL

REAR ELEVATION

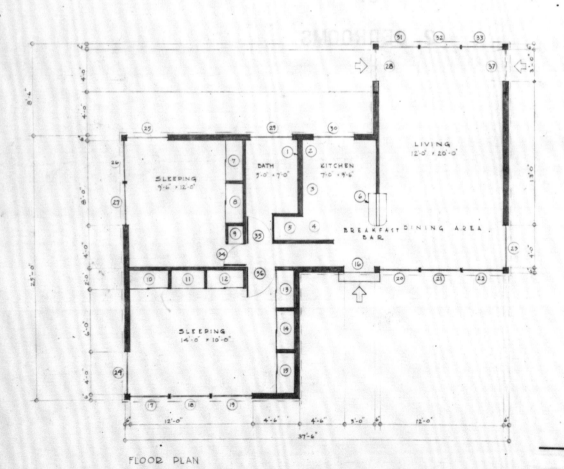

FLOOR PLAN

LIVING
12'-0" × 20'-0"

SLEEPING
9'-6" × 12'-0"

BATH
5'-0" × 7'-0"

KITCHEN
7'-0" × 9'-6"

BREAKFAST   DINING AREA
BAR

SLEEPING
14'-0" × 10'-0"

$6,778

① ALL PLUMBING FOR RANGE, SINK
   REFRIGERATOR, HEATER IS IN THIS
   WALL PANEL · PRE-ASSEMBLED
② SINK
③ RANGE
④ REFRIGERATOR
⑤ HEATER
⑥ DROP LEAFS · FORMING BREAKFAST
   BAR
⑦ ⑧⑩⑫⑬⑭⑮ ALL THESE
   CLOSETS STRUCTURALLY
   IDENTICAL
⑩⑪⑫ INTENDED FOR WIFE
⑭⑮ INTENDED FOR HUSBAND
⑪ BUILT IN DRESSING TABLE WITH
   SHELVES ABOVE MIRROR
⑮ DRAWERS · MIRROR · SHELVES
⑧⑩⑫⑬ CLOTHES HANGER
   CLOSETS
⑯⑱⑰ EXTERIOR DOORS
⑰⑱⑲⑳㉑㉒㉓㉔㉕㉖㉗
   IDENTICAL WINDOWS
   PREASSEMBLED
㉙㉚ IDENTICAL WINDOWS
   PRE-ASSEMBLED
㉛㉜㉝ IDENTICAL WINDOWS
   PRE- ASSEMBLED
㉞㉟㊱ IDENTICAL INTERIOR DOORS
   PRE-ASSEMBLED

8 0 2 SQ. FT.
8787 CU. FT.

632 SCALE: 8 FEET TO THE INCH SHEET 115
AND AS SPECIFIED FOR DETAILS
HOUSE 271 - MINIMUM

NORMAN BEL GEDDES · DESIGNER · 350 PARK · NEW YORK 22

language that was in sync with current trends: His own version of the Cape Cod cottage and the Ranch House were nearly identical to Levitt's versions. Geddes offered a third alternative in his Modern Low-Cost House, a diminutive of House Number 3 (FIG. 4). When compared to Levitt's Cape Cods, Geddes's design was certainly modern in appearance. It was, however, in no way revolutionary. The house drew heavily on the minimalist International Style

good design and, more specifically, on his ability to configure space efficiently (and therefore increase value for the consumer)—primarily through the reduction of waste in "non-enjoyable hallways."[21] In his low-cost houses, he transferred that savings into square footage for closet space and bedrooms. This savings formula was the core of his project, and Geddes believed he had found a competitive advantage through this simple design strategy.

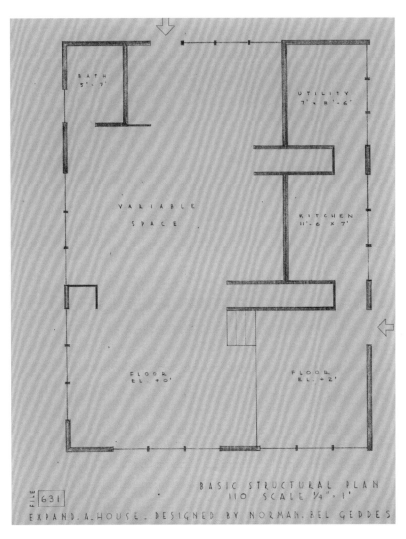

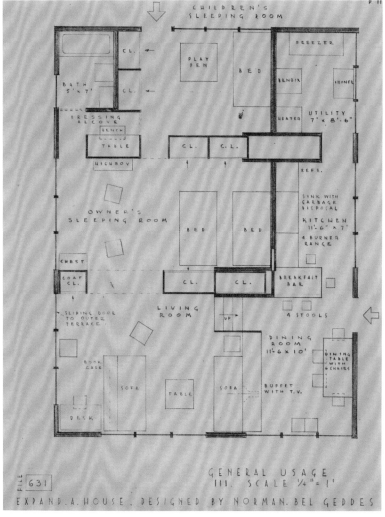

projects developed in Europe during the late 1920s, such as the housing enclaves designed by Mart Stam and J. J. P. Oud, or perhaps Richard Neutra's contemporary work, such as the Channel Heights development in Los Angeles (1940–42).[20]

It seems, then, that in 1950 Geddes was more interested in exploring low-cost housing as a business opportunity than a design challenge. Even so, the success of Geddes's business strategy relied on

While he was developing the Low-Cost House, Geddes began work on his next project, The Norman Bel Geddes Expand-A-House: Tomorrow's House Today.[22] With this innovative dwelling, Geddes offered both a critique of contemporary design and a set of solutions that, if built, would have truly reformed American domestic life. By 1950 Geddes had invested two decades in housing research. He had concluded that while domestic life could be reduced

FIGURE 7 (LEFT)

Entertaining plan for Geddes's Expand-A-House, c. 1950. Photostat, 8½ x 11 in., 21 x 28 cm

FIGURE 8 (RIGHT)

Bed storage system for Geddes's Expand-A-House, c. 1950. Photostat, 8½ x 11 in., 21 x 28 cm

to four functions (sitting, sleeping, eating, and cleaning), each task required a different kind of space and different furniture or equipment.[23] Modern life, and the modern house that supported it, demanded flexibility. With the Expand-A-House, Geddes created a "new formula of house planning" in which interior space could be allocated as needed, simply by pushing a button to remove restrictive walls (**FIG. 5**).[24] In this concept, only the kitchen, bathroom, and utility

partitions could be retracted to open space or extended to enclose more intimate areas. In the second system, sliding closet units (rectangular in plan and volume) doubled as wall partitions.

Geddes further developed a full line of furniture to complete this flexible house: The Expand-A-Bed was a critical component to the success of the plan (**FIG. 8**). The modular bed, which lacked both headboard and footboard, could be rolled (or pro-

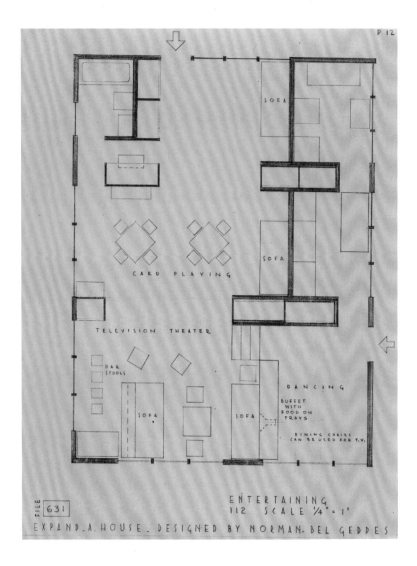

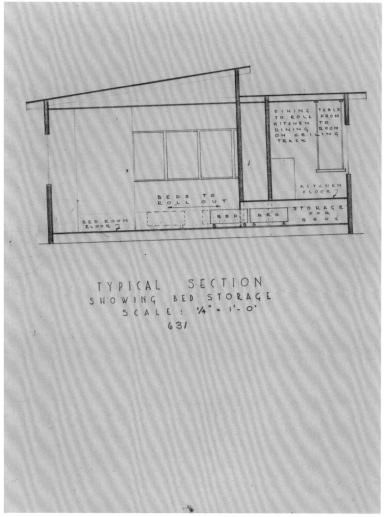

room perimeters remained static; all other walls could be dynamically reconfigured to accommodate a range of activities during daytime, nighttime, guest visits, and entertaining (**FIG. 6, 7**). The rectangular plan of the Expand-A-House measured 26 by 31 feet, but could be flexibly configured by two systems of sliding walls: the movable partition and the "disappearing closet."[25] In the first system, thin moving

pelled by motor) anywhere in the house or stored in two-foot spaces built into the raised floor level of the dining and kitchen areas. While Geddes failed to sell the Expand-A-House concept to an industry sponsor or builder, he continued to pursue the disappearing bed project. By 1954, he was promoting "An Unnamed Idea which is a New Way in Everyday Living," namely, the elimination of the bedroom in favor of

FIGURE 10 (TOP)
*Unsigned rendering of
the Walless House outdoor
dining area, c. 1954.
Pencil on paper,
25½ x 9⅞ in., 64.8 x 25.1 cm*

FIGURE 11 (BOTTOM)
*R. David Rowland aerial
view rendering of the
Walless House swimming
pool, c. 1954. Pencil on paper,
25½ x 9⅞ in., 64.8 x 25.1 cm*

configurable space. Geddes offered the Expand-A-Bed as a space-saving piece of movable furniture that could increase usable floor space, particularly in small houses, apartments, and hotels.[26] This project, however, was also left on the drawing boards.

Although Geddes's ideas were creative and well developed, he discovered that similar ideas had already been patented or existed in other venues, such as Gerrit Rietveld's Schröder House (1924). Nevertheless, built or unbuilt, the Expand-A-House marked a turning point in Geddes's explorations as he sought to redefine postwar living patterns. In a market that was still dominated by traditional construction techniques, conventional building materials, and—to some extent—historicist form language,

this project also represented a considerable leap for American housing.

Geddes continued his exploration of movable walls with his Walless House in 1954.[27] Unlike previous designs, the Walless House was designed for a specific climate and lifestyle. Developed primarily for temperate or tropical climates, where residents could open up entire walls for natural ventilation, this design concept allowed any room in the house to be free of outside walls at the push of a button (FIG. 9). The basic form of the house was rectangular or, in more complex versions, comprised intersecting volumes not unlike House Number 3. A simple structural system was key to the technological mechanism: The house was constructed on a slab founda-

FIGURE 12

Sketch plan for the Walless House, also known as the Edith House; so named for Geddes's wife, Edith Lutyens Bel Geddes, February 1, 1954. Pencil on paper, 11½ x 9 in., 29 x 23 cm

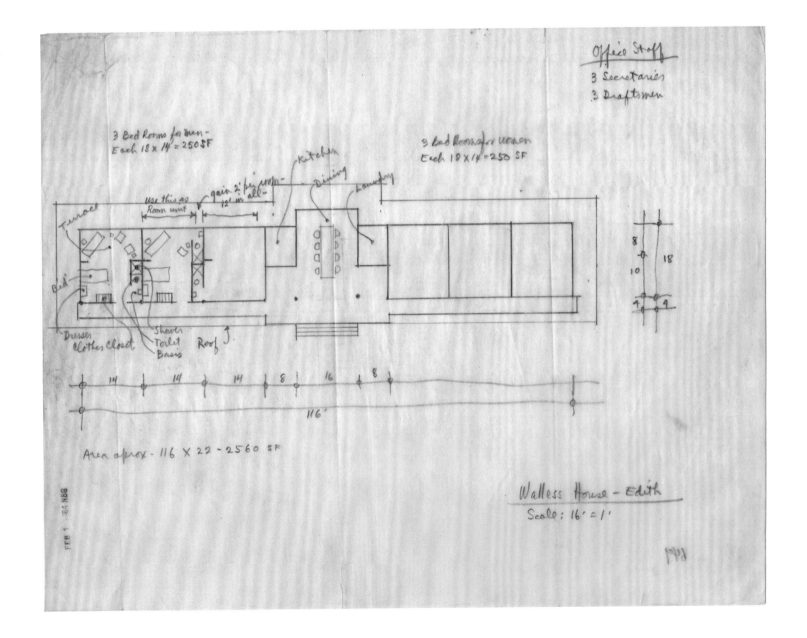

tion, with wall supports formed by 4-inch columns spaced at 12-, 16-, or 20-foot intervals (FIG. 10). The wall planes between each support were connected to the structure at the roofline. The wall functioned as a pivoting screen and, when open, "disappeared" into the ceiling plane, operating like a garage door—or like Geddes's source of inspiration, the door for an airplane hangar.[28] When the wall was open, the interior and exterior combined into a large, single-space, roofed pavilion (FIG. 11, 12).

With the Walless House, Geddes continued to explore his long-standing interest in spatial efficiency, now maximized by the complete elimination of boundary walls. The project's significance lies not only in Geddes's technological explorations of the movable wall system but also in his new desire to design dwellings that were not universal, but individual, regional, and local. This shift was indicative of current trends. By 1953, and certainly by 1956 when Geddes filed for a patent for the house, the context for American postwar housing had changed significantly.[29] The United States had rebounded from the Depression, the country had recovered from the war effort, and the building industry had met the national demand for housing units. Prefabrication and low-cost housing were no longer of immediate interest. What did persist for Geddes, and those designers who would follow him, was a sustained interest in good design, with an eye on the horizon of changing domestic habits and tastes.

ENDNOTES

1 Norman Bel Geddes, *Horizons* (Boston: Little, Brown, 1932), 14.

2 Geddes, "The House of Tomorrow," in *Ladies' Home Journal* 48 (April 1931): 12. Full-size overruns collected in Oversize Box 11, Folder 206.2, Geddes Papers.

3 Geddes, *Horizons*, 122, 13.

4 Ibid., 3.

5 Ibid.

6 Geddes presents "rest, eat, and play" as the three

primary functions a house must provide. Ibid., 124.

7 Ibid., 128.

8 Ibid., 4–5.

9 Ibid., 128.

10 Geddes, "The House of Tomorrow."

11 Ibid.

12 Geddes, *Horizons*, 138.

13 Geddes, "The House of Tomorrow."

14 The Museum of Modern Art exhibited the work of European modernists in "Modern Architecture," which opened in February 1932. See Terence Riley,

The International Style: Exhibition 15 & The Museum of Modern Art (New York: Rizzoli, 1992).

15 Geddes, *Horizons*, 277.

16 In his discussion of House Number 3 in *Horizons* (129–139), Geddes only vaguely refers to "European styles" that might have provided a precedent for his work and only refers generally to "architects [who] have attempted to solve the problem of domestic architecture in terms of the present age" (*Horizons*, 122). He later mentions modern architects who were "a long time ahead of [him]," such as Frank Lloyd Wright, and those who had a "major influence upon architecture," specifically Le Corbusier and J. J. P. Oud. See *Horizons*, 276–277. Geddes does not reference any specific text by Le Corbusier, though his chapter title "Towards Design," as well as his discussion of skeletal construction systems, curtain wall construction, bands of continuous windows (analogous to strip windows), and flat roofs used as terraces (see *Horizons*, 130–135) seem to reference Le Corbusier's *Towards a New Architecture* and Five Points. Though Geddes does not offer evidence of any correlation, he does mention that in 1927 he shifted from theater design to "experiment in designing motor cars, ships, factories, railways—sources more vitally akin to life today . . . " (*Horizons*, 5).

17 Ibid., 129.

18 Ibid.

19 Revere Copper and Brass, Inc., "Tomorrow's Homes for the Many, as Conceived

by Norman Bel Geddes," Box 23, Folder 400.6, Geddes Papers.

20 While Geddes left little specific evidence regarding his sources of inspiration, his mention of architects (such as Raymond Hood and Le Corbusier), his use of contemporary images in *Horizons* in 1932 (work by artists and architects such as Margaret Bourke-White and Albert Kahn), and his clippings files now deposited in his archive demonstrate that he was very much conscious of design developments in the United States and abroad. It is likely that he would have been aware of and perhaps inspired by the postwar residential work of designers such as Richard Neutra, Walter Gropius, and Buckminster Fuller, for example.

21 Geddes, "The Norman Bel Geddes Low-Cost House" (23), Presentation Book, Box 49, Folder 460.1, Geddes Papers.

22 Geddes, "The Norman Bel Geddes Expand-A-House: Tomorrow's House Today," Presentation Book, Folder 631.1, Geddes Papers.

23 In *Horizons,* Geddes originally discussed three functions (rest, eat, play); by 1950, he added "cleaning" as the fourth function. Though he does not specifically discuss this addition, it may have been a recognition of changing social norms for domestic work, particularly within the intended "low-cost" market for this house; presumably, families who would perform their own domestic duties in the absence of servants would be more concerned with space for laundry and cleaning. For

functional categories, see Geddes, "The Norman Bel Geddes Expand-A-House: Tomorrow's House Today," Presentation Book, Folder 631.1, Geddes Papers.

24 Ibid.

25 Ibid.

26 Geddes, "An Unnamed Idea which is a New Way in Everyday Living," 28 October 1954, Box 49, Folder 631.9, Geddes Papers.

27 Geddes, "The Walless House: One of the Most Important Contributions to Housing in Recent Years," Presentation Book, Box 51, Folder 649.4, Geddes Papers.

28 Geddes was interested in adapting doors used for the aviation industry, particularly movable hangar doors. His files for the Walless House contain a note and a brochure for aviation hangar doors made by Byrne Doors, Inc., of New York. See Byrne Doors clipping, Box 51, Folder 649.4, Geddes Papers.

29 U.S. Patent #2941794, granted to Norman Bel Geddes, Edith Lutyens Bel Geddes executor, 21 June 1960, Box 51, Folder 649.2, Geddes Papers.

13

WORKPLACES

Katherine Feo Kelly

Throughout his long career, Norman Bel Geddes designed environments for a variety of businesses. Built or unrealized, each of these projects incorporated elements of Geddes's particular interests, such as attention to audience, new technology, and flexible spaces. Whether as an aesthetic expression or a fixation on ideal workflow, the most consistent theme in Geddes's workplaces was a focus on streamlined efficiency. This concept characterized his vision for two projects that serve as valuable case studies: a factory complex for the Toledo Scale Company in the late 1920s and a series of proposals for the National Broadcasting Company (NBC) in the 1950s. At the Toledo Scale factory complex, Geddes prioritized the aesthetics of efficiency over mechanical requirements, shaping a progressive image of the company through architecture and interior design. At NBC, Geddes promoted his belief in the need to modernize television production by modeling his studio designs on a factory system of mechanized line production. Forgoing the Toledo factory's emphasis on *aesthetics* and the look of a business space, Geddes's television designs focused on the *mechanics* of efficiency and the speed of production.

In 1929, Geddes began redesigning the factory and grounds of the Toledo Scale Company in Ohio. While understanding the need to create a space for efficient industrial manufacture, Geddes's designs for the Toledo Scale factory also stressed the commercial advantage of beautiful architectural forms, the necessity of flexible workspaces, and the long-term benefits of a total workplace environment with on-site recreational provisions and spaces for employee education. Though the project was never built, he later called his work on the complex "one of the most satisfying experiences of my life—an adventure in factory design."[1]

The Toledo assignment was Geddes's forte: holistic design thinking on a grand scale, consisting of a master plan for a twenty-acre built environment on an eighty-acre site.[2] Geddes considered the finished product a sales tool for the company. A beautiful working environment—free of the usual "factory ugliness"—would be inspirational to employees and consumers alike.[3] The laboratory and factory buildings were modern in style, featuring cantilevered construction with long, uninterrupted, horizontal strips of windows and smooth, rounded corners; an imposing administrative building was fronted by a 120-foot-diameter reflecting pool and rows of poplar trees (FIG. 1).[4]

Clean, streamlined aesthetics were of paramount importance to Geddes for the interior of the working spaces. In the laboratory, factory, and machine shop (FIG. 2), all mechanical functions were hidden, eliminating dust-catching features by concealing ducts and conduits. All waste management and water, electrical, steam, and telephone utilities were housed in a service basement.[5] Instead of overhead shafting and belts in the factory, "with the inevitable accompanying dust and dirt," machines had individual motors to keep ceilings clear. This strategy also allowed temporary partitioning of the space to make the factory a "perfectly flexible, working instrument."[6]

Geddes framed the streamlined aesthetics and light-filled interiors as a benefit to employee welfare, but also included recreational spaces such as tennis courts, a stream-fed swimming pool, a baseball field, and a wooded picnic area. These spaces, along with an airfield for executives, covered parking for 2,500 cars, and spaces for restaurants, lounges, and employee education, rounded out the image of Toledo as a model of "progressive industrialism."[7] Although the company's president supported Geddes's proposal through the completion of plans in February 1930, construction was delayed by city issues until the worsening Depression made Geddes's grand vision economically infeasible.[8]

Geddes's venture into factory design continued, albeit with a very different program, two decades later in Manhattan. In early 1951, Geddes began a five-year attempt to convince NBC executives that a redesign of the network's studios would optimize the production of television by eliminating the current "wasteful, makeshift adaptation of traditional forms, structures and mechanics."[9] In an uncharacteristic turn, Geddes jettisoned all of the persuasive and dramatic design elements he had developed as a successful theater designer and parlayed into the factory environment at Toledo. Instead, at NBC, he focused entirely on mechanical, economic, and production concerns to create a new

FIGURE 1

*Toledo Scale factory, aerial
rendering of machine shop,
laboratory, and assembly
shed, 1929. Photograph by
A. B. Bogart, 9½ x 7½ in.,
24.1 x 19 cm*

type of television studio theater. Geddes argued that
this streamlined system of television production
required a bold departure from traditional theatrical forms: "This building, although we will speak of
it as a television studio, is more properly a television
factory."[10]

Sensing potential in the new medium of
television, Geddes sent proposals to the three major
networks in 1950–51, offering his services as a consultant to reimagine television studios along more
"scientific" lines.[11] "Television resulted from years
of scientific development," he argued, "yet the studio
and stage phases of it still depend on antiquated,
expensive methods inherited from radio, the movies and theaters."[12] Sylvester "Pat" Weaver, head of

programming, later president of NBC, and one of
television's true pioneers, took up Geddes's offer in
1951. Two years earlier, in 1949, Weaver had set up a
Television Program Department at NBC with the express purpose of producing more programs in-house
and thus controlling the network's entire schedule.
(At about the same time, NBC was shifting from
broadcasting programs underwritten by a single
sponsor, which gave the sponsor's advertising agency
great power over programming, to ones underwritten
by many different sponsors, which gave the network
greater control.) Shifting the production of shows
entirely to the network, however, meant higher costs.
Geddes's pitch to NBC focused on alleviating the
network's new financial and production burden, with

presentations revolving almost entirely around how to increase NBC's "production flow" by maximizing the efficiency of auditorium broadcasting spaces. Weaver, who subscribed to a "spend money to make money" policy for outsourcing creative services, looked to Geddes to lend his design expertise to this new need for studio space, claiming "there are plenty of people around here that are paid to advise me and the only one that I have met so far who knows something that I don't know, or at least I feel that way, is you."[13] Thus, in August 1951, Geddes began a three-month contract for a one-story television studio in Manhattan, with no fewer than fifteen hundred seats

bile stages were the design solution not just for maximizing space, but also for maximizing profit through increased broadcast capability. Geddes's preoccupation with the financial advantages of his plan might have resulted from his perception that the network's changing production model required a less theatrical and more economically efficient approach. Each of Geddes's four proposals for NBC—the Factory Studio, the Atlantis Studio, the Pilot Theater, and the Broadcast Horizontal Studio—was based on the studio-as-factory concept, abandoning cohesive architectural and theatrical design in favor of highly mechanized systems of mass production.

and space for large-scale, multi-hour "spectaculars."[14] However, transcripts of early conversations show a disconnect between Geddes's ambition to create the "visionary thing" for the future of television production and Weaver's request for an interim plant "that will be most useful to us now."[15]

Geddes's approach to NBC centered on the economic efficiency of increasing the total number of shows recorded per day through a mechanized, mobile stage system. The mechanical stage concept was reminiscent of Geddes's theatrical design for a staging of *The Patriot* in 1928—in order to use the entirety of the stage for each set, he created multiple scenic "platforms" that could be dropped in on steel wires from the flies.[16] In its incarnation for NBC, mo-

Drawing a direct analogy to line production techniques perfected in the auto industry fifty years earlier, Geddes framed what would be his first presentation for NBC, the Factory Studio, using standards of industrial efficiency.[17] The complex scheme was a far cry from Weaver's original request for two contiguous theaters with a common operating unit in a one-story structure.[18] In early 1952, Geddes showed an elaborate model of a 60,000-square-foot interior space—the "guts," as he termed it—with six levels stretched into a ten-story-tall space (**FIG. 3, 4**).[19] The main thrust of the proposal was the mobile stage system; there was no plan for the exterior or interior design of the building. NBC's current method of production required crews to spend multiple days building

FIGURE 2 (LEFT)
Toledo Scale factory, rendering of experimental machine shop interior, c. 1929. Photograph by A. B. Bogart, 9½ x 7½ in., 24.1 x 19 cm

FIGURE 3 (RIGHT)
Factory, or Vertical Broadcast Studio. Longitudinal rendering, interior, by Alexander Leidenfrost, c. 1951–52. Photograph, 12 x 10 in., 30.5 x 25.4 cm

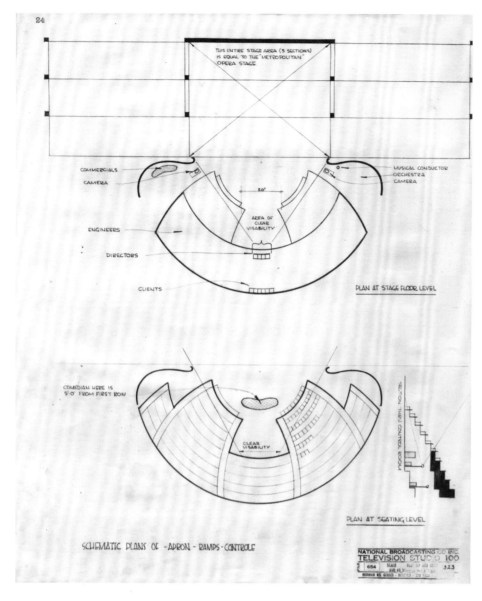

THIS ENTIRE STAGE AREA (3 SECTIONS)
IS EQUAL TO THE "METROPOLITAN"
OPERA STAGE.

COMMERCIALS
CAMERA

MUSICAL CONDUCTOR
ORCHESTRA
CAMERA

ENGINEERS

AREA OF
CLEAR
VISABILITY

DIRECTORS

CLIENTS

PLAN AT STAGE FLOOR LEVEL

COMEDIAN HERE IS
5'-0" FROM FIRST ROW

CLEAR
VISABILITY

PLAN AT SEATING LEVEL

SCHEMATIC PLANS OF - APRON - RAMPS - CONTROL

NATIONAL BROADCASTING CO. INC.
TELEVISION STUDIO 100

FIGURE 4
*Factory, or Vertical
Broadcast Studio.
Schematic plans of apron,
ramp, control, c. 1951–52.
Photostat, 10 x 12 in.,
25.4 x 30.5 cm*

scenery, dressing, and lighting a set on a single stage, leaving time for only one short rehearsal before a final broadcast. Geddes's plan allowed nine stage sections to move from floor to floor via an elevator shaft and a rolling track system, thus freeing up the building's six auditorium spaces to be used for numerous stage sets in a single day. By Geddes's figures, this version of a television studio would increase total production from three to forty-nine programs per week.

The stress on production efficiency in Geddes's presentation books overshadowed some of his more interesting design developments for television environments. Relocating the control room closer to the stage from its existing position in the back of the room, for instance, gave directors easier access to actors and allowed sponsors prime seats for viewing. In eliminating the traditional theater proscenium, Geddes sought to create an intimate live-viewing environment "devised exclusively for television."[20] With no separation between seating and stage,

performers would have the ability to walk right up to their audience, cultivating immediacy with both live audience members and at-home viewers.

A variety of issues kept plans for the Factory Studio from moving forward. NBC was operating in the red financially, and Weaver was skittish about leasing a large new property to accommodate a new complex.[21] Additionally, claims that movable sets and overhead rigging would reduce labor by up to seventy-five percent, combined with titles in Geddes's presentation book like "Mechanization Replacing Human Element," caused concern about potential discord with labor unions.[22] Most importantly, NBC was unsure of the reliability—and necessity—of a fully mechanized theater; at one point, Weaver told Geddes, "I don't have any faith in mechanical things."[23] Although the economy of space in Geddes's plan was obvious, one NBC manager noted that the high up-front cost of mechanization, plus several foreseeable engineering problems and the potentially devastating impact on the production schedule in case of a failure, made actual savings dubious.[24]

Geddes worked with NBC executives to develop a new proposal dubbed Atlantis, which in actuality offered very few changes from the Factory system: twenty-nine performance spaces spread over eleven floors hardly simplified the potential engineering issues. With this second proposal, Weaver grew disappointed in Geddes's abandonment of architectural considerations, and Geddes was frustrated that Weaver had "no comprehension of the major economical advantages" of his plan.[25] Nonetheless, in 1954, Geddes negotiated a third contract to return to Weaver's original request: a design for a single television theater with an "architectural shape that is the direct expression of its use."[26] In the request for a proposal, Weaver asked for "one good picture, Norman; rather than a lot of plans, space studies and economical comparisons."[27]

The outcome of this effort, a proposal for the Pilot Theater, was a 60,000-square-foot amphitheater-style theater that represented a return to a more traditional theatrical model.[28] This circular studio was a departure from the Factory plan. To start with, Geddes's Pilot model showed a holistic architectural form and interior space, not just the engineering "guts" of movable stages. Geddes described the building's conjoined circle shape as "a Television Studio-Theater in its pure architectural form" that "should be a showcase for NBC Television."[29] Moving away from the complexity of the Factory Studio, the Pilot's single stage functioned for both rehearsals and broadcast performances. Mechanization and efficiency still figured strongly, however. The stage was conceived as a "Double Circle Theater," whereby concentric "setting rings" would move dressed sets via "silent roller mechanisms" around a small, fixed center stage area where actors could wait and tall set pieces would remain while scenery would rotate around them (**FIG. 5, 6**).[30] One large auditorium space and a stage area with adaptable "rings" that could be dressed or left bare as necessary accommodated a wide variety of programming needs, from comedy shows to revues to "spectaculars" (**FIG. 7**).

A key element of the Pilot Theater was an expansion of Geddes's earlier gesture toward the importance of intimacy in television's distinctive performer-audience relationship. Good comedic television, Geddes argued, required a space that allowed for the "comic's susceptibility to audience reaction."[31] To achieve this, Geddes conducted interviews on audience interaction with three comedy legends, Bob Hope, Sid Caesar, and Steve Allen. The design outcome of this research—removable audience seating and a 40-foot, adjustable camera ramp—provided the means to change the studio environment to suit the requirements of each comic: a traditional, eye-level theater environment for Hope, space for camera close-ups for Caesar, and room to walk among audience members for Allen. Geddes contended that prioritizing design that brought out the best of the interaction between comedian and audience would not just make for a more "alive" performance but would also enhance NBC's image in the eyes of its viewers. This showed a renewed interest in the persuasive power of design that he had abandoned in the Factory and Atlantis plans.[32] Geddes argued that by providing a more traditional viewing space, complete with wide aisles, comfortable seats,

FIGURE 5 (BELOW)
Pilot or Producer's Showcase. Photograph of model, side angle. Photograph by Fred Roha, 10 x 8 in., 25.4 x 20.3 cm

OVERLEAF
FIGURE 6 (LEFT)
Pilot or Producer's Showcase. Overhead photograph of model with scenery (horses), c. 1955. Shows cameras on elevators. Photograph by unidentified photographer, 10 x 12 in., 25.4 x 30.5 cm

FIGURE 7 (RIGHT)
Pilot or Producer's Showcase. Photograph of model, Car Spectacular. Photograph by unidentified photographer, 10 x 12 in., 25.4 x 30.5 cm

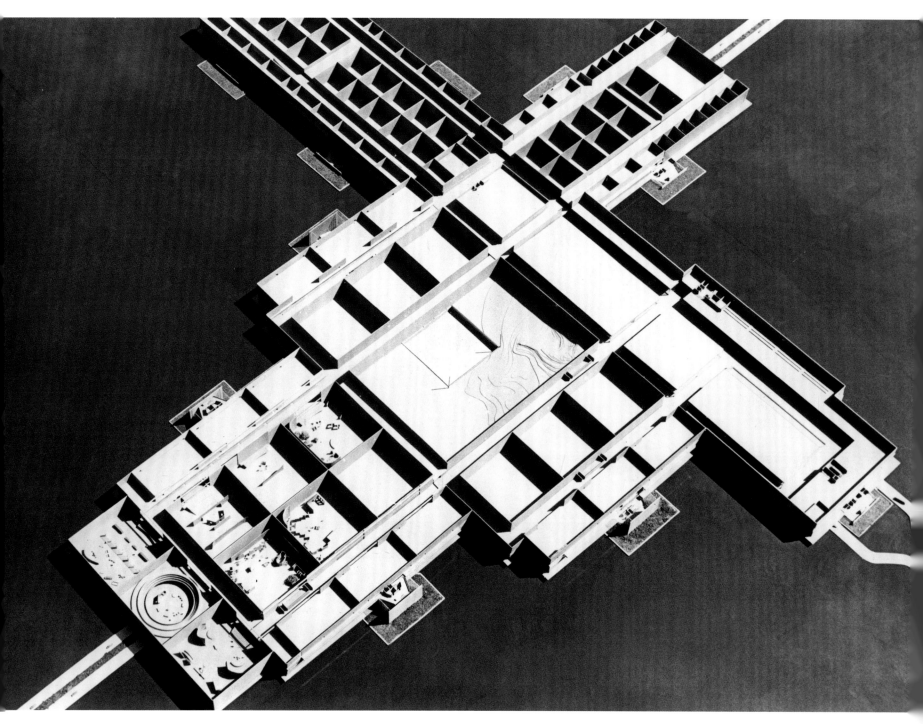

FIGURE 8

Horizontal or Broadcast Horizontal Studio, aerial photograph of model (full "cross" view). Photograph by unidentified photographer, 9½ x 7 in., 24.1 x 17.8 cm

and easy entrances and exits "audiences will leave this theater shouting the praises of the National Broadcasting Company."[33] As he had with the Toledo Scale factory, Geddes returned to the belief that beauty and sensibility in the exterior forms of the building would not only become a "trademark" for NBC, but would be viewed as a "new contribution to daily life." Unfortunately, however, the Pilot Theater was never built; NBC didn't have the funds to lease the necessary land, and the relationship between Geddes and Weaver was breaking down. By 1955, for example, Geddes was drafting unsent letters to Weaver threatening to discontinue work for NBC unless Weaver was "willing to take the stand that

much better studio facilities are necessary to the type of highly imaginative and expansive programs that he believes in."[34]

Geddes's last proposal for NBC, the Broadcast Horizontal Studio, commissioned in March 1956, returned to a fundamentally industrial-production model of television studio. Instead of moving stages vertically through the building, a series of grids shifted "modules"—much like shipping containers—laterally on tracks around the building, providing the same spatial efficiency in set dressing and rehearsing as the Factory Studio plan (FIG. 8, 9). NBC was "Big Industry," Geddes contended in his Horizontal presentation, and thus required the

same space considerations as businesses that were "manufacturing automobiles, deep freezing food, and producing thread from chemicals."[35] Geddes was also committed to solving "major bottle-neck problems in today's production methods" and looked for ways to eliminate any piece of equipment or personnel from the stage floor "other than actors, director and camera," recommending "segregation of traffic and occupational areas between actors, stagehands, technicians, scenery movement, electricians, clients, visiting public."[36]

Although a few members of the NBC team supported Geddes's ambitious plans throughout the early 1950s, Geddes continually clashed with Weaver over his belief in an industrialized television studio.[37] Over the course of their correspondence, Weaver seemed disappointed that Geddes's designs centered on a radical reconfiguration of television production methods rather than a simple, architecturally distinct building for NBC. From a practical standpoint, the network was never in a financial position to lease land appropriate for the scale of Geddes's proposals, and many of the more complicated plans were unsound from an engineering perspective. Nevertheless, Geddes remained loyal to his futuristic ideas, telling his agent, "I never believe in myself more than I do with regard to what I can contribute to the practical production side of television."[38]

FIGURE 9
Horizontal or Broadcast Horizontal Studio, aerial photograph of model, detail of scenery in mobile grid, October 1956. Photograph by unidentified photographer, 7 x 4½ in., 17.8 x 11.4 cm

The arc of Geddes's designs for workplaces demonstrates his commitment to the principle of efficiency—a commitment, in the case of NBC, that he advocated almost to a fault. While Geddes's attention to the primacy of design and theatricality might have shifted over time, these elements, when put to practice in the Toledo Scale factory, were integral to the larger goal of providing efficiently used spaces. A beautiful environment was, to Geddes's mind, just another method of promoting and increasing the influence of the business it housed. When Geddes ceased to incorporate aesthetic considerations of space into his designs for NBC, his clients balked, not only because his radical changes to production were risky from an engineering standpoint, but also because NBC didn't like Geddes's trying to streamline production without providing the streamlined look for which he was so famous. Geddes's futuristic projections about the ideally efficient workplace existed in a delicate balance with his theatrical sense of space. While working with NBC, he chose to focus almost entirely on the "guts" of a fully mechanized version of a theater, losing the strength of his vision and the power to sell it.

ENDNOTES

1   Norman Bel Geddes, *Horizons* (Boston: Little, Brown, 1932), 206.

2   Agreement, 10 April 1929, Box 8, Folder 153.1, Geddes Papers.

3   Geddes, *Horizons*, 200, 206.

4   Jeffrey L. Meikle, *Twentieth Century Limited* (Philadelphia: Temple University Press, 1979), 53. See also Meikle's essay in this volume.

5   Geddes, *Horizons*, 215.

6   Ibid.; publicity release, n.d., Box 9, Folder 153.5, Geddes Papers.

7   Nicolas Maffei uses the term "progressive industrialism" to explain the intended effect of Geddes's designs for Toledo on the community. Nicolas Maffei, "Designing the Image of the Practical Visionary: Norman Bel Geddes, 1893–1958." PhD thesis, February 2000, Royal College of Art, 116.

8   Copy of letter from Hubert Bennett to the University of the State of New York, 9 September 1951 (original date 1931), Box 8, Folder 153.1, Geddes Papers; Jeffrey L. Meikle, "Weighing the Difference: Industrial Design and the Toledo Scale Company, 1925–1950," in Dennis P. Doordan and Davira S. Taragin, eds., *The Alliance of Art and Industry: Toledo Designs for America* (New York: Hudson Hills Press, 2002), 137.

9   Undated proposal, William Morris Agency letterhead, Theater Box 164, Folder J-1, TV-1, Geddes Papers.

10 Factory, or Vertical Broadcast Presentation booklet, 23 April 1952, 6, Oversize Box 22, Folder 9.16, Geddes Papers.

11 Geddes also spoke to CBS, NBC's rival network, about contracting his services to propose a new method of housing television production, but they never "took the bait." Letter from Geddes to George Gruskin (his agent at William Morris), 12 July 1951, Theater Box 165, Folder J-7, TV-2, Geddes Papers. See also draft contract, 16 January 1951, and contract with ABC, 22 August 1950, Theater Box 165, Folder J-7–8, TV-2, Geddes Papers.

12 Letter from Geddes to David Sarnoff, 12 May 1953, Theater Box 164, Folder J-5, TV-1, Geddes Papers.

13 Mike Mashon, "NBC, J. Walter Thompson, and the Struggle for Control of Television Programming, 1946–58," in Michele Hilmes, ed., *NBC: America's Network* (Berkeley: University of California Press, 2007), 144; transcript of phone conversation between Geddes and Pat Weaver, 16 April 1951, Theater Box 165, Folder J-8, TV-2, Geddes Papers.

14 Letter from George Gruskin to Fred Wile, 29 August 1951, Theater Box 165, Folder J-7, TV-2, Geddes Papers.

15 Transcript of a conversation between Geddes and Pat Weaver, 27 July 1951, Theater Box 165, Folder J-8, TV-2, Geddes Papers.

16 Christopher Innes, *Designing Modern America: Broadway to Main Street* (New Haven: Yale University Press, 2005).

17 Factory, or Vertical Broadcast Presentation booklet, Geddes Papers.

18 Undated proposal, William Morris Agency letterhead, Project #656, Theater Box

164, Folder J-1, TV-1, Geddes Papers.

19 Transcript of interview with Fred Coe by Geddes, 23 November 1954, Theater Box 165, Folder J-3, TV-2, Geddes Papers.

20 Factory, or Vertical Broadcast Presentation booklet, Geddes Papers.

21 Memo from Geddes to George Gruskin, 3 September 1952, Theater Box 164, Folder J-3, TV-1, Geddes Papers. See also transcript of interview with Fred Coe by Geddes, Geddes Papers.

22 Letter from Richard Pinkham to Joe McConnell, 30 January 1952, Theater Box 164, Folder J-6, TV-1, Geddes Papers. Factory, or Vertical Broadcast Presentation booklet, 23 April 1952, 31–32, Oversize Box 22, Folder 9.16, Geddes Papers.

23 Transcript of interview with Fred Coe by Geddes, Geddes Papers.

24 "Report—Atlantis Project," Chester Rackey, Manager of Audio and Visual, 15 February 1952, Theater Box 164, Folder J-4, TV-1, Geddes Papers.

25 Letter from Geddes to George Gruskin re: "Points to tell Sarnoff," 2 June 1953, Box 164, Folder J-3, TV-1, Geddes Papers.

26 Transcript of interview with Fred Coe by Geddes, Geddes Papers.

27 Pilot or Producer's Showcase Theater Presentation booklet, n.d. (carbon copies are stamped 24 June 1955), 1, Theater Box 172, Folder X-7–8, Geddes Papers.

28 Undated proposal, William Morris Agency letterhead, Project #656.

29 Pilot or Producer's Showcase Theater Presentation booklet, n.d. (carbon copies are stamped 25 June 1955),

3–5, Theater Box 172, Folder X-7–8, Geddes Papers.

30 Ibid., 55.

31 Ibid., 10.

32 Ibid.

33 Ibid., 60.

34 Draft of letter from Geddes to Pat Weaver, 14 November 1955, Theater Box 165, Folder J-7, TV-2, Geddes Papers.

35 Horizontal, or Broadcast Horizontal Studio Presentation booklet, March 1956, 4, Oversize Box 23, Folder X-1–3, Geddes Papers.

36 Ibid., 11, 87.

37 Fred Coe, an NBC producer and director, told Geddes that his presentation of "assembly line television production" was "not only the most visionary but also the most practical analysis of television's inherent program problems I have ever seen." NBC letter from Fred Coe to Geddes, 28 April 1952, Theater Box 164, Folder J-2, TV-1, Geddes Papers.

38 Letter from Geddes to George Gruskin, 25 May 1952, Theater Box 164, Folder J-3, TV-1, Geddes Papers.

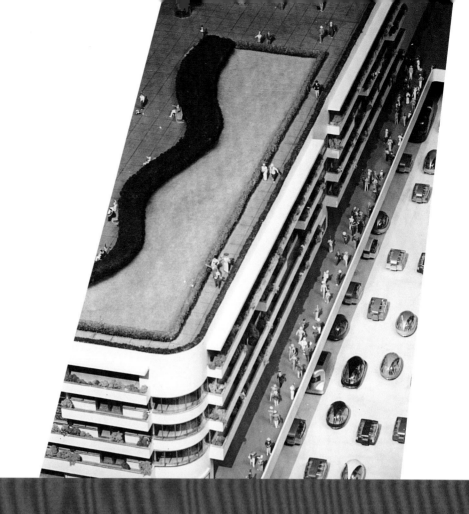

14

FUTURAMA

Lawrence W. Speck

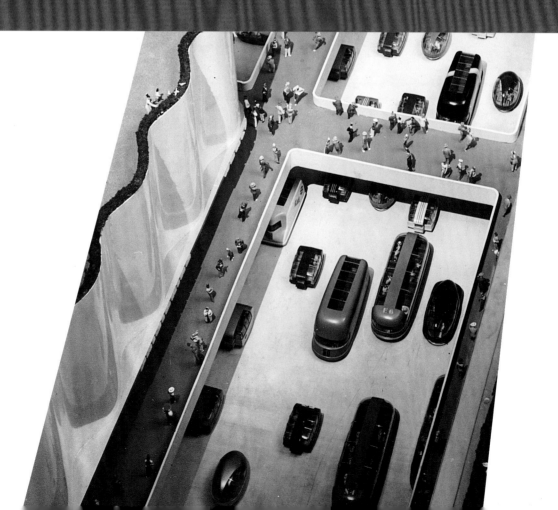

orman Bel Geddes opened his 1940 book, *Magic Motorways,* by crowing,

Five million people saw the Futurama of the General Motors Highways and Horizons exhibit at the New York World's Fair during the summer of 1939. In long queues that often stretched more than a mile, from 5,000 to 15,000 men, women and children at a time, stood, all day long every day, under the hot sun and in the rain, waiting more than an hour for their turn to get a sixteen-minute glimpse at the motorways of the world of tomorrow. There have been hit shows and sporting events in the past which had waiting lines for a few days, but never before had there been a line as long as this, renewing itself continuously, month after month, as there was every day at the Fair.[1]

Ever the showman, Geddes took great pride in creating a blockbuster hit that he considered "the most popular show of any Fair in history."[2] In many ways his work for General Motors at the 1939–40 New York World's Fair was the culmination of his ambitious, eclectic career, showcasing the very broad range of skills and disciplines he had mastered over the previous twenty-five years.

Both buildings and exhibits for Futurama were theatrical and dramatic, drawing on Geddes's years as a set, lighting, and production designer. His love of spectacle and his penchant for the grandiose found full expression in both the scope and the sweep of this extraordinary show. The project also mined Geddes's long love affair with transportation, speed, and the automobile. His sophisticated thinking about cars and their rapidly increasing technical capabilities sparked a vision of America where automobile transportation transformed both lives and landscapes. But it was Geddes's decades of dedication to projecting an optimistic new American culture that showcased best at Futurama. This was an opportunity to demonstrate a whole new way of living that expressed the freedom, individuality, progressive perspective, and can-do attitude that Geddes hoped for in America. At Futurama, his consummate skills as a showman and designer were ultimately secondary to his larger role as visionary and futurist.

Geddes's detailed projections for America portrayed a life of personal choices enabled by technological advances, increased leisure time, and far greater mobility.[3] His cities were sleek, logical, and efficient. Their slender, dramatic skyscrapers, widely spaced to optimize sweeping views, housed powerful captains of industry who were lords of the domain they overlooked. Traditional city landmarks such as churches and civic buildings were dwarfed by powerful new towers for business that clustered in polycentric arrays rather than in a central downtown node. Generous parks brought natural beauty as well as healthy recreation to the densest parts of the city, while broad streets provided rich pedestrian experiences and a thriving mercantile environment. Geddes's exhibition "translated the future into a grand spectacle in which an ecological package of 'abundant sunshine, fresh air, and green parkways' seamlessly blended with a massive traffic infrastructure, streamlined skyscrapers, and futuristic airports."[4]

Many inhabitants of Geddes's future took advantage of their personal automobiles to flee the density of office and mercantile concentrations at the end of the workday to residences in gracious leafy suburbs or even nearby small towns. Expressways took them easily and quickly to neighborhoods dotted with lakes, marinas, amusement parks, and golf courses. On the weekends, their newfound freedom of movement as well as their greater leisure time created by a technologically enhanced workplace enabled them to take long car trips out of the city to picturesque resort towns, spectacular religious retreats, and vast nature preserves. The countryside they passed through on these trips was dotted with industrialized farms that employed chemical fertilization, greenhouse climate control, and advanced plant hybridization to reduce the farmers' working hours as well as their financial risks.

Geddes's future was uncompromisingly positive. Outmoded business areas with their harsh sweatshops and residential slums with their narrow, dark streets lined by tenement houses would be replaced by a bright, shining "wonderworld" created by progressive ideas and technological know-how. In a short twenty years, America could remake itself into a thriving, dynamic economy based on creating

FIGURE I

*Geddes model of
the General Motors
"Highways and Horizons"
exhibition campus, c. 1938.
Photograph by Richard
Garrison, 10 x 8 in.,
25.4 x 20.3 cm*

more things for more people. In the process, it would generate new opportunities, new places, and new ways of living that would become a model for the rest of the world to follow.

THE GENERAL MOTORS EXHIBITION IN CONTEXT

More than 44 million people visited the 1939–40 New York World's Fair in two summer seasons.[5] After a decade of suffering through the Great Depression, the entire fair—with the theme "Building the World of Tomorrow" and opening slogan "Dawn of a New Day"—offered to lift the spirits of Americans through a vision of a brighter future driven by technological and industrial progress. The 1,200-acre fair site was divided into different zones that radiated

from a central Theme Center marked by the iconic Trylon and Perisphere.[6] Located near the Theme Center, the General Motors exhibition building was the centerpiece of the Transportation Zone and by far its most popular feature (**FIG. I**).[7]

Exhibitions of the three primary U.S. auto manufacturers adjoined each other at the head of the Transportation Zone and were conceived by three top designers of the 1930s—Geddes, Walter Dorwin Teague, and Raymond Loewy.[8] The Ford Motors building featured Teague's "Road of Tomorrow," where visitors could test-drive cars along a spiral ramp. The Chrysler Motors building housed several Raymond Loewy exhibitions, including one called "Rocketport" that used models, animated maps, projected images, sirens, flashing lights, and

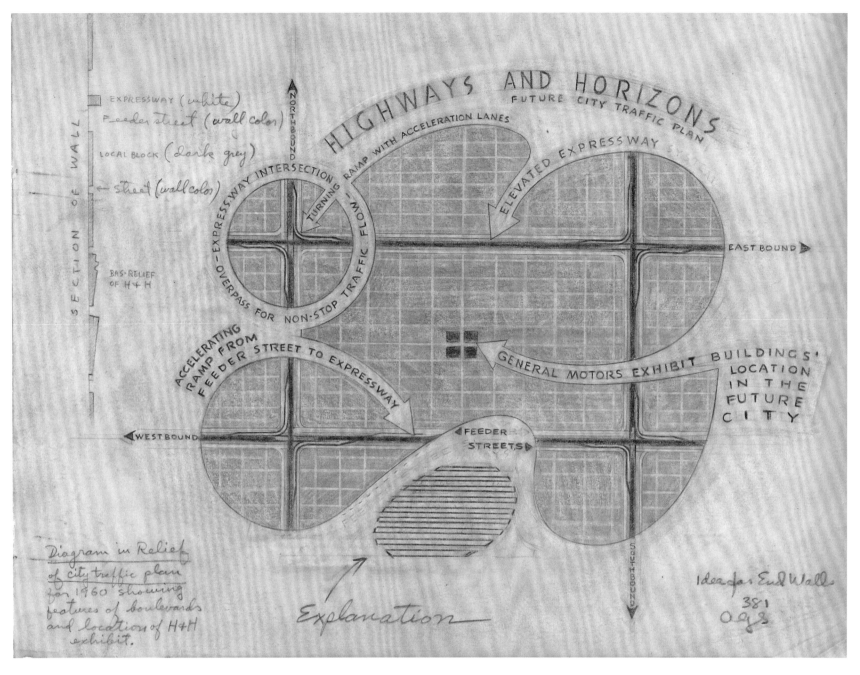

EXPRESSWAY (white)
Feeder street (wall color)
LOCAL BLOCK (dark grey)
street (wall color)

SECTION OF WALL

BAS-RELIEF OF H+H

HIGHWAYS AND HORIZONS
FUTURE CITY TRAFFIC PLAN

NORTHBOUND

TURNING RAMP WITH ACCELERATION LANES

EXPRESSWAY INTERSECTION

OVERPASS FOR NON-STOP TRAFFIC FLOW

ELEVATED EXPRESSWAY

EAST BOUND

ACCELERATING RAMP FROM FEEDER STREET TO EXPRESSWAY

GENERAL MOTORS EXHIBIT BUILDING' LOCATION IN THE FUTURE CITY

WESTBOUND

FEEDER STREETS

SOUTHBOUND

Diagram in Relief of city traffic plan for 1960 showing features of boulevards and location of H+H exhibit.

Explanation

Idea for End Wall
381
OGS

simulated sounds of explosions to depict a fantastic, one-hour New York–to–London commuter space flight.

In the face of the Depression's significant challenge to capitalism, the fair (and the Transportation Zone in particular) offered some of the nation's business giants an opportunity to convince the public of the trustworthiness of corporations and the brighter future offered by industrial capitalism. The goal was to sell ideas rather than goods. Exhibitions were intended to make Americans comfortable with mass production and with a new consumption-oriented way of life. Exhibitions used drama and spectacle to educate consumers. Enhanced capabilities of industrial production infused the medium as well as the message. Muscular new machines and gadgets

created spectacular experiential effects. Designers challenged themselves to produce exhibitions that would give fairgoers jaw-dropping tales to tell the folks back home. Norman Bel Geddes was in his element at the 1939–40 New York World's Fair.

THE EXHIBITION BUILDING

The General Motors exhibition building resulted from a collaboration between Albert Kahn as architect and Norman Bel Geddes as designer.[9] Having designed the enormous General Motors building in Detroit in 1922, Kahn already had a long history with General Motors.[10] The collaboration between Kahn and Geddes produced a building that was striking and sculptural, though something of a pastiche of disparate parts. Geddes designed the

FIGURE 2
Norman Bel Geddes & Co.'s "diagram in relief of city traffic plan for 1960 showing features of boulevards and location of Highways & Horizons exhibit," c. 1938. Pencil on paper, 11 x 8¼ in., 27.94 x 20.95 cm

building as a wrapper for the exhibit with "imposing, unembellished, curved surfaces that would look up to convey a sense of power yet conceal the actual shape of the Futurama with its massive surprise ending" **(FIG. 2)**.[11]

The building's north and west sides featured a mammoth, solid curvilinear wall that terminated at the southwest corner of the site, where it swept out to cup the major access point for Futurama. A spaghetti bowl of serpentine ramps snaked up to a dramatic vertical slice through the thick wall that formed the actual entry portal, flanked by a stylized *G* and *M*. The shapeliness as well as the enigmatic blankness of the building on this very prominent site facing the Theme Center provoked curiosity as well as created a tight, minimal enclosure for the elaborate exhibit device contained within.[12]

MAP LOBBY

Once visitors entered the west portal of the building, they were transported to the exciting new world of Futurama. As he had done so dramatically in *The Miracle* fifteen years earlier, Geddes immersed his audience in a carefully orchestrated theatrical experience. Lights slowly dimmed as visitors left the bright glare of the outdoors and descended zigzag ramps into the cavernous space of the Map Lobby.

The edges of the room were obscured in a misty blue-gray zone of illumination wherein an enormous map of the United States seemed to hover magically over visitors. The map highlighted major cities as well as geographical features, but its primary focus was on roadways. First, strips of light depicted the current roadways of 1939 in bright red. Then, lights demonstrated the congestion that was expected to occur on this network with the phenomenal growth in automobile ownership projected for 1960. A third shift in lights and configuration envisioned a new system of superhighways that would link the country in a logical, efficient web of interconnectivity.

Like a modern-era Lewis and Clark, Geddes was infected with the notion that the east and west coasts of the country needed to be drawn together in order to create economic and political unity. He was distressed by the difficulty of crossing the country: "Even today, in cars that can go 70 miles an hour, many motorists take ten days to cross the continent."[13] The excessive cost in time, money, and energy to do long-distance transport was hampering progress and was due, primarily, to outdated attitudes toward roadways.

Geddes's extensive experience with auto manufacturers convinced him that "Engineers could readily design trucks, buses and passenger cars to operate at 100 miles an hour, if proper roads were available for their use."[14] The Map Lobby created a vision for how those roadways could connect all major American cities and enable travel from the Atlantic to the Pacific on land in twenty-four hours. With characteristic bravado, Geddes proclaimed, "It may sound fantastic. At least it sounds remote. But it can be done. The need for quicker and safer and more economical transportation demands it. The imagination and courage of America will attend to it."[15]

Public investment in this infrastructure was, of course, in the interest of General Motors, the exhibit's sponsor. Growth in markets for automobiles was heavily dependent on improved roadways, and the emerging American automotive industry desperately needed publicly sponsored highway construction to thrive. Highways were previously the domain of state and local authorities, but there was increasing pressure for the federal government to take responsibility for this nationwide challenge and to play a decisive role in creating a sophisticated interstate highway system. With an audience of 25 million visitors, it is not surprising that the first message at Futurama's entry was a plug for ambitious roadway construction.

As the audience moved in carefully choreographed lines through the Map Lobby, a soothing, authoritative voice explained the map and its message. At the end of the room, visitors were ushered into two-person compartments gliding along a moving sidewalk.

MOVING SOUND CHAIRS

Each of the six-foot-high capsules was upholstered in deep blue mohair that provided a sense of theatrical elegance as a quiet conversational voice began the narration of a journey into the world of 1960. The innovative stereo sound system, conceived by Geddes and built by Western Electric, allowed messages to be synchronized to exactly what viewers were seeing at any given moment. Visual and audio messages converged to create an intense and carefully orchestrated total experience.

The sound chairs were mounted on an elaborate contraption envisioned by Geddes as part escalator, part elevator, and part conveyor belt. Dubbed the "carry-go-round," it was engineered by Westinghouse Elevator Company and was an impressive technological accomplishment in its own right. Chairs swiveled slightly while moving smoothly up and down elevation changes of approximately twenty-three feet along a complex figure-eight route of just over one-third of a mile.

The sound chairs provided an orderly means for moving 2,150 people per hour, roughly 28,000 per day, through Futurama. More importantly, however, they allowed Geddes to create something much closer to a theater experience rather than conventional exhibition fare: The foot-weary viewer was seated and comfortable, the message was delivered orally, and the experience was one of constant motion— no written text or static visuals. Geddes immersed visitors in the world of 1960 by making them feel a part of it as they glided dramatically over the vast landscape of the future he had created (**FIG. 3**).

THE FUTURAMA MODEL

Below the track of sound chairs, the largest animated model ever built stretched to what seemed to be the distant horizon (**FIG. 4**). Covering almost four-fifths of an acre and requiring the talents of 180 craftsmen, the model comprised more than half a million individually designed buildings, a million trees resembling thirteen different species, and more than fifty thousand automobiles (including ten thousand that moved).[16]

The model depicted America in 1960—beautiful, unspoiled countryside, progressive farms, orchards of blooming fruit trees, hydroelectric dams, power plants, water treatment plants, resorts, religious retreats, amusement parks, airports, small towns, and great metropolitan areas. During the short tour of the future, darkness fell over the landscape at one scale and then turned into dawn,

FIGURE 4
Futurama metropolis, aerial view, 1939. Photograph by unidentified photographer, 10 x 8 in., 25.4 x 20.3 cm

NORMAN BEL GEDDES DESIGNS AMERICA

introducing a larger, more detailed scale. The buildings of the future were simple and modern but also streamlined to give a sense of dynamic progress. The towers, some intended to be a quarter-mile tall, featured landing pads on top for helicopters and autogyros.

The Futurama model's most prominent feature was its innovative motorway system of the future (**FIG. 5**). Great highways wound their way through the countryside, negotiating steep mountains and hillsides in complete accord with the breathtaking scenery. Expressways accommodated seven

lanes of traffic in each direction, with safety curbs between lanes. Radio control kept all traffic moving at uniform speeds of 50, 75, and 100 miles per hour. Remote control bridges, suspension viaducts over vast valleys, and broad tunnels through mountains facilitated fast, smooth auto movement over any landscape condition.

A VISION FOR 1960

Though many of Geddes's particular approaches to problems of the future were not entirely original, the amalgam of them was something truly new. He was a master of stitching together ideas that were "in the wind" and formulating a holistic vision from them. The idea that the automobile gave an opportunity to live with less congestion and in greater communion with nature inspired many of the concepts Frank Lloyd Wright incorporated into his Broadacre City project of the 1930s.[17] Futurama's self-sufficient farming communities and satellite towns located in the countryside echoed Wright's predilection for personal independence, rural living, and dependence on a network of highways for interconnectivity.[18] In Futurama's densest urban areas, the spacing of tall buildings surrounded by "sunshine, light and air," as well as the emphasis on efficient mass-produced middle-class housing, bore strong resemblance to the work of Le Corbusier, whose urban schemes were familiar to Geddes as well.[19] The distinctive genius of Futurama's vision was that it seemed appealing, achievable, and real. The additive, incremental quality of its great metropolis seemed much more authentic than the crushing geometric order proposed by polemicists like Le Corbusier.

HIGHWAYS AND HORIZONS

Visitors' final view of the vast Futurama model was a large-scale representation of an intersection in the city of 1960, with auto-oriented passages on the ground and wide pedestrian sidewalks one level above (**FIG. 6**). As visitors exited, their sound chairs, eased onto a moving sidewalk, and then alighted on solid ground, they found themselves at that same intersection at full scale. They had actually entered "the world of tomorrow"—and were given a pin that said "I have seen the future" (**FIG. 7**). Each building at the intersection played a role in depicting the lifestyle of 1960 as well as promoting the interests of General Motors. These included the GM Auditorium, which featured the "Previews of Progress" stage show intended to position the company as a leader in scientific innovation; a glass-faced auto showroom displaying new GM cars; a department store filled with the latest Frigidaire appliances; and a modern apartment house. At street level, cars, buses, and trucks occupied the roadway Geddes had designed to operate without interference from pedestrians,

while the elevated sidewalks were free of car conflicts and traffic signals.

IMPACT

The long-term implications of Futurama were fully appreciated by thought leaders of the era as diverse as urbanist Lewis Mumford,[20] journalist Walter Lippmann,[21] and economist Stuart Chase.[22] They understood (sometimes critically) that Geddes's vision implied extraordinary changes in both the scope and the direction of city and regional planning in the United States and a fundamentally different role for governments, especially in transportation planning. As Mumford noted, "These express highways will by their nature create a new type of motor transportation—trains of motorcars, beside which our present feeble attempts at trailers will look piffling."[23]

After viewing Futurama, President Franklin Roosevelt asked Geddes to advise the country on a comprehensive cross-country auto transportation network. The Federal-Aid Highway Act of 1944 that followed called for a national system of interstate highways that closely resembled in concept the network Geddes envisioned in the Map Lobby.

That system as we know it today, with its fourteen-lane freeways, loop roads skirting major cities, and broadly arced flyover intersections, is remarkably like the motorways of Futurama.[24]

Also bearing a strong resemblance to the density and fabric of Geddes's metropolis are American Sunbelt cities like Houston, Dallas, and Atlanta, with their polycentric, broadly spaced clusters of tall buildings and their soft green suburbs. Their lifelines of limited-access roadways that link distinct urban and exurban worlds and their separations of residential, commercial, and industrial districts create patterns of living that are not so different from the culture of mobility, independence, and leisure envisioned for Futurama.

Though one can see glimmers of Geddes's visions in the work of urban planners and thinkers who were coming of age at the time of Futurama, such as Edmund Bacon and Kevin Lynch, his ideas are much more prominent in the work of the doers of the post–World War II era than in the work of thinkers. Futurama was aimed at the masses, not the cognoscenti, and its fruition came in the vernacular of America more than in academe or on the pages of serious journals. The city Geddes envisioned was created by developers like William Zeckendorf and Gerald Hines and by urban impresarios like Robert Moses. That city was built on optimism, entrepreneurship, and a positive sense of always moving forward. A powerful theme of Futurama was that new ways of thinking and living laid the foundation for what was best in life, and that progress—replacing the old with the new—was a fundamental part of "the Great American Way."

The United States got the world that Norman Bel Geddes dreamed into reality. The consortium of industrial giants, including Geddes's clients General Motors and Shell Oil, acquired the subsidies in the form of investment in roadways that were needed to make them dominant global economic forces. The car-dominated culture of urban sprawl, social alienation, voracious energy consumption, and increased greenhouse gases that they fueled bears a strong resemblance to the culture that would likely have inhabited the world of Futurama. Geddes envisioned an extraordinary, optimistic image of a utopian future, but he did not foresee the concomitant problems that are so apparent to twenty-first-century society today.

Norman Bel Geddes's boundless energy, visionary imagination, consummate design skill, and extraordinary salesmanship are all abundantly evident in his work at the 1939–40 New York World's Fair (FIG. 8, 9). The indiscriminate enthusiasm for progress and confidence in a growing industrial power structure that characterized his era are clearly there as well. For better and for worse, the vision Futurama described so viscerally in 1939 lives on three quarters of a century later in the expressways and the cities of America as well as in the lifestyles and social structures they have engendered and supported.

FIGURE 9 (PRECEDING SPREAD) *Geddes, holding blueprint, standing on a section of the unassembled Futurama model, 1939. Photograph by Gjon Mili, 10 x 8 in., 25.4 x 20.3 cm*

ENDNOTES

1 Norman Bel Geddes, *Magic Motorways* (New York: Random House, 1940), 3.

2 Ibid.

3 For other general descriptions of Geddes's vision for America depicted in Futurama, see Donald J. Bush, "Futurama: World's Fair as Utopia," *Alternative Futures* 2 (Fall 1979): 3–20; and Barbara Hauss-Fitton, "Futurama, New York World's Fair 1939–40," *Rassegna* 60 (Spring 1994): 54–69.

4 Adnan Morshed, "The Aesthetics of Ascension in Norman Bel Geddes's Futurama," *Journal of the Society of Architectural Historians* (September 2004): 74.

5 The fair's first season opened 30 April 1939 (the anniversary of George Washington's inauguration as president in New York City) and closed 31 October 1939. Because of its great popularity and because its costs had not been recouped, it reopened 11 May 1940 and closed 27 October 1940.

6 The Theme Center was designed by the New York architectural firm Harrison and Abramovitz and housed the second most popular exhibition at the fair, Democracity, conceived by the well-known designer Henry Dreyfuss.

7 Roland Marchand, "The Designers go to the Fair, II: Norman Bel Geddes, the General Motors 'Futurama,' and the Visit-to-the-Factory Transformed" in Dennis P. Doordan, *Design History: An Anthology* (Cambridge, MA: MIT Press, 1995), 104.

8 Another design giant, Donald Deskey, created "The World Day After Tomorrow" for Bristol-Myers elsewhere at the fair.

9 Kahn also collaborated with Walter Dorwin Teague on the Ford Motors building immediately next door.

10 Much of Kahn's Detroit-based practice was for automotive companies, including Packard, Ford, Chrysler, and the Fisher Body Company in addition to General Motors. See Albert Kahn, *The Legacy of Albert Kahn* (Detroit: Detroit Institute of Arts, 1970), 21.

11 Marchand, "The Designers go to the Fair, II," 111.

12 The sculptural ramps were compromised somewhat in the later stages of the fair by the addition of metal and canvas shade structures to keep the summer sun off fairgoers who had to wait for hours to enter this west face of the building.

13 Geddes, *Magic Motorways*, 146.

14 Ibid.

15 Ibid., 164.

16 More than forty thousand new moving cars, trucks, and buses were added for the 1940 version of Futurama.

17 Geddes first met Wright when they were both working with Aline Barnsdall in Los Angeles in 1915–16.

18 Jennifer Davis Roberts, *Norman Bel Geddes: An Exhibition of Theatrical and Industrial Designs* (Austin: The University of Texas at Austin, 1979), 46.

19 Ibid.

20 Lewis Mumford, "The Skyline in Flushing," *New Yorker* (29 July 1939): 38–41.

21 Walter Lippmann, "A Day at the World's Fair," *New York Herald Tribune* (6 June 1939): 25.

22 Stuart Chase, "Patterns for a Brave New World," *Cosmopolitan* (January 1940): 38–9.

23 Mumford, "The Skyline in Flushing": 40.

24 Lawrence W. Speck, "The Shaping of Things to Come," *OMNI* (October 1989): 87.

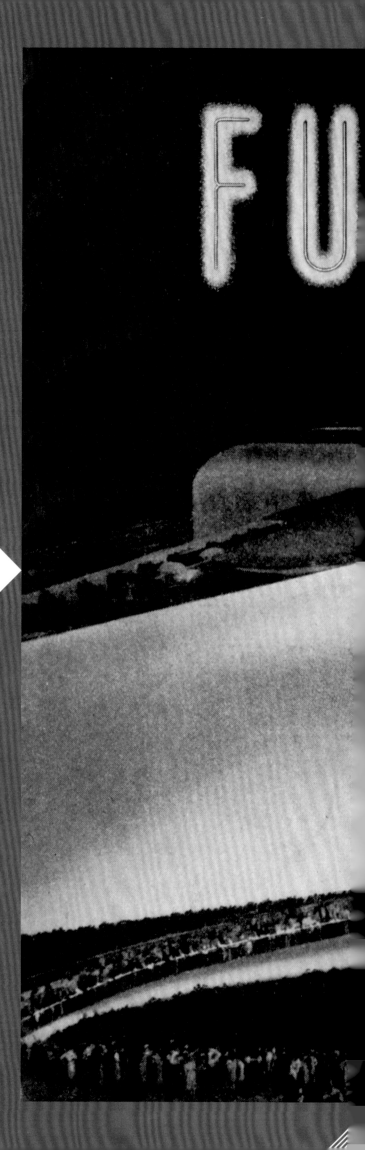

FUTURAMA PORTFOLIO

FIGURE 10
General Motors' souvenir booklet for its "Highways and Horizons" exhibit at the 1939–40 New York World's Fair.

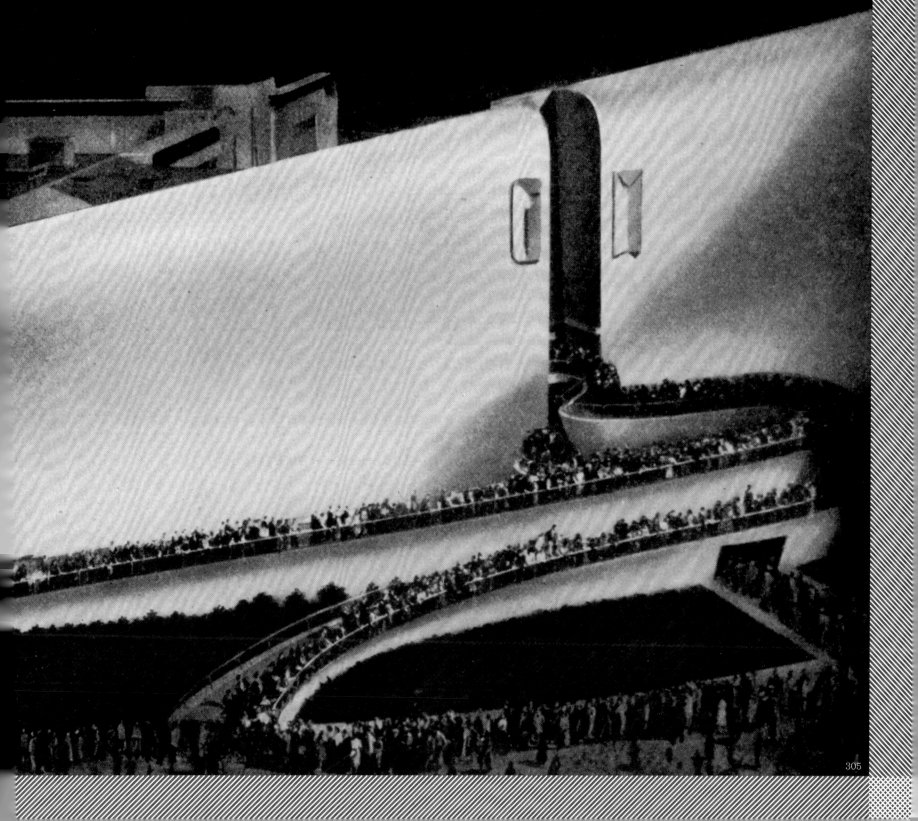

TURAMA

FIGURE 11 (OPPOSITE)
Worker installing bridge
on Futurama model, 1939.
Photograph by Richard
Garrison, 8 x 10 in.,
20.3 x 25.4 cm

FIGURE 12 (ABOVE)
Workmen among
Futurama model build-
ings, 1939. Photograph,
10 x 8 in., 25.4 x 20.3 cm

Geddes-designed green and yellow model cars for Futurama exhibition, c. 1939. Mixed media, 8 x 3 x 2 in., 20.3 x 7.6 x 5 cm (green car); 6 x 3 x 2⅜ in., 15.2 x 7.6 x 6 cm (yellow car)

FIGURE 14 (OPPOSITE)

Worker placing model cars on Futurama downtown street, 1939. Photograph by Richard Garrison, 8 x 10 in., 20.3 x 25.4 cm

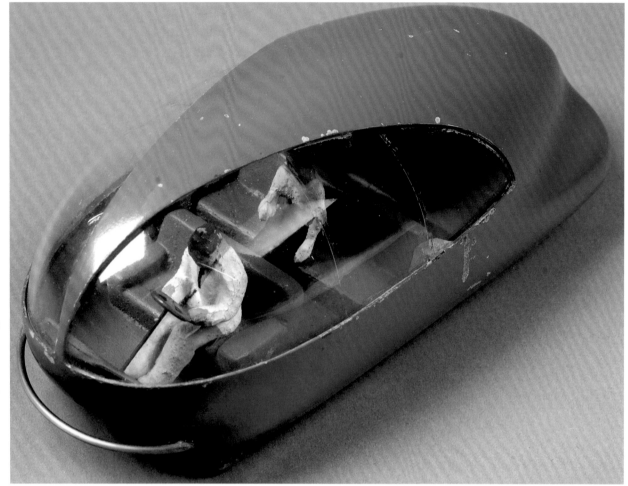

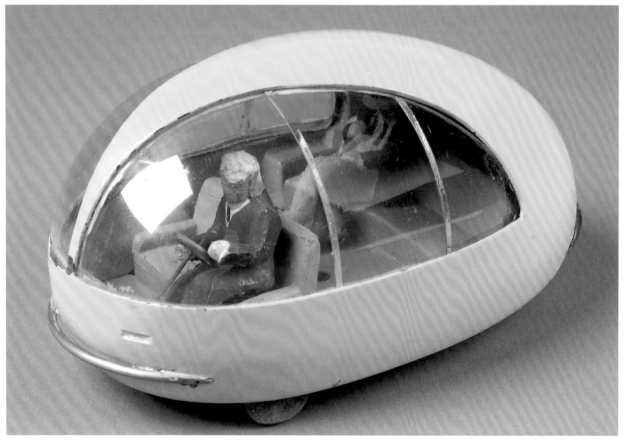

FIGURE 15 (LEFT)
*Futurama airport, 1939. Photograph by
Richard Garrison, 8 x 10 in., 20.3 x 25.4 cm*

FIGURE 16 (RIGHT)
*Futurama cityscape, 1939. Photograph by
Richard Garrison, 10 x 8 in., 25.4 x 20.3 cm*

FIGURE 17 (OPPOSITE)
*Futurama model dam, 1939. Photograph by
Richard Garrison, 10 x 8 in., 25.4 x 20.3 cm*

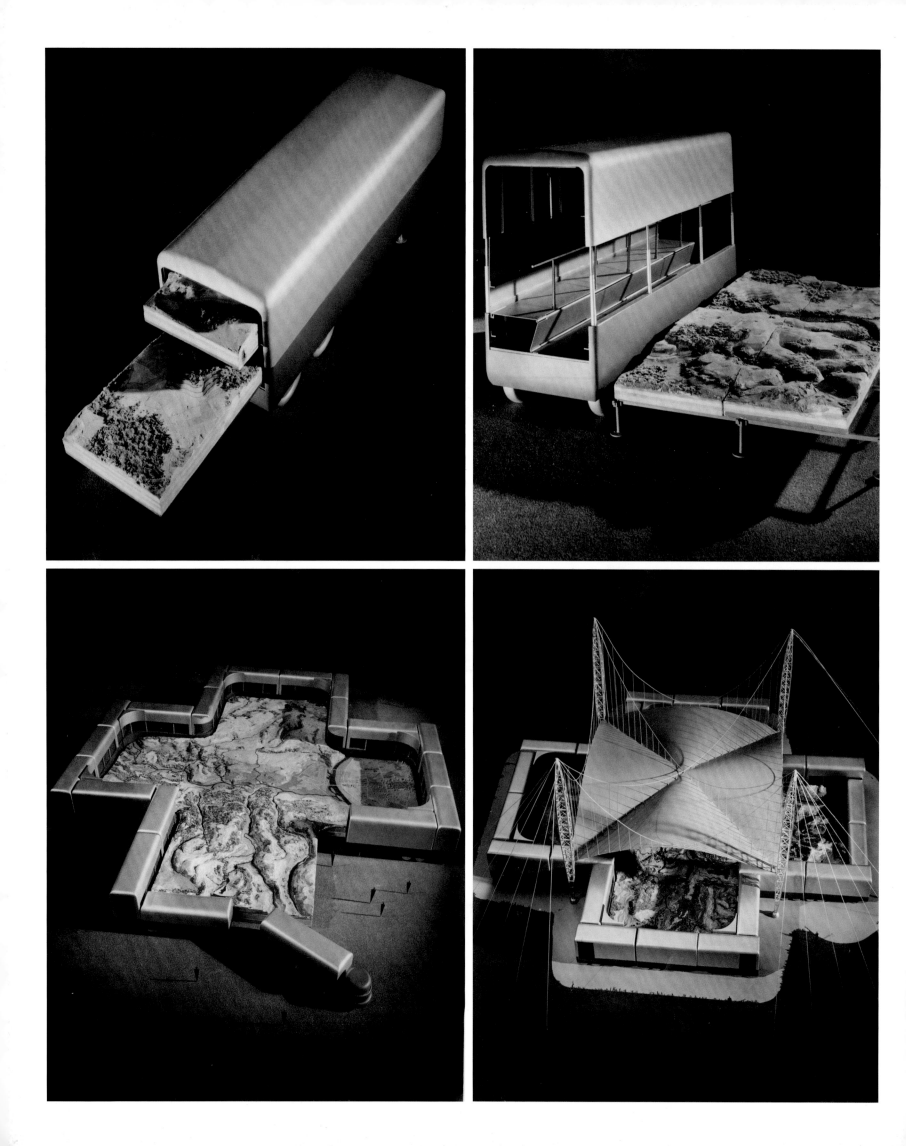

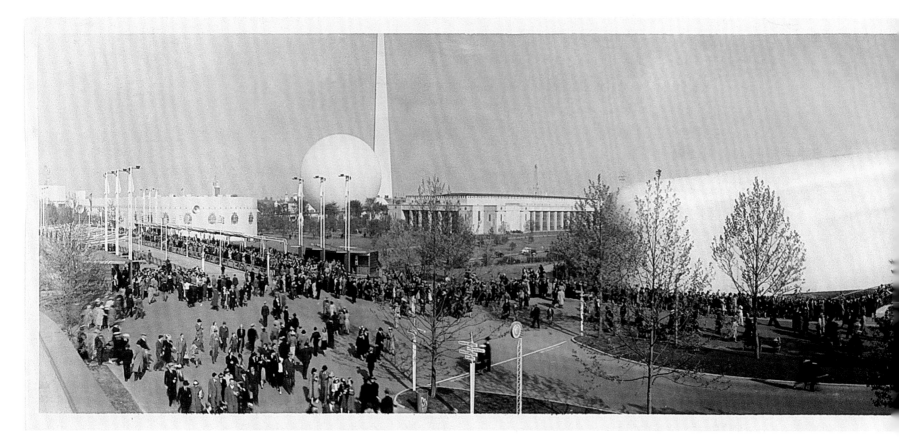

PRECEDING SPREAD

In an effort to perpetuate Futurama after the close of the World's Fair, General Motors solicited ideas from Geddes, who proposed shipping the Futurama model by either zeppelin or truck caravan. The zeppelin option was deemed impractical, and these model photographs document Geddes's plan for how Futurama would be shipped and reassembled as a traveling exhibition using ground transportation.

FIGURE 18 (TOP LEFT)
Futurama Caravan trailer with panels loaded, c. 1940. Photograph by unidentified photographer, 8 x 10 in., 20.3 x 25.4 cm

FIGURE 19 (TOP RIGHT)
Futurama Caravan trailer with panels ready to load, c. 1940. Photograph by unidentified photographer, 8 x 10 in., 20.3 x 25.4 cm

FIGURE 20 (BOTTOM LEFT)
Futurama Caravan panel and trailer assembly, c. 1940. Photograph by unidentified photographer, 8 x 10 in., 20.3 x 25.4 cm

FIGURE 21 (BOTTOM RIGHT)
Futurama Caravan fully assembled and tented, c. 1940. Photograph by unidentified photographer, 8 x 10 in., 20.3 x 25.4 cm

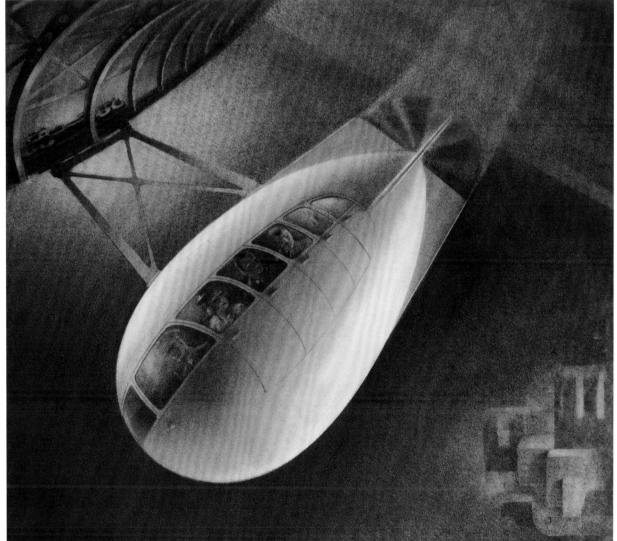

PRECEDING SPREAD, CONTINUED
FIGURE 22 (RIGHT)

In 1940–41, Futurama traveled with the General Motors "Parade of Progress" exhibition that was developed following the 1933 Chicago World's Fair "to show . . . how industrial research and constantly advancing industrial techniques contribute to the strength and vigor of the nation." General Motors "Parade of Progress" exhibition installed in an unidentified city, c. 1936. Photograph by unidentified photographer, 8 x 10 in., 20.3 x 25.4 cm

FIGURE 23 (ABOVE)

Panorama of the General Motors Highways and Horizons building at the 1939–40 New York World's Fair, May 16, 1939. Photograph by unidentified photographer, 42¼ x 10 in., 107.3 x 25.4 cm

FIGURE 24A, 24B (LEFT AND OPPOSITE)

Two renderings for a Geddes-proposed Sky Ride concession for the 1939–40 New York World's Fair, c. 1937–38.

15

THEATER OF WAR

Christina Cogdell

Few people know that Mr. Geddes has probably devoted a greater part of his life to the subject of military and naval matters than he has to design.
—Internal office memo from Geddes to his employee, Pemberton, September 27, 1939[1]

It is not generally known that Norman Bel Geddes is one of the best informed men in the country on military strategy, war maps and things pertaining to the present conflict. Known mainly as a leader in his field of design, it is interesting to note that for every book in his extensive library on his own subjects he has two books on naval and military subjects. (then lead to the story of the war game.)
—Internal office memo from Pemberton to Geddes, titled "Suggested material for wire to be sent to prospective clients," September 27, 1939[2]

Just a few weeks after the outbreak of World War II, while the General Motors Futurama exhibition was still on display at the 1939–40 New York World's Fair, Norman Bel Geddes began fashioning himself, in his usual grandiose style, as one of the nation's leading experts on war. Interoffice memos and meeting notes from the days leading up to the war demonstrate that he clearly hoped to capitalize on the international military escalation. His motives, however, were not just related to profit or circumstance. As the internal office memos between Geddes and his employee Pemberton suggest, Geddes had both a long-standing interest and expertise in the history and strategies of war. He owned almost seven hundred books about war and claimed his collection included every official record ever published on any war in history.[3] Furthermore, he actually read these books, digesting land and naval strategies in consideration of particular geographies and available technologies. Journalist Edwin C. Hill, writing for the *New York Sun* in 1931, affirmed that Geddes "can quote you von Clausewitz by the yard and reel off whole pages of 'Jane's Fighting Ships.'"[4] Geddes materialized his fascination with war by designing a series of elaborate war games, the first of which he made during World War I in 1915, the same year as his earliest known theatrical model. One highly popular version of this game was played in the 1930s

by New York intelligentsia, designers, and military men at Geddes's Manhattan apartment, in weekly sessions notable enough to be written up in the local papers and reprinted as far away as Florida, Texas, California, and even Shanghai (**FIG. I**).

Interestingly, two of these news stories highlight with irony that Geddes was "an out-and-out pacifist" who was arrested and "languished in jail for two days" during World War I for writing articles opposing the draft and United States entry into the war. "He hates war with an unholy hatred," wrote Hill, "says that it settles nothing and that war makers are the world's greatest criminals."[5] Perhaps Geddes's obsession with war was like that of pacifist H. G. Wells, who also created war games during World War I with the rationale that war games are more entertaining and less deadly than real war and could serve as a suitable replacement for it.[6] This seems a stretch, though, given the serious focus, lengthy duration, and types of military-related play that Geddes pursued, as well as the very real work he did for the U.S. armed forces during the early to mid-1940s. Furthermore, given Geddes's mantra of "the imagination creates the actual" and that many of his projects demonstrated his implementation of this axiom, it would be inconsistent to interpret his fascination with war gaming as a substitute for actual warfare. Rather, it is more likely that Geddes viewed his lifelong explorations of war in the literary, historical, and gaming realms as virtually real experiences and, therefore, preparation for actual work for the military. His and Pemberton's press-release verbiage asserts as much, that is, that his gaming and study of military history and strategy credentialed him as an expert ready to contribute high-level designs to prospective military clients.

A number of overlaps exist between Geddes's design work of the 1920s and 1930s and his war work: Some of his biggest theatrical and industrial design successes shared their conceptual and technical innovations with techniques he developed in his war games and work for the U.S. military. For example, his first war game was structured to simulate distant aerial viewing for its players, who stood around a large model of two mythical countries whose terrain closely mimicked the entire European western front with adjacent seas. According to Hill, it established "a bird's eye view of modern warfare for players who can see like a bird and reason like mathematicians." He praised it as an "extraordinary" war game, "vast and complicated; as involved as a labyrinth; chess on a heroic scale" (for chess, too, is a war game).[7] Geddes's use of this same aerial perspective technique in his work for Shell in 1937 (**FIG. 2**) and in the Futurama model of the United States two years later (**FIG. 3**) was merely an extension and elaboration of a process perfected over the preceding two decades through improvements made to his war game and techniques he developed for his Animated Battle Map project between 1927 and 1935 (**FIG. 4**).[8]

move along the interstate highways of the future, pulled by the same kind of mechanical track system.[11] Finally, in 1943–44, he used 216 motors with chains and pulleys to move tanks and ground troops over uneven terrain in what may have been the first-ever mechanically operated battle simulation room (**FIG. 5, 6**).[12] The 60-square-foot realistic terrain model was built by Geddes for the Army Air Force School of Applied Tactics (AAFSAT) and was scaled to represent 150 square miles of territory with troops and all accoutrements. Clearly, Geddes did not compartmentalize his techniques to just one area of his creative activities.

Understanding Geddes's deep interest in—and detailed designs pertaining to—war adds yet one

Another example of the relationship between Geddes's technical innovations and his war games was his creation of the first-ever mechanized mobile theatrical set design, which used offstage motors to efficiently move scenery into place in *The Miracle,* staged in New York in 1924.[9] In 1925, he integrated a similar mechanical apparatus into a 25-foot-long horse racing game, also played in his apartment. Motors beneath the track were calibrated for each horse's speed; they worked with a pulley and track system to move as many as twenty horses down the track, while a weighted ball contraption introduced an element of chance into the horses' speed.[10] In his Futurama model fifteen years later, Geddes upped the mechanical ante by having fifty thousand cars

more layer to our knowledge of his paradoxical character. He was a pacifist obsessed with war, a naturalist who loved technology, a socially liberal eugenics supporter, a designer who made realistic models of infinitesimal detail representing places he'd never seen and spaces like Futurama that purportedly existed twenty years hence. His immersion in theatricality was total. By integrating an understanding of Geddes's designs for the theater of war from their onset in 1915 through the 1940s, we gain a much more complete picture of Geddes and the innovative technical and conceptual leaps he made between theater, industry, and warfare.

Strong precedents for some of Geddes's greatest design successes using models in the late 1930s

FIGURE 4
*Geddes placing a military
unit on a terrain model he
most likely created in 1927
for his Animated Battle Map*

*films, c. 1933. Geddes's first
war game was created
c. 1915 and had a grid surface
dictated by the rules of play
(see fig. 7). Photograph by*

*(Florence) Vandamm Studio,
10 x 8 in., 25.4 x 20.3 cm*

were set by Geddes's early war game and Animated Battle Map project. His 1915 war game was made from cork, overlaid with gridded graph paper painted different colors representing geographic features, printed with text and symbols identifying cities, towns, industrial centers, roads, and railroads (FIG. 7, 8). A photograph (FIG. 4) from about 1933, however, shows Geddes with a different war model, whose layers have been covered with moss, sand, and other materials to simulate an aerial view of actual terrain. This shift from abstraction toward greater realism reflects broader trends in regionalist art of the thirties away from Cubism, as well as the contrast between the Expressionist New Stagecraft that Geddes espoused and his smash-hit realist sets such as for *The Miracle*. This trend toward realism in Geddes's war terrain models also presaged the minutely detailed, realistic modeling techniques he perfected for the 1937 Shell City of Tomorrow and Futurama at the 1939–40 New York World's Fair.

The mythical opponents of his 1915 war game occupied two countries named Yelozand and Redegar. Each had armies with different divisions, including standard numbers of infantry, cavalry, tanks, and aircraft, while their navies possessed many different types of ships as well as planes, troops, artillery, and anti-aircraft guns.[13] Other components included

import routes and major industries—steel, iron, coal, munitions, agriculture, motors, shipbuilding, textiles, cattle, sheep, and petroleum (if the first five were overtaken, a country had to surrender).[14] All were represented by pushpins (up to 7,500 per team) of variable sizes and shapes with different symbols on them (FIG. 8) that were deployed on a 64-square-foot relief map.[15]

The war game's forty-five-page rule book was based closely upon American, British, French, and German histories and manuals of warfare.[16] The rule book was passed out to teams along with sheets for writing down General Headquarter Field Orders and maps for plotting out the next week's strategy. Play began at eight P.M. sharp once a week; each side had thirty minutes to complete all moves equivalent to one twenty-four-hour period before the turn passed to the other side. The game continued until midnight with no time-outs. In the pre-computer era, this game was not for the faint-hearted; because a single "war" could last longer than a year, players had to be seriously committed.

The game attracted not only military leaders to its fold—Vice Admiral William B. Fletcher, Lieutenant General Sir Compton Packenham, even General Count Igor Moravsky from the Russian White Army, among other soldiers and cognoscenti—but also

FIGURE 5 (LEFT)

Geddes "Synthetic Training Model" or "Air Tactical Trainer," Army Air Force School of Applied Tactics, Orlando, Florida, 1943–44. The control panel for moving ground and air forces is on the far back wall on the right. Spotlights shone in from both sides to light the model; those simulating the battle were above, looking down. Photograph by Norman Bel Geddes & Co. for the United States Army, 10 x 8 in., 25.4 x 20.3 cm

FIGURE 6 (RIGHT)

Support structure and mechanical motor, chain, and pulley system (visible interspersed between the support jacks) in the basement beneath the AAFSAT model (fig. 5), Orlando, Florida, 1943–44. A similar system likely operated the moving vehicles in Futurama. Photograph by Norman Bel Geddes & Co. for the United States Army, 10 x 8 in., 25.4 x 20.3 cm

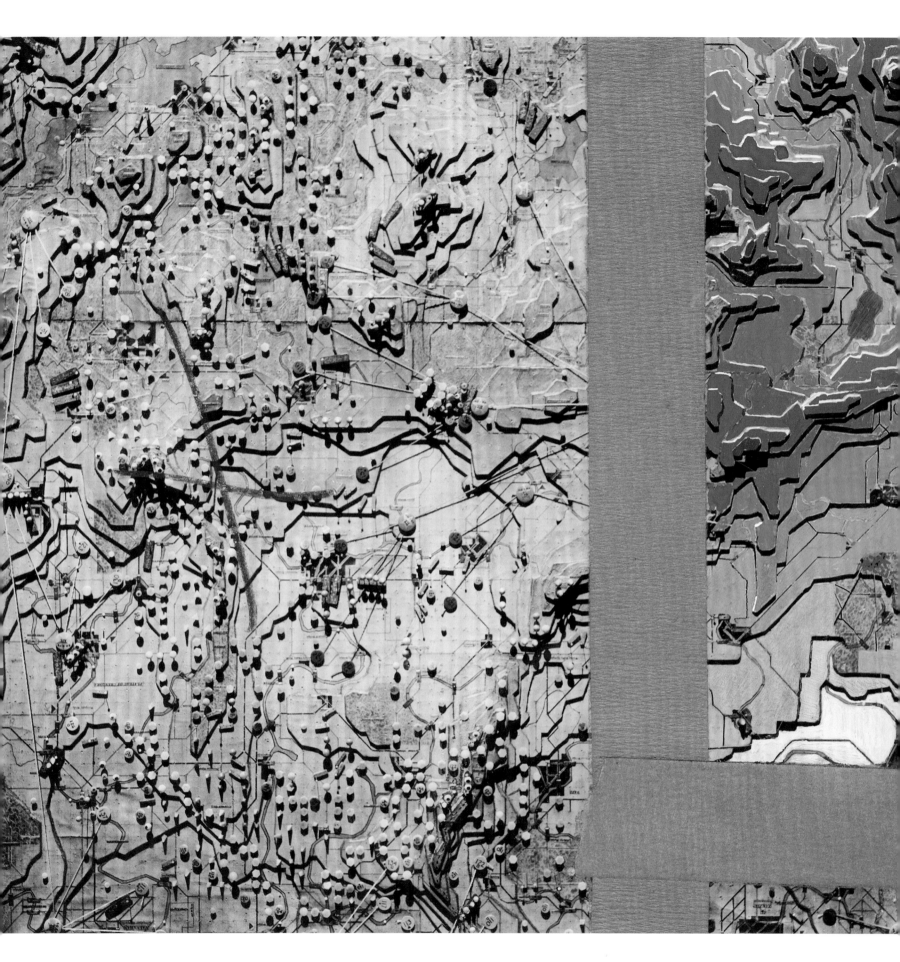

FIGURE 7
Geddes's first war game
(created c. 1915) in play (see
detail, fig. 8), September 20,

1939. Photograph by Richard
Garrison, 10 x 8 in.,
25.4 x 20.3 cm

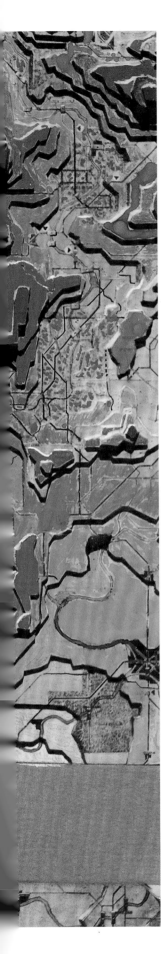

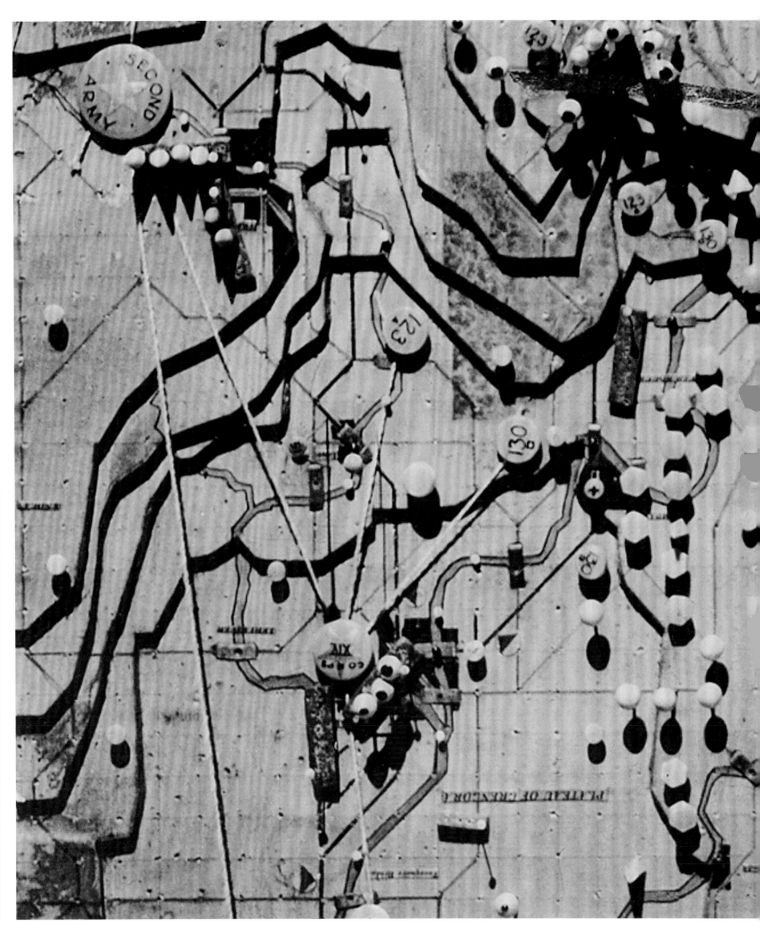

FIGURE 8
Detail of Geddes's original war game, left-side center toward bottom, showing the model's topographic layers, the printed text marking features on the map, and some of the different types of pushpins (varied by size, shape, color, and symbols) used to mark troop numbers and size, the "Second Army" headquarters, and various types of equipment and artillery.

chess champions. The American national champion Edward Lasker was a regular, and one evening when the world champion Russian Alexander Alekhine knocked on the door of Geddes's apartment hoping to join the game, Geddes sent Lasker down to welcome him. "Alekhine had read about the game in a White Russian newspaper in Paris, and brought me the clipping," Geddes wrote, saving the clipping for his archive.[17]

As part of his Animated Battle Map project, Geddes made three films in 1927 that represented reenactments of the Battle of Tsushima from the Russo-Japanese War, the Shenandoah Valley Campaign from the U.S. Civil War, and the Battle of Waterloo from the Franco-Prussian War.[18] Although these films have been lost or degraded beyond salvage, other documents describe in detail his plan to record thirty-six of "The World's Great Battles in Motion Picture Map Form," provided he could find a financial backer. The idea was developed in conversation with Packenham and other military players of his game, who advised him that the project "will receive unanimous support of the War and Navy Departments of all governments" for its immense educational value. "I would add a P.S. saying something about your stage work," Packenham wrote Geddes in 1929, encouraging him to emphasize his theatrical expertise, now applied to the arena of war, in his pitch to prospective sponsors. He added, "Make some reference to the fact that you have a large and thoroughly experienced technical staff, of draftsmen, etc.," referring to Geddes's growing industrial design firm.[19]

Credibility as an expert was required because of the huge sums Geddes was seeking, for he estimated the cost of just one film at over $31,500.[20] His conceptual goal was just as lofty, as he strove for both a fantastic level of realistic detail as well as the historical "truth," a "single authentic connected account" arrived at through "exhaustive research" in "consultation with recognized authorities," including translators who would compare historical battle narratives written by all of the opponents.[21] Geddes imagined that these experts would report "accurately on all phases of the organization of the various armies, troop movements for every hour during

the . . . days of the battle" and would record "this data on comparative charts." Small notebooks and loose-leaf diagrams in his archive reveal, however, that he was his only expert, preparing the narratives for three self-produced battle films that probably did not fully realize his elaborate vision. Examples of his isolated, in-depth studies include tracking of the hourly movement of ships in the Battle of Tsushima, mathematically plotting their turns at different scales, and for the U.S. Civil War's Seven Days Battle at Richmond, calculating the time and distance for a company of infantry, cavalry, and wagons to move down a road.[22]

Geddes extended this same level of realism to the scale and features of the terrain model and the re-creation of weather and lighting conditions, as well as to the camera distance from and angle to the surface in relation to the speed and length of the film. "One minute of battle time equals one second of film time. . . . Battle time equals film time equals film length," he specified.[23] Similarly, for a scale of "1 foot equals 1 mile," a more detailed map of the battlefield of Waterloo "would be approximately 10 by 12 feet," whereas "a map of the area of operations will be approximately 25 by 30 feet." He wanted these maps "to be built up in layered relief, painted and upholstered in various textures to represent the different characters of terrain," such as the 1933 model (which was probably made for these films) and those he would later create (FIG. 4). Unlike the surface of his first war game (FIG. 8), these three-dimensional maps would be "devoid of any lettering or anything of ordinary map character which would destroy their realism. The maps will be given the appearance that we get of a geographical area from an airplane."[24] Troops "will appear to be moving of their own accord," which he probably planned to accomplish either through the same mechanism he constructed for his 1925 horse race game or through a stop-motion technique (in the "stop" periods, he would move the pieces by hand, suspended over the model by a catwalk if necessary). "Trains and motor lorries being loaded with troops or supplies, ships being refueled, and aircraft at various heights will be clearly visible. When important, mess, rest and bivouac periods and Engineering preparations such as trench digging, bridge building, and sapping will be graphically portrayed." Using lighting and

FIGURE 9
Geddes with map and ship models, c. late 1939. Photograph by A. F. Sozio, 8 x 10 in., 20.3 x 25.4 cm

other atmospheric techniques from the theater, such as a smoke machine, he planned to clearly replicate "day or night, land and sea conditions, weather and visibility" as well as "[t]he direction of the sun, which is most important, especially at sea and in hilly or mountainous terrain."[25] In order to keep continuity in the filming and in the scale and action of the battle, he planned to film with a camera primarily fixed above the map, "as from an airplane," but to move the camera closer or to a different angle when he needed to show greater detail or give greater clarity.[26]

As these details suggest, inspired by his 1915 war game and in the context of developing his Animated Battle Map project between 1927 and 1935, Geddes envisioned almost all of the major techniques that he would later employ in his films, models, model photographs, and exhibitions of those models from the late 1930s onward, including those for Shell, General Motors, and his wartime work for *Life* magazine and the U.S. Navy. These techniques included highly realistic model making, variable scaling for variable distance, representing temporal and atmospheric conditions, simulating motion, positioning the audience to have an aerial point of view, and correlating camera/viewer distance and angle to match the scale and narrative of the model. Only technical inventions, such as Futurama's complex sound system and conveyor and remote-controlled model aircraft for the AAFSAT simulation room, added new mechanisms to his already well-equipped repertoire of theatrical tools.

Yet, as Packenham noted in 1929, what Geddes really lacked was not sophisticated ideas but credibility outside of the theater. "With such a large undertaking ahead of you," he had told Geddes, referring to the Animated Battle Map project, "it might be well to point out that you have been in the habit of doing bigger things and getting away with them."[27] Although this was indeed true in the theater world, it was not yet true for his newfound career of industrial design. It wasn't until after Futurama at the 1939–40 New York World's Fair more than a decade later that Geddes finally obtained an audience with the military men whom he had approached with his various ideas derived from the Animated Battle Map project. Their attention in October 1941 was undoubtedly

due to their sense of the pressing immediacy of U.S. entry into World War II as well as to Geddes's fame as a man with technical ingenuity and a flair for drama who could get grandiose jobs done. Never one to think small, by 1940 Geddes had graduated from a 64-square-foot war game with fifteen thousand pieces (**FIG. 1**) to a 35,738-square-foot model of the United States in 1960, comprising 408 model sections each measuring 5 feet by 20 feet, on which were placed fifty thousand moving automobiles, 500,000 miniature buildings, and one million miniature trees (**FIG. 3**).[28] His estimation of his own ability to bring about "reality"—both future and past—through his imagination and talent, or at least to impart trompe l'oeil visual and material form to accounts of "reality," had similarly matured. Whereas visitors to Futurama left wearing buttons stating "I have seen the future" (more than that, they had physically walked into it), viewers of Geddes's 1927 film reenacting the Battle of Tsushima from 1905, or the U.S. Navy officers who commissioned him in 1945 to create the official photographic record of the Battle of Midway from 1942 (because enough high-quality "real" photos did not exist), could believe that they had indeed seen "the past."

Editors and general managers at major newspaper syndicates during the first two months of World War II, however, were skeptical when, in the absence of regular news coming from the front, Geddes tried to convince them to run a "news" column provided by Norman Bel Geddes & Company. He suggested the title "What Is Happening in the War Zone?" and promised that in consultation with a "strategy board" appointed by him, his company would "provide the reader with a understanding [*sic*] of what was going on in a manner not otherwise obtainable."[29] Geddes's office developed this idea in a meeting in September 1939, when he showed his first war game of 1915 to his staff. In four hundred telegrams sent to news agencies, he offered to provide a daily "cartoon strip" showing the sequential movement of troops and supplies, created by photographing the placement of different types of pushpins on new topographic relief maps of Europe his office was constructing (the first of these is shown in **FIG. 9**). Arrows superimposed on these photos and

FIGURE 10 (OPPOSITE)
FIGURE 11 (OVERLEAF)
Cover and inside spread of Geddes's "Batlrama" map produced by McClintock Publishing Company, c. late 1939–early 1940. 21½ x 28¼ in., 54.6 x 71.8 cm (fully unfolded)

NORMAN BEL GEDDES'
BATLRAMA

10¢

ACTUAL RELIEF MAP OF NORTHWESTERN EUROPE

An exclusive new kind of map giving the geographical features that influence military operations—mountains, ridges, passes, hills, valleys, rivers, and showing other features such as bridges, railroads, motor roads, canals, cities and towns.

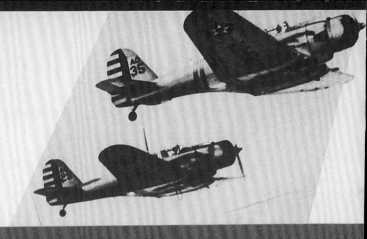

Estimated Strength of the Various Nations at War and the Neutrals.

Approximate Figures Derived From Best Sources Available

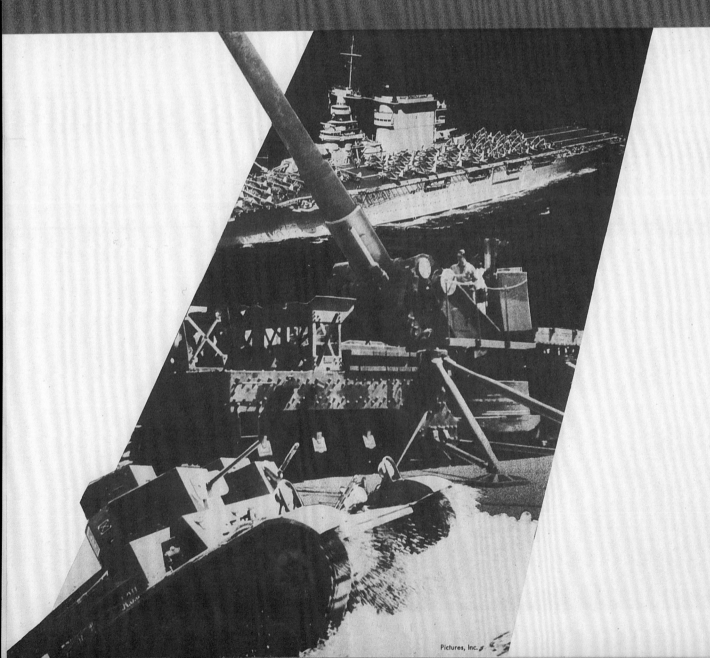

Country	Regular Army, Plus Trained Reserves	Navy Tonnage	Merchant Marine Tonnage	Air Force Total Planes	Monthly Plane Replacements	Populations of Countries
Great Britain	640,000		17,540,000	4,800	1,000	46,688,000
British Dominions and Colonies	1,100,000	1,850,000	3,085,000	250	——	445,000,000
France	6,115,000	796,000	2,800,000	3,200	1,000	41,900,000
Germany	3,470,000	517,000	4,350,000	7,500	1,300	90,000,000
Russia (U.S.S.R.)	13,040,000	302,000	1,320,000	7,500	750	165,750,000
Italy	4,230,000	641,000	3,340,000	4,200	500	43,700,000
Belgium	780,000	none	435,000	350	——	8,300,000
Netherlands	415,000	60,000	2,750,000	350	——	8,640,000
Switzerland	450,000	none	none	500	——	4,170,000
Spain (1936)	150,000	80,000	1,000,000	150	——	24,575,000
Portugal	450,000	negligible	260,000	negligible	——	6,825,000
Denmark	150,000	14,000	1,100,000	100	——	3,750,000
Norway	125,000	32,000	4,600,000	100	——	2,900,000
Sweden	850,000	100,000	1,500,000	250	——	6,265,000
Finland	250,000	15,000	550,000	150	——	3,805,000
Hungary	700,000	negligible	negligible	100	——	10,615,000
Rumania	1,810,000	12,000	90,000	500	——	19,535,000
Greece	550,000	45,000	1,900,000	100	——	7,020,000
Turkey	680,000	56,000	200,000	600	——	16,429,000
Yugoslavia	1,550,000	10,000	380,000	800	——	15,400,000
Bulgaria	350,000	negligible	negligible	100	——	6,320,000

ALPHABETICAL LIST OF CITIES AND TOWNS WITH GRID REFERENCE NUMBERS

To locate a town: First number after name of town indicates its position from top to bottom; second number indicates town's position from left to right.

Town	Down	Across
Aix-La-Chapelle (Aachen)	37	31
Alford	4	6
Altkirch	68	31
Amiens	39	8
Amsterdam	20	28
Antwerp	30	23
Apeldoorn	23	34
Argenteuil	48	5
Armentieres	32	13
Arnhem	25	33
Arzfeld	44	30
Aschendorf	17	42
Bachum	31	40
Bailleau	31	13
Barmen	33	39
Basle	69	34
Bendorf	42	39
Benfeld	62	33
Bentheim	24	41
Bielefeld	28	48
Bitburg	46	31
Bitche	55	36
Bonn	39	37
Boston	7	4
Boulogne	30	6
Bourges	66	1
Breisach	65	34
Brigg	1	4
Bruges (Bourges)	28	17
Burgh le Marsh	5	6
Brussels	34	22
Calais	28	8
Cambridge	14	2
Chalons-sur-Marne	51	17
Cleethorpes	1	5
Coblenz	43	39
Colmar	64	33
Cologne	36	37
Crefeld	32	35
Croningen	14	39
Courtray	32	16

Town	Down	Across
Darmstadt	49	44
Deding	25	37
Delft	22	25
Diedenhofen	50	29
Dijon	68	18
Dordrecht	25	26
Dortmund	31	41
Duisberg	31	37
Dullingen	41	29
Dunkerque	28	11
Duren	37	32
Dusseldorf	33	36
East Retford	1	1
Eindhoven	29	29
Elberfeld	33	38
Elten	26	34
Emden	14	43
Emmen	19	41
Emmendingen	62	37
Enschede	24	39
Erstein	62	35
Essen	31	38
Ettingen	57	40
Eupen	38	30
Forbach	53	32
Frankfurt	47	45
Fraulautern	51	32
Freiburg	64	36
Fumay	43	21
Gainsborough	1	1
Geldern	32	33
Gelsenkirchen	31	39
Genep	27	33
Ghent	30	19
Gillingham	22	2
Givet	41	22
Gladbach	33	34
Grantham	6	1
Great Yarmouth	13	12
Grimsby	1	5
Guthau	24	40

Town	Down	Across
Haarlem	20	27
Hagen	33	41
The Hague	22	25
Haguenau	58	37
Hamm	30	43
Hastings	27	1
Heerlen	35	31
Heidelberg	53	43
Heilbronn	56	46
Hengeloo	23	39
Hilversum	22	19
Horncastle	4	4
Immingham	0	5
Ipswich	17	7
Kaiserslautern	52	38
Karlsruhe	56	40
Koevorden	20	39
Lahr	61	37
Lauterbourg	57	39
Leer	15	45
Leiden	21	26
Liege	37	28
Lille	33	14
Lincoln	3	2
London	20	0
Longwy	49	27
Lorrach	69	34
Louth	3	5
Ludwigshafen	52	42
Luxembourg	48	29
Maastricht	35	29
Mablethorpe	3	6
Mainz	48	42
Malines	32	23
Mallenthal	40	31
Mannheim	52	42
Market Rasen	2	3
Maubeuge	39	17
Mechelen	34	30
Merzig	50	31

Town	Down	Across
Metz	52	28
Mezieres	44	21
Montherme	43	21
Montmedy	49	26
Mulheim	36	37
Mulhouse	67	33
Munster	27	43
Nancy	57	27
Neuenhaus	21	40
Neufreistett	59	38
Neuss	33	35
Newark	4	1
Nichtendu	59	38
Nijmegen	26	32
Nordheim	22	41
Norwich	12	10
Offenbach	47	46
Offenberg	60	38
Oggersheim	52	41
Orleans	57	1
Osnabruck	25	46
Paris	49	5
Pforzheim	59	43
Pirmasens	54	37
Popenburg	17	43
Prum	42	31
Rastatt	58	40
Razebrouck	31	13
Remscheid	34	38
Rheims	48	16
Rheydt	34	34
Roermond	34	31
Rotterdam	24	25
Rouhaix	33	15
Saaralbe	55	33
Saarbruecken	53	33
Saarlouis	52	32
St. Amand	36	16
St. Denis	48	6
St. Michel	42	17

Town	Down	Across
Salt Fleet	3	6
Sarreguemin	55	34
Sasbach	64	34
Schiedam	23	25
Schlestadt	63	34
Schliengen	67	34
Sedan	46	22
Seraing	38	28
Sierck	50	30
Skegness	5	6
Sleaford	5	2
Southend-on-Sea	20	4
Spilsby	5	5
Spurn Head	2	7
Strasbourg	60	37
Stuttgart	60	45
Terberg	26	35
Thann	66	32
Tilburg	28	28
Tournay	34	16
Trier	48	33
Tuxford	2	1
Udem	27	34
Ulm	65	49
Utrecht	23	29
Valenciennes	37	16
Venloo	33	31
Versailles	49	4
Warfleet	6	6
Wiesbaden	47	42
Wilhelmshaven	13	48
Wissembourg	56	38
Witten	32	40
Worms	51	42
Worth	56	39
Wragby	3	3
Ypres	31	14
Zweibrucken	53	36

FIGURE 12 (BELOW)
A jeweler working for Norman Bel Geddes & Co. alters a model ship with jeweler's and dental tools to conform to precise scale (1 inch to 100 feet) of current ship details, per plan shown on the clipboard. Photograph by unidentified photographer, 10 x 8 in., 25.4 x 20.3 cm

FIGURE 13 (OPPOSITE TOP)
Ship Models for "Submarine Attack Teacher MKs and Mods.," Navy Ordnance Contract NXSo 14763. Models and photograph by Norman Bel Geddes & Co. for the United States Navy, 9½ x 7¾ in., 24.1 x 19.7 cm

FIGURE 14 (OPPOSITE BOTTOM)
Norman Bel Geddes & Co. presentation booklet page titled "A Submarine Range Finder / Providing quick and positive identification of any naval vessel within periscope range and establishing distance and angle of the target," c. 1941–42. Photograph and typed text, 8½ x 11 in., 21.6 x 28 cm

accompanying text would explain the strategies being implemented by France and Germany.[30] Members of the press uniformly declined, telling Geddes it was "too hypothetical," to which he replied that he was "certain that the service would be accurate within 80 to 90 percent."[31]

At the same time, Geddes convinced McClintock Publishing Company to produce copies of a map called the "Batlrama," based on a photograph of the same topographic model of Europe (FIG. 10, 11). This map would be available for purchase by the public for ten cents, so they too could place pushpins on their own maps and follow along with Geddes's interpretation of the war. Confusing his previous war-related creations with his proposed representations of current war events, Geddes had trouble

keeping separate the phrases "war game" and "war map." Documents in the files for the News Syndicate War Map and the Batlrama projects repeatedly and significantly interchange these phrases in an imposition of Geddes's imagination and knowledge of war over actual current history in the making.[32]

Consistent with his usual modus operandi to secure work for his office, Geddes set his staff in motion effecting the work he envisioned in order to show prospective clients the possibilities. As early as March 1940, at his own expense, Geddes's office constructed a concrete "ocean," replete with waves that realistically simulated "mid-ocean conditions" and "smooth areas representing inlets and bays."[33] On the model Geddes staged ships in formation, including their wakes, using his model ship collec-

tion of the world's navies (**FIG. 13, 17**). After *Popular Science* magazine ran an article in November 1941 featuring Geddes's model photographs of staged battles and actions at sea, Geddes received a letter from Commander C. G. Moore that culminated in his first contract with the U.S. Navy, signed soon after the U.S. entry into the war after the bombing of Pearl Harbor on December 7, 1941.[34] The final agreement stipulated a rush order of fifty photos each of fifty enemy ship models on the "ocean," taken at specific horizontal and vertical angles, to be completed in seven weeks for a sum of $25,500.[35] This assignment demanded the alteration of selected ship models to match the most up-to-date confidential Navy intelligence. Geddes rented a room adjacent to his office, taped off the windows, restricted access to only those employees assigned to the job, and installed a locked vault that was opened and closed only under observation of Navy personnel, who also removed all films from the cameras.[36]

What followed over the next twenty months was a series of confidential model ship making and model photography projects for the Navy, including those used in training servicemen in enemy ship and plane recognition, as well as ship-formation still photographs and stop-motion films, one of which was executed in collaboration with Pathé News.[37] Geddes brought several jewelers onto his staff (**FIG. 12**) to help execute a series of enemy ship models (**FIG. 13, 17**) for "Submarine Attack Teacher MK2s and Mods" commissioned by the Navy's Bureau of Ordnance. The purpose was suggested by a presentation booklet made by Geddes's office, whose first page reads: "A Submarine Range Finder / Providing quick and positive identification of any naval vessel within periscope range and establishing distance and angle of the target." Another page (**FIG. 14**) projects a double overlay of model photographs of the Italian ship *Littoria*, viewed at a 75-degree angle, to simulate the view through a torpedo gun sight so that the gunner could ascertain correct identification, angle of approach, and distance from the target simply through a quick comparison of the length of the "projected image" with that of the ship as seen through the gun sight—the "target image." The blackness of the surrounding page evokes the precise

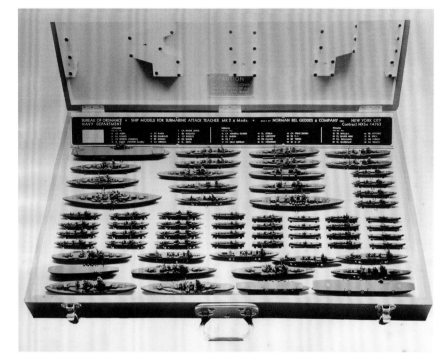

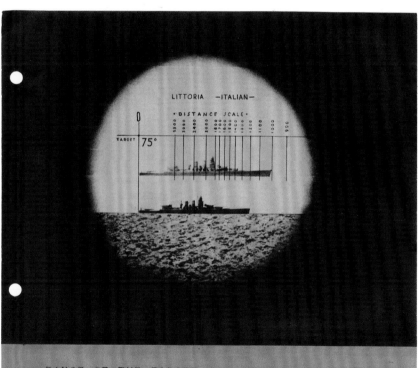

FIGURE 15 (ABOVE)

*Model of Guadalcanal,
Solomon Islands, shot
for* Life *magazine, assignment 08, setup 01, take
08, in "Presentation
Book—Geographical
Model Photography."
Photostat, 9⅝ x 6½ in.,
24.4 x 16.5 cm*

FIGURE 16 (RIGHT)

*Lead image used in "Coral
Sea: Norman Bel Geddes's
Models Re-enact Naval
Battle,"* Life *magazine,
May 25, 1942. The actual
Battle of the Coral Sea
took place May 4–8, 1942.
Copyright © 1942 The
Picture Collection Inc.
Used with permission. All
rights reserved.*

and deadly outcome of perfectly scaled model ship photography put to this use (which hardly seems the vision of "an out-and-out pacifist").[38]

While he was developing these projects for the Navy, Geddes began doing model photography assignments for *Life* magazine.[39] Geddes used the non-confidential versions of his model ships to reenact the Battle of the Coral Sea in his first assignment, which ran as a "photojournalistic" piece on May 25, 1942, less than three weeks after the battle ended (FIG. 16).[40] Geddes made many claims about the superiority of model photography over real photos taken on site in the midst of the action. In the case of naval battles like the one on the Coral Sea, few real photos usually existed. In the rare instances when soldiers were shooting film instead of artillery, or journalists were along for a life-threatening ride, camera lenses could usually only capture a fragment of the action, which often was obscured by smoke or clouds or darkness. Yet, in the absence of photographs documenting a battle, Geddes had no concern about filling in with his imagination, as demonstrated by his attempts to entice newspaper syndicates with his "news" column.

Geddes was able to convince *Life* of the "journalistic" value of model photography, although in the Coral Sea article they made sure to stress their "supervision" over the creation of "realistic" images from the "known facts."[41] *Life*'s readers took little persuading, as their letters to the editor called

Geddes's photos "amazing," "magnificent," the "best" and "most exciting," "the Futurama of war reporting!" One photo mailed in showed Navy Lieutenant Commander Sampson using Geddes's photos of the Coral Sea battle to train cadets at Ellington Field.[42] The theatrical talent of Geddes's employees—making a concrete ocean, wakes of salt, billowing smoke from cotton and wire armature, and oil spills with paint, matching lighting and atmosphere to actual conditions, keeping all to scale, and photographing as if from the cockpit of a plane overhead, won Geddes more than fifty subsequent assignments from *Life* over the next two and a half years. The Coral Sea battle was immediately followed by the Battle of Midway (FIG. 18), as well as by geographic model photography of sites such as Guadalcanal in the Solomon Islands (FIG. 15), that oriented *Life*'s readers to distant locations where the war was being fought.[43] In 1945, after the war's end, when it was decided that Midway had been the war's turning point, the U.S. Navy commissioned Geddes to create the official historical photographic record of the battle, a seven-month task so huge his crew set up shop in a rented warehouse space at Manhattan's South Ferry (FIG. 19). This commission surely affirmed his lifelong study of the official records of the world's major battles that he began before 1915.[44]

In early 1943, Geddes's work for the military expanded into a major project for the U.S. Army Air Force at the new, but short-lived, School of Applied

FIGURE 17
Photograph of model Japanese ship formation used as the lead image in "Model Ships Show World's Navies," article in Popular Science, *November 1941.*

NORMAN BEL GEDDES DESIGNS AMERICA

Tactics in Orlando, Florida (**FIG. 5, 6**). Geddes pushed the limits of technology on the cusp of the digital age as he applied all of his skills from theater, design, and war gaming in the creation of an analogue, three-dimensional battle simulation room, replete with remote-controlled aircraft, directed through an electrical control panel.[45] Like the position of fairgoers in New York, the "aerial" position of the soldiers at AAFSAT was well above the mechanically operated battlefield, and they too were sealed off from it by glass windows. Two hundred officers and soldiers, split into the "Reds" and the "Blues," looked down through glass windows to the model below and placed their commands to drop bombs and move forces electronically using the control panel. Airplanes made of Lucite operated through remote control, and bomb hits created light flashes on the model below. No photos of battle simulation in action at AAFSAT exist, leaving us to wonder if this ambitious project ever actually worked or was used as intended; one can only imagine something equivalent to Geddes's "Landing on the North Sea Coast" in real time (**FIG. 18**). The model replicated central Florida in miniature, the very "theatre of operations" in which soldiers at AAFSAT practiced war against each other (this was, after all, the School of *Applied Tactics*), hurling their bodies over sand dunes and hiding behind bushes before coming in for the purely mental exercise of simulated battling using Geddes's "Synthetic Trainer #1."[46]

While Geddes was in Florida building his masterpiece of war theater, his staff was installing an exhibition of their work for *Life* magazine at The Museum of Modern Art in New York City, one of several of the museum's exhibitions that highlighted contributions to the war effort. For the first week after the January 1944 opening, Geddes's model makers were in action on set constructing a "river crossing model" in a space cordoned off to museum-goers but visible through a glass window. At least two of the models, most notably "Landing on the North Sea Coast" and "Attack on Gibraltar," were not historical reenactments of World War II battles at all but rather were predictive enactments created by Geddes showing "logical" military "possibilit[ies]." The photos of "Attack on Gibraltar" had been created in mid-1942,

before the Allies defeated Germany at El Alamein in North Africa, when Geddes thought such an attack was likely. The catalog accompanying the exhibition exposed Geddes's and *Life*'s intentions: "The sequence of *such an* attack, *if it had happened*, is shown in these models that were built and photographed at that time *in preparation for such a news break*."[47] Geddes's photos seemingly would have run in *Life* as "news" (or something "such as" news) despite the fact that his "photojournalism" was completely fictional.

Even if Geddes's predictions were "accurate within 80 to 90 percent," as he asserted when publicizing his syndicated war maps concept, he apparently had no problem imposing his own interpretation on the facts of history, past as well as current—in spite of being a self-taught student of all "official histories" of previous wars, or rather perhaps because of being a self-taught student. Geddes had little time for academic pursuits and even less patience for a particularly academic type of methodological rigor. He did, however, excel in the skills needed to create breathtaking illusions that could transport the imagination. He came of age during World War I and matured professionally in the theater and in the pumped-up, Gatsbyesque business world of the Roaring Twenties. It is probably no coincidence that he first proclaimed his mantra, "the imagination creates the actual," around 1926, an idea that fit well with his Christian Science beliefs as well as with the giddy optimism of the age. Perhaps it is surprising, however, that the Great Depression did little to daunt his energy and vision and failed to bring him back to reality.[48] Instead, he doggedly persisted for decades in blurring the lines between the imagined and the actual, as seen in his inability to distinguish between a "war game" and a "war map," in his cavalier treatment of what counted as "news," and even in the models and images he made for the Submarine Attack Teacher (all the while considering himself a pacifist). This belief ran deep throughout his endeavors in the theater, industrial design, and his projects pertaining to warfare. The war game he created in 1915 thus established an approach that he closely adhered to throughout his diverse career.

FIGURE 18 (OPPOSITE)
Setup 06, take 08, for Task Force Operation model photography sequence most likely completed for Geddes's third assignment for Life *magazine, c. July 1942, documenting the Battle of Midway, which actually happened June 4–7, 1942. Model and photography by Norman Bel Geddes & Co., 10 x 14 in., 28 x 35.6 cm*

FIGURE 19 (OVERLEAF)
Image showing the creation of the official historical photographic record of the Battle of Midway for the U.S. Navy, 1945–46, at the ferry house at slip five, South Ferry. The project employed up to thirty people and cost the U.S. Navy $65,000. Photograph by Norman Bel Geddes & Co. for the United States Navy, 7³⁄₄ x 8 in., 19.7 x 20.3 cm

ENDNOTES

1   Memo from Geddes to Pemberton on 27 September 1939, Box 23, Folder 402.1, Geddes Papers.

2   Memo from Pemberton to Geddes on 27 September 1939, titled "Suggested material for wire to be sent to prospective clients," Box 23, Folder 402.1, Geddes Papers.

3   Ruth Pickering, "Games Worth the Candle—Sport for Kings and Good Fellows Fought Out on the Playing Fields of Mr. Geddes," *Arts and Decoration* (February 1933): 18–20, 62, Box 6, Folder 56.11, Geddes Papers.

4   Edwin C. Hill, "In Spite of Kellogg Treaty, War Again Rages on Wide Front," *New York Sun* (12 January 1931), Box 6, Folder 56.11, Geddes Papers.

5   Ibid., and Pickering, "Games Worth the Candle": 18.

6   On H. G. Wells, see Ed Halter, *From Sun Tzu to Xbox: War and Video Games* (New York: Thunder's Mouth Press, 2006), 61–62, and Peter Perla, *The Art of War Gaming: A Guide for Professionals and Hobbyists* (Annapolis, Md.: Naval Institute Press, 1990), 34–35.

7   Hill, "In Spite of Kellogg Treaty."

8   For a very insightful article analyzing the aerial perspective trope so present in much of Geddes's work, see Adnan Morshed, "The Aesthetics of Ascension in Norman Bel Geddes's Futurama," *Journal of the Society of Architectural Historians* 63:1 (March 2004): 74–99, and his book, *The Architecture of Ascension: Airplanes, Skyscrap-*ers, and the American Imagination of the Master Planner, 1919–1939 (Minneapolis: University of Minnesota Press, 2011).

9   Norman Bel Geddes, *Miracle in the Evening* (Garden City, N.Y.: Doubleday & Company, 1960), 293.

10 Pickering, "Games Worth the Candle": 18–19, and Flat file, Folder 107.1, Geddes Papers.

11 Footage showing miniature model cars moving along the highways of Futurama in film "k-11 World's Fair, General Motors Exhibit," and also in a black-and-white film opening with a marquee saying "General Motors invites you to tour the future," digitally reformatted from original reel film, Geddes Papers. See also Jennifer Davis Roberts, *Norman Bel Geddes: An Exhibition of Theatrical and Industrial Designs* (Austin: Humanities Research Center, University of Texas at Austin, 1979), 43–44. The 1940 version of Futurama had fifty thousand moving autos; the 1939 version had only ten thousand.

12 On Geddes's AAFSAT model, see John F. Rudy, "Air Forces School Works Out Battle Tactics Here for Aerial Combat Zones," *Orlando Morning Sentinel* (12 May 1943), Box 34, Folder 487.1, Geddes Papers, as well as other documents in this folder, and information in Box 34, Folder 487.2, "AAFSAT/Contracts Feb 1943," Geddes Papers.

13 Types of ships included battleships, cruisers, destroyers, submarines, patrol boats, minelayers, minesweepers, tenders, transports, and cargo ships; see "Rules of Play / Record Copy, 7th War Game," page III-1, Box 5, Folder 56.4, Geddes Papers; and G. Deming Seymour, "War has broken out again in East 37th Street," *Utica [N.Y.] Press* (6 November 1929), Box 5, Folder 56.10, Geddes Papers. Standard war games pitted Red versus Blue; see Halter, *From Sun Tzu to Xbox*, 41, 91, and Perla, *The Art of War Gaming*, 55.

14 "Rules of Play / Record Copy, 7th War Game," pages II-1, IV-1, IV-2, Geddes Papers.

15 "Geddes Provides 'War' As a Game for Guests—Fleets and Armies Clash at Call of Players at Big Board Devised by Artist," *New York Times* (6 March 1929), and Richard Massock, "About New York," Providence *Tribune* (13 March 1929), Box 6, Folder 56.11, Geddes Papers.

16 Range of fire was also adjusted based upon relative terrain position. White paper strips with these range tables are in Box 5, Folder 56.4, Geddes Papers. See also "Rules of Play / Record Copy, 7th War Game," pages IV-3, VI-1; and "Table of co-ordinate Maxima for diagonal Ranges from 7 to 30 kilometers," Box 5, Folder 56.4, Geddes Papers.

17 Geddes, *Miracle in the Evening*, 233–34; on Lasker's attendance, see letter from Igor Moravsky to Geddes, 11 May 1930, Box 5, Folder 56.1, Geddes Papers. Alekhine's news story in Russian is in Box 6, Folder 56.11, Geddes Papers.

18 Geddes claimed he made these three battle films in 1927 in his description of the history of model photography in "Presentation

Books—'The Bel Geddes Process for Television, Motion Pictures, Graphic Illustration,'" 26, Oversize Box 11, File 672.1a, Geddes Papers.

19 Letter from T. C. Packenham to Geddes, 24 June 1929, and "A Project for Recording The World's Great Battles / Revised Draft Feb 1935," as well as an earlier draft entitled "Brief Outline of a Project For Recording The World's Great Battles in Motion Picture Map Form," all in Box 10, Folder 179.1, Geddes Papers.

20 "Estimate for Test Animated Battle Map / Shenandoah Valley," dated 16 March 1935, predicts "say $23,000" for that film; also "Brief Outline of a Project For Recording The World's Great Battles." A letter from Henry Allen Moe, of the John Simon Guggenheim Foundation, to Geddes, 21 July 1937, reveals that Geddes had approached the Guggenheim Foundation to inquire about a fellowship to fund his Animated Battle Map project, which Moe declined, Box 10, Folder 179.1, Geddes Papers.

21 "A Project for Recording The World's Great Battles / Revised Draft Feb 1935."

22 Diagram of "Marching Time," Box 10, Folders 179.1 and 179.2, Geddes Papers.

23 See notes and diagrams, Box 55, Folder 672.1, Geddes Papers.

24 Description for Geddes's proposal for the Battle of Waterloo, in "Brief Outline of a Project For Recording The World's Great Battles in Motion Picture Map Form."

25 For an example of his technique, see Geddes's footage of the Shell Oil Company City of Tomorrow project, included in the film titled "Norman Bel Geddes Collection 2000 Rollo etc.," from minute 25:29 through 29:24, Geddes Papers. This film has outstanding live studio footage showing the smoke machine, camera height and angles, and the lighting Geddes used to stage the photographs he made for the Shell model of the City of Tomorrow.

26 "A Project for Recording The World's Great Battles / Revised Draft Feb 1935."

27 Letter from T. C. Packenham to Geddes, 24 June 1929.

28 Roberts, 43–44.

29 Minutes of a promotional meeting about "Use of War Map by the Associated Press," 17 October 1939, Box 23, Folder 402.1, Geddes Papers.

30 Long version of minutes of meeting regarding War Map, 27 September 1939; "Miscellaneous Notes on the Map Syndication idea" memo from Geddes to Barker, Pemberton, and Ettinger, 2 October 1939; and minutes of a meeting between Wilbur Forrest and Harry Staton of the *Herald Tribune* with Geddes, Barker, and McClintock, 13 October 1939; all in Box 23, Folder 402.1, Geddes Papers.

31 Geddes also stated, "If we are wrong in our reasoning, then the next day we will move our pins back," in long version of minutes of meeting regarding War Map, 27 September 1939. The minutes of this meeting are revealing of Geddes's confidence in his ability to predict war maneuvering based on his understanding of war strategy and his eagerness to capitalize on the war and push his ideas off to the public. See also minutes of a promotional meeting about "Use of War Map by the Associated Press" and "memo from Ettinger in Geddes's office re: meeting with Mr. Wilbur Forrest of the *Herald Tribune*," Box 23, Folder 402.1, Geddes Papers.

32 Minutes from a luncheon about War Map, 20 September 1939, with Geddes, Pemberton, and Capt. Delano, state, "After Mr. Geddes outlined the three phases of the War Game . . ." See also letter from Henry Snevily, general manager of the Bell Syndicate, Inc., to Geddes, 18 September 1939, who called it the "War Game Map." Both in Box 23, Folder 402.1, "Newspaper Syndicate War Maps—Memoranda," Geddes Papers. See also letter from George McClintock on Batlrama letterhead, 23 May 1940, in Box 24, Folder 404.1, "Job 404 Battlerama, Client Correspondence," Geddes Papers, which states, "In September 1939 when the map was first thought of, the plan was to produce a sort of War Game."

33 "Model Ships Show World's Navies," *Popular Science* 139:5 (November 1941): 116–19, Box 55, Folder 672.14, Geddes Papers. The first photographs of "Jap Ship Formations" and Geddes's staging of naval battles were made on 8 March 1940 by Richard Garrison and A. F. Sozio for Job File 403, "Navy Ship Models Photographic Record," which almost certainly were not done for the U.S. Navy as the title of the folder might seem to imply but rather were photos of Geddes's "navy ship model" collection (as in *Popular Science*'s article title), Box 30, Folder 453.9, Geddes Papers. Other photos are dated 10 May 1940; 20 June 1940; 3 July 1940; and 8 July 1940; all of these photos, I believe, are stamped with Job File 403. Some of these are listed in the photographic record sheets as taken for "Ship Model Proposal" for use in a "presentation book" (used by Geddes's office to pitch projects) being made by R. Day. Also, one of these "Jap Ship Formation" photos, dated 19 July 1940, is in Photo Box 14, Folder 453, "LIFE Naval Battle—16 photographs of model building and battle models," Geddes Papers, although it is doubtful that this photo was taken for *Life* at the time it was made. Also, a photo very similar to this one ran in *Popular Science* and is not credited to *Life*. Note finally that the Newspaper Syndicate War Maps project was given Job File 402, the Navy Ship Models Photographic Record Job File 403, and Batlrama Job File 404, suggesting that these three projects originated in Geddes's office at about the same time.

34 The phrase "time is of the essence" is the last clause in "Agreement Between the United States of America and Norman Bel Geddes & Company," 7 January 1942, Box 29, Folder 446, Geddes Papers.

35 Letter from C. G. Moore, Commander, U.S. Navy, to Geddes, 24 October 1941, referencing "the November issue of *Popular Science*," followed up with a letter from Moore to Geddes, 13 December 1941, and Geddes's response to Moore on 18 December 1941, all in Box 29, Folder 446.3, Geddes Papers. Later their agreement was adjusted to include some ship formations, per letter from Moore and Samuel A. Smiley to Norman Bel Geddes & Company, 28 February 1942, in the same box.

36 "Otto Wester and Herman Rath have been hired to start on the ships Monday morning. Mr. Geddes will have to start the first revisions on the model ships which Mr. Smiley selected on Monday morning," per interoffice memo from Geddes, 30 December 1941, Box 29, Folder 446.3, Geddes Papers.

37 Memo from Schoenberger after phone call with Mr. Adams, Pathé News, 23 October 1942, Box 32, Folder 475.1, Geddes Papers; letter from Schoenberger to Orville Goldner, Lt. U.S.N.R., Training Film Section, Photographic Division, Bureau of Aeronautics, 13 January 1943, Box 32, Folder 477.1, Geddes Papers; letter from Clay Adams of Pathé News, Inc., to Geddes, 10 January 1943, Box 34, Folder 485.1, Geddes Papers. See also discussion in the correspondence about a stop-motion film that Geddes's office made in 1943 to demonstrate their technique, Box 34, Folder 485.2, Geddes Papers; this film may be film k-5 "Navy Ship Motion Study" in the Geddes Papers.

38 Geddes's first project for the Navy, completed in

March 1942, was to photograph fifty ships from fifty different positions, at fifteen-degree angles both horizontally and vertically. Navy project #2, to create thirty-three replicas of enemy model ships, began in the same month. Perhaps the Navy wanted the scaled miniature replicas for training submarine torpedo gunners. If so, then Geddes's presentation booklet may have gotten him the second job. A May 1943 news article describes training very similar to this at the Army Air Force School of Applied Tactics, where Geddes was working: "There's a long box type machine which operates electrically to improve a gunner's estimation of ranges. Planes move around in it at various distances. The gunner can estimate the distance in actual firing yards, then check it on the machine." See John F. Rudy, "Air Forces School Works Out Battle Tactics Here for Aerial Combat Zones."

39 Geddes mentions *Life*'s interests in model photographs of naval reenactments at the staff meeting on 27 September 1939; see also memo from R. Nowland to A. C. Barker on 26 September 1939, both in Box 23, Folder 402.1, Geddes Papers. See also letter from C. G. Moore to Geddes on 13 December 1941.

40 Geddes's collection of model ships, quite a few of which were made from sterling silver, grew to around thirteen thousand by the war's end. After the war, he sold the collection to New York attorney Harry Beethoven to recoup some of his substantial monetary losses from his costly work for the U.S military. That Geddes invested a huge sum of his own money in these projects reveals his strong personal commitment to them. Geddes claimed he "had all of my capital wiped out during the war" in a letter to Rear Admiral Arthur K. Doyle, Commandant, U.S. Navy Operating Base, Bermuda, 19 September 1947; letter from A. K. Doyle, Rear Admiral, U.S. Navy, to Vice Admiral A. W. Radford, U.S. Navy, Commander Second Tank Fleet, Naval Air Station, Norfolk, Va., 26 August 1947; both in Box 30, Folder 458.5, Geddes Papers; also letter from Harry J. Beethoven to Geddes, 3 April 1951, Box 55, Folder 672.2, Geddes Papers.

41 "Coral Sea: Norman Bel Geddes' Models Re-enact Naval Battle," *Life* 12:21 (25 May 1942): 21–25.

42 "Letters to the Editor," *Life* (15 June 1942): 2.

43 See lists of *Life* projects and dates completed, Box 30, Folder 453.4, Geddes Papers.

44 See Box 105, Folder 972.3, Geddes Papers.

45 On the relation of the first video game to computers in the 1940s, see Halter, *From Sun Tzu to Xbox*, 7.

46 John F. Rudy, "Air Forces School Works Out Battle Tactics Here for Aerial Combat Zones."

47 Text for "Attack on Gibraltar," *Norman Bel Geddes War Maneuver Models Created for* Life *Magazine* (New York: Museum of Modern Art, 26 January to 5 March 1944), italics added. See also the press release for the exhibition written by The Museum of Modern Art, "War Maneuver Models Shown at Museum of Modern Art," 26 January 1944, Box 35, Folder 499.3, Geddes Papers.

48 Christina Cogdell, *Eugenic Design: Streamlining America in the 1930s* (Philadelphia: University of Pennsylvania Press, 2004), 293, no. 62.

16

THE BEL GEDDES PROCESS

Andrea Gustavson

Throughout his long career as a stage and industrial designer, Norman Bel Geddes built scale models of his designs and photographed these miniature theaters, buildings, and cities in an attempt to blur the line between representation and reality. In a similar vein, he crafted large model sets on which he staged and photographed World War II battle scenes or re-created and photographed the building of the Egyptian pyramids. Between 1924 and 1957, Geddes developed a method of photographing models that he termed the Bel Geddes Process (**FIG. 1**). Applied to theatrical work, consulting for the U.S. Navy, or projects for *Encyclopaedia Britannica*, the Bel Geddes Process took several forms, from detailed photographs of a single building to aerial images of naval battles fought in the Pacific. Each iteration, however, involved the practice of photographing models that created realistic images otherwise impossible to capture. Although Geddes had been photographing models for years, in the 1950s he retroactively named all earlier instances of model photography for theaters, corporations, and the military as the Bel Geddes Process in order to market it as a technique bearing his brand.

By 1957, Geddes had created a series of elaborate photo-textual presentation books that showcased his model photographs to potential clients and proclaimed the many benefits of his technique. These books describe model photography as a "new form of illustration" able to convey truth even when depicting fictional subjects because it was "predicated on a photograph of something conveying more than reality."[1] Geddes insisted that model photography could capture anything available to the imagination, holds both "popular appeal" and "entertainment value," and would be "applicable to the fields of Education, Journalism, Television, Text Books, Movies, Museums."[2] According to Geddes, his technique could represent subjects as diverse as weather patterns, Einstein's Theory of Relativity, and football plays. Developed through a series of model-making projects over a thirty-three-year period, the Bel Geddes Process evolved into a form of illustration that Geddes insisted could render realistic even the most fantastical of subjects.

DEPICTING *THE DIVINE COMEDY*

In early instances of model photography, Geddes drew on his experience with theatrical design to dramatically light and photograph his models so they aligned almost exactly with his renderings (**FIG. 4**). Geddes dated the origin of the Bel Geddes Process to his never-produced stage adaptation of Dante's *The Divine Comedy* in 1924. His model stage was photographed following the conventions of formal portraiture, dramatically lit and set at a three-quarter turn relative to the camera lens (**FIG. 3**).[3] He insisted that all his images "were of photographic subjects [of] a special kind of three-dimensional model—with illusion, realism, atmosphere, and drama designed into them." To Geddes, the Bel Geddes Process conveyed an "impact of reality more impressive than first-person experience," so that viewers could not distinguish between representation and reality.[4] His model photography would, he claimed, seem more real than actual photographs of finished projects and real-world events.

IMAGINING THE TOLEDO SCALE FACTORY

The first commercial applications of the Bel Geddes Process were for the Toledo Scale factory complex in 1929. These photographs of Geddes's models ranged from "aerial" images of the master plan for the factory complex to extraordinarily detailed images of each building. Just as Geddes's presentation books were crafted narratives to guide the reader's imagination, his model photographs were often intricately lit to direct the viewer's attention.

Geddes often oscillated between asserting the realism of his model photographs and highlighting their dramatic possibilities. The photographs in some ways solved the problem of the models' inherent lack of realism (**FIG. 2, 5**). He worried that the miniature nature of his scale models would fail to signify their masterful design and insisted that his production teams strive to create "models that photograph real instead of as toys."[5] For instance, Geddes had photographs taken of each model building within the Toledo Scale factory complex to depict their grandeur and to convey a sense of their future reality. Geddes insisted that because photography was associated with "current factual subjects," his

THE WATER SURFACE, 80 PERCENT OF THE
WORLD'S WARSHIPS, ATMOSPHERE, DRAMATIC
LIGHTING, GUNFLASHES, SHELL BURSTS, HITS,
MISSES, DEPTH CHARGE EXPLOSIONS, SINKINGS,
AERONAUTICAL COMBAT, TORPEDO TRACKS, SUB-
MERGED SUBMARINES, SMOKE SCREENS, ARE ON
CALL.

images conveyed a level of truth; although not "on-the-spot news photographs . . . not even 'real' photographs," his images would "carry those convictions due to being photographs instead of drawings."[6] Geddes's images, however, often looked more like studio portraits than documentary images. Photographs of the model of the factory complex's machine shop are marked with Geddes's instructions to "rotate light from outside instead of inside" so that the dramatically lit building would seem to glow.[7] So, although Geddes's rhetoric about photography pointed toward his desire for veracity, in fact, he often relied on the-

atricality when selecting his images and editing his presentation books.

PHOTOGRAPHING FUTURAMA

Geddes's Futurama exhibit for General Motors at the 1939–40 New York World's Fair was certainly his most photographed model (**FIG. 6–8**). Drafting his presentation books years later, Geddes returned to Futurama as an example of the benefits of the Bel Geddes Process. A presentation book compiled in 1957 for the Ford Foundation relies on the realistic photographs of Futurama, drawing an explicit

FIGURE 6 (LEFT)

*Spectators viewing
Futurama from the "carry-
go-round" conveyor, c. 1939.
Photograph supplied to
Geddes by General Motors,
10 x 8 in., 25.4 x 20.3 cm*

OVERLEAF
FIGURE 7 (LEFT)

*Model-maker constructing
a bridge for the General
Motor's Futurama exhibi-
tion for the 1939–40
New York World's Fair.
Photograph by Richard
Garrison, 8 x 10 in.,
20.3 x 25.4 x cm*

FIGURE 8 (RIGHT)

*General Motors publicity
photograph for Futurama,
1940. A short press release
about the image reads:
"These two Manhattan
youngsters, in search
of unusual Eastertime
adventure, explore the now
famous General Motors
Futurama, dazzling world
of the future, visited by
millions at the New York
World's Fair. Here, nestled
in a small-town church-
yard, Mildred Cozzens and
Wylie McCaffrey discover
a nest of brilliantly colored
eggs. The efficient motor
traffic of the Futurama
halted to witness the
Easter spectacle, but will
be resumed for the public
on May 11, reopening date
of the World's Fair . . ."
Photograph by Gjon Mili,
11 x 14¼ in., 27.9 x 36.8 cm*

FIGURE 9, 10 (LEFT AND RIGHT)

Geddes presentation book titled "The Bel Geddes Process of Television, Motion Pictures, Graphic Illustration," 1957. Geddes's photo-textual presentation book to the Ford Foundation touted the benefits of the Bel Geddes Process by drawing an explicit comparison between a diagram used by Life *magazine to explain an amphibious landing and a montage of model photographs built to convey the same information.*

comparison between renderings of the model and photographs of the finished building. Captioned with statements proclaiming the realism of his Bel Geddes Process, this book juxtaposes an artist's rendering of the "designer's concept of a segregated Street Intersection drawn before it was built" with a photograph of the General Motors building and intersection after it was built. These images are followed by a comparison between a diagram used by *Life* magazine to explain an amphibious landing and a montage of model photographs that convey the same information **(FIG. 9, 10)**. As with his work for the Toledo Scale factory, the models and renderings

Life magazine, that he had the opportunity to bring the Bel Geddes Process to a wide public audience. Soon after, he began working with the U.S. Navy to photograph models of potential military targets and recently waged naval battles.[8] His work for the military allowed him to continue crafting models on the same grand scale as he had for Toledo Scale and General Motors.

Geddes's work creating model photographs of war led to an increased insistence on realism. His pictures of models of military targets and re-creations of actual battles, although lit dramatically and staged elaborately, were always marketed to

offered the opportunity to envision the future, but the photographs lent that possible future the appearance of reality.

RE-CREATING WAR

Years later, as he pitched the Bel Geddes Process to potential clients, Geddes would return to his work re-creating key battle scenes in model form and consulting for the military during World War II. Geddes had been making war-themed models for decades prior to the war, but it was not until 1942, when he developed a series of model photographs for

potential editors and military officials with assertions about their veracity. Geddes developed formulas for placing the camera at the angle that would maintain the sense of scale and best convey the elevation of the actual geography **(FIG. 11)**. Geddes even highlighted the technique's ability to surpass the work of professional photojournalism, labeling it the "ideal illustrative medium for any illustratable subject where on-the-spot photographs were not made or cannot be made" **(FIG. 12)**.[9] Geddes included testimonials in his presentation books, labeling the process as a "new dimension [that] has been added to war reporting" and "the finest method for visualizing history."[10] When marketing his model photography process to the military or to news media, Geddes proclaimed its realism, arguing that accurate representation of geographic regions and battle scenes would be crucial when planning aerial attacks, training military personnel, or even when selling the public on the reasons for the war.

ENCYCLOPAEDIA BRITANNICA: PHOTOGRAPHING HISTORY

Translating his experience building models for the military into something more marketable in the post-

In December 1944, he prepared an extensive proposal for the encyclopedia company, suggesting more than a hundred possible model photography subjects that might appeal to both adult and adolescent readers. Designating his model images as a new form of instructional communication, Geddes insisted that his photographs would move the encyclopedia company far beyond their typical clunky diagrams. Geddes suggested subjects whose value he deemed educational—models of weather patterns, fallen civilizations, or the workings of the locks at the Panama Canal. In one of many letters to *Encyclopaedia Britannica,* he assured the company's president that "we can tell the model

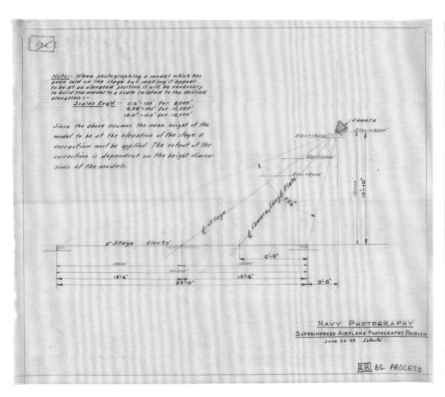

war period proved challenging for Geddes. He noted that making and photographing models, as he had for the Navy, was extremely expensive, "but it was during the war and the government didn't give a damn. They just said go ahead and do it."[11] Later it became difficult for Geddes to procure the kind of patronage necessary to underwrite the cost of production for the models he wanted to create and photograph.

Toward the end of the war, Geddes began cultivating a relationship with the editors and president of *Encyclopaedia Britannica,* attempting to persuade them of the educational value of model photography.

photography stories so that they will explain themselves to a fourteen-year-old mind and to a forty-year-old mind, without either treading on the intelligence of the younger or insulting the intelligence of the older person."[12] Geddes noted his model photographs could communicate knowledge without language and, therefore, would open up new potential markets around the world, assisting in "educating the illiterate."[13] Not content with simply reworking illustrations, Geddes added suggestions for carrying cases and illustrated atlases to his long list of proposed potential encyclopedia projects.

Although Geddes initially secured a budget of $5,000 a month and an agreement to create six models—the Panama Canal, the building of the Pyramids in Egypt, an "ideal farm," and three others to be determined—his imagination outgrew his budget, and he finished only the first two of these projects. One completed series presented a photographic narrative of the construction of the pyramids over several phases (**FIG. 13-15**). Each model was staged with thousands of miniature slaves in various work poses. The photographs document the gradual building of

the model while simultaneously depicting the story of the building of the pyramids. Years later, insisting on the educational value of these images for textbook publishers and museums, Geddes noted that his representation of historic subjects would appeal to young readers because "youthful minds are literal; they want three dimensional realism." The Bel Geddes Process could, he claimed, photograph even historic events that occurred thousands of years before the invention of the camera.

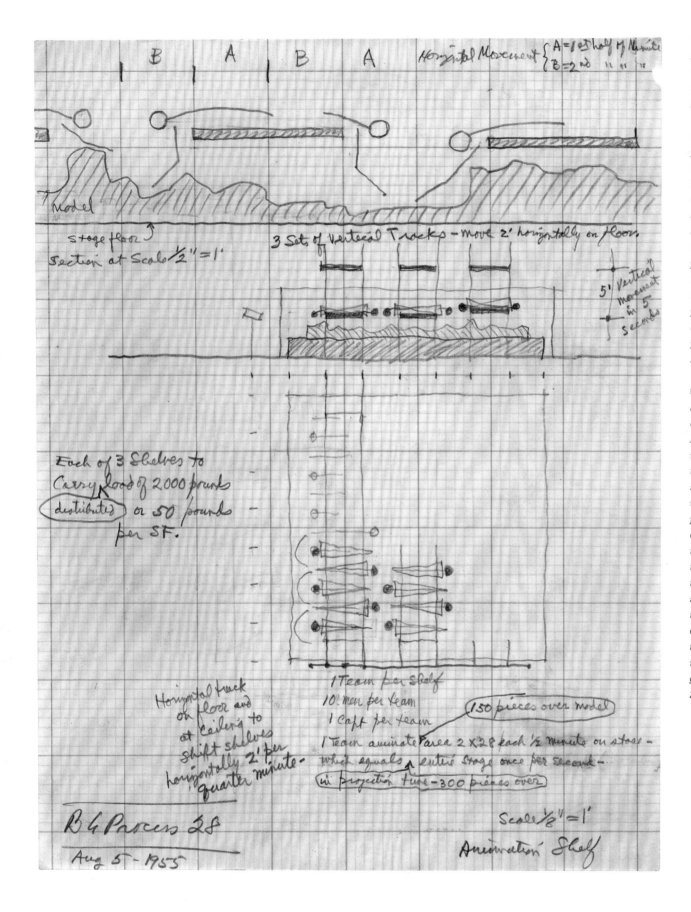

B   A   B   A   Horizontal Movement { A = 1st half of Minute
                                              { B = 2nd   "   "   "

↑ Model

stage floor ↑
Section at Scale ½" = 1'

3 Set of Vertical Tracks — Move 2' horizontally on floor

5' Vertical movement in 5 seconds

Each of 3 Shelves to Carry load of 2000 prints (distributed) or 50 pounds per SF.

Horizontal track on floor and at ceiling to shift shelves horizontally 2' per quarter minute.

1 Team per Shelf
10 men per team
1 Capt per team

1 Team animate area 2 x 28 each ½ minute on stage — which equals entire stage once per second — in projection time — 300 pieces over

150 pieces over model

Scale ⅛" = 1'
Animation Shelf

B 4 Process 28
Aug 5 – 1955

FIGURE 13, 14, 15 (OPPOSITE)

Egyptian pyramids construction model and photography by Norman Bel Geddes & Co., Inc., 1945. Many of the model photography projects Geddes pitched to the Encyclopaedia Britannica *were intended to illustrate entries on historical events or on agricultural or architectural processes, as with these three images showing the building of the pyramids. Photographs by unidentified staff photographer, 8 x 10 in., 20.3 x 25.4 cm*

FIGURE 16 (LEFT)

Sketch of stop-motion animation rigging, August 5, 1955. The rigging allowed ten men to lie face down and side-by-side on large, wooden suspended platforms that floated over the model every thirty seconds, allowing the workers to move thousands of pieces slightly forward before the platform was pulled off to the side to allow the camera to record the next frame. Pencil on graph paper, 8½ x 11 in., 21.6 x 27.9 cm

THE BEL GEDDES PROCESS

Although he had been photographing models for years, by the 1950s Geddes drew on all his previous experience working with model photography for theaters, corporations, and the military to conceptualize and market his Bel Geddes Process as a method in itself. Believing his technique to be applicable to a range of businesses, he circulated his presentation books to television producers and filmmakers as well

sums spent commissioning illustrations of historic events or staging large-scale scenes. Geddes insisted that the technique would increase the realism of book illustrations and would save filmmakers the unpredictability and expense of on-location shots.

Geddes also billed his Bel Geddes Process as a method for constructing visual narratives for textbooks and stop-motion animation. Potential clients could commission models of almost any imagin-

FIGURE 17

Alexander Leidenfrost rendering of rear-projection in a television studio, not dated. Geddes promoted the Bel Geddes Process to film studios as a cost-saving technique, suggesting they project stop-motion animation footage of his models on a screen placed behind actors filming their scenes. This rear-projection would, Geddes claimed, save the expense and the unpredictability of large-scale, on-location shooting. Photograph by unidentified photographer, 12 x 10 in., 30.5 x 25.4 cm

as textbook publishers and educational foundations. Seeking a new way to underwrite the expense of models built to match the grand scale of his imagination, Geddes tried marketing the Bel Geddes Process as a cost-sharing endeavor that would save subscribers millions of dollars. Filmmakers and publishers would jointly underwrite the expense of building massive models on studio lots. This shared, up-front expense would save potential clients the extravagant

able subject, provided they could align their needs with those of other funders. Geddes provided these possible clients with a list of hundreds of possible subjects to be preselected and proposed compiling teams of model makers, photographers, lighting specialists, and animation workers. The models would be staged with movable figurines, lit from several angles, and equipped with up to twelve cameras to photograph and film the action. Negatives would be retouched, prints developed with Geddes's approval, and the images collected into illustrated stories and news features or printed as short stop-motion animation films (FIG. 16). Although very few films were finished, Geddes proposed that footage of large-scale action scenes or complicated location shots would be brought to the studio and rear-projected on screens placed behind the actors (FIG. 17).

The scale of his imagination plus the skill of his execution allowed Geddes to photograph subjects that would be impossible to capture with a camera for years to come. Geddes insisted that there was nothing his model photography could not represent and turned his attention toward capturing "impossible assignments," including images of Atlantis or of New York City as it might appear several decades in the future. Geddes claimed that he was able to build models and to provide photographs of "scenes apparently taken anywhere in the world, at any period of the past, present or future."[14] None of the techniques he incorporated into the Bel Geddes Process—model making, retouching negatives, or stop-motion animation—were innovations in visual representation. Model making had long been an established architectural practice, and stop-motion animation was a popular filmmaking technique by the time Geddes turned to both.[15] Although his technology was not innovative, his imagination went far beyond the capabilities of the camera. The Bel Geddes Process, as Geddes conceived it, anticipated a relationship between photography and fantasy not possible until the advent of programs to digitally manipulate images. Selling the Bel Geddes Process, with all the broad claims he could leverage, Geddes promised both still and moving images that would go beyond the limits of traditional representational practice—realistic images of fantastical subjects.

ENDNOTES

I am grateful to the many people whose insightful comments or patient rereadings guided my writing and research, including Katherine Kelly, Christina Cogdell, Helen Baer, Rick Watson, Charlotte Nunes, and Emily Bloom.

1   Norman Bel Geddes, "Bel Geddes Presentation Book for Television, Motion Pictures, Graphic Illustration," 9, Flat Box 14, Folder 672.1b, Geddes Papers.

2   Ibid., 15.

3   Norman Bel Geddes, *A Project for a Theatrical Presentation of The Divine Comedy of Dante Alighieri* (New York: Theatre Arts, 1924). Illustrated by Francis Joseph Brugière.

4   Geddes, "Bel Geddes Presentation Book for Television, Motion Pictures, Graphic Illustration," 5 February 1957, Oversize Box 5, Folder 28.17, and Geddes, "Model Photography—Draft Case History, USN, Life, Encyclopedia Britannica 1941–1946," 1941, Box 55, Folder 672.1, both in Geddes Papers.

5   "'Data Subjects' in BG Process (Model Photography Since 1951), 1952–1958," Box 4, Folder 28.15, Geddes Papers.

6   Geddes, "Bel Geddes Presentation Book for Television, Motion Pictures, Graphic Illustration," 8.

7   Geddes, "Photograph of Toledo Scale factory machine shop," Photo Box 3, Folder 153.1, Geddes Papers.

8   For more on Geddes's use of models and his relationship to war, see Christina Cogdell's essay in this publication.

9   Geddes, "Bel Geddes Presentation Book for Television, Motion Pictures, Graphic Illustration," 5 February 1957, Oversize Box 5, Folder 28.17, Geddes Papers. The Geddes archive contains multiple copies of presentation books, each often slightly different.

10 Testimonials credited to The Museum of Modern Art, "Editors of *Life* Magazine," and "James V. Forrestal, Secretary of the Navy" in "Bel Geddes Presentation Book for Television, Motion Pictures, Graphic Illustration," 39, 52, Flat Box 14, Folder 672.1a, Geddes Papers.

11 Geddes, "Transcript of phone conversation between Geddes and Lewter Cowan regarding the Bel Geddes Process," 23 February 1957, Box 4, Folder 28.1, Geddes Papers.

12 Norman Bel Geddes, "Letter from Geddes to Mr. E. H. Powell, President," 3 January 1945, Box 37, Folder 531.2, Geddes Papers.

13 Geddes, "Bel Geddes Presentation Book for Television, Motion Pictures, Graphic Illustration," 69, Flat Box 14, Folder 672.1a, Geddes Papers.

14 Geddes, "Letter to Mr. Sam Zimbalist, Metro Goldwyn Mayer, Culver City, California," 2 January 1958, Box 4, Folder 28.1, Geddes Papers.

15 For more on model making as an architectural practice, see Mark Morris, *Models: Architecture and the Miniature* (Chichester: Academy Press, 2006) and Albert Smith, *Architectural Model as Machine: A New View of Models from Antiquity to the Present Day* (Boston: Architectural Press, 2004). For more on the history of stop-motion animation, see Ray Harryhausen and Tony Dalton, *A Century of Stop-Motion Animation: From Méliès to Aardman* (New York: Watson-Guptill, 2008).

17

GRAPHIC DESIGN

Peter Hall

In January 1940, the trade journal *Advertising Age* ran a quarter-page ad announcing the "exclusive employment in the magazine field of Norman Bel Geddes" on three leading magazines published by the Crowell-Collier Publishing Company. For Geddes's firm, this was a major coup: At the time, the three magazines—*Collier's*, *The American*, and *Woman's Home Companion*—had a combined circulation of over eight million.[1] More significantly, Geddes was not known for his accomplishments in the field of graphic design and magazine art direction. As a publicity brochure printed with *The American* magazine noted (FIG. 1, 2), Geddes's vaunted conquests, from theater design to locomotives to the "unforgettable" Futurama of the previous year, had yet to include this new territory:

To one important field of industrial endeavor Mr. Geddes has heretofore not turned his talents. That is the field of the mass stimulation of people through the medium of the printed and illustrated word, as exemplified and typified by the national magazine. [2]

To refer to magazine design as the "mass stimulation of people" recalled the "consumer engineering" language of the adman Earnest Elmo Calkins, whose case for kick-starting the stagnant economy by stimulating people to "abandon the old and buy the new to be up-to-date" was common parlance by 1940.[3] The newly conceived profession of industrial design was cast as the prominent means of stimulation. "Industrial design itself, according to the publicists, would streamline the industrial system and bring the nation out of the Depression."[4] If Geddes could stimulate five million people to visit and marvel at the Futurama exhibit he had designed a year earlier, then surely he could stimulate the readers of magazines and, in doing so, "provide better attention-value for advertisers."[5]

Geddes's brief but well-documented flirtation with a magazine publishing house provides an intriguing insight into both the giddily nervous climate shortly before the United States entered World War II and the working methods of a design studio that was in many ways at its peak in 1940. A picture emerges of a celebrated designer struggling to sustain his reputation as a visionary and to stay on top of an unwieldy

project at a complex and political organization. For Geddes, who practiced design as an art of rhetoric and persuasion, the project would take considerable persuasive talents, not only to stimulate readers, but also to convince the entrenched editorial staff at Crowell-Collier to adopt his ideas. Ultimately, it was a relationship destined to fail.

Geddes's first forays into graphic design were considerably earlier. The account in Geddes's autobiography, *Miracle in the Evening*, portrays a penniless, plucky twenty-year-old hero working the Detroit advertising scene. After a two-week position producing black-and-white pen illustrations for advertisers came to an end at the Peninsular Engraving Company in 1913, Geddes persuaded the company president to hire him on commission to produce color drawings.[6] When the president invited Geddes to enter a competition to design covers for the programs of four local theaters, he won for all four covers, was put on a salary of $40 a week, and before long found that his "bold drawing in comparatively flat color" was starting to become popular in the advertising industry (FIG. 3). At this point, the tale gains a fast-forward quality, giving the reader the impression of a precocious negotiator, gifted with an intuitive eye for upcoming trends. After several months of working at "top capacity," bringing revenues of more than $800 a week to the company, Geddes tells the president that he will be leaving to go freelance, where he can earn "ten times as much in half the time." Deploying dialogue worthy of Horatio Alger, Geddes the narrator recounts an exchange that ends with the president doubling Geddes's salary, effective immediately, and Geddes calling him "unappreciative."[7] By the time he is twenty-one, Geddes has rented a house for his family in Detroit, is running a studio with revenues of $5,000 a week, and has launched his own magazine, *Inwhich*, an illustrated monthly described by Geddes as "a book in which I say what I think." Issue number one included a design for a theater that reemerged in *Horizons*, the book that established Geddes's prominence as an industrial designer in 1932.

Geddes's use of editorial design as a means of extended persuasion becomes most evident in his

FIRST...

Léon de Vos

NORMAN BEL GEDDES stands in the very forefront of those who are changing the face of America. Born and reared in the Middle West, Mr. Geddes came to New York in 1918. His first interest was the theatre, upon which he had a profound effect. He then pioneered in the field of designing for industry, combining the elements of good design with the same dramatic presentation and knowledge of mass psychology that had placed him in the forefront of the world of the stage.

FIGURE 3
*Geddes golf-swing poster
for Peninsular Engraving
Company, c. 1914.
Serigraph, 12⅜ x 24¼ in.,
31.4 x 62.9 cm*

NORMAN BEL GEDDES DESIGNS AMERICA

best-selling book *Horizons* and its successor, *Magic Motorways*, published in 1940. *Horizons* is a significant landmark in the history of streamlining, but as a work of graphic design offers nothing typographically groundbreaking. Text is set in a stately, justified serif face (Caslon Antique) with only a jazzy dropped-cap sans serif at each chapter opener and an all-type Futura cover to position the book as forward-thinking. The book is, however, *paced* in a quite sophisticated way. The text, which opens with Geddes's call for a new kind of artist whose materials are not paint and stone but the tools of the industrial age, is repeatedly punctuated by inset photographs and drawings (**FIG. 4**). The images are selected and ordered to form a kind of visual argument reminiscent of the juxtapositions used by Le Corbusier in *Towards a New Architecture*. For example, Geddes advocates art being "released from its picture frames and prosceniums and pedestals and museums and bursting forth in more inspired forms." He echoes this rhetoric with progressions of images: a Paul Cézanne still life, a Ralph Steiner photograph of a tree wrapped in barbed wire, an Imogen Cunningham flower, and a Margaret Bourke-White photograph of plow blades. He writes:

Has it ever occurred to you that a photograph of a flower, even though devoid of color, might be as thrilling as a painting of it, or that six plow blades, laid side by side and photographed would form a striking pattern?[8]

Horizons leans heavily on Le Corbusier's work for this persuasive visual rhetoric. Geddes acquired a copy of *Towards a New Architecture* shortly after its translation in 1927 and marked it heavily, adapting its argument that architects should learn from the engineer's aesthetic.[9] Both designers juxtaposed images of geometric ancient architecture with architecture of mass production, but Bel Geddes upped the ante, using expressive images of dynamos and grain silos by Bourke-White, where Le Corbusier represented objects in a more documentary fashion. The differing use of images reflects the designers' differing motives. According to design historian Nicolas Maffei:

Le Corbusier was primarily interested in grafting the sober aesthetic of the engineer onto modernist architectural design, while one of Bel Geddes's primary goals was to engineer increased consumption through the use of expressive design and imagery. . . . Horizons was a product of pure salesmanship. It was fantastic, dramatic, and sensational.[10]

The visual rhetoric developed by Le Corbusier in his slide lectures of the 1920s—a prototype for the book—was not based on any watertight proof. His one hundred–slide "films" that supposedly pursued "the awesome strides of logic" to argue that the Machine Age required a new architecture were based on effects rather than syllogisms, on inductive rather than deductive reasoning.[11] Le Corbusier's rhetorical armory of methods included running a sequence of images of modern industrial forms, from ocean liner, to airplane, to automobile. Designed to elicit a laugh (which a critic called a "shock technique"), these were contrasted abruptly with a meretricious-looking Chateau de Fontainebleau.[12] In *Magic Motorways*, Geddes's manifesto for future transportation, the author gives Corbusian visual rhetoric a vaudevillian boost, adding tabloid-style captions and switching with gay abandon between expressive photography, information graphics, and photojournalistic modes of representation. An account of the control towers of Geddes's envisioned future superhighway—which would monitor the hypothetical radio-controlled cars speeding at regulated distances below—is supported by a full-page image of a naval officer peering through binoculars from the bridge of an ocean liner (**FIG. 5**). An image of a matador and bull bears the caption: "The American national sport is dodging a car." The image selections are thus subtle and clumsy, metaphorical and outright corny.

The Geddes of *Magic Motorways* is somewhat more cocksure and less circumspect than the narrator of *Horizons*. According to a back cover blurb on *Magic Motorways*:

He is a man of almost unbelievable energy, irascible and unpredictable at times, but loved and admired by a vast circle of friends that even includes his publishers.[13]

Throughout the book are constant, unabashed plugs for Futurama, with dramatic photographs of the model city's experimental road layouts, suggesting that the automotive futures envisioned in the text had already been tried and tested. Indeed, the entire book is presented in Geddes's introduction as a kind of post-production analysis of Futurama, with a theatrical metaphor:

This book will take you backstage. It will answer the many questions which the Futurama left unanswered.[14]

By the time Geddes was hired by Crowell-Collier to redesign its magazines, he had crafted a larger-than-life public persona and established an approach to editorial design premised on the reader as an audience member, to be stimulated, entertained, tricked, and persuaded. This would be achieved through the deft organization of text and image into a visual argument that appealed on a variety of levels—through humor, sentimentality, high drama, and diagrammatic explanation. This approach was considerably different from the editorial and form-driven developments in publication design happening elsewhere.

At *Vogue,* for example, the Russian émigré M. F. Agha had introduced the role of the art director to the American magazine, as a figure who shared responsibility with the editor for shaping both the content and look of the magazine. Recruited by Condé Nast in 1929, Agha had introduced sans serif typefaces, rejected existing tenets of page layout, and invented the pictorial feature and fashion art, working with a roster of experimental photographers on the title, including Edward Steichen, Cecil Beaton, and Charles Sheeler.[15] Alexey Brodovitch, another Russian émigré, joined *Harper's Bazaar* in 1924 and pioneered a logotype and a more integrated treatment of type and image, where type would mimic, mirror, or create dynamic space around photography. Like Agha, he brought a stable of extraordinary talents to the magazine, including Man Ray, Irving Penn, Henri Cartier-Bresson, and Jean Cocteau, and introduced full-bleed imagery, montage, and the strategic sequencing of photographs.

The comparison is, of course, slightly invidious. Where *Vogue* and *Harper's Bazaar* were magazines in the business of introducing innovative visual ideas and fashions from Europe to upper- and middle-class women, *Woman's Home Companion,* as its name suggests, delivered a broad staple of household tips, stories, and advertisements to a vast number of housewives and their families. High advertising revenues, high circulations, and longstanding editors at the three Crowell titles also ensured that any proposed design changes would warrant close scrutiny and resistance. In 1940, *Woman's Home Companion* had a circulation of 3.49 million and an editor, Gertrude Lane, who had been there since 1919.[16] (Its rival, *Ladies' Home Journal,* with circulation hovering around the same number, that year claimed the largest circulation of any magazine in the world.) *The American,* a general interest, mixed content monthly, had a circulation of around 2.25 million.[17] *Collier's,* a weekly with a venerable history for social and political commentary, was, at the time of Geddes's appointment, enjoying a circulation surge, to 2.88 million[18] under editor William Chenery, who had been there since 1925.[19]

Most significant, Geddes was hired by Crowell-Collier as an *external* consultant, whereas Brodovitch and Agha were *internal* art directors. This would effectively limit the amount of day-to-day influence Geddes had on reshaping the three publications with the in-house art and editorial teams. Given Geddes's celebrity status and the demands on his time, this external position was a necessity. A memo to the publisher from January 1940 spells out clearly the terms of Geddes's consultancy. For $25,000 a year, Geddes writes:

I am to be under no obligations to devote any definite part of my time to your service. I am, however, to appoint an assistant who shall devote his entire time to the above described affairs of your company, and who will report to me. You are to pay his salary in monthly installments.[20]

From the start of the project, Geddes sounded more like an advertising man than an art director. The extensive documentation of meeting minutes,

mately twenty cents per day per passenger. Owing to the fact that air cooling is incorporated at the start in my design, the cost of maintaining this feature would be somewhat lessened. The present design calls for the steam-vacuum cooling method of the Carrier Engineering Company. This system requires less steam for cooling the car in summer than for heating the car in winter. Thus, the locomotive steam load is not increased. The fact that it is now feasible to supply railway cars with conditioned air is sufficiently remarkable,

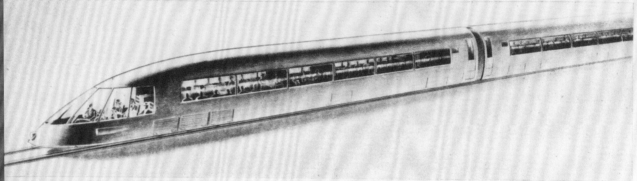

61 · REAR (LOUNGE) CAR NUMBER 4   DESIGNED BY NORMAN BEL GEDDES 1931

particularly when we recall that air-conditioning systems for buildings require very large space. It is more remarkable still that the compact air-cooling systems designed for railway cars operate so economically that they add little to the cost of traveling.

Throughout the train, as regards interior arrangements, first consideration has been given to comfort and convenience of passengers rather than maximum capacity. In the day car, there are seventeen swivel armchairs with

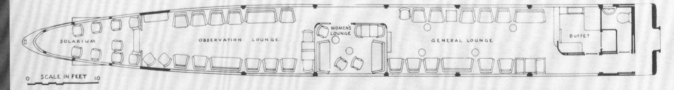

62 · REAR (LOUNGE) CAR NUMBER 4: PLAN   DESIGNED BY NORMAN BEL GEDDES 1931

NORMAN BEL GEDDES DESIGNS AMERICA

memos, and letters from the Crowell-Collier job reveals that the former advertising designer had little regard for the sanctity of an editorial-advertising separation. Geddes focused on magazine cover design as a means to establish "trade-marks,"[21] looked for advertising "tie-ups"[22] with editorial, and pushed for more "effective distribution" of advertising and editorial.[23]

The editors, of course, resisted. At an internal meeting at Geddes's office after the unveiling of a prototype design for *The American*, the first of the three magazine "dummies" commissioned by Crowell-Collier, Geddes summed up the situation:

[There are] some people over at Crowell-Collier who are not sold on the idea of NBG & Co. contributing anything as an outsider to their publication. After The American *dummy presentation quite a few have been won over, but things are still in a dubious stage.*[24]

Geddes's subsequent post-rationalization of the project suggests that the firm undertook extensive market research as it developed the three dummies: gathering data on popular preferences in magazines, interviewing "hundreds of men and women on color preferences" (women liked red, men liked blue), and analyzing the kinds of editorial ideas "most appealing to advertisers, women readers, men readers, young people from 20 years to 25 years." Typography "authorities" were consulted on legibility and layout. Weights of paper, logotypes, binding methods, and types of finish were also studied. The objective was to seek out the magazine elements that had "the most human appeal to the greatest number of Americans."[25]

The meeting minutes of the period, however, suggest a stronger driving force was Geddes's desire to make a big splash in the magazine world. Early into *The American* redesign, Geddes held a meeting with five of his staff members to discuss what each of them considered the major objectives of the job. After two employees spoke up, Geddes jumped in with his version, which he saw as a "totally new concept in getting up a magazine." He added (and a secretary underlined the remark in the meeting minutes):

It has got to be as new as bleed was before it was thought of. It's got to be definitely startling in its freshness![26]

The reference to "bleed" undoubtedly called to mind the enormous impact that *Life* magazine had made on the publishing industry. Launched by Time Inc. in 1936, *Life* was the country's first popular magazine to use images—including full-bleed photographs—to communicate editorial direction, which, as a news weekly with a fast turnaround, required a number of developments in letterpress printing, coated paper, and ink technologies.[27] Like radio, the news weekly provided a quicker return for advertisers than monthly magazines, and its popularity among readers was phenomenal. Circulation had soared to 2.5 million by 1939.[28] A Geddes office analysis of the magazine alongside *Reader's Digest*, which was a market leader by 1940, noted:

Brevity and pictures are the two lessons to be learned from these two publications. This fast moving world demands brevity. This fast moving world is picture minded.[29]

But Geddes's "totally new concept," as it emerged in *The American* magazine of March 1941, was in advertising, not editorial design. Four new ways of selling ad space, described as "animated spreads," were trumpeted in a media kit as "the first really new thing in publication advertising since the half-tone!"[30] Most priority was given to the "zigzag" spread (**FIG. 6, 8**), which ran advertisements across the top of one page, down a column of the facing page and then exited page right. Editorial content was annexed to small boxes on the bottom left and top right of the spread. Similar efforts at "effective distribution" of advertising and editorial, as Geddes called it, were achieved with the "strip spread," which consigned editorial to a center strip (**FIG. 7, 13**), and the "horizontal spread," which ran advertisements across the bottom of a two-page spread. Both methods gave the effect of two pages of advertising for the price of a single page, as the promotional material duly noted (**FIG. 9**). The fourth innovation, a

FIGURE 5
Illustration captioned "Control Bridge: Ocean Liner Style" in Magic Motorways *(1940). Image credited to Kurt Schelling.*

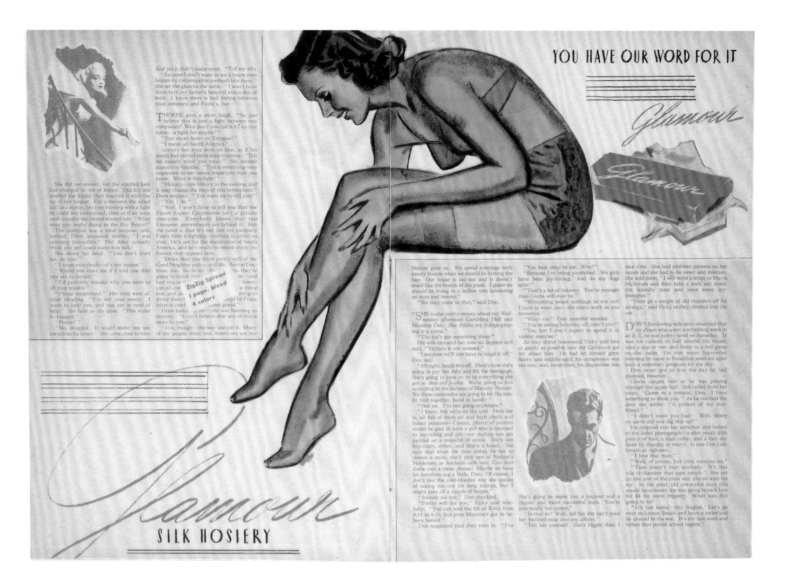

YOU HAVE OUR WORD FOR IT

Glamour

Glamour

Glamour
SILK HOSIERY

FIGURE 6

Geddes-designed Glamour Silk Hosiery "zigzag" spread for Crowell-Collier, c. 1941.

"bookmark third cover," was a half-page flap added to the back cover that could be used as a bookmark, with the table of contents printed on the folded front. The inside provided a page and a half of high-visibility advertising space.

Lavish supplements were published by Crowell-Collier to promote the animated spreads idea, with transparent overlays printed with highly saturated color ads peeling gently from editorial spreads, as if to suggest a respect for the independence of editorial content. In the actual magazines, however, the overlay would vanish, enhancing the sense that Listerine, Sunrise Cereal, and Studebaker had infiltrated the editorial heart of the organ.

Geddes struggled to win over the editorial staff and gain more control over the project. In his prototypes, some effort had been made to increase editorial impact, such as designing covers distinctive to each title, controlling the color palettes, developing a more flexible layout system, and making simple readability improvements such as a binding that would allow the magazines to lie flat and eliminating article run-overs. But every move was also in advertisers' interests. The response to Geddes's dummy of *Woman's Home Companion* was not positive:[31] In editor Gertrude Lane's view, the magazine's mission was not to stimulate its discerning readers of serious fiction with advertising.[32]

Lane's retirement in 1941 provided Geddes with the chance to redesign the magazine. Crowell-Collier gave his firm *Woman's Home Companion* to develop as a "test case."[33] But some frank discussions took place first. Robert Staples, the art director of *Woman's Home Companion*, had "reservations" about how the Geddes operation might work

This is a "comprehensive" of a full-color food advertisement as it might appear in a 680-line page in the large page size magazines.

The transition of the elements of this advertisement to the 429-line type page of The American Magazine is shown to the right. ➡

This Strip Spread is one page bleed . . . in area it is only 5 square inches less than this 680-line page: area + scale + freshness + directed reader traffic! More interesting, more exciting, more attractive!

FIGURE 7

"I Never Dreamed I'd Rush to Breakfast…" Geddes-designed "strip spread" for Crowell-Collier.

FIGURE 8 (OVERLEAF)

Promotional piece for Geddes-designed zigzag spreads, c. 1941.

THE AMERICAN MAGAZINE

the first
OF THE
ZIGZAG
SPREADS

HISTORY IS MADE *Inside...*

Keeping up with Hollywood

Touring the sets this month we found Spencer Tracy on the Woman of the Year set, in which he co-stars with Katharine Hepburn, studying his next script, This Strange Adventure. In this Spencer will play the role of a traveler of the seven seas who believes in no God but is eager to know all about the plan of things. Spencer is also slated to appear in Tortilla Flat.

On the set where They Died With Their Boots On is being made Errol Flynn was using his idea of sign language to converse with one of the imported Indians, before he discovered that the man was a college graduate.

Monty Woolley is probably the first actor in Hollywood to have a "sit in." In his role as The Man Who Came to Dinner, practically all of his scenes are in a wheel chair.

On the One Foot in Heaven set, Martha Scott told us that it is her secret desire to play a modern role—she never has.

Two hundred pounds of moth balls were used as hail in All That Money Can Buy and then reclaimed for use in studio drapery.

● HERE are some of Gracie Allen's latest inventions: a transparent newspaper so the wife can see her husband at breakfast; a building that goes up and down so that elevators are not needed and a shaving mirror with the upper half of Clark Gable's face on it, so that one does not tire of shaving the same old face.

Count Oleg Cassini designed the costumes for his bride, Gene Tierney, in The Shanghai Gesture.

● BARBARA STANWYCK suggests that the next time you serve creamed chipped beef for Sunday breakfast, you season the sauce with prepared mustard and thicken with beaten egg yolk. Lovely color—lovely taste!

● TO PREVENT DRY SKIN and dry hair, Priscilla Lane has discovered that it is important to include a pint of milk, two leafy vegetables and at least one citrus fruit in her daily diet. She often goes on a two-day diet of fruit juices and raw vegetables to counteract the tricks of the California sun.

Dickie Hall was born five years ago in Brooklyn but does not want to go back. Even at this tender age he has several concert recitals at Carnegie Hall and Steinway Hall to his credit. But what he is most proud of is his role of Nick Charles, Jr., in Shadow of the Thin Man, starring Myrna Loy and William Powell. Myrna Loy let him use her dressing-room between scenes and there Dickie composed his first piece, The Adventures of a Zebra. His next role is in Babes on Broadway. Dickie's mother died when he was born and his grandfather has taken care of him ever since. They live close to the studio in a bungalow court, where Grandfather Hall keeps house, sees that Dickie practices his piano, takes him to school and to work. Dickie is allowed to be quite independent, he is very courteous and not at all self-conscious. He loves airplanes and is making a collection of models. He adores his alley cat that he found on the street and a huge rubber fish is his favorite possession. As a special treat the five-year-old is allowed to parade around the house wearing the medals his beloved grandfather won in two former wars.

KAY MULVEY

DON'T MISS

- **THE MAN WHO CAME TO DINNER: Monty Woolley and Bette Davis in sophisticated satire.**
- **H. M. PULHAM, ESQ.: J. P. Marquand's best seller with Hedy Lamarr as the career girl and Robert Young as the man who allowed family tradition to upset his life.**
- **KING'S ROW: Strong human emotions of rich and poor in small town. Ann Sheridan, Ronald Reagan, Robert Cummings, Betty Field.**
- **LOUISIANA PURCHASE: Bob Hope in film version of the colorful musical comedy hit.**
- **ALSO RECOMMENDED: The Lady Is Willing (Dietrich as screw-ball actress adopts child) • Kathleen (Shirley Temple growing up) • Shadow of the Thin Man (more laughs) • Design for Scandal (Judge Rosalind Russell and news photographer Walter Pidgeon) • Swamp Water (Walter Huston, Walter Brennan) • Bahama Passage (Madeleine Carroll, Stirling Hayden) • Remember the Day (Claudette Colbert, John Payne in thoughtful drama).**

Johnny's so long at the Fair

NELIA GARDNER WHITE

Lexie learns what Johnny meant by being free—and is free herself

ILLUSTRATOR: MARIO COOPER

CONCLUSION

So Lexie met the death of her husband, Johnny Duval. Alone with the proud woman who was Johnny's mother. She could not be with him as he lay dying; she could not hear his last words. He did not lie dying anyway. He died swiftly in a battle in the sky.

She walked over and took the official letter from Mrs. Duval's hands. This was not truth, this plain unadorned statement. This was not Johnny they spoke of.

She looked from the black official letters on the white page to the bony wrists of Mrs. Duval. And suddenly the wrists were real to her, more real than this letter. They seemed to contain all the sorrow of the world, all the suffering of all proud mothers in the universe.

"I will make you some tea," Lexie said. What a futile thing—a silly thing to say to sorrow so complete! And yet what other road was there through tearlessness?

She went to the little kitchen, put the kettle on, stood beside it till the water boiled. She brought the silver tray and the silver pot, the finest cups. She carried the tray in, set it on the round table.

"Come," she said. "You must drink some tea."

Mrs. Duval rose and walked to the chair by the hearth, sat down and Lexie poured her a cup of tea. Lexie had an instant of wild longing for her mother's loving anxious blue eyes, her mother's arms about her; then she took a cup of tea, sat on the stool quite near to Mrs. Duval, knowing that there was a kind of comfort in coldness, in reticence, too.

Then she could not bear coldness, reticence. She put her cup on the tray, leaned her head against the black dress of Johnny's mother. And presently, slowly, reluctantly, the thin hand rested on the sandy hair, pushed the hair gently back.

"Poor child!" Mrs. Duval said very quietly. "You did not know that it would be this way."

"It can't be. It isn't true," Lexie whispered.

"It is true," Mrs. Duval said in that same quiet voice. "It is true, Lexie."

"Not Johnny," Lexie said. "Not Johnny."

The thin hand kept stroking her hair steadily. Lexie was quiet, though the cry kept pressing from her heart: "Not *Johnny!*" and all the hours she had spent with him crowded at her and the gay sound of his voice, the blueness of his eyes, the bright blond of his hair, the strength of his arms, the life in him.

Then Mrs. Duval [CONTINUED ON PAGE 32.]

A new car finds a new friend

in talented Mrs. Lawrence Tibbett, former Jane Marston of New York and San Francisco, who recently selected a distinctively styled new Studebaker Land Cruiser. Mrs. Tibbett dresses smartly, is an enthusiastic golfer, good horsewoman and skilled gardener. She and her distinguished husband have a collection of show dogs on their farm.

THE BRIDE'S HOLIDAY

(*Continued from page 29*)

and I want to say, 'Yes; but I can write advertising copy that will pull like molasses candy.' But I've arranged for golf lessons and bought a bridge book, which looks worse to me than a stockbroker's sales analysis.

"We're still with the senior Shepherds, but Bill has finally mentioned a house, praise Allah. I'm wild for a little privacy, but Ellie insists that there's no hurry, and that we'll save time by waiting until we find *exactly* what we want. (As if anybody ever did.) Ellie is a revelation to me, by the way, and upsets all my misconceptions about Southern women. She looks like porcelain and she's a generalissimo.

"And I'm about to decide that she's fairly typical. That baby-doll manner common to Southern gals is a racket, probably developed after the Civil War to meet competition in a glutted matrimonial market, and persisting to the present day. But it works. Even Bill, as smart as he is, falls for his mother's act and thinks it's a comic coincidence that all her departments function so perfectly.

"I'VE read this over and decided that it sounds smart-alecky. I don't mean to. Really they are charming, friendly people who are anxious to make me feel at home. The fault is mine, because I don't speak the language, but it shall be remedied as soon as I can possibly learn. Let it never be said of Kit Mallonee that she busted an assignment.

"Write to me, you bum. I miss you more than I would have believed possible. When I get a house you must come down and have a good laugh at the spectacle of me, picking over vegetables at the market." . . .

Summer released its grip with the coming of October. The heat had been bad, Kit realized, but this gracious coolness was worse. In South Carolina you relaxed under the heat, letting it have its way with you; but the presage of autumn did things to your blood. Ambition stirred; the desire to resume your job prodded your brain and your muscles. And still, after more than a month, she was having her breakfast in bed and following a program that would have delighted a debutante.

"Do they keep this up indefinitely?" she asked Bill one night as she kicked off her evening slippers for the climb upstairs.

He grinned and picked up the slippers. "Whenever they can find a pretext. You're it, right now, and they love you."

Strangely enough, they did. Because she was intelligent she had decided to put on an act of her own: Kit Shepherd, a poor Yankee city girl who had never really lived before. Everything was new, and so she asked questions and made mistakes, laughing at herself as she did it. But the act was wearing thin, she decided; not for them, maybe, but for her. Kit Mallonee had been a woman of action.

She scrubbed her beautiful Irish skin and creamed it thoughtfully. "Everybody's been lovely, Bill—Ellie and Dad the nicest of all. But I feel like a blooming parasite."

He bent and brushed his lips against her shoulder. "Try feeling that way for a while, sweet. You've supported yourself for eight years and you deserve a vacation."

"But I've had it—the vacation, I mean. Now I want to start learning my new job."

HE STOOD behind her, smiling at her face in the mirror. "Do you know the first thing about housekeeping, Kits?"

"Not the first or the second. We paid Stella seventy-five dollars a month to do it for us."

He chuckled. "I'm in for a bad time. I feel it coming."

She turned and looked up at him. "When?"

He got it. Marriage hadn't dulled his perceptions. But he sparred. "Do you hate it here, beautiful?"

"Of course not! But we ought to be moving on, Bill. To an apartment, if we can't find the right house."

"I'm so delighted with our new Studebaker," says

Mrs. Lawrence Tibbett

CHARMING WIFE OF FAMOUS OPERATIC STAR

"I really selected our new Studebaker as a surprise for my husband," says Mrs. Tibbett, "because he gets so much relaxation out of motoring and driving himself. But I have found it such a comfortable and easy-driving car, it's hard to believe it wasn't built to order. The designer Raymond Loewy does have a genius for individualizing everything he styles."

THOUSANDS of other families, whose pride is their instinct for good taste and their alertness to good value, are doing as the Tibbetts did and buying distinctively styled new Studebakers this year.

You may purchase a smart 1941 Studebaker Land Cruiser—on either the Commander Six or President Eight chassis—for surprisingly little money. See your local Studebaker dealer now and go for a thrilling, convincing trial drive. Low down payment—easy C.I.T. terms.

DISTINCTIVELY SMART, NEW

STUDEBAKER LAND CRUISER

AVAILABLE ON COMMANDER SIX OR PRESIDENT EIGHT CHASSIS

(*Continued from page 94*)

"I'm a mug, I guess," he confessed slowly. "You've seen the apartments, and there's not a really decent one in town—not one good enough for you. It's the same with the houses we've looked at. I thought we might consider building if we don't find something soon."

Her throat ached with loving him. "But that would take months, Bill. If we had an apartment I might—practice on it."

He nodded abstractedly. "Okay. We'll see which we consider the least of the evils."

They left it that way, but Kit had a sense of frustration for the first time since she had known him.

Two days later he telephoned her from the mill and there was excitement in his voice: "Got time to look at a house with me?"

Her heart sang. "Of course. I'll be ready when you get here."

When he saw her face he realized how much it meant to her, and he tried to prepare her for a possible disappointment: "They aren't sure yet when it can be sold. It's an estate proposition, and you know what they are. But we can at least look at it."

The house stood on a hill and held out its arms to them. It was a rambling, whitewashed brick house with a mellow slate roof, and Kit thought, "This is It." "Oh, gosh, Bill!" she breathed.

He slanted his beautiful grin at her. "Easy, baby. Don't fall in love with it yet."

"I already have," she admitted. "Sometimes you see things and claim them for yours; sometimes you see them and they claim *you*. This house has already put the Indian sign on me."

He nodded gravely. "I know. I'm afraid it's done the same thing to me. Let's go in."

The house was perfect; somebody, she thought, with an ache, had loved this place to death. She left it reluctantly, with more than one backward glance; already she saw herself in it, taking care of Bill.

But the next evening when he reported on his findings her heart dropped again. "It'll take several weeks to get in touch with all the heirs and get the necessary signatures," he told her regretfully. "I guess you'll have to be patient, sweet."

"I won't!" she wanted to scream. "I've had all I can take of this upholstered life and Ellie's sirupy sweetness. I'm tired of being patronized as a child bride." . . . In spite of her resolutions she burst out desperately, "Oh, Bill! Can't we move in, and rent it until then?"

"And move right out if they won't sell?"

"Yes," she insisted stubbornly. "Or take an apartment."

"For a month, maybe? Or less? Wouldn't that be a slap at Mother? She loves having us here." ("Of course she does," Kit thought; "it keeps you under her thumb!") He searched her stormy eyes. "Do you hate it as much as that, Kit?"

Reason came back. "Of course not," she said more gently. "But it's her house and I'm so useless; she won't let me lift a finger. And I'm not accustomed to feeling useless."

"I see."

But somehow his voice was too quiet. Somehow she felt that he didn't understand;

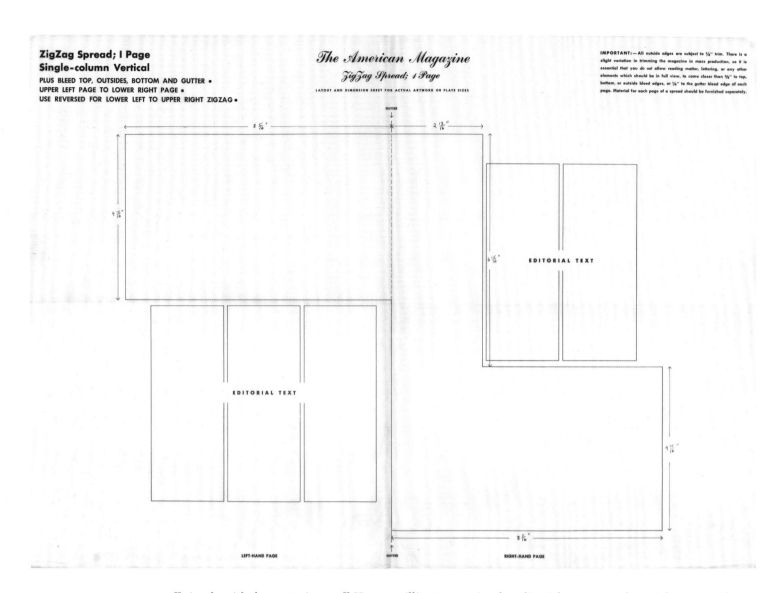

FIGURE 9 (ABOVE)
Printed diagram of Geddes's advertising layout innovations for Crowell-Collier. 22½ x 16 in., 57.2 x 40.6 cm

FIGURE 10 (OPPOSITE)
Cover of the Geddes-redesigned Woman's Home Companion, *January 1942.*

efficiently with the magazine staff. He was willing to give it a three- or four-month trial. Willa Roberts, the managing editor and soon-to-be editor, was blunter, according to Geddes's notes:

She doubts whether Geddes is the right organization to handle a woman's publication; not questioning Geddes ability, but believed that Geddes is good for doing a big dramatic job, and projects himself too much into the future instead of today's needs. She believes that the Woman's Home Companion *dummy was very interesting; more for advertising ways instead of editorially.*[34]

A subsequent office memo notes that Geddes "will try to handle Miss Roberts informally at lunch."[35]

The Geddes test case of *Woman's Home Companion* came out in January 1942 (**FIG. 10**). Clearly some advances had been made to enliven and reorga-

nize the editorial content and art. A feature on "better meals" had been designed with an illustration made up of component parts and a table of information as the central focus, suggesting a more user-friendly way of divulging information quickly (**FIG. 11**). Another feature on home improvements with "needle, shears and paste" had a similarly cohesive approach to breaking up blocks of text into captions beneath illustrations (**FIG. 12**). Tint blocks were used to suggest a continuation of photographic images across a body of text (**FIG. 14**). Other editorial spreads set images at dynamic angles or included a dotted line grid to suggest that recipes could be cut out as cards. Another spread, presumably aimed at children and to promote American Hispanic relations, featured "Rosita, our good neighbor," a paper doll with a variety of exotic outfits. Most of these ideas had been discussed in the spring of 1940. But none of them

CHRONOLOGY

The following chronology is modified from the one in Jennifer Davis Roberts's *Norman Bel Geddes: An Exhibition of Theatrical and Industrial Designs*, published by The University of Texas at Austin in 1979. Not an exhaustive listing of designs and projects by Norman Bel Geddes, this chronology shows the broad scope of his involvement in American art and industry and relates to material explored in this book.

1893

Norman Bel Geddes born in Adrian, Michigan, on April 27.

1908

Geddes's father, Clifton T. Geddes, died on June 22 in Sylacauga, Alabama.

1914

Began designing *Thunderbird* (produced in 1917) after spending a summer on the Blackfoot Indian Reservation.

Wrote "Main Features of a Theatre for a More Plastic Style of Drama," which promulgated a "diagonal axis" layout for theater interiors.

1915

Published *Inwhich* magazine through 1916. Invented his first war game.

1916

Married Helen Belle Sneider on March 19 in Toledo, Ohio; adopted the name Norman Bel Geddes.

Introduced the first focus (spot) lights as sole means of stage lighting.

Moved to Los Angeles and designed children's theater for Aline Barnsdall there.

Designed an abstract staging using only six screens for *Nju*.

Created designs for a never-realized production of *King Lear*.

Daughter Joan Bel Geddes born December 2 in Los Angeles.

1917

Moved to New York City in December; worked for the Metropolitan Opera.

1919

Designed *Boudour Ballet* for the Chicago Opera Company; originated the first combined focus and flood lamp.

Exhibition of designs at the Art Institute of Chicago, where he studied briefly.

1920

Devised apparatus for the creation of abstract sounds and their amplification and distribution to various parts of the stage.

Designed a stage and setting for never-realized 1921 production of Dante's *The Divine Comedy*; published the project in 1924.

1921

Designed first quick-change pivot stage for Ray Goetz.

1922

Designed Palais Royal Cabaret Theatre for Sam Salvin in New York City.

Exhibition of theatrical designs at Victoria and Albert Museum, London, and Municipal Museum, Amsterdam.

Daughter Barbara Bel Geddes born October 31 in New York City.

1923

Designed Theater Number 6, which morphed into the Repertory Theatre design for Chicago's 1933–34 Century of Progress International Exposition; grouped three separate auditoriums around a central tower for repertory organization.

1924

Designed Island Dance Restaurant for Cecil B. DeMille in Hollywood.

Designed *Feet of Clay* for Cecil B. DeMille and Paramount in Hollywood.

The Miracle opened at New York City's Century Theatre, redesigned by Geddes as a Gothic cathedral.

Designed *The Comic Supplement* for Flo Ziegfeld in Washington, D.C. and New York City.

1925

Invented a mechanical horse race game.

Designed and directed *Jeanne d'Arc* in Paris.

Wrote articles "Modern Theory of Design" and "The Theatre and Motion Pictures" for the 14th edition of the *Encyclopædia Britannica*.

Designed *Sorrows of Satan* for D. W. Griffith and Paramount Pictures.

1926

Designed Macy's Christmas Parade in New York City.

1927

Designed display windows for Franklin Simon & Company in New York City.

1928

The Patriot opened in New York City, featuring novel set-changing mechanism.

Drafted announcement of the formation of Norman Bel Geddes & Co. for industrial design work.

Designed Motorcars #1–5 for the Graham-Paige Motor Company.

Designed metal furniture for the Simmons Company.

1929

Designed Cole Porter's *Fifty Million Frenchmen* in New York City.

Designed a conference room for J. Walter Thompson Advertising Agency in New York City.

Appointed designer of illumination for all buildings and grounds of Chicago's 1933–34 Century of Progress International Exposition and consultant to the fair's Architectural Commission; designed Divine Comedy Theatre, Theatre Number 14, Water Pageant Theatre, Temple of Music, Open Air Cabaret, and Aerial Restaurant.

Designed counter scales and factory complex for the Toledo Scale Company.

Designed Air Liner #4.

1930

Awarded a prize for design of the Ukrainian State Theater at Kharkov.

Developed plans for the Rotary Airport in New York City, off the tip of lower Manhattan.

Exhibition of designs for Chicago World's Fair buildings at the Architectural League of New York City.

An article about Geddes is published in July issue of *Fortune* magazine.

1931

Hamlet produced at New York City's Broadhurst Theatre.

Articles "The House of Tomorrow" and "Ten Years from Now" published in *Ladies' Home Journal*.

Designed kitchen ranges for Standard Gas Equipment Corporation.

Completed designs for streamlined Locomotive #1.

Developed line of teardrop-shape cars, typified by Motorcar #9.

"Grand Master of Modernism" article published in the *New York Herald Tribune*.

1932
Horizons published by Little, Brown, and Company.

Designed streamlined ocean liner.

Designed refrigerator with top monitor enclosed in body for General Electric Company.

Geddes featured as the subject of a *New Yorker* cartoon.

1933
Married Frances Resor Waite in March; introduced to her uncle, Stanley Resor, of the J. Walter Thompson Advertising Agency.

Designed medallion commemorating the silver anniversary of the General Motors Corporation.

"A Peep Into the Future by the Spectacular Norman Bel Geddes" feature published in the *Detroit News*.

1934
Designed for Socony-Vacuum Oil Company a prefabricated service station with traffic flow diagrams painted on pavement.

Designed oceangoing streamlined yacht for Axel Wenner-Gren.

Created advertising and designs for Chrysler Motor Company.

Designed airplane interiors for the Pan American Clippers.

Designed housewares for Revere Copper and Brass.

Designed a vacuum cleaner for the Electrolux Corporation.

"Streamlining" article published in November *Atlantic Monthly* magazine.

1935
Dead End, designed and produced by Geddes, opened at the Belasco Theatre in New York City.

Established a short-lived partnership with architect George Howe.

1936
Designed and produced *Iron Men* at the Longacre Theatre in New York City.

Featured in Sheldon and Martha Cheney's *Art and the Machine*.

1937
The Eternal Road opened at the Manhattan Opera House in New York City.

Designed "City of Tomorrow" advertising campaign for Shell Oil Company.

Profiled as "Norman Bel Geddes, Master of Design" in *Pencil Points*.

1938
Designed the Barberry Room addition to New York City's Berkshire Hotel.

1939
Geddes design projects opened at the 1939–40 New York World's Fair: exhibit and building for the National Dairy Company, the Wilson Packing Company, Futurama in the General Motors "Highways and Horizons" exhibit, Crystal Lassies novelty.

President Franklin Roosevelt invited Geddes to join the National Motorway Planning Authority.

Redesigned *Collier's*, *Woman's Home Companion* and *The American* magazines for the Crowell-Collier Publishing Company; designed new typography format for the *New York Post*.

Norman Bel Geddes & Co. new offices opened at Rockefeller Center, New York City.

1940
Designed radios for the Emerson Radio and Phonograph Corporation.

Magic Motorways published by Random House.

1941
Designed poleless tent, cages, costumes, acts, and trucks for Ringling Brothers and Barnum & Bailey Circus.

Designed, built, and photographed reconstructions of naval and military battles for *Life* magazine.

Designed aircraft identification system for the U.S. Army.

Profile of Geddes published in the *New Yorker*.

1942
Designed new self-camouflage technique for the U.S. Army Engineers.

Advised U.S. Army on blackout technique for the greater New York City area.

Designed radios and phonographs for RCA.

Tomorrow's Homes for the Many booklet published, featuring a modular home system designed by Geddes in 1940 for the Housing Corporation of America.

Geddes's redesigned *Women's Home Companion*, featuring zigzag and strip spreads, is published.

1943
Designed electric, radio-controlled model aircraft for Strategic Command, Army Air Force, and supervised construction in Orlando, Florida.

Produced "Civilian Defense in Action" for New York City at Madison Square Garden.

Designed a variety of products for IBM beginning in 1943 culminating in the design, with Eliot Noyes, of the IBM Electric Executive typewriter in 1948.

1944
War models exhibited at The Museum of Modern Art, New York City.

Designed Coca-Cola vending machine for Mills Industries.

Married Anne Howe Hilliard on December 20.

1945
Designed a fifty-year master plan for the redevelopment of Toledo, Ohio.

Prepared model photography stories on the building of the pyramids in Egypt and the construction of the Panama Canal for *Encyclopaedia Britannica*.

1946
Designed line of radios and the company trademark for Federal Telephone and Radio Corporation.

Constructed models and advised on preparation of the official record of the Battle of Midway for the U.S. Navy.

Closed large office to focus on pure design rather than project management.

1948
Designed Copa City for Murray Weinger in Miami, Florida.

1949
Designed all-weather, all-purpose stadium for the Brooklyn Dodgers.

Designed a "consumers' building" for General Motors Corporation in New York City.

1950
Proposed Expand-A-House prefabricated home construction franchise.

1951

Developed Boca Raton master plan for the hotel owner and real estate developer J. Myer Schine.

Designed Factory TV Studio for NBC in New York City.

Began development of Walless House, culminating in Edith House of 1954.

1953

Married Edith Lutyens on June 7.

1954

Designed Pilot TV Studio for NBC in New York City.

1955

Commissioned to remodel the British Colonial Hotel, Nassau, Bahamas.

1956–1957

Developed a proposal and designs for a resort on the Mediterranean near Malaga, Spain.

1958

Died of a heart attack on May 8 at age 65.

SELECTED
BIBLIOGRAPHY

Albrecht, Donald, and Phil Patton. *Cars, Culture, and the City.* New York: Museum of the City of New York, 2010.

Albrecht, Donald, Robert Schonfeld, and Lindsay Stamm Shapiro. *Russel Wright: Creating American Lifestyle.* New York: Harry N. Abrams, Inc., 2001.

Albrecht, Donald, ed. *World War II and the American Dream.* Washington, D.C.: National Building Museum; Cambridge, MA: MIT Press, 1995.

Behr, Shulamith, David Fanning, and Douglas Jarman, eds. *Expressionism Reassessed.* Manchester, UK: Manchester University Press, 1993.

Blaszczyk, Regina Lee. *Imagining Consumers: Design and Innovation from Wedgwood to Corning.* Baltimore: Johns Hopkins University Press, 2000.

———. *American Consumer Society, 1865–2005: From Hearth to HDTV.* Wheeling, IL: Harlan Davidson, 2009.

Bragdon, Claude. "A New Kind of Theatre by Norman Bel Geddes." *Architectural Record* 57 (March 1922).

Bush, Donald J. *The Streamlined Decade.* New York: George Braziller, 1975.

Calkins, Earnest Elmo. "Beauty the New Business Tool." *Atlantic Monthly* (August 1927).

Cheney, Sheldon. *The New World Architecture.* New York: Longmans, Green, 1930.

Cheney, Sheldon and Martha. *Art and the Machine.* New York: Whittlesey House, 1936.

Clarke, Sally H. *Trust and Power: Consumers, the Modern Corporation, and the Making of the United States Automobile Market.* New York: Cambridge University Press, 2007.

Cogdell, Christina. *Eugenic Design: Streamlining America in the 1930s.* Philadelphia: University of Pennsylvania Press, 2004.

Corn, Joseph J., ed. *Imagining Tomorrow: History, Technology, and the American Future.* Cambridge, MA: MIT Press, 1986.

Corn, Joseph, and Brian Horrigan. *Yesterday's Tomorrows: Past Visions of the American Future.* New York: Summit Books, 1984.

Doordan, Dennis P. *Design History: An Anthology.* Cambridge, MA: MIT Press, 1995.

Doordan, Dennis P., and Davira S. Taragin, eds. *The Alliance of Art and Industry: Toledo Designs for America.* New York: Hudson Hills Press, 2002.

Ferriss, Hugh. *The Metropolis of Tomorrow.* Princeton: Princeton Architectural Press, 1986.

Flinchum, Russell. *Henry Dreyfuss, Industrial Designer: The Man in the Brown Suit.* New York: Rizzoli International Publications, Inc., 1997.

Flink, James J. *The Automobile Age.* Cambridge, MA, and London: MIT Press, 1990.

Geddes, Norman. *Inwhich.* Detroit: self-published, 1915–1916.

Geddes, Norman Bel. *A Project for a Theatrical Presentation of The Divine Comedy of Dante Alighieri.* New York: Theatre Arts, Inc., 1924.

———. *Horizons.* Boston: Little, Brown, and Company, 1932.

———. "Streamlining." *Atlantic Monthly* 154 (November 1934).

———. *Magic Motorways.* New York: Random House, 1940.

———. *Miracle in the Evening: An Autobiography.* William Kelley, ed. Garden City, NY: Doubleday, 1960.

Gerlernter, David. *1939: The Lost World of the Fair.* New York: Free Press, 1995.

Gutfreund, Owen D. In *Robert Moses and the Modern City: The Transformation of New York,* Hilton Ballon and Kenneth T. Jackson, eds. New York: Norton, 2007.

Hellman, Geoffrey T. "Profiles: Design for a Living—II, Norman Bel Geddes." *The New Yorker* 16 (February 8, February 15, February 22, 1941).

Hilnes, Michele, ed. *NBC: America's Network.* Berkeley: University of California Press, 2007.

Hunter, Frederick J. *Catalog of the Norman Bel Geddes Theatre Collection at The University of Texas, Austin.* Boston: G. K. Hall, 1973.

Innes, Christopher. *Designing Modern America: Broadway to Main Street.* New Haven, CT: Yale University Press, 2005.

Kras, Reyer. *Streamline: The Dawn of Tomorrow.* Amsterdam: Stedelijk Museum, 2001.

Kuksa, Iryna. "Scenography and New Media Technologies: History, Educational Applications, and Visualization Techniques." Doctoral dissertation, University of Warwick, 2007.

Leach, William. *Land of Desire: Merchants, Power, and the Rise of a New American Culture.* New York: Pantheon Books, 1993.

Maffei, Nicolas. "Designing the Image of the Practical Visionary: Norman Bel Geddes, 1893–1958." Doctoral dissertation, Royal College of Art, London, 2000.

Marchand, Roland. *Advertising the American Dream: Making Way for Modernity, 1920–1940.* Berkeley: University of California Press, 1985.

Meikle, Jeffrey L. *Twentieth Century Limited: Industrial Design in America, 1925–1939.* Philadelphia: Temple University Press, 1979.

———. "Norman Bel Geddes and the Popularization of Streamlining." *The Library Chronicle* of The University of Texas at Austin, New Series Number 13 (1980).

Morshed, Adnan. *The Architecture of Ascension: Airplanes, Skyscrapers, and the American Imagination of the Master Planner, 1919–1939.* Minneapolis: University of Minnesota Press, 2011.

Norman Bel Geddes War Maneuver Models Created for Life *Magazine.* New York: Museum of Modern Art, 26 January to 5 March 1944.

Nye, David. *American Technological Sublime.* Cambridge, MA: MIT Press, 1994.

Porter, Glenn. *Raymond Loewy: Designs for a Consumer Culture.* Wilmington, DE: Hagley Museum and Library, 2002.

Postman, Neil. *Amusing Ourselves to Death: Public Discourse in the Age of Show Business.* New York: Viking, 1985.

Rassegna 60 issue is devoted to Norman Bel Geddes (1994).

Rile, Terence. *The International Style: Exhibition 15 & The Museum of Modern Art.* New York: Rizzoli, 1992.

Reid, Kenneth. "Masters of Design: II—Norman Bel Geddes." *Pencil Points* 18 (January 1937).

Roberts, Jennifer Davis. *Norman Bel Geddes: An Exhibition of Theatrical and Industrial Designs.* Austin, TX: The University of Texas at Austin, 1979.

Samuel, Lawrence. *Future: A Recent History.* Austin, TX: University of Texas Press, 2009.

Russell, G. Norman. *Norman Bel Geddes and the Art of Stage Lighting.* San Jose, CA: G. N. Russell, 1974.

Rydell, Robert W., and Laura Burd Schiavo, eds. *Designing Tomorrow: America's World's Fairs of the 1930s.* New York: Yale University Press, 2010.

Schrenk, Lisa D. *Building a Century of Progress: The Architecture of Chicago's 1933–34 World's Fair.* Minneapolis: University of Minnesota Press, 2007.

Susman, Warren. *Culture as History: The Transformation of American Society in the Twentieth Century.* New York: Pantheon Books, 1984.

Walker, Nancy A. *Women's Magazines, 1940–1960: Gender Roles and the Popular Press.* New York: Bedford/St. Martin's, 1998.

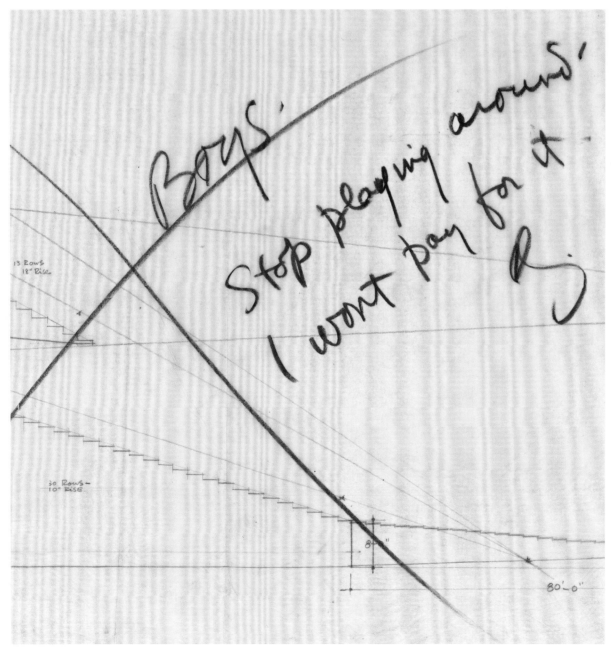

Geddes berates his staff, 1949. In a succession of draft drawings for an all-weather, all-purpose stadium, Geddes had asked his draftsmen to leave out a particular detail that he considered proprietary and did not want to present to the client unless absolutely necessary. His "boys" kept including it, thus his note.

CONTRIBUTORS

DONALD ALBRECHT is curator of architecture and design at the Museum of the City of New York and an independent curator. His exhibitions include international traveling retrospectives of Eero Saarinen and Charles and Ray Eames as well as thematic shows such as *Paris/ New York: Design Fashion Culture* and *The American Style: Colonial Revival and the Modern Metropolis.*

REGINA LEE BLASZCZYK is an historian and author who specializes in business, technology, innovation, design, and fashion. Her books include *Imagining Consumers: Design and Innovation from Wedgwood to Corning* (2002); *American Consumer Society, 1865–2005: From Hearth to HDTV* (2009); *Rohm and Haas: A Century of Innovation* (2009); and *The Color Revolution* (2012). She is a visiting scholar in the Department of the History and Sociology of Science at the University of Pennsylvania and an associate editor at the *Journal of Design History.*

CHRISTINA COGDELL is associate professor of design at the University California at Davis and author of *Eugenic Design: Streamlining America in the 1930s* (2004), winner of the 2006 Edelstein Prize. She is co-editor of *Popular Eugenics: National Efficiency and American Mass Culture in the 1930s* (2006) and a special issue of *Boom: A Journal of California* on California Design (2012), and has published in *Design and Culture, Design Issues, American Art,* and *American Quarterly.* She is currently researching the influence of popular scientific theories of self-organization and its emergence in contemporary architecture, and teaches courses in the history of art, architecture, design, and American culture.

DAVE CROKE is a graduate student in the Department of American Studies at The University of Texas at Austin.

CHRISTIN ESSIN is an assistant professor of theater history at Vanderbilt University in Nashville, Tennessee, and a graduate of The University of Texas at Austin with a PhD in performance as public

practice. Further research on Geddes's career as a theater designer will appear in her upcoming publication *Stage Designers in Early 20th Century America: Artists, Activists, Cultural Critics* (Palgrave, 2012).

KATHERINE FEO KELLY is a doctoral candidate in the Department of American Studies at The University of Texas at Austin. She received her master's degree in design history from the Royal College of Art and has published in *The Journal of Design History, Design and Culture*, and *Fashion Theory: The Journal of Body and Dress.*

ANDREA GUSTAVSON is a doctoral candidate in the Department of American Studies at The University of Texas at Austin. Her dissertation is on personal photography, affect, and the Cold War. She has published in *The Journal of American Studies.*

PETER HALL is a design critic and former senior lecturer in design at The University of Texas at Austin. He is currently a senior lecturer in the Design Futures Program at Griffith University in Brisbane, Australia.

CHRISTOPHER INNES is a professor of English and holds the Canada Research Chair in Performance and Culture at York University. He has published widely on modern and contemporary theater, his most recent books being *Designing Modern America Broadway to Main Street, Modern British Drama— The Twentieth Century*, and *Directors/Directing.* His research is profiled on his website: www. moderndrama.com.

SANDY ISENSTADT teaches the history of modern architecture at the University of Delaware. His writings center on postwar reformulations of modernism, contemporary architecture, and the spatial implications of material culture. His 2009 book, *The Modern American House*, describes the visual enhancement of spaciousness in the architectural, interior, and landscape design of American domestic architecture.

INDEX

Process

Animated Battle Map, 318, *320,* 321, 325–26

Batlrama relief map, *327–29,* 330

Battle of Midway model, 333, *334, 335, 336–37, 342*

Bel Geddes Process in, 348–49

Coral Sea Battle model, *332,* 333

films of battle reenactments, 325

model photography for U.S. Navy, *330,* 331, *332, 333*

"news" column, proposed, 326, 330

News Syndicate War Map, 326, 330

ocean model, 330–31, 333

relationship with theater projects, 318

ship and plane recognition training, 331

ship models, *324, 330,* 331–33

three-dimensional terrain models, 325–26, *327–29,* 330

United States model, 326

war games, 317–21, *322–23,* 325

Warren Rome Metallic Bed Company, 215, *216*

watercraft design

"Control Bridge: Ocean Liner Style," *362*

Wenner-Gren yacht, 96–97, *98–99,* 106, 112

Water Pageant Theater, *179*

Weaver, Sylvester "Pat," 278–80, 284–85

Weill, Kurt, 22, *36*

Weiner, Howard A., 82

Weinger, Murray, 125–26, 128

Welles, H. G., 317

Wenner-Gren yacht, 96–97, *98–99,* 106, 112

White City, World's Columbian Exposition, Chicago, 136, *137*

Wilcox, William R., 144

window displays. *See* store displays

"Wings" jewelry, *82*

Woman's Home Companion

advertising spreads in, 364

circulation of, 360

redesign of, 368, *369, 370, 371, 374*

women, as consumers, 78–80, 90

Woolworth, Frank W., 77

workplace design, 277–87. *See also* Toledo Scale Company

chairs, *224–25,* 226

desks, 217, *220*

NBC studios, 277–86

production efficiency, 279–80, 286

tables, 226, *227*

typewriters, 24, 65, 67, *248, 249*

vending machines, *246*

World's Columbian Exposition, Chicago, 136, *137*

"Worth of Paris" window display, *72–73*

Wright, Frank Lloyd, 116, 145, 296

Wright, Russel, 55–56

Y

yacht design, 96–97, *98–99,* 106, 112

"Your Home of Tomorrow," *150*

Z

Zeckendorf, William, 302

Ziegfeld's Follies, 14, *33*

"zigzag spread," 363, *364, 366, 367, 368,* 374

Support for this book's publication has come from the trustees of the Edith Lutyens and Norman Bel Geddes Foundation, the Graham Foundation for Advanced Studies in the Fine Arts, Furthermore: a program of the J. M. Kaplan Fund, and Janet and Jack Roberts.

Support for planning the exhibition has been generously provided by the National Endowment for the Humanities, the Graham Foundation for Advanced Studies in the Fine Arts, and the Marlene Nathan Meyerson Family Foundation. An FAIC/Tru Vue Optium® Conservation Grant has greatly enhanced the display of key images in the exhibition. IBM has provided significant in-kind support.

Project Manager: Andrea Danese
Designer: Sarah Gifford
Managing Editors: Tamara Arellano, Jen Graham
Production Manager: Anet Sirna-Bruder

Library of Congress Cataloging-in-Publication Data

Norman Bel Geddes designs America : I have seen the future / edited by Donald Albrecht.
     pages cm
  Includes bibliographical references and index.
  ISBN 978-1-4197-0299-0 (alk. paper)
1. Geddes, Norman Bel, 1893–1958—Criticism and interpretation.
2. Design—United States—History—20th century. I. Albrecht, Donald. II. Geddes, Norman Bel, 1893-1958. Works. Selections. 2012.
  NK1412.G43N67 2012
  745.4092—dc23
                                        2012008312

Introduction copyright © 2012 Donald Albrecht; "Norman Bel Geddes and a Spiritual Philosophy of Art and Inspiration" copyright © 2012 Danielle Brune Sigler; "Practical Vision and the Business of Design: Norman Bel Geddes Incorporated" copyright © 2012 Nicolas Paolo Maffei; "Imagining Consumers: Norman Bel Geddes and American Consumer Culture" copyright © 2012 Regina Lee Blaszczyk; "On the Road to the Future" copyright © 2012 Dave Croke; "'A Few Years Ahead': Defining Modernism with Popular Appeal" copyright © 2012 Jeffrey L. Meikle; "The Future Is Here: Norman Bel Geddes and the Theater of Time" copyright © 2012 Sandy Isenstadt; "Theater Productions" copyright © 2012 Christin Essin; "Theaters" copyright © 2012 Laura McGuire; "Modular and Mobile" copyright © 2012 Christopher Innes; "Furniture" copyright © 2012 Christopher Long; "Domestic Media Designs" copyright © 2012 Nick Muntean; "Housing" copyright © 2012 Monica Penick; "Workplaces" copyright © 2012 Katherine Feo Kelly; "Futurama" copyright © 2012 Lawrence W. Speck; "Theater of War" copyright © 2012 Christina Cogdell; "The Bel Geddes Process" copyright © 2012 Andrea Gustavson; "Graphic Design" copyright © 2012 Peter Hall

Cover photo copyright © Estate of Margaret Bourke-White/ Licensed by VAGA, New York, NY. *Spectators viewing the Futurama exhibition*, c. 1939. Photograph by Margaret Bourke-White, 10 1/4 x 13 1/2 in., 26 x 34.3 cm. Norman Bel Geddes Collection, Harry Ransom Center, The University of Texas at Austin

Printed and bound in Hong Kong

10 9 8 7 6 5 4 3 2 1

Abrams books are available at special discounts when purchased in quantity for premiums and promotions as well as fundraising or educational use. Special editions can also be created to specification. For details, contact specialsales@abramsbooks.com or the address below.

ABRAMS
THE ART OF BOOKS SINCE 1949

115 West 18th Street
New York, NY 10011
www.abramsbooks.com